Essential Software Development Career + Technical Guide

Essential Software Development Career + Technical Guide

ENGINEERS/DEVELOPERS/ PROGRAMMERS: INTERVIEWING, CODING, MULTITHREADING, MANAGEMENT, ARCHITECTURE, AGILE, CRYPTO, SECURITY, PERFORMANCE, UI/UX, HARDWARE, NETWORKING, ENCRYPTION, DATABASES + MORE!

AppJungle.NET LLC

ISBN:
ISBN-13:

Dedication

To my family: Lisa, Bradley, and Kyle. Thanks for the enthusiasm to get this book published!

Table of Contents

Foreword

Who Is This Book For?

If you are in high school/college or are currently a software engineer, developer, programmer, or engineering manager, or planning to become one, this book is for you.

This book provides a varied set of mini topics, including career, technical, and process advice from the beginning of your career to senior engineer, lead engineer, and management for both technical and soft skills.

This book is arranged in collections of those topics that you can read all the way, skim through, or look up whenever you need some guidance.

Let this book provide suggestions and technical advice and offer ideas, suggestions, and more throughout your career.

This book will employ practical, real-world solutions that cover a wide array of topics to give you a broad idea of the career and technologies that developers will use. It will also take a deep dive into some topics to provide valuable details and opinions/advice.

Yes, I know this book can't obviously have everything about software engineering in it; otherwise, the book would be so big you couldn't pick it up. :)

However, it does try at a high level to cover areas most software engineers might run into.

Beginner, High School, or College

If you are just considering a career or have started your path toward a software engineering degree/job, then this is the book for you. You will learn about the best things to do to prepare yourself, classes to take, languages to learn, steps to prepare for interview, best places to work, and much more.

Starting Your Career to Mid-level

There are lots of things that you likely weren't taught in college about what life would be like once you start your job. These tips, techniques, and advice will provide the information you need, so you don't have to learn it the hard way. There is plenty of both career and technical advice, so you don't make the mistakes others have. Avoid the pitfalls and accelerate your career.

Senior to Expert Level

I'm sure you have read all of the books and know a lot of the material. But I bet you will still find information in this book that you will make you glad to have bought it. It can help you take your career to the next level, if you desire.

Disclaimer

F40542EF617277AC147502965855DA70

CHAPTER 1

Intro

Introduction

Congratulations on acquiring/purchasing this book! This book is an overview of everything related to software engineering. If you are currently wondering if software engineering is right for you, this book will help you decide that by letting you see all that is involved in software engineering: learning, interviewing, working, problem-solving, and much more.

This book covers from high school, beginner to seasoned veteran topics. If you are a beginning software engineer wondering what it's all about, this book is for you, since it will have to provide coverage of many topics and areas you might encounter, giving you confidence in your role. If you are a seasoned software engineer, this book is also for you, as it has references, tips, and reminders on areas that you might not have been involved with all the time, and it will be helpful as a reference when you do. The topics covered will range from the beginning decision to be a software engineer all the way to daily life as a software engineer. This book will help you solve problems you might encounter and provide a reference for you throughout your career for learning things you have not yet learned or remembering things you've forgotten. It will also offer more practical examples rather than the idealism you will find in the industry.

You might ask, what background do I have that is relevant? I was interested in computers at a young age, probably around seven. I started writing programs as a young child over 40 years ago with Basic, then C, Assembly, C++, C#, Java, Pascal, COBOL, Fortran, Lisp, Prolog, and more. I wrote the first program that I sold at around the age of 15. It was similar to a spreadsheet. The program was written for a shoe store on a TRS-80 computer. As a kid, I wrote shareware software for a bulletin board systems (BBS), used by many folks, including, I found out, a navy sub commander!

Later, while going to college, I also worked with friends to create our own software products. We got our product onto the store shelves. After college, I've worked for some of the largest and most well-known companies in the world on large software products: AT&T, Unix System Labs, Novell, Hewlett-Packard, SunGard, and Citigroup, for example, as well as some smaller, lesser-known companies. I also wrote some financial shareware that made its way into Barron's financial paper in a review. So I've seen small software shops all the way to some of the largest.

I'm a hands-on (still technical) software development manager at a large multinational firm. I'm a hiring manager and am thoroughly versed in the interview process. Hopefully, my experience can help beginners and seasoned engineers understand the things managers are looking for in an interview. The book provides experiences with becoming a manager and helpful real-world hints and advice on situations you may encounter.

I will offer information that I believe is worth knowing, along with suggestions, solutions, and more learned over the years, to help you along your career journey. This book has articles that span topics from before becoming a software engineer to taking next-level steps in your software engineering journey to real-world advice and solutions on topics software engineers/developers/programmers might encounter. Don't wait to look through the book now. Skip to the chapters that interest you.

I'm hoping some of the information and examples amassed over my 40-plus years of working with software can help you and perhaps prevent you from making some mistakes I made. :)

CHAPTER 2

Should You Become a Developer?

Should I Become a Software Engineer/Developer?

This certainly is a big question: "Should I become a software engineer?" If you have already been doing some programming/coding, you might know the answer to this question already. If you really like coding to see the computer do things and figuring out how to make it work, spending endless hours trying things . . . then there is a pretty good chance that being a software engineer might be a good career for you.

A long time ago, in a place not far away, there was a boy at a young age who was dropped at the arcade in the mall. His mother would drop him there to occupy him while she shopped. Directly across on the other side of the mall was a RadioShack. Instead of playing at the arcade, he walked across the mall to the RadioShack and spent an hour or more programming the TRS-80 Model 1. This would happen on a fairly regular basis.

If that little boy sounds like you, then you definitely should consider a software engineering career. That level of passion isn't required for a good career in the field. However, the passion helps, since it likely means there is a deep interest in learning the craft and the work itself.

If you like many of these, Software Engineering might be a good career path:

- Making a computer do things.
- Figuring out how computers/coding works.
- Making software for other people to use and seeing how they use it.
- Really learning the correct and best ways to do things efficiently.
- Find programming fun to do (not a requirement but certainly helps).
- Dealing with things at a very detailed level.
- Software engineers make decent pay in many locations.
- Have a love for tech.
- Solving detailed problems.
- Enjoy digging to figure out how things work at the lowest level to fully understand what's happening (not a requirement, though this might show exceptional interest in this field).
- Learning new things: Development languages and technologies change often, and keeping up with the latest information on everything is probably impossible, but keeping up to date on technologies you work in or that will help you in the future will aid you in a software engineering career. You are good at learning on your own from a book or video, or online info.
- Very logical, detail oriented, analytical.
- Not required, but if you've been programming as a kid and liked it and you still are interested.

- Ability to work in a team (you might do a lot of coding alone, but many other things require teamwork and collaboration).
- Strategy, games, and puzzles.
- Trying new technology (drives you to learn new things).
- Some software engineers either have done something with music in the past or present (optional), but if you are musically inclined, there are aspects that might incline you to be a software engineer.
- If you get a good feeling thinking about someone using something you wrote to benefit them or others.
- Lots of patience: Coding can be very tedious and time consuming, with sometimes spending long amounts of time looking at the same code and trying to figure out why it is not working... until hours later, something clicks, and you find something or figure it out or ask someone for help.
- Doing things like making sure you put things in your refrigerator in the most efficient location for both sizes (i.e., don't put lots of small things on the shelves with large space to fit larger items like milk jugs and instead make sure they go on smaller fit areas). If you are seeking order, you probably have an underlying skill/talent for seeing order in other things like coding.
- Professional pride in always trying to become a better software engineer.

The career path may not be for you if:

- You don't like spending hour upon hour in front of a computer.
- You mind spending less time with people and more time working with a computer. Yes, you get to work with others, but you

will spend a lot of time on your own coding . . . this isn't for everyone if you don't enjoy working independently.

- You don't enjoy talking or dealing with semantics or lots of tiny details. Coders often have lots of discussions like these, and if stuff like this isn't your cup of tea, it might set you on edge. Some even seem trivial, like spaces vs. tabs, but can be almost a religion with some folks.
- You don't enjoy spending hours diagnosing why something doesn't work . . . and it's critical that it does . . . like now! Debugging can be quite stressful when you know there is a customer issue happening now, and it needs to be solved.
- Software developers/engineers are often on the escalation path for issues, meaning that your company could call you late at night to work on a production issue. In many places, this doesn't happen often, but at some jobs it can be more frequent. Something to think about, as this can impact work-life balance. For most places I've worked, this didn't happen enough to be a big issue, but I've heard stories of other people who were not as fortunate. If that's something you never want to worry about, this might not be for you. Many jobs, though, might ask you to do some work after hours in emergencies . . . even for non-software engineer jobs.
- You don't like to have your work criticized. Code reviews are a regular feature of software engineering, which means other people will review and comment on your work all the time.
- You don't like deadlines. It can be like having deadlines every two weeks. It's often flexible for sprint deadlines but less so for when there are close release dates to get your software out or there are urgent issues that need to be resolved.

As a Software Engineer, what would you do?

If you wanted to know what a computer software engineer does, read on:

- Work on a team with other engineers, testers, business analysts.
- Help work through user scenarios/stories and understand how users would use new functionality in software to understand the value of the software/service for the company's clients/customers (or at least get that information from the business analyst).
- Help architect/design software, services, and algorithms achieve the goals brought up in the user scenarios/stories. That includes thinking through how you will release/deploy/support this when it's in customers'/clients' hands, often trying to find the best compromise of what is possible to do in the time the customer/business analyst would like it done.
- Implement some portion or all of the features through coding or other means necessary to achieve the outcome desired from the user scenarios/stories. You will work with many tools to get this done.
- Fix other people's code that may have been written long ago. No one might know how it works, and it would be up to you to figure it out.
- Often implement unit testing to test the code you created (writing code to test other code; yep, it's a thing).
- Implement functional and/or integration automated testing (yes, more code to test the code you wrote from a higher-level functionality). Testing your code can sometimes take three times the time it took to write it (sometimes more or less).

- Work with the QA (Quality Assurance) team to, you guessed it, test your code again! Yes, we do a lot of testing.
- Support the product once released with questions customers have on why something works the way it does or doesn't work the way they expect.
- Fix bugs that are found by QA or worse, by the customers, which sometimes includes (usually not too often in larger companies) being on the phone with rightfully cranky customers about why the software is not working the way they expect.
- Not always, but developers have been known to drink large quantities of coffee and work often stops temporarily when the coffee machine stops working (not a requirement, just something I've noticed). :)
- Work in nearly any industry that uses computers and needs code written or supported.

What Is a Day as a Software Engineer Like?

Days can be very varied as a software engineer, based on what is going on at the time at your company. For example, working on a new, as they say, green field product vs. an existing product can have some significant differences in what your day looks like. Some companies have layers of people fielding customer support requests before they get to a software engineer, to prevent them from being interrupted too often. Other organizations have fewer layers and more interruptions due to support issues.

Here are some example days: Sometimes, you can get a mix of types of work on any day just based on what is happening. Don't assume these example days come one right after the other; they may or may not.

Day: Working on a Story/Feature

8:00 a.m.: Coffee and start your day reading/responding to e-mails. You start to look at where you were in your code the previous day and what you are planning to do today.

9:00 a.m.: Scrum meeting, where everyone tells what they worked on yesterday, what they will work on today, and anything blocking them from getting their work done (ideally lasts only 15 minutes, but often there is what they call post scrum to get into some details facing the team that day).

9:30 a.m.: Working on either minor architecture/design of classes or implementing the feature. Perhaps implementing a piece of functionality like a form on a web page that saves the data the user entered and adds some logic for checking the data. Like perhaps verifying a street address, city, and state. Some debugging of that logic.

11:00 a.m.: Not done with the saving logic yet, but did some cleanup on the web page. Making the page for where the user entered data look a little better, fixing colors, and styles . . . needs more work, but it is easier to stare at, now.

12:00 p.m.: Lunch, either at your desk reading some random news or articles, or couldn't get your brain out of the code and got back to debugging. Or sometimes, you might just need a break and go take a walk after lunch to clear your head. Sometimes, go out for lunch with the team or on your own.

1:00 p.m.: A colleague catches you either coming back from lunch or grabbing your nth cup of coffee. They ask you to see if you have ideas about what could go wrong with an issue a customer is having with a part of the product. You both discuss some ideas.

1:30 p.m.: Focus back on trying to get all the saving and validation (code that checks data) logic to work correctly. Coding and debugging to get it all to work.

3:00 p.m.: Grooming meeting (a usual meeting as part of a sprint). You look up from your code and realize, "Uh-oh," you have a meeting starting right now! A grooming meeting is one that happens every other week to go over stories to flush out the details with the team and try to get them ready to be worked in a future sprint and estimate how long they might take. Typically, a business analyst walks through the stories, asks if it has enough details to be understood, and estimates them. If not, the team discusses and adds details until they can estimate it. If you hadn't had this, you would have been coding, debugging, or building automation testing for your story being worked for the day.

4:30 p.m.: Back to adding a few changes to your saving code . . . still not done. More debugging and coding. You try to tune out the surrounding discussions to focus on your code.

5:30 p.m.: You look up and realize it's already past five. You take some notes for yourself for tomorrow and save your work for the day (perhaps pushing to your fork on a git repo). Some issue with the code you can't figure out right now . . . it's going to bug you till you figure it out.

6:00 p.m.: Yep, worked a little late for the day. Happens naturally, just thinking about code and trying to get things done. Time to stop thinking about code for the day . . . but occasionally, the problem of the day creeps back into your brain later.

Next day:

6:00 a.m.: The next morning, while in the shower, your brain suddenly comes up with the answer to the coding issue you had been working on yesterday. Yes! You think, why the heck does my brain think of this stuff while in the shower . . . Oh well, thanks, brain. One problem might be solved.

Note: You might not even code every day as a software engineer. Sometimes not for many weeks, when working on support issues or documentation.

Production Issues

Depending on the type of software and the company, developers are called on to support the software when there is a customer issue or production issue. Sometimes, these can be, at some firms, in the middle of the night if you are on call. Some firms use a "follow the sun for support" approach so that you might support production issues from 8:00 a.m.–8:00 p.m., or something like that, and another location on the other side of the world supports 8:00 p.m.–8:00 a.m.

At smaller shops, or even some larger shops in certain groups, you might be on a rotating on-call schedule for those hours or round the clock. The financial industry sometimes has round-the-clock coverage for certain groups and services, for example. Other industries may do this as well.

During a production issue, you might need to discuss the issue with operations and other development teams and groups to determine where the problem is and determine a workaround or fix if one can be done soon or perhaps scheduled for later, depending on how severe the issue is.

Not all jobs have this requirement, but quite a few do, again depending on the software, customers, service, company, etc.

Why Should I Want to Work as a Software Engineer?

- Software engineering pay is pretty good, depending on the economy and location, of course, but usually significantly better than many other jobs. Check job sites to see what they pay in your area.
- Software engineers are in good demand—again, depends on the economy, but someone has to help create all of those websites, right?
- If you want to work inside in an office environment, most of these jobs will fit that (air conditioning in the summer and heat in the winter is pretty nice!).
- If you like making things with code, it can be very fulfilling. Making things that other people use can be fun. You can do front-end screens or back end and solutions that make the whole thing work.
- You can learn to build your own phone/mobile apps to have a side gig, if you desire (just make sure it doesn't conflict with your day job/policies).
- Think about all the functionality you carry on your smartphone. Software engineers created all that software on your phone! Phone calls, calendars, voicemail, calculators, camera apps, etc., all because of your friendly neighborhood software engineers. :)
- You can learn to write your own games, if you desire. :)

Where Do Software Engineers Work?

I would say that in nearly any industry, you will find software engineers. You likely won't find them working in small retail businesses (only contracted perhaps to help with their website or something along those lines). Mom-and-pop retail likely wouldn't have a long-term need for those skills or probably couldn't afford them.

You see software engineers in either small startup software businesses or medium-sized companies and larger of nearly any business that needs to build software for their company or integrate it. Of course, big businesses might have hundreds or even thousands of software engineers, depending on how much software/integration their company needs.

Summary

You've now read about some software engineers' traits and the red flags for things that might mean you aren't ready for that type of role. You have read what a day might be like for a software engineer. If you still have interest and think there are things you could learn and you don't find any concerns too problematic, you could still think about improving those areas to see if you feel you are interested after all.

I knew many people who had never touched a computer before college, and I asked them how they decided they would like this. It's certainly not a pre-requisite. Many of those folks went on to be software engineers. Some were better than others, but they still decided to stick with it and do it.

I've known others who learned and decided they wanted to work with people more. Just purely sitting in front of a screen coding was not pleasurable enough for them to stick with it (even though it might pay more than other options).

If you still think it might be for you and you haven't coded yet, try it and see if you like it. Watch a video on coding and get started, and see how it goes.

CHAPTER 3

What to Learn in High School

What Should I Learn in High School to Help Me Become a Software Engineer?

If you have a computer at home, try anything you are interested in to get you coding. Here is a list of ideas that could help you in high school for software engineering. For those skimming this book and thinking about a career in software development while you are still in high school, here are some things to consider.

Please take advantage of the opportunities that present themselves. One student in a high school computer class finished his coding assignment and helped the other students having trouble completing theirs. The teacher noticed this and asked the student if he would like to work on a side project with him. The project was to collect the data from a little league and process it for the league. This was an excellent opportunity to learn about programming for a purpose rather than just a class exercise.

Some ideas:

- If you have computer programming classes at school, take one and see how you do. That should be a sort of mini job. Your teacher will give you tasks that you will need to complete. If you do well and like them, you are on the road to being a software engineer. (Take the opportunity to learn and be sure if this is for you.)
- Find the college you think you might get into and look at their first semester course work for the program you would look to attend. That should give you an idea of what you are heading into.
- Learn to type properly if you haven't already; it will help writing code more quickly and accurately.
- Write a "Hello World" application in a language of your choice (C#, Java, Ruby, PHP, or anything else, take your pick).
- Write a small program.
- Create a small website.
- Create a simple game (it doesn't need to be complicated or pretty).
- Find a software project you would like to work on online or on your own.
- Find an Arduino or Raspberry Pi project to which you would like to make your own coding alterations. Mixing hardware and software can be a lot of fun.
- Math and science classes are often a staple in many computer science degrees, if that is what you are going for eventually at a four-year college.
- There are options other than a four-year traditional college. You could find a vocational tech school that has some multi-year computer programming courses. (Not the high school courses, but the sort of ones that offer an alternative to regular college

for programming.) They may have degreed and non-degreed programs that can provide different cost/time options compared to a traditional college. A traditional computer science degree may help you land your first job more quickly. After a few years of work for a company, the school you went to won't matter as much. Just read up on reviews of people finding jobs or not from that school to ensure the program is accredited and legit. A well-known school or provider can help you land jobs more quickly.

- Consider if a college that supports co-op is right for you. Colleges that support it let you go to school for certain semesters and then work for a semester, switching at different intervals, giving you a mix of real-world and school experience. Co-op can make it much easier to find your first job.
- If you already have some computer skills, look if there are any internships for juniors or seniors during the summer. This can be a great way to earn money and experience simultaneously.

The Internet is filled with information to help you. You can find videos on YouTube that can teach you how to code or write a game for free. Try those first. If you are having trouble finding some quality coding videos, you can take a look at https://www.pluralsight.com/. They have a lot of videos on technical topics.

Learning a Programming Language

Learning programming languages and technology is pretty much the same as the way you learn other things, so if you are looking to learn a programming language or the best way to learn a programming language, read on.

Your choices range from any combination of the following or more:
Reading (online or a book)

Watching (either online or in person)

Doing (actually trying it out yourself)

You might like to read something and then try it. You might like to watch some training and then try. Or you might like a combination of reading, watching, and then trying, or any combination of the above.

Once you understand it enough, you could get it and try it for yourself.

Video Training Site

You can find a lot of information online. A good video course site is www.pluralsight.com. Reasonably priced to try for a month and watch any of their hundreds of courses.

Your method of learning may be different from someone else's. I like to switch between watching and reading and then trying, depending on how complex the topic is. If it's a brand new language I'm trying to learn, I might buy the best book I can find at a reasonable price and read/skim through it cover to cover just to get a feel for the language. Then I might go back and look in detail at areas of interest. Then I might watch some training on the topic. Once done with those, I'd be ready to sit down and give it a try.

General Overview of Aspects of Programming Languages

When learning a new language, there are often similarities to other languages in some ways. Also, just due to the nature of languages and computers, there are some common areas of a language or API.

Syntax/definitions: The syntax of the language itself, defining variables, functions/methods blocks of code, etc.

Code like int myTimeoutValue; OR; void; Method(); {} define the layout or details of your program.

Control keywords: Statements that allow you to decide on certain conditions change the flow of the running program in some way. In some languages, you might see keywords like IF, THEN, ELSE, DO, WHILE, FOR, etc. Those types of statements help you decide which things to execute.

Assignments, comparison, arithmetic operations: You know, a=0; a<1; a=a+1; etc.

Framework/OS/or Standard API calls: All the previous items mostly don't need the support of the underlying operating system or any framework API. Definitions, Assignments/Arithmetic, and Control are usually core language functionality. Framework/OS or API calls sometimes need to interact with the underlying operating system or some underlying framework to do some more complicated actions.

Writing to a file involves an API/framework calling the operating system to do that work. The good news is that a lot of languages these days have standard APIs/frameworks that work similarly on different OS platforms (e.g., Java, C#.NET, etc.), so if you learn the API, it can be helpful anywhere. That wasn't always the case with other languages like C++, where some operations were standard in C++ that you could do, but doing more OS-specific actions involved calling the Windows APIs directly. C#.NET has a pretty robust framework that can work similarly on Windows or Linux now, for example. Java has some similar functionality. C++ can also use the .NET framework as well now to take advantage of the functionality there.

Many languages have features, even similar features like the above, and sometimes it's the syntax of the language that is the main difference between one language and another. Still, all the features mentioned above possibly work in similar ways. That's how it can be relatively easy to learn one language or another. Since most languages are English, it's like learning the difference between US English and UK English—they might use different words to mean the same things, such as football vs. soccer, etc. Once you learn the different formatting and words you need to use them, you can get through the basics.

Idioms: Each language has standard ways of doing certain things. This could relate to the specific way keywords are used or to how a set of statements are often used together to achieve a particular result. If you code without knowing these, someone who knows the language well will recognize you aren't a native to the language. Sometimes, those idioms are not required, but other times, they were put in place to solve potential issues/concerns with code. Reading, watching, training, and looking at code will help you recognize common bits of code used this way.

Naming conventions: Some languages have evolved a sort of standard naming convention. You should see how people name things in the language of your choice. It won't change how it works, but it may change readability and future support. If you use an odd naming convention, folks might recognize you haven't used the language in practice. Some languages use variable names like myVariable, with the first word in the variable lowercase. If your language has classes, they might be named like MyClass, with each word capitalized.

Summary

Don't worry too much about all that stuff yet. If you try stuff, just get something working. If coding is something you enjoy, you are more likely to stick with it, and getting something working from code is the start.

What Programming Language to Learn First?

This is almost like asking what second spoken language you should learn. Python is presently a popular first language. I wish C# had existed early in my career. It didn't, so I originally learned C, assembly, C++, BASIC, pascal, prolog, lisp, and a few others. Why do I like C#/Java? They are object-oriented languages with type safety built in. Learning a language that would be useful to you in the future, I think, is better. Most websites probably use technologies like PHP, Ruby, C#, Java, and JavaScript. Most applications are web-based these days, so picking a popular language might be a good start. I prefer compiled languages over scripting to improve performance and reduce errors. I've been living on Microsoft platforms, so C# in that case can be an option. For non-Microsoft platforms, maybe Java.

The best thing to do is search job boards to find the language with enough jobs to support a living in your area. Compare the language you chose to the most popular languages to see how it compares to the number of jobs in your area.

Why Should You Learn Programming?

If you like learning how to make computers do something, then you might want to learn programming. Software engineers can make reasonably good pay over their career. If you are a maker, you can expand the types of things you can make with a little programming and an Arduino, Raspberry Pi, or PC.

Arduino hardware applications are easy to put together by assembling the hardware and coding the software. I experimented with Arduino to make a sound amplifier for a radio. I also put together a UV light sensor project that was pretty cool. Using a 3D printer, I printed the case for it as well. It can be exciting to build your hardware/software projects.

How to Learn Programming for Beginners?

You could follow any of the ideas at the top of this section. Reading, watching, and/or doing, whichever is better for you, can work. I've used all of those and/or combinations to learn to program. A good series of video courses can make it easier to follow along. Most people are visual learners, so having the video aspect can help.

CHAPTER 4

What Computer to Buy

Which Type of OS/Computer Should You Buy for School/College for Someone Interested in Being a Software Engineer?

Wow, this one can evoke near religious zealotry even among normal users, and perhaps even more so for software engineers. So please don't spam me. Everyone has an opinion, and these are mine.

I'm going to lay out the criteria that I'm considering for this discussion:

- The computer should be able to perform any school/college tasks with ease and be easy to support/maintain.
- The computer should be cost effective, giving you ample computing power for the price.
- If you like games, take that into account so you don't end up getting a machine that can't handle them. (Hey, it's ok to like games. I still do and wouldn't want a machine that couldn't handle some.)
- It should have enough disk space, CPU, and memory to let you try out all sorts of capabilities and software.

- It should be compatible with the greatest majority of software available so you can run all the tools you want/need.
- You should consider the target job/platform you have an interest in for future jobs (if you know) to make sure it can handle what you need.
- It should match as closely to what future work software/computers you might use to give you a leg up at work and get experience. (This isn't always exactly possible, but there are options I will explain.)
- Decide if portability is more important than power—laptop vs. desktop. In a desktop, you can almost always get a more powerful computer for a comparable price.

So again, this will be controversial, but I'll start right off the top here. A Mac/MacBook may not meet all these criteria well. There are some businesses that use them, and a few a lot, if the software they make is relevant for them or for other reasons, but they are not the most common. There were maybe 100 million Mac users and probably 1.5 billion Windows users at this point in time, as per a 2017 article, "Apple Reveals Windows 10 Is Four Times More Popular than the Mac," *The Verge*, n.d. They are definitely more common for teams developing iOS apps. If your goal is to develop iOS apps, then yes, you will need some type of Mac.

Why may Mac not always be a good option?

- May not be cost effective. You can sometimes get a much more capable Windows computer at a lower price.
- An educated guess, given the imbalance of Windows vs. Mac computers, is there would likely be less software specific for Mac.
- Not an issue, unless you are a gamer: You can't usually play heavy graphics games with a standard Mac or MacBook. The hardware/really isn't available easily for it. The drivers aren't really designed for it. Many AAA heavy graphics games are probably

going to be for Windows or a hardware platform (Xbox, PlayStation, etc.) If you get a MacBook and play graphic intensive games, you will probably be unhappy.

- Businesses that are not targeting software for Mac/iPhone may not use them, so getting used to more standard platforms in the workplace will be useful, like Windows, which is probably the number one desktop computer in the world for business. ("The World's Second-Most Popular Desktop Operating System Isn't MacOS Anymore," *Ars Technica*, n.d.)
- I don't believe Macs are used much as servers, so this may not match a target platform you would write to if you were a web development software engineer. They most likely would be generic PCs with Windows or Linux.
- Some software development tools need right-click options, and from a MacBook, it's not built in (you could buy your own mouse and run Windows).
- Yes, you can run Windows on a Mac, but you still can't right-click easily without a new mouse (I believe), or play graphics-intensive games, usually because they don't have support for the latest graphics cards or the drivers aren't great. Dual booting means you will take up a lot of your disk space with another OS, and the price still can be higher than other options.
- Windows has, in the past, had better development tools. This is changing a little, with Microsoft porting Visual Studio to other platforms. Also, Visual Studio code provides a better development editor for more languages and platforms.
- Apple uses hardware to set itself apart from others and does not bring disparate hardware together like Windows or Android.

If you plan on developing for Mac or iPhone, you will need a Mac computer. If you were developing for Android, you could develop on any computer. iPhone is a great platform and market, though Android seems bigger overall but fractured by OS versions and variations.

Mac is popular for certain software in specific industries that are typically non-development oriented, like movie editors, publishing, and music. If building software targeting iPhones, the Mac is the only game in town. There are a lot of iPhones. But, currently there are still more Android devices, so we should keep those in context. There was some news the balance may be starting to change.

I do like the MacBook UIs for a Unix computer. It may be the best for desktops, even among Linux machines. It is an excellent practice to develop on the platform you are targeting, if that is reasonable, as when you are testing, you might find specific bugs earlier. You obviously can't do that for iPhone/Android, since you can't develop on them, mainly just target them.

An example was at a financial firm I worked at where we built server trading systems. We had a Windows server as our desktop, so we were developing as close to our target environment as possible. We also had workstations (near server class machines) to get closer to the production machine environment.

Why Not Linux? Most Web Servers Are Linux

While, to the best of my knowledge, most web servers are Linux, and the OS is free, it doesn't satisfy the criteria. It probably doesn't have the most available software and good game support (again, if you play games).

Linux is less often used as a desktop and more often as a server, so most business desktops, I believe, are Windows.

You can always run a VM on a Windows machine to run Linux or even just run the command line natively.

What Hardware Do You Need for Your Windows PC?

Ok, so now the question is, what do you need in a computer? A Windows computer for your desktop is an excellent option.

When you are building code and need to compile it and edit and run it, you want it to be fast. A good CPU and Solid State Disks (SSD) disk can help.

At this point in time, if you can afford it, I'd recommend the latest i7 processor (or one generation behind to save some money). Buying that processor level keeps your computer purchase powerful for a reasonable life span. You want this computer to last you at least three years. New software that comes out may run too slow if you buy a less powerful computer or older hardware. With that said, if an i5 is more affordable for you, it should be good enough to buy. (Just make sure it will run any games you desire.)

For disk, at least a 1TB SSD disk would be ideal if you plan to install developer tools. Get a minimum of 16 GB of memory. If you want to run lots of VMs on your machine and servers to not mess up your host OS, then even more memory may be at least 32 GB and more disk space if you can afford it. You can sometimes add memory or disk later if you need, so you don't necessarily need to buy it upfront. However, there is often only one slot for an SSD disk or drive on a laptop and only one slot for a PCIe disk on a desktop (sometimes two), so if you plan to upgrade later, figure out what that would cost you. Consider a recent graphics card that will run the games you want today and some possible future AAA games you might want to play.

If you can't afford those specs, it is ok to compromise a little. Check the games you are interested in. Don't purchase the minimum spec; at least get the recommended if you can afford it. Remember, you want this computer to last you at least three years.

For monitors, the OLED monitors are nice, or even some of the newer LCD monitors are very nice. Make sure the graphics card you buy supports at least two monitors and potentially even three. As a new developer, you can live with one or two. Three monitors are really nice if you can afford them, though only recommended once you have a job that can pay for your computing habit. For work, it's nice to have your calendar on one monitor, e-mail/or Dev IDE on another, and your group chats on another monitor.

In terms of where to buy, a good place to buy machines for less money can be from Dell Outlet. You can get new, scratch-and-dent, and certified refurbished devices there at discount prices. It's possible to save as much as 40 percent or more on some purchases compared to new ones, so it is a great way to get more computing power for less money from a company you trust. Be willing to watch the site for a few weeks to see the hardware that comes and goes so you get a feel for what is a good price or not. If new hardware is on the main site but not in the outlet yet, don't despair. If you can wait for a few weeks, the newer hardware will usually start showing up in the outlet.

CHAPTER 5

College

Choosing a College/School to Be a Computer Software Engineer

Many years ago, one high school student looked at colleges for a computer career. At the time, it appeared that most computer science curricula would be considered part of the math department in colleges. There was just one college he found at the time that had its own college of computer science at the school. The college also had a co-op program, basically a work-study program that was interesting as well. His mother had recently given him a book to read about mega universities. Mega universities are colleges with tens of thousands of students. It turned out that, at the time, the only college with a college of computer science (that I was aware of) was a mega university, and that was Northeastern University.

There are so many things to consider in choosing a college, not even just what school or major. If you want to find out what college you need for a software engineer or what school for a computer software engineer, read on.

You don't need a traditional college to be a software engineer. You could get training from a multi-year tech school on programming/computers. It might be harder to get some jobs for the first couple of years that way, but after that it should be easier. Name-brand tech schools might help a little. Make sure they are accredited and offer job placement services and they can tell you their success rate on placements.

For a more traditional college, let's start with what you want to do for your major. (Read this entire section first, then come back and think about your major again. You might change your mind.)

That question is difficult even after you have decided that you want to be a software engineer. There are many branches of information systems and computer science now.

The core seems to be (some of these from college websites):

- Computer Science BS: focusing on the math and science underpinnings of computers and coding as well as the coding itself. Courses might comprise things like:
  - Computer courses: Intro to Computer Science, Data Structures, Discrete Structures I/II, Computer Architecture, CS Electives 1, 2, 3, 4, 5, 6, 7, Design/Analysis of algorithms
  - CS Electives like: Software Methodology, Systems, Programming, Principles of Languages, Numerical Methods, Intro to Imaging and Multimedia, Internet Technology, Computer Architecture 2, Compilers, Operating System Design, Distributed System Concepts, Computer Security, Modeling and Simulation of Continuous Systems, Brain Inspired Computing, Intro to Computer Graphics, Software Engineering, Database Systems Implementation, Introduction to Data Science, Intro to Artificial Intelligence, Topics in Computer Science, Formal Languages and Automata, Intro to Computational Robotics
  - Math/Science: Calculus ½, Linear Algebra
  - General: General electives (15 of these)

- There are many more degrees at some schools (take a look at Northeastern University. For example *Programs—Khoury College of Computer Sciences,* n.d.) https://www.khoury.northeastern.edu/programs/#jump-0) has some or all of these:
  - BA Computer Science
  - BS Comp Sci/Media Art
  - BS Comp Sci/Political Science
  - BS Comp Sci/Economics
  - BS Comp Sci/Design
  - BS Comp Sci/Sociology
  - BS Comp Sci/Philosophy
  - BS Comp Sci/History
  - BS Comp Sci/English
  - BS Comp Sci/Criminal Justice
  - BS Comp Sci/Biology
  - BS Comp Sci/Linguistics
  - BS Comp Sci/Computer Engineering
  - BS Comp Sci/Game Development
  - BS Comp Sci/Music
  - BS Comp Sci/Communication
  - BS Cybersecurity/Economics
  - BS Cybersecurity
  - BS Cybersecurity/Criminal Justice
  - BS Cybersecurity/Business Admin
  - BS Datascience
  - BS Datascience/Biochemistry
  - BS Datascience/Journalism
  - BS Datascience/Business Administration
  - BS Datascience/Psychology
  - BS Datascience/Mathematics
  - BS Datascience/Environmental Science

  - BS Datascience Ecology and Evolutionary Biology
  - BS Datascience/Behavioral Neuroscience
  - BS Datascience/Biology
  - BS Datascience/Health Science
- Given how many programs there are, you can find programs tailored more to the work you might like to go into. Not all schools have as many programs.
- Information Technology areas may cover things like security, data/information, web design/development, or video game production.
- In some schools, this might just be a subset of courses to take, or for an extra year, earn a master's degree too in an area: Examples include human-computer interaction, web design, database technologies, networking, advanced web design technologies, information visualization, electronic commerce, with minors in business tech writing and art.

So How Do You Decide Your College/Major?

- Choose the top five areas that interest you and rank them as best you can.
- Use job boards to see how many jobs in your area match the education path/jobs you will look for.
- If it's above, let's pick a number and say, 1000 jobs in a commutable area, that could be a viable job market—more is even better.
- If it's below a couple of hundred available jobs in your area, it could be harder to find work for that type of role.
- Also, do some reading to try to forecast if the job market you are looking at is expanding or contracting. You should target expanding markets ideally and not contracting, unless perhaps

it's a really huge market and only going down a little and is likely to remain a significant market for obviously more than four years, so when you get out of college, there is work. You should try to forecast a minimum of 10 years (which can be hard, but if you see a large, expanding market that has been expanding for the last 10 years, it's a good bet that it will keep going unless there is a technology shift that may change that).

- Think about the job you would want and perhaps the industry you might work in. Maybe you want to work in the finance industry building stock market software, or perhaps you want to work in the healthcare industry. The good news is that general computer science or associated degrees can apply to almost anything. Some industries can be a little trickier to get into if they like to see folks with some additional base of knowledge and experience first. The finance industry can be a Catch-22. For example, they like to see industry experience when they hire. They will hire others, but they would prefer industry experience. Other industries might be like that as well. Right now, this may just help you visualize where you would want to be and help tailor the courses you take toward the industry you desire.
- Hint: There probably will be lots of web development jobs for a long time at this point. There are varying technology stacks—Windows or Linux, C#/asp.net/JavaScript/SQL, Ruby, JavaScript/MySQL, PHP/JavaScript/MySQL, and I'm sure many variations.
- Compare the results in a major metro area vs. your area for a number of jobs. If the population in your area is lower and businesses are fewer, there might not be that many jobs in your area. Take the numbers in your area in context with what is available in a major metropolitan area vs. your closest major metro area,

if that is commutable, of course (or if you think you would be ok with moving there for a job).

- If you found enough jobs that look for the degrees you would be going for, then great. You have found a good viable option, at least to earn a living.
- Think about it: Are you happy in that job and interested? If not, go back and find one that fits the other criteria and would make you happy. If happy is not the right word, satisfied, interested, willing to perhaps work in that career for a long time,.
- Next, look at your major or select one that best fits what your sort of general area of job would be.
- Check the required course list and see if you believe you will excel in them. If not, maybe you should look at other programs. For example, if one program is heavy on math (e.g., calculus) and science (physics, etc.), and if you aren't great in that area and think that will be incredibly hard, consider if there are other programs available. Be open to a little challenge, but if that is just really not something that makes sense for your career path and your skills, think hard before you start. Not all computer degrees require heavy math and science. Perhaps a particular program at a specific school may be better for you. I wasn't thrilled with taking so much math, physics, and calculus. It was very hard for me. I am glad I made it through those, even though I've never needed those for a job.
- Make sure the classes really look like they cover the skills you would need for the job area you are looking for. It doesn't need to be a 100 percent, as many job requirements aren't covered at colleges, so as much as is reasonable to expect from the college classes as per typical computer degree programs.
- Do you need a degree? Some jobs may require it. Others may be more flexible. Having a degree might be easier to land your

first couple of jobs that way. When you don't have a degree, there might be some folks who ignore your resume when you only have had a couple of jobs. After you've had a couple of years of employment, it will probably matter less. You can probably still find jobs without BS/BA degrees in computers. It can sometimes be harder to land the first couple of jobs that way, though. Bootcamps or technical schools can be enough to get into some jobs. Once you have a year or two of experience, some companies may allow the experience in place of a Computer Science or related degree. Your safest bet to get a job is a reasonable computer college degree.

College Locations

If you decide to get a full college experience at perhaps one of the biggest college cities in the world, New York, Chicago, and Boston are probably some of the most significant college towns. Boston is a big college area: Harvard, Boston College, Tuft, and MIT. Those big cities can be good if you like that sort of thing. Some folks aren't thrilled with being in a sizable city and the crime that often goes with that. I had my heart set on a particular college, and I liked the college and the experience; it was nice in some ways not having to deal with a car, being on campus.

Moving far away from my home location made me miss my many friends from high school. I made some new ones in college, but since they were near Boston and I moved back home many hours away, it's harder to maintain those friendships. If you make friends quickly, perhaps you have nothing to worry about. If not, something to consider if going to school closer to home (presuming some of your friends do also) is that it might keep you a little more connected. Things are much more virtually connected today, but virtual is not quite the same, so I would say that that was one regret I had. Other than those things, the Boston experience was busy and exciting.

I also regret not learning the piano/keyboards, but that's a different story.☺

Can You Become a Software Engineer without a Degree?

Yes. But you will probably not be as proficient as new engineers out of college who took the time to develop a deeper background in data structures/algorithms. This can make finding your first couple of jobs harder. You probably need some significant education you can put on your resume that shows you know how to code. A well-known technical trade school or training class, for example. You might need to start as an intern if you are on the younger side and still in school. An internship is possible for juniors/seniors from high school but is more common for college students. Having some significant classes that show you have learned the skills or capability to do what the business needs might help get you to get in the door. Some jobs require certain degrees. Others may accept experience in place of one.

This can be a lot harder to get in and may depend on if the job market is very short on developers (which can then make it easier). I heard someone recently with no experience other than a 12–18 week boot camp got a $100k-plus offer (NYC area), but I don't have the details on if this person also had a college background, at least. If you can afford it, the safest bet is to get a college education. This doesn't need to be ivy league. Even a reasonable local college can greatly improve your chances of getting a job. Bootcamps are great for learning a language/environment, but they don't teach you all the foundational things you would learn in college. When interviewing, it will be easy for someone to tell if you have only some of the foundational knowledge by asking questions. It is possible to learn foundational computer science on your own. It would just require diligence, experience, and perseverance.

I've been hearing rumors about some untraditional technical training schools offering training for the ability to pay it when you get a job. I don't know much about them and, as such, would not recommend them. My personal recommendation is to find well-known, well-established, accredited companies that have been teaching for over 10 years, with a documented track record of placements, comparable to a local county college or other accredited colleges with technical programs. Do your research.

What Does a Software Engineer Education Cost?

This is just the cost of the professional training or college you choose. It will probably range from in the thousands for a technical training course to many thousands or more a year for a college degree (and varies by the colleges you choose). For community colleges, you might start your degree program for the first couple of years under $9,000 or $12,000, depending on where you live and the college. For more name-brand colleges, it can cost you a lot more. Research the school or technical training school and look at what job placement programs they have. Please find out how successful they are at helping place students once they graduate. Name-brand schools can make it a little easier to land your first job, but you will often pay a significantly higher cost for those that probably wouldn't be worthwhile in the long term. You need a school that is good at teaching the material you need at reasonable prices and is an accredited educational institution so you can transfer credits to another school, if you need to.

How Much Do Software Engineers Make Out of College?

This can vary by your location and by the company/sector you go into. For example, the New York City metro area will pay more on average ($72k–150k) than out in Montana on average ($64k–110k). Still, these are good salaries overall. Always check job sites to see current salaries, since these can change with the area and with the economy.

Co-Op

One consideration when going to college is to see if your college supports a co-op program (if you are interested). Some schools offer this where, for part of your degree program, you go to school for a semester or a quarter, then work for a semester or quarter (this can extend the time to complete your degree). The positive side is that sometimes the schools offer placement services to help you get these jobs. When you are done with the degree, you will have a leg up on others since you will come out of school with work experience already (plus you have made some money to help with school as well). It's a win/win and can make finding your first job much more manageable.

Intern Programs

For traditional college, where you have a summer break for your junior year or after your senior year, you can see if companies are looking for interns.

You can check on the company site or job posting platforms like Indeed.com, Monster.com, LinkedIn, etc.

These are often paid, though not always. Sometimes, the pay can be pretty good, depending on the company and the economy. See if you have skills equal to or close to what they are looking for, and apply. Keep an eye out for this early, probably in the March, April, and May time frame, or your slots will all be taken. These programs can be a great way to get your foot in the door. If they like you, they may offer you a job when you get out of college.

Some companies try to put a very positive foot forward with interns by finding them some interesting short-term assignments and treating them as well as possible, so this can be a very interesting experience.

One Person's Experience

This is just one person's experience. Everyone is likely to have a different experience. My experience may not have been the typical co-op experience, since most of the official co-op jobs were near the college in Boston and I had decided to go back home many hours away, so there were few available official co-op job listings there. I had to find co-op jobs on my own.

A Company that Helped Manage Money

This company had software they gave to account executives to go out and sell their retirement money management services. The team I worked on helped improve that product. I also helped come up with a copy protection scheme to protect the 3.5" disks they sent to their account representatives. This prevented it from being copied and the software from being used by unauthorized people. It required monthly software codes to be entered to allow it to keep working. Even after I returned to school, they let me do some side projects for them while at school and bill the hours I worked.

A Consumer Electronics Firm

Here, we worked on coding in a Visual Basic-like language for DOS using a product called HyperPad. We built executive user interfaces. Imagine a map of the United States with areas where there were production plants showing in either green, yellow, or red to indicate their status. An executive could click on a plant to get detailed information. While working there, my coworkers and I decided to write two products that work with HyperPad. One we called HyperFont, and the other we called debugging assistant. We even got the Brightbill-Roberts company that made HyperPad include fliers for our products in their box. We had a separate company to market those. My coworkers and I even visited the company in upstate New York.

For My Company with a Friend—Not Co-Op

This wasn't officially co-op, since I did it on the side during this time. A coworker/friend from the previously mentioned company later helped me produce another product we called Virtual Monitors (a virtual desktop-like product). We sold through a publisher that got products into retail software stores at the time (Egghead Software). It was pretty cool being in college and being able to go to a retail store and see the product you created on the shelves there. IBM at the time was looking to port software to OS/2, and they lent me what was probably a $7,000 IBM ps/2 at the time. I had it in my apartment to try to convert Virtual Monitors and other software to OS/2. I had some direct contact with developers on OS/2 in Florida when there were issues. Another benefit of publishing products at the time was getting a free CompuServe account. It was a sort of the precursor to Prodigy and AOL. It was one of the most significant services of its time.

A Small Start-Up Document Imaging Company

There was a two-person startup: the owner and me. I was tasked with creating software that could batch scan and index documents, writing the code in C. We put together enough of a demonstration so that we could demonstrate on the trade show floor of COMDEX. It was fun being able to show the code you just wrote (hoping it all worked well) to prospective customers.

Planning Your College Courses with an Eye toward a Software Engineering Job/Programming

Look over the curriculum that you plan to choose carefully. Don't overload your semesters with tons of challenging classes, especially if you have lots of math/science and computer classes in that semester. Many computer science courses require lab or development work and can take a load of time. Having other time-consuming courses won't make your job any easier. It is not always possible to do this, but do what you can.

If you don't think you will do well with math and science, if possible, find another curriculum that can still achieve your goals. Many computer programming jobs don't need calculus or physics, so unless you plan to work in a field you think it is necessary, you could probably get away without it. There are plenty of jobs without those requirements. You will need basic math skills for most software engineer jobs. Sometimes, knowledge of statistics could be helpful. There are a lot of times you will be working with large amounts of data. Many folks have gotten by without formal statistics classes that can be recalled, and it's not a requirement that we've seen at most jobs.

Other types of math courses or other courses I have some comments on:

- Discrete Math: You might see classes about discrete math or some variation on courses like that. That course is interesting but more challenging than you might think. That is Boolean logic/math. You could live without it, but you may be a better algorithm designer with it. I'd say I haven't had to use that knowledge very often directly, but at least that math applies to the work you could be doing.

- Linear Algebra: Again, a little harder than it seems. Unless you are doing computer graphics or matrix manipulations, you probably won't use this knowledge often in most general business applications I've run into. I've done some matrix-like operations, but at least for me, it was string-related, not math-related many times.

Some other classes that were interesting:

- Computer Engineering/Electronics: Wow, I liked and had trouble with this course at the same time. Using basic logic gates, we would build simulation circuits on a simulator to simulate logic gates and build adders or other higher-level electronic circuits and simulate them. Very cool, though the tests in this class are hard. Nearly everyone in the class was failing. Then, everyone in the class learned we went to the wrong but similar class. Hence, we had to petition the dean to allow the course as a replacement (nearly the whole class showed up at the dean's office when someone heard it was the wrong course. Luckily, they accepted it; with our grades, that was lucky). Is this required to be successful in computers? No, not at all. But if you really like to know what's going on in the guts of a computer, it can be very interesting.
- Automata: Very applicable, but testing was harder than I expected. This teaches things like parsing and processing text and making decisions (could be any text/language processing) or really any type of a state machine, for that matter, where

input causes a change of state to process things differently. It is like regular expressions if you are familiar with that and how you can process those. It's like if you do not know the language Perl and someone asks you to take a test on it. If you read up on Perl one day (well, see some examples of code), you'll see why that might have been mildly funny . . .)

- Compiler Design Class: This class was fun but a little hard. Also, probably not something most people will be using after school, unless you plan on writing a compiler of some type, I guess.
- Artificial Intelligence: This was a very interesting course, using Lisp to simulate neural networks and various processing. This wasn't a very popular field when I took it, I believe. Now, however, machine learning is getting pretty popular.

Look through the computer electives and determine things that would be useful to your future job, as well as a couple that might interest you. Always keep an eye on what you might do in your future job. For example, I thought taking compiler design would be a great idea . . . but I haven't used much of that knowledge in almost 30 years. Interesting, yes, perhaps, but not useful in most jobs. There are exceptions, of course. I did take artificial intelligence, which had not been useful for years, but is becoming really popular now (I wonder how much I still remember). I also surveyed a graduate cryptography course that was interesting.

General Electives

If you are like me and find your other regular classes are challenging enough, you might decide to pick some easier general electives where you can, such as Intro to Rock Music, Music Appreciation, etc. (Yes, I took those.) I did take one actual science elective, Astronomy, since it was an interest of mine. I was just hoping it wouldn't be too hard.

You can challenge yourself or have fun with your electives if you have all of your other required courses out of the way. It's your choice.

What Computer Language Classes to Take?

You may be allowed to take classes for different computer languages as elective computer courses. The best thing is to consider which languages will be most beneficial for your career. Languages that have a lot of jobs in the area you live would be an excellent way to tell if that language will be a good choice. Check out job sites like Indeed.com and search for jobs for the languages you are interested in and compare popular ones like Python, PHP, C#, Java, Ruby, JavaScript, C++, etc. Also, realize that some different languages are sometimes used for different things. Some languages might not be normal to use to write websites, for example, while other languages would be. So find ones in an area of your interest with the most jobs so that even coming out of school, you will have more marketable programming knowledge.

Planning to Transfer in the Future?

If you are planning to do a portion of your classes at one school and transfer to another, you might want to try to confirm that the credits would transfer before you take them. It's no fun after you take classes and you want to transfer, finding out they don't transfer. If possible, get the info in writing. An example case might be if you start by going to a two-year school for an associate's degree and later want to transfer to a full four-year college to complete your degree. Knowing your curriculum maps well would be good, as well as that the other school will accept credits.

Often, you need to confirm they would accept credits from your school at all, then next check individual courses. They would compare the course descriptions credit syllabus/overview to see if it matches a comparable course that your new school has.

Even if you aren't sure now, knowing that the curricula are close between your current and future school can make things much easier.

If You Prefer To Go Full-On Computer Science

If you are looking to get into science with an eye toward jobs that will need it or for the challenge and go full-on calculus, physics, etc. and you think you can pass all of that or at least want to go for it. For some folks, it's easy. Some folks, it's not. Plant me firmly on the not side. I did like learning about it. I just can't claim I was good at it, and you certainly don't like something as much when you aren't good at it.

(Nearly everything on this page is an opinion, so do your own research on what you might need. Mine is just one person's experience.)

Surviving College as a Computer Science Major (or a Variation of That)

Hopefully, you are a coffee drinker (if not, you will be . . . you will be), and you will probably need a caffeine jolt. Nearly every morning began with some form of coffee.

At some point, you will be staring at a screen for hours and can't figure out what is wrong with your program as your eyes start to glaze over . . . Don't worry. It will usually come to you. If it doesn't, hit up a friend in your class to review your code (if your teacher/school allows that). You'll often find that they can spot the thing you've been staring at for hours and somehow missed, and in like two minutes, they go, "Why the heck did you do that?"

If you are a computer major, you probably won't have as much time to party as some of the other majors do at college. Or at least I could recall feeling that way. Not that I was the type to party, so I guess that didn't really matter much.

While college is a bit hazy in the rearview mirror, I do recall nearly living in the computer labs to get some work done. Though some of it I was able to do remotely . . . remember though, this was BI (Before Internet), well before the Internet as you know it today. It existed at the time, but it was nothing like what it is today. You could e-mail, FTP, and connect to remote messaging systems or remote into a Unix-like system to run some command-line functionality. At the time, we had access to, surprisingly, some Macs, some probably second generation PC clones, maybe 80286 at the time, some Unix system (Sun, I think), and a DEC-VAX.

The good news is, this generation of computer science engineers wouldn't need to use slow modems to connect to the Internet. Modems sounded like a fax machine. They were about 14 k, 28 k, or 56 k bits per second at the time, which is way slower than today's speeds measured in megabits or gigabits per second. The point of that is, your remote options will probably be pretty good now, with access to on campus systems remotely over the Internet from your home PC, which most of you probably have some form of or will, for college.

I'm guessing these days that computer labs aren't as popular with so many good remote options, though the pictures on one of the sites showing a nearly full lab makes me wonder. They do mention plenty of remote options and remote printing.

Computer Labs/Home Computers, Assignments, and More

To make some extra money, I worked as a proctor in the computer labs, getting printouts and running antivirus on machines or re-installing as needed, helping people with issues, and so on. This can be a good option for some extra money, to meet people, and to have access to the lab.

Having some sort of computer at your home or dorm, though, will make your life a lot easier, not needing a free machine at the lab and being able to get work done whenever you need. Make sure what you have will work to help you at college. It might be easier to use a Windows PC than a Mac, for example. In business, there are generally more Windows PCs than Macs, so getting and learning it will serve you well. Macs are around at some businesses but usually at most companies in small numbers, of course with some exceptions at certain companies where they sell Mac software or use it for a particular reason. They are much more popular today, though, in business than in years past, but I believe they still do not make up a significant number in most firms that I have worked at.

The lab can be a good place if you are struggling with assignments, though, and need help. You may see someone working on your assignment and can ask for their help. If you've made some friends in your classes, you can get in touch remotely for help as well.

Also, professors usually have office hours. You can get their help in person or, these days, I'm sure remotely as well.

Multi-Person Programming Projects

At some point, you will probably be asked to do a multi-person project. That will sort of simulate what you might have to do at work one day. Pick your team carefully, and make sure if you get to choose your project, it is actually achievable in the time you have. Don't put it off. Programming nearly always takes longer than you expect it will. Make sure your team agrees on the project and who will work on which parts.

Design it together or propose an architecture and get accepted by the team, then lay out your plan for everyone's work on it.

These projects can be harder than you think due to the team dynamics, lack of experience working on multi-person projects, personalities, and expectations.

Some Other General Trivia

Comp Sci/engineering friends can make good roommates for apartments/dorms. Help with projects is always nearby, and some common experiences seem to fit well. Don't get me wrong, you can cohabitate with other majors. It's just that you might not have as much in common. We got along ok with the other majors, though perhaps the only activity I can recall doing with them was watching a zombie movie. I'm probably not the standard you should go by, though I will say a lot of the other majors always seemed to have a lot more parties.

What Do You Do If You Have Trouble with Your Classes?

Remember the teacher, your friends/classmates, or if need be, a tutor can be helpful. Yep, even in college.

If you need to retake a class, that is possible, and you can even do it at another school. Just get it pre-approved that the credits will transfer if you just need a couple of extra credits. Talk to the counselors. It could be that some classes have different placement levels, like math or science you should be in.

When You Have Finished Your Degree

Make sure you get your final transcript that proves you graduated and make copies of your final transcript. Many jobs nowadays do background checks, and they will call your college to check on your degree. There are two important parts about college: learning and them telling the companies that you did, in fact, graduate from there. Occasionally, colleges mess up on one or the other, and I can tell you it's rather unpleasant to get called by a company you are trying to get hired by and be told that your college said you don't have a degree. Make sure you have those copies of the final transcript and graduation certificate to prove it.

Just thinking back on my college days . . . unless you really like it spicy, don't try suicide wings . . . Just don't.

CHAPTER 6

What They May Not Teach You in School

What They May Not Teach You in School about Working as a Software Engineer

For instance, I didn't learn to juggle (badly) in school. That might not be too useful for software developers, but below you will find a lot more useful stuff.

These are just some of the things you sometimes don't learn in school:

Time Management

Arguably, as I'm sure this is taught in some schools, learning where and how to focus your time can be helpful.

There are many popular methods, and each technique could probably take up a book, so I'll summarize it here.

Look at the book *Getting Things Done*. It's a pretty popular methodology. I knew someone who started their own business who used this. He grew it into a multimillion-dollar business and sold it for even more to a megacorp. He liked this methodology, and I've used it as well, and it seems to work reasonably well.

I'd recommend giving it a try. It might help you keep track of things and prevent you from procrastinating on things you could do.

Source Control and Branching

At least I didn't learn this in school. Of course, that could be because there were not the variety of source control options that there are today. Today, there are a plethora of good options: Git, SVN, Team Foundation Server, Perforce, and plenty more. There was a Unix version of SCCS that was out much earlier, but that had not made its way to Windows yet. We'll cover this later in another section, though.

Business Focus/Prioritization

This mixes time management, money management, and feature/fix management. One approach applying to software is what people call MVP, or a minimum viable product. What minimum product could you put out to satisfy customers and keep your business alive or to grow it? Some folks don't like this term, as they believe it goes against customer value. They restate it as something like Minimum Valuable Product—though similar in concept, what is the minimum product you could deliver that is valuable to customers, with the apparent implication of also being valuable to your company to stay alive or grow? College and school teach you the "right," way, and you must do it "right," or your grade will suffer. Colleges often teach ideal circumstances and emphasize for that perfection to achieve those 100 scores.

Small business/startup to mid-size business can be as brutal or more. It can come down to . . . if we don't get a product into customers' hands they are willing to pay for, the company will go bankrupt, and all of its employees will be out of work, with perhaps not enough money to provide for their families. When you are starting up or running a business, you want to keep your end goal in focus, but you will probably need to make some tough decisions sometimes for a company to survive. I saw these play out in real time, and I've seen these decisions made and how a company thrived because of them.

That could mean implementing something in the easiest/fastest way possible, not the best way possible. While they say if you settle for good, you won't get to great, also note that perfection can be the enemy of "good enough for now." If your competitor gets a feature out before you do, they could take business and money away from the company that you need to keep it running. You need to weigh time as money (as a business owner, you are paying employees, and that can cost a lot of money); you need payback on that money to stay in business.

It would help if you also recognized when it might be time to pay for the short-term gains you've made due to your time-to-market method of implementing software. At some point, your software may start to pay the price for that, where you would need some better architecture that will take longer.

Features/functionality don't need to be implemented in black or white, perfection or nothing. You can instead have a long-term goal in mind to plan for your future. But implement a minimum viable solution on your path to reaching your end goal with a plan to take some steps to improve in the middle. Get your time to market on valuable features faster with a plan for the future.

Folks running the business will often appreciate hearing about the options available in terms of achieving some gains earlier rather than later. Sometimes, it will make sense to go for the long-term solution. Just think things through from a business perspective—what makes the most sense for the business and what makes the most sense for the project—and perhaps they can meet in the middle somewhere and eventually get to where you would like to be.

The Rules and Business

Throughout school, you have been told that you must follow the rules, and if you don't, you will be penalized. They will mark off your grades, etc. I'm sure there are some rules in school you bend when you shouldn't. You should follow your school rules, as they're likely strictly enforced. The business sometimes operates a little differently. If it's NOT illegal, your business might consider bending the rules they made for themselves. You should follow the rules, as it's likely only folks at the proper levels that can alter them without ramifications (depending on the org). I'll give an example: You are told by your risk management team that never is a developer allowed database access to production. It's against corporate policy. It cannot happen EVER! For the past three years, they have held to that, and you've heard that. Your boss tells you, "Look, we need to solve this problem. You need to get access to the production DB." You tell your boss, "NO, it can't happen. The risk team will never let that happen." Your boss goes to the risk team and says, "We need this and now." The risk team is like, "Umm . . . hmm . . . ok, but we will require management to sign a risk exception form."

You've just learned two valuable lessons: one, be careful about telling your boss no, and two, the rules are not as strict as you might have thought.

If there is a good business reason to do something, as long as it's not illegal, the business might consider it, even if they have all sorts of rules and processes against it. In business, it's best not to talk about absolutes such as "can't do this" or "must do that" for the rules, since it can depend on the situation sometimes. A better phrase is "our SOP

(Standard operating procedure) is to (insert thing here)." If you talk about things in absolutes, you may look foolish when you find out they are not so absolute.

Working with Others and the Art of Influence and Leadership

Let's face it. Most people don't like to be told what to do. If you are told to do something, you will probably do it if you have to, but you may not like it. In school, you are often told what you need to do. That's what schools do to teach you. Business is often a team effort, needing to work together to achieve more than individuals could achieve alone. Sometimes, you will be working on a team of peers or with disparate groups. You will probably need to work together to achieve your goals. If everyone has the same goals, hopefully, there can be some agreement with the teams to move forward. Sometimes, it takes leadership from someone. Sometimes, that is someone who has no authority to lead but lead by example. They devise a plan and communicate effectively about it to the team, helping make the plan happen. Others join in and agree on the plan. These plans can call for compromise/negotiation, networking, selling your plan or someone else's plan, or potentially call for leadership, depending on the situation.

One of the older books still talked about today is *How to Win Friends and Influence People*. Some people today misinterpret influence as take advantage of, but it's not that. It's a mutual understanding of wants/needs and helping satisfy them. The book is stuffy. I went looking for more modern-day equivalents. Haven't read this book, but *Principle Centered Leadership* is on my to-read list.

I would recommend not just becoming a scholar of technology but also learning more about people. Learn how they work together. Make it one of the things you continue to learn throughout your life. Pick up a book or audiobook on it once in a while to keep your mind refreshed on the topic. Perhaps some folks can recommend other books on this topic.

Also related is the art of negotiation (e.g., salary, what you are working, what you need, etc.). A popular book is *Getting to Yes*, though there are many others.

Continual Improvement

The end of school is not the end of your journey to being a software engineer. It is just the end of your beginning. Software engineering is a vast set of fields, now. No person can master them all. You will need to stay concurrent with technology and continue to improve your skills, because training to be a software engineer is not being one. If you tried to learn karate from a book, after completing the book, you would not consider yourself a master. The book was just the start of the journey, and now actually using those skills will be required to keep you on the road to continual improvement.

Creativity

School may teach you some creativity, and there certainly have been some notable people who were creative while in school. A lot of notable creativity happens outside of school or after your years of school, though. Creativity is both a talent and something you can exercise to try to continue to be creative. There is some creativity in every bit of software you write, but sometimes, that is limited. I recommend you practice it yourself. This can be important if you want to come up with your own apps, products, or just designs for the current ones you work on.

What Do You Want?

And What Are You Capable of? What Roles Should I Target for My Career? Work-Life Balance

This goes to the drive of what you want to do/work on, things you like, and what has meaning to you.

Why, you ask, does this matter in a discussion about software engineering? Perhaps it could change what industry you want to work in, and thus what area you want to live in, and impact what jobs are available to you. It can affect how much you want to give to your work vs. how much to your personal life. It can help you decide the career path you will pursue. It's something you should think about as you go through your career.

For example, there is an inclination by some software engineers to go into management. By its very nature, management means there are fewer jobs available in your role than if you do the work (i.e., the people that would work for a manager). The higher up you go, the fewer jobs there are typically, and at some level, that can mean you need to move to find the jobs you desire. It can be harder to find jobs at higher levels. If you are unable to work with people or empathize with them, you might not go far in management.

Do you want to work in financial areas to make more money but have less personal time? Being in higher-level management may also mean less personal time (not always, but it can).

Your ideas about what you want can hold you back or lead you in appropriate or inappropriate directions. You need to think carefully about these things to decide what you want and what you are capable of (being honest with yourself).

Creating Your Own Opportunities or Taking Advantage of Them

You don't need to work for others if you can find a way to be a consultant or work for yourself. This might be easy if your money expectations/needs are low and very hard if you have greater needs/money expectations.

You could create your own software/service, start your own company, and create your opportunities. Or you can take the traditional route and work for a company and work on their products. Even by doing that, you can create opportunities when you see them. I knew some developers who created their own web version of a thick client product and basically created a new group just for those folks to work on it.

Or you see someone leave the firm, and they had a position you believe you can take, and you are sure you would want it. Ask for it (don't wait. Be sure it's right for you, then decide and take advantage of the opportunity if you can). That doesn't mean it will always work out for you, but sometimes, luck, timing, and creating your opportunities are part of your growth path.

If you are really stuck at a firm, not given more responsibility/pay, and want/need it, and can't get it internally, it might be time for you to look elsewhere if that fits your overall plan and desires.

I knew someone in a different type of job who, by agreeing to move around the world and work for well-known companies, got salaries/bonuses that would make your jaw drop to the floor. Someone with the skills and is willing to move to and go to the right places and change jobs to get bigger pay to do it can achieve things if they are capable. Of course, you need to have decided if that type of life is the one for you. Money isn't everything. Moving isn't painless.

Perfect Is the Enemy of Done/Money

When you are working for a company, for the most part, they are there to make money. They often do that by satisfying customers, but that doesn't mean your product needs to be "perfect." If, for example, your company was having trouble making payroll in the next month and you could make some money by releasing a feature that would make you money next month vs. taking two more months to make it perfect, which do you think the company would choose? It would probably prefer to stay in business and get the feature out now rather than later. It doesn't even need to be as evident as this scenario. Companies prioritize making money sooner rather than later in general. If you can learn to design software and a release schedule to bring value to the company/customers sooner rather than later, you will be a more valuable asset to your company.

Software Development Life Cycle (SDLC) and Auditing

Your school may or may not have much information on a business-level SDLC. You may have learned about parts of it like Agile Scrum, or you may have even gone through an overview of some lifecycles. Understanding how that affects your day-to-day work in real life might be something else. You will learn how your ticket systems are used within your company's SDLC and the procedures needed at various stages of the process. Each company tends to have broad similarities but many specific differences. Ticket system implementation is often customized for a company or even a group. Understanding what it takes to deliver and maintain a product in a production environment is probably not something they teach in school.

You'd be surprised at how many business processes are driven by audits of business processes, especially in highly regulated industries like financial or medical. Some businesses are burdened with significant effects just due to audit requirements.

Audit requirements can sometimes require two people for what was done before by one (look up segregation/separation of duties). At some point, you may need to learn the mental skill of a Zen master and the equivalent of psychological judo. Plus, you will need sound business practices to come out of an audit unscathed. If an audit finds issues with the business process, it could result in as little as just needing to document or correct it. Alternatively, it could end up being something more serious such as financial penalties or, in the worst of cases, loss of business depending on the audit or industry.

Coding for a Production Environment

Not sure if schools are teaching this today, but when I learned, you could write most code that worked and didn't necessarily handle all failure scenarios. For production coding, your code must properly handle any known conditions or potentially unknown errors that could come up in a reasonable way and keeps your system and data integrity and reliability to levels required by your business environment. Often, this also means logging all significant errors so that you can support and maintain the code. In addition, monitor it for potential upcoming or current issues.

Professionalism

Take pride in your work and learn to improve, meaning do it well and learn to do it well. Some of these are very general.

Consistently arrive on time, and work at least your required hours (don't skip out early).

Treat others with respect as you would want to be treated.

Don't discuss your or other people's salary with other people, especially other people at work.

Don't leave for hours for long lunches, breaks, and so on. Even if your office has flexible hours, confirm what is the norm and stay within reason.

If you took a longer break, make up your hours or take PTO otherwise, if allowed. Make sure the work that was supposed to get done is done, if at all possible.

Take pride in your appearance and your odor/smell (hopefully lack of smell). Shower daily, please.

When you need to criticize things, don't criticize people; instead, discuss the specific process or behavior, and be constructive, not destructive.

Give two weeks' notice if at all possible if you need to leave your job (or whatever the notice requirements are).

Don't accept a job and immediately leave to go to another position to accept another offer. That will be looked at poorly by the firm you left.

Schedule your days off. Don't spring it on your manager that you need to take off tomorrow unless it is an urgent one-off need. Running a business with people randomly needing to leave is hard, especially for smaller companies.

The Art of What You Should or Shouldn't Say No To

NO isn't always the best thing to say. It's often good to ask about better directions to take on something rather than saying no. No one likes to hear no, especially in business. Sometimes, no is the right answer, but you should think very carefully whether you can use another method. For instance, asking questions about another direction would be better.

A lot of people in businesses may ask for your help, and it may, in some cases, benefit you to say yes or even benefit you to say no. But think about what is right for the company, you, your team, and your manager before you terminate a request with the dreaded no. Sometimes, an answer could be, "I don't think today, but how about tomorrow?" Sometimes, it's as simple as that.

They didn't teach you that in school. Saying to your teacher no, you aren't going to do that assignment, probably wouldn't go over well. But perhaps some of you did learn the art of negotiation, asking for a little extra time with a valid reason (and not the dog ate your homework sort of reason).

Also, you might be confronted with something that seems like a yes or no. Think about if there is another option. Sometimes, there is a gray area that helps keep things beneficial for all.

Interviewing

This is a topic covered later in more detail. At least, as far as I can recall, most colleges don't cover this topic very well or at least not specific enough for software engineers. Questions can range from knowledge questions, to whiteboard problems questions, to all out coding/debugging solutions, or even puzzle problems. *Cracking the Coding Interview* by Gayle Laakmann McDowell is a popular book on this topic (see Interviewing).

Working with Your Manager

Yes, your parents have been training you for years to do what they tell you. Schools have been teaching you to do what they tell you for years. So you would think that would have prepared you for everything you might encounter at work. Sort of, but there are a lot of nuances and dynamics at work that there were not in those cases that can significantly change what you are trying to do.

What does your manager want from you? This can vary from manager to manager and based on your work. In general, your manager wants you to do the tasks you picked up or were assigned in as time-efficient a manner as possible and as autonomously as possible or as the task requires while following all the required business rules and procedures. Your manager wants you to know how to do your job independently or collaboratively as the task requires, involving your manager in the minimum amount needed (or as much as the manager desires).

Figuring out how much communication and collaboration your manager wants can sometimes be tricky, as it can vary based on what you are doing or what the manager likes to be involved in. The best thing you can do if you are new to navigating this type of management is asking to start to get a feel for what they want: "How much communication do you want on the task or tasks I will be working on? And how would you like the communication, e-mail? and how often?"

Some managers like to be somewhat hands-off and only want to know about risks that could affect the product/schedules, quality, and significant effort that would be outside the norm or the expected. Other managers like more frequent updates to stay in touch about what is going on. If you don't know what your manager wants, asking questions like that will help clarify. You will have to learn to use your judgment based on the information you feel you need to communicate and how urgently you feel they need to get the information you need to tell them. If it's not urgent, an e-mail may work. Something more urgent may require a call or text message, for example.

Managing Stress

Yes, school can be stressful. No one wants to fail a class. It's tough preparing for in-class presentations or hard tests. None of those match the level of stress when you need money, and you need to find a job. When your job is having layoffs and the economy is down, it's hard to find new work. That's a whole new level of stress.

Things you can try:

- Exercise: Walk, workout, etc. Exercise can be a great stress reliever. Try it regularly. Take a walk every day.
- Once you know you have done all you can do for now, try to let go and do an activity you enjoy. Reading, hiking, a hobby building things, whatever it is that you can do to take your mind out of the stress to something you like.
- Code something you would like to do to keep your skills up. Perhaps a game or just something using a technology you've wanted to learn.
- Listen to calming music.
- Take a vacation. Maybe it's time for a break. I've known people who got laid off from work and had a great time between jobs. Or just a normal vacation from your job, of course.
- Make sure you are getting enough sleep. All-nighters in school were great, right? Work and all-nighters usually aren't quite as fun.

Warning: I'm not a doctor or medical expert, so just opinions, use at your own risk.;)

I'm sure you can check the Internet for more ideas. If nothing is working, your doctor may be able to help with some suggestions.

Teamwork

What experiences have you had working in a team? In this case, a team creates business value for the company's customers. How can you work together and coordinate your activities to deliver value? We'll be going over the Agile Scrum framework in this book as one way to at least create a helpful process. It alone won't get things done. Only actual teamwork will do that.

CHAPTER 7

Where to Work

Here Are Some of the Best Places to Work for a Software Engineer

What are the best places to work for software engineers? One thing to note is that as a software developer, many businesses are pretty good places to work. In most industries, software developers get paid reasonably. Those are generalizations. There are exceptions to every generalization, of course.

Another such generalization is that software developers are treated better (pay, hours, benefits, etc.) in companies or divisions of companies where they are building a product/service that is directly responsible for significant revenue for the company. It's possible that software engineers, even in the same company, don't get equivalent pay and benefits if they work in an area that doesn't directly contribute to a product's revenue.

For example, if you were a developer working on Microsoft Office or Microsoft Windows, those products contribute directly to the company's bottom line.

I've heard/read that it doesn't apply in all industries. For example, gaming software developers are rumored not to be paid as well or given as many perks (except perhaps the ability to play games all day... joking...)

Some industries get a sort of reputation in the software field. An industry that is generalized to ask developers to put in long hours and work when on call 24/5–24/7 is the financial industry. The financial industry in the past has been generalized to pay better than other industries. As with any generalization, it is not always accurate. It can vary significantly based on the company, division, and product being worked on. Pay can significantly depend on the division or group that you are in. It can even vary from group to group within large companies.

Within a particular company, try to work for a growing product that makes a lot of money in the organization. It's much easier to work in a business line that's making a lot of money than one that isn't or is losing money, so picking the most significant growing product at a company can offer benefits. There could be benefits to a smaller, significantly growing product with a promising future, but that future is often harder to predict.

How Company Size Can Affect Your Experience

Small: (2–100 people)

This could be a startup if it's new and offer the possibility of options/ stock payout if it is promising and plans to go public. Or it could be a small, existing company. In a small company, people are probably doing multiple roles. This provides an opportunity to learn different tasks but also likely means more responsibility and less ease to take time off, as you have little to no backup. If your business requires 24/7 support, it's possible you would be that support. Before joining such a business, clarify all this, so you know what you are getting into.

Another good side of this is that it may be easier and faster to grow into a higher-level role. There is excellent potential for growth in small companies. With so few people, it can be easy to rise higher quickly, sometimes even by someone higher up leaving, when they need to fill a role soon. At the same time, it could cause stagnation, with only a few other groups internally. If the management chain stays in place, it could prevent rising up the chain. Growth or need could also come naturally. As the business expands, leaders will need to guide many new people as they join. For example, by being one of the first software engineers, if the business takes off, you might end up in a natural leadership role, perhaps even a manager or a higher level one day.

Medium: (101–1000 people)
These companies usually offer more job security, since the business has grown to the point it's at least mildly successful. There should be enough people to allow for easier time off than at a small business. There should hopefully be at least a rotation for support roles. It might be a little harder to move up to higher roles in such an organization, since there is likely a well-established structure.

Large: (1001 and above)
Large companies usually offer lots of stability, structure, and process. There are usually enough people to support rotation and allow time off more easily. It will be harder to move up roles in an existing structure, though one benefit is that there are so many areas in the organization that one area might be a bit different from another, offering opportunities if you need to move groups.

Software Companies

These can be great places for developers to work, since software engineers are the key to making money for these companies. They are often treated better than other employees, sometimes even within the same firm. Some of these firms may be cloud software firms that use their product to create a service, which can be even better, since there is a continuous revenue stream.

It's hard to describe the difference between working at a software company and working at a company that isn't doing software. At one non-software company, we were there to service, providing the executive team with information. They needed to get information, and they needed it now. There was not much of an SDLC or process you would have at a software company. We weren't making money for the business. We were providing data to show the business where they were making money and where they were not. It was still a reasonable place to work.

Perhaps part of the appeal of working at a company that makes software for other companies/people is knowing your software gets used around the country/world and interacting with people and users that use your software. It's pretty cool to meet people out in the world who are using the things you have written.

Regulated vs. Unregulated

Regulated businesses like the financial or medical field often have more process, validation, and audit requirements than unregulated businesses. This adds overhead to the development process so that the business meets the regulatory requirements. If you haven't worked in an area like this before, it can be an eye-opener to see how much process there is. Larger businesses often have even more processes.

The requirements around this are usually a rigorous, well-documented process that reduces the risk of certain types of events occurring. It is also about auditing the software development process to determine if there are any holes in its implementation. At one of the companies I worked, we had several significant audits a year, taking several weeks. Some were more detailed than others. To give you an idea of the type of process they put in place, they had requirements that developers could not do any official builds, and they couldn't have access to the machines that could do the builds. The build machine also had to record a hash of what was built. Then that would be verified by testing before being used in production.

Working in a Place You Like the Most

Often times, this will come down to:

- You like the work.
- You like the technology.
- You like the people you work with.
- You like your manager.
- Your company is doing well.
- You are paid reasonably.
- You are appreciated and treated well.
- You continue to learn things and do not stagnate.
- You are working in a field that you are passionate about and/or help people and society in some way.

The last item can add a new dimension for folks who perhaps felt that something was lacking in their job but didn't know what. Having a job that makes you feel good about what you do can add that extra dimension to the work you didn't have earlier. For example, imagine being a developer at one of the companies that helped make the vaccines to save possibly millions of lives from COVID or other diseases. Jobs like that can fill in that missing piece you didn't even realize was missing or when you couldn't tell what was missing until you found it. Everyone might have their own opinion on what that is. If you can find what makes you feel good about a job, perhaps you can find that extra dimension in your next position or your present one.

Organization Culture

Many organizations have their own sort of culture. Some are driven by their leadership, employees, or both. This culture can take many forms. Some businesses might have a culture of frugalness, not wasting things. One organization I know wouldn't even buy Post-it notes for their staff, as they were often pricey. During the dot-com boom, some start-ups had things like game rooms, open offices, free snacks and drinks, and even alcohol in some places. Some businesses offer flexible hours and work-life balance. Other companies might like big parties, office lunches, team lunches, and more. Two different companies I worked at had ping pong tables. Two also offered free snacks and drinks. One even had free alcoholic beverages. At one company I worked at, people would keep hard alcohol bottles on their desks. One company had a culture of touting other people's work and helping internal people solve the product's software issues. One company had an open office-type environment, and another had two-person offices. Some had a culture of people working late and paying for taxi/limo rides home past a specific time. Others had a culture of a weekly meeting that always had a free lunch. One had a game room with a pool table and an Xbox.

It can be more than what they offer, though. Some environments are open and friendly, where people come up to you and ask what you do. They give credit to others' efforts and more.

COMPS

An acronym to help you remember what to consider:

Culture: Is the company culture something you like?

Organization: Is the company and its product something you connect with and feel good being a part of?

Money: Is the pay reasonable compared to the average in the area?

Product: Is software or service the product where developers are the ones creating profit for the company, or is the software being written purely as an expense? It's better when your job directly helps make products or services the company sells.

Size: Think about the size of the organization and the possible mobility that may or may not give you.

What Area of Software Engineering Should I Go Into?

This is a tricky question unless you have strong opinions on these areas.

There used to be just two high-level areas: front-end and back-end developer. Now, with full stack developers doing front end and back end, that's a little less of a thing than it was before, but some companies/products sometimes still work that way.

There are so many technologies and niches now: artificial intelligence, database, web, distributed systems, e-commerce, compiler design, data science, driver development. Nearly every industry has some form of specialty now.

Let's face it, though. The world is on the Internet, so web developers have plenty of jobs. Mobile developers are becoming quite popular as well for Android/iOS.

You might want to start thinking about what you want to work on. Always keep in mind how many jobs are available in the area. Make sure there are a lot in your area or the place you plan to live so that you will always have opportunities.

Sometimes, you end up in areas you never expected because a job interested you. You might have one idea but see an attractive alternative opportunity elsewhere. Again, just think about whether your job takes you in the direction that makes you more marketable so that you will always be able to find work.

When I started looking for work, I looked for big name-brand companies that people would recognize. I figured that just seeing those names on my resume would give me some credibility vs. companies folks don't recognize. I don't know how much that helped, but it was just a thought.

At least have some things in mind that will help guide you in decisions for your choice of college, college courses or education, and possibly eventually jobs. If you see other opportunities that interest you and would keep you marketable or make you more marketable, these could be considered.

Once you are in a particular type of job/skill set, it can be hard to switch to another unless you've had the opportunity or some training you could put on your resume. For example, without experience, many companies probably wouldn't consider you for a switch in types of development like moving from thick client Windows apps to working on web apps. I decided a while back that the world was switching toward the web rather than thick client apps, and if I had the option to make the switch, I should consider it, since there would likely be more opportunities there. Luckily, I had a little background and a company that provided an opportunity.

Financial firms pay more money on average in the New York metro area but may ask more of you, such as working late nights and even being on call 24 hours for some types of trading systems.

Which Tech Stack Should You Learn/Work In?

You might like free tools so you can learn them without paying, like Linux, Apache, MySQL, and PHP (sometimes referred to as LAMP). PHP may be losing a bit of popularity recently in favor of other languages, perhaps Ruby or others.

Or you might like the above using Windows (WAMP) or use a pure Microsoft stack like Windows, ASP.NET, and C#/SQL if we are considering web stacks.

If you want more desktop or server development, perhaps consider Java or C# Linux/Windows.

I've preferred the Microsoft stacks. They still offer the lower-end tools free, and the tooling is better, easier to use, and more productive. The C# language is moving forward well, with lots of features and options.

Some industries tend to use more of one stack than another. In the financial sector, for servers, there is a lot of LAMP stack usage. Even Internet web servers or back-end servers use Linux in financials a lot. A few years back, it was around 70 percent Linux web servers vs. about 30 percent Windows. It was probably that way because of the cost, since Linux can be free. But frequently, big corporations want to support, so they end up paying for Red Hat Linux and a support contract, so the costs are about equal.

I still prefer the Windows OS, as it's much more UI based and has many more apps and tools on that platform. The desktop window manager and the whole UI seem much more refined, along with the apps that keep you away from the heavy command-line parameter-driven configuration of Linux.

I had always wanted to work for a financial company. My previous manager left and went to one. Late one summer, he asked if I wanted to go see what they do. It was maybe July or August 2001. It was kind of like a startup still but grew a bit. Its location was nice, high up in the north tower of the World Trade Center.

I had been there maybe a year or so earlier for a one-week training on user interface design, so being back there felt familiar. It had always worried me a little after the 1993 bombing of the World Trade Center. It was always with a bit of trepidation I went there. I was going to see what they were up to, but I probably should have guessed they wanted to interview me. What I saw was great, and they offered me the job. I said I'd think about it. I wasn't ready to commute to New York City and wouldn't have been thrilled about working in the World Trade Center, given my concerns about it. I would have had some great options, had I joined at that point, but I didn't.

Of course, everyone knows what happened on 9/11, and it then caused an economic downturn, which was probably partially the cause of me ending up being laid off in January 2002. Luckily, the company that had been in the trade center survived and was set back up in another location, and they said they could still hire me in a couple of months. The source code luckily survived because an employee had taken it home the night before on a laptop. My previous manager had been the only person injured in the company. He was taken away in an ambulance but accidentally left the computer he still had with him at the scene. Someone found his laptop and brought it to him.

When working on stock market applications, everything is centered around the markets such as Nasdaq and NYSE. If your application only trades those, the main action happens between market hours, 9:30 a.m. and 4:00 p.m. If your systems can trade other venues, then you may have trading activity before the market opens and after the market closes.

Those markets would sometimes have test days on weekends, when they were implementing significant new market functionality. One of my entire teams worked the mornings every Saturday for almost the whole summer to make sure our systems would work with the Nasdaq changes.

After market hours, data is sent for settlement of trades. Some systems still would use the FTP protocol for settlement data. If a trading error of some sort happened during the day, then people could end up working late into the night to make sure all of the trade data got fixed if needed to send out prior to the next day's trading. Developing was similar to developing at other companies. We did have a shared market simulator environment that would replay the previous days' data so that we could test our systems on real market data. If there were serious bugs found, they might literally need to be fixed that day before the next trading day started. That didn't happen very often, but it did occasionally.

For specific objectives, it was easy to get the money for new hardware if it had a good business purpose. If you can reduce trade latency, you needed 300 GB of memory for all machines, high-end SSDs, 40 Gbps networking, nanosecond packet tracing devices, and time clocks, all with no problem. When the business would make a decision that we could improve the speed by spending months working on the code or could just buy some hardware, we would often be able to throw hardware at improving performance/scalability. It would make sense in many cases where the lost opportunity cost of something else software-wise we were working on was better for the team to work on and buy hardware where we could in order to help performance.

After some market crashes and some trading venues having performance issues, it was pretty widely adopted that everyone should be able to handle 3X (three times) the max trading volume you currently have. We would test many of the components until they would fail under load to see just how much data we could handle. Luckily, our design could scale horizontally pretty easily by stock symbol ticker ranges like A-I, and so on. If the volume was getting higher to maintain 3X, we could add in a new set of servers and split the ranges equally among them to reduce the load each server would take.

There were times I would get calls in the middle of the night for support issues related to installing and setting up new software overnight. Not too often, but in the middle of the night, a few times can seem like a lot. The pay was pretty decent, though, so if you had to work at night, it was just part of the job.

CHAPTER 8

Preparing to Find a Job

Your Resume

Your resume is for marketing you. This should be well written with zero spelling or grammar mistakes. Historically, people liked to keep this document short. If you have 10 years' experience, perhaps you could have five pages if you had to. Keep it short. Your resume is not a book. It's a summary list of your jobs, dates, positions, and work.

Include on Your Resume the Following Details:

- Summary of your role and experience
- Areas of technical skill/knowledge
- Your per job information and experience

For Each Job, Include:

- Company name (if it's a current position, you could say large communications company if you don't want them to know your current company)

- Month, Year (start of employment)–Month, Year (end of employment)
- Your title/role
- A summary of your experience for the job. Mention the projects you worked on, the technology you used to do it, and specifically the major features/functionality you implemented.
- Mention the significant projects you worked on and the technologies used.

Additional Items

Mention what projects you worked on, the technology you used to do it, and the major features/functionality you implemented.

Open-Source Software

If you have the time to contribute quality code to open-source software and you can include this on your resume, it lets potential employers see how you code, which can be a great way to show off your skills. You can add a link to the project on your resume.

The Top of an Example Resume Below:

John Doe
1 Main St., New York, NY 10014
212-555-1212 john.doe@myemaildomain.com

Company Name, New York, NY
1/2021–Present
Software Engineer, Development

Built a web-based stock-trading application. Full stack using C#/HTML/CSS/JavaScript/SQL/ASP.NET. Implemented order entry screen on the web UI. Implemented API support on the back end using C#/WebAPI. Designed UX for order entry displays.

You would just add more detail to the job and replace the format for other jobs. It should be about a paragraph per job, smaller when your resume is longer (over 5–10 years' experience). You can go to two to five pages if you need to. It's not supposed to be a book, just a high-level summary of where you worked, when you worked there, what your title was, what did you work on, and what technologies you used. You can add a summary section above your job experience to summarize your current skills.

There are many sites online to help you build your resume.

One example is https://www.canva.com/create/resumes/

You can search online for more.

Consulting

Consulting companies make money by charging an hourly rate to the hiring firm and paying the consultant less per hour than they make. How much less can vary from firm to firm, situation to situation, company to company, and even person to person, so you will need to negotiate the most reasonable deal possible.

W-2 vs. 1099 vs. Corp to Corp

W-2 is a form used to pay employees. If you work for a consulting firm, they may pay you as an employee, and you would have a W-2 form. This is more like an employee pay than a consultant, though, usually. The benefit of being on W-2 for a consulting firm is you that don't have to worry about your own taxes from a payroll standpoint.

The downside is that you can't use the pre-tax money for other things that you could expense. Some consulting companies will offer health benefits that you could pay for out of your pay. Unlike normal companies, they will likely pass the full cost down to you, which can be significantly more than what you would normally pay as an employee by possibly double or triple. You usually have less negotiability on the hourly rate you can make on a W-2, as the consulting company is often handling some of the taxation and other benefits for you.

1099

1099 is an IRS form for paying individuals or businesses, meaning that the consultant is responsible for paying their taxes and not the firm paying. Most companies these days want you to go through a consulting company and not be a direct consultant for them, as it offers a level of shielding from liability to the firm. The benefit of being paid this way is that you can possibly use some of the pre-tax money for things like training, computers, etc. This gives you more flexibility in using your pay. However, there are lots of IRS requirements, so you will likely need a tax professional to help you with what can and can't be expensed.

Corp to Corp

This is basically one business paying another business. This means you would need to create and maintain your own business entity, which will cost money. Depending on the corporation set up, you may also need to pay payroll tax when you pay yourself. This method, however, can offer the most flexibility on paying expenses pre-tax or expensing items over time, but it also requires more tax and business knowledge and is often more costly. Not all consulting companies offer this option.

Health benefits still may be an option through your company deducted from your pay but again will be pricey.

Consulting vs. Full Time

Working for a company as a consultant, you can sometimes be treated like an outsider. You likely won't be invited to some company meetings and will possibly be treated a little differently as they hired you for a specific job, and they will want you to focus on that. Even though you are paid hourly, they may have rules. They may tell you not to bill over 40 hours, and they may still ask you to work longer. Yes, that should not be allowed, but I know it has been done.

As mentioned above, you will probably be responsible for the full cost of benefits, which can be quite expensive, possibly double or triple the cost you might pay as an employee sometimes. If it's offered through the consulting firm, you might get a slightly better deal but still pay a lot.

Many companies have a policy that they don't want consultants working for them as a consultant for over one year. This is because many court cases have decided that at that point, you are just basically an employee and, in some cases, told the company that hired them that they owe back benefits and taxes because of it. To avoid that liability, companies work through consulting firms and try to limit the time consultants are working for them.

After your time is up, some consulting companies offer to allow the hiring company to hire you as an employee (at a price paid to the consulting firm; often significant). Other consulting firms might want you to just move on to another project, and if you aren't hired, that would be what you need to do, anyway. So you might have jobs that only last from months to a year, and you might need to move around a lot to stay employed.

Consulting can sometimes be easier when just starting out to help you get a job, and if you don't have a family, it might be easier to deal with jobs that move around, different hours, and not have steady pay all the time. They usually want someone with considerable experience, so it would probably not be something you could get right out of school, but after a year or two, it might be easier to find some consulting work. But it is not impossible to get out of school for the right job if you had the right skills, perhaps did co-op, and if the market is hot for developers.

You should know that most consulting companies are body shops, as they call them. They bill the firm you work for perhaps 50–95/hr, for example, and pay you less, so they make the difference. Sometimes, that difference is quite considerable. Some companies may put you on bench pay for a short time between jobs, trying to keep you. Others won't pay you if you don't have an active job.

Consulting can be a good way to switch between jobs more often to get into different industries. However, it has lots of downsides too. There is no career path. You might be treated like an outsider at a company (no company parties, etc.), so it isn't for everyone.

A Consulting Gig

One of the largest projects I have seen with consultants on it had hired well over a hundred consultants, perhaps 200 people total, on the project. It was working on an internal system to move equipment between offices, contract agreements with external firms, and more. It was my first job after college. They gave us a written test to see if we knew how to program for Windows. One of their questions on the test seemed like a bad question, so I corrected it. I got the job, so I'm guessing I got some of them correct.

They had so many consultants in this one building, which apparently was a large data center for communications equipment. Most of the space for the consultants had cubes, but they ran out of room there, so they put people side by side and on the opposite sides of what seemed like just long tables you might set up for a picnic. They squeezed a bunch of consultants pretty tightly into this shared space. The room had a big window on the side you would come in, so we nicknamed it the fishbowl.

So many people were being hired, it wasn't clear they even cared if the consultants knew the tech stack or not. I don't think that is typical for most consulting jobs that are looking for people with the skills to jump into a project and be productive quickly.

They had some regular employees there working with the consultants. There were also managers from the company to manage the consultants and employees. There were back-end programmers working on Oracle databases and front-end developers working on thick client Windows apps or integrated Microsoft Word using their Visual Basic-like language.

Most meetings would be for everyone discussing the project, but some meetings were employee-only meetings where consultants were excluded.

For this project, they wanted all the hours consultants were willing to work to get this done sooner. Some of us would come in at around 6:00 a.m. and leave around 11:00 p.m. Sometimes working six days a week. It was common for people to bill 90+ hours per week. On consultant's pay, that was pretty nice just coming out of college.

As the project was winding down, they started to want a much tighter account of consultant hours. They started asking us to account for every 15 minutes of our day. I think I took a long time in the bathroom one time, and one of the managers asked where I was. I knew at that point it was probably time to start looking for another gig.

The building we were in was rather a drab data center across from a beautiful glass building. We would go across the parking lot to the glass building to have lunch. Our badges worked to get us in for lunch. The cafeteria was rather nice, overlooking the back of the building, which had loads of greenery and a pond. The cafeteria was even multitiered, having people sitting on different levels in this glass-enclosed space.

One day, we decided to take a walk around this nice building. We got to one area that had a revolving glass door. One of the people in our group went in and pushed the door to get through. Lights and alarms started sounding, and it said "door backing," as it trapped our coworker inside (it was a man-trap security door). We tried to use our badges to get him out, but it didn't work. We asked a female employee if she could help. She said, "Boys will be boys," as she used her badge to release our coworker. We didn't go wandering around the building after that incident.

They started to not have enough work for all the consultants, but they didn't want to let them go since it was not complete yet, even with the project well over budget. As I didn't have enough work, I asked if I could put an easter egg in the app. It was a cool end credits screen with all our names scrolling by if someone knew the right key combination. Shortly after, I found my next consulting gig.

What Is a Full Stack Developer?

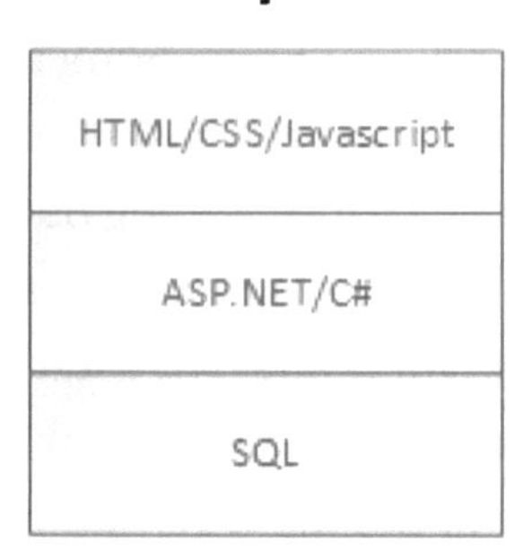

A full stack developer is someone who claims to be able to work on front-end and back-end development for an entire tech stack. This is just an example of one stack.

For example, someone skilled in:

- ASP.NET
- C#/ASP.NET: a language/framework
- SQL: a database language
- JavaScript: front-end scripting
- HTML/CSS: front end

A person who is skilled in and has development experience and is comfortable in developing all of these technologies would be considered a full stack developer.

Rarely is anyone an expert in all of these technologies, and thus, there are different levels of proficiency among developers. Often, developers with this set of skills are more weighted in C#/SQL or HTML/JavaScript or somewhere in between.

As long as you think you have a reasonable ability to operate from front end to back end on the tech stack that a company is interested in, then you could consider yourself a full stack developer.

Blazor/WebAssembly

There are quite a few different technologies to learn to be a full stack developer. One new technology that could reduce the need to use JavaScript is Blazor/WebAssembly. For example, in a typical Microsoft full stack, you might need to know HTML/CSS/JavaScript/SQL/C#. With Blazor/WebAssembly and C#, you could have C# run in the browser and do the work of JavaScript. This would reduce the need to learn JavaScript in that stack.

This is an exciting set of technologies to keep an eye on.

Staffing Firms and Recruiters

There are staffing firms looking to hire developers for either consulting roles or full time. These firms are sometimes working with the companies they are trying to place people for or try to submit people, even though they aren't directly working on a position for a company if they know a position is open or may open. For example, a firm called StaffingIsUs might try to find people for a position at a company called GreatBuys.

For consulting roles, they typically charge an hourly rate to the hiring firm and then give a portion of that money to the person being hired either hourly or as a salaried W-2.

Sometimes, they make a contract to hire for a position where it is a contract for a few months (e.g., three months) with a right to hire if they like the person. If the firm agrees to hire, typically, the hiring firm would pay a percentage of the person's salary for the year to the staffing firm (around 10–15 percent or more), as a one-time lump sum.

When recruiters are recruiting for a full-time role, the hiring firms are typically asked to pay around 10–15 percent or more of the person's offered salary as a one-time lump sum.

Recruiters, if they are well connected, could be a benefit to your search, since they can sometimes get your resume reviewed by a hiring manager where they would otherwise sit in an electronic pile somewhere, never being seen. That's if the recruiter has a working relationship with a particular firm. Recruiters might try to submit your resume even without a relationship with the firm, which may not help you at all. Therefore, it might be good to ask if that firm has recently placed any candidates with that company and if they have direct communication with the hiring manager.

Be careful when submitting your resume via a recruiter. If you submitted directly as well, that could be a potential conflict. If they hired you, the recruiter/recruiting company might request their fee, but the hiring firm might say you submitted directly, so they don't owe them the fee. In a case like this, unless they really like you as a candidate, they might just toss your resume into the electronic trash bin rather than have to worry about whether they have to pay the recruiter or not. Therefore, definitely let the recruiter know if you submitted directly to a company previously, when, and for what job, and consider if you want to do that or not.

Also, hiring firms sometimes have a limited budget to use external recruiters, so they might choose to go with a candidate who submitted directly if they had equivalent experience, skills and skills.

If you are ok with consulting, recruiters are probably the way to go, since most firms want an approved consulting firm to work with and don't want to work with a candidate directly. There are tax risks to working directly with candidates. Plus, it's just a matter of scale.

When looking for full-time work, direct rather than using a third-party recruiter is probably a better option if you have the time to do the job search yourself.

If you are really having trouble finding the time to do the direct job search yourself, you could consider a well-connected recruiter at a staffing firm you trust. Just realize the above mentioned pros and cons of this.

Do You Need Certifications?

Do you need any certifications? In general, in a lot of cases, no. There are probably cases and scenarios where that could be helpful, and in some cases required. If you have very little experience but have a Microsoft certification in C#, and you were going for a C# job, it might give a company more confidence to hire you. Some jobs have started looking for Amazon Web Services (AWS) or Microsoft Azure certifications, so you might look and see if the type of jobs you are looking for would require or be benefit from having some types of certifications.

Finding a Job

Where should you start when looking for a job? The answer: EVERYWHERE. Hey, when you need a job, you need it. When you are looking for a job, you should do it like a job and treat it like your most important job ever. That means be systematic about it. Keep a track of where you are posting your resume.

Start with the Job Boards:

indeed.com
ziprecruiter.com
simplyhired.com
careerbuilder.com
linkedin.com
dice.com

Post your resume to these boards so prospective companies can find you. Also, look for and apply to as many jobs that fit your experience. If you don't have experience yet, then look for entry-level jobs. Indeed has an option to filter by entry-level jobs, for example.

Searching for jobs, you will need to find the right keyword for the technology you have experience with or are interested in. Search to find some jobs. Look at what the jobs say that is close to what you are looking for. Find some of the unique technology words that those contain to help refine your search, such as full stack developer, WAMP, LAMP, ASP.NET, .NET, .NET framework, etc.

Check individual company sites for jobs.

You can try these staffing firms:

https://www.randstadusa.com/
https://www.mykellyjobs.com/
https://careers.actalentservices.com/

Colleagues, Friends, and Family

Reach out to former colleagues to see if they know of any jobs available. Many jobs are found through referrals by colleagues, especially people that you worked with a while and you worked well with. They might be willing to get your resume in front of the right people who can get you an interview. If you worked well earlier with a former manager at a different firm, they might just hire you. Other times, you might need to interview like others, but getting the interview is a big deal. A referral that knows your work and trusts the work you do on the job is priceless and might make getting your next job easier.

CHAPTER 9

Interviewing

Learning how to interview is going to be an important area of your career.

Software engineers aren't just asked soft skill questions and questions about the background of what they worked on. You can expect to be queried on anything overlapping in your resume, especially anything with the skills the company you are interviewing for is looking for, and perhaps more. These questions can span from general technology to architecture/design/implementation to language choices, and so on. Plus, you could and probably will write code, debug, and code review code. Some companies ask problems like brain teasers. Be prepared to write code on a whiteboard, on paper, or on a computer (if you are lucky, in an appropriate editor that folks use for your tech stack).

The book *Cracking the Coding Interview* by Gayle Leaakmann McDowell is a popular book to get to help you walk through the types of problems/coding they may ask you to solve.

You might ask, is this fair? Yes, and no. Companies need a way to evaluate if the software engineers they hire can code and solve problems efficiently. The problem is figuring out how to do that. Coding something should be fair. Remembering how to implement academic algorithms off the top of your head is not, in this author's opinion, fair without offering the ability to look up details on the Internet like any developer coding in a job would do. However, that doesn't mean you won't be asked to or won't have to do it. So the best thing is to practice those.

Research the company you will interview for so that you know about the business they are in and the products they sell. This context could be important when interviewing, as you might understand what they are trying to get at with their questions. Also, they might ask if you understand their business, and it looks better when you have done some research to understand what it is they do.

Bring hard copies of your resume, and make sure you have digital copies you can e-mail if needed. Also carry a notepad and a pen if you would like to take notes of some sort. If you have a portfolio, you could bring that too. Collect marketing information, along with awards, reviews, screenshots, and write-ups of software you have worked on, into a binder to bring with you to jobs to show folks that are interested. Keeping a collection of your work to show people can help you stand out among the crowd (that's not a typical thing people do, but I believe it can be useful and give you an edge). It allows them to see the type of software you have worked on in a bit more detail. Unless you worked on something really popular, like the Windows OS, Microsoft Office, or something like that, folks might not know a lot about the software you wrote.

For the interview, the dress code is, by default, suit and tie for men, unless they tell you the dress code is different. For women, there is more flexibility. Something business appropriate would likely be fine.

Some places might want a phone interview first and then in person, or these days, perhaps both will be on some web conferencing system like Zoom, WebEx, Hangouts, etc.

If you have the option, have benefits discussions with the recruiter rather than interview folks (unless that is the recruiter). Stay away from salary discussions unless they ask. An interview is about getting them interested in you first. You already would have told the recruiter your salary requirements by this point, so you are likely in the range they would be willing to pay.

Reminder: in some states, you are not required to provide your previous salary, so in those states, they shouldn't ask. Even if your state isn't one of those, you don't necessarily need to provide your previous salary. Just say "I'm looking for $XXXXXX," or just say, "I'm open. If you can give me the range, I can see if that is a fit." If you mention a specific salary you are looking for, that should ideally be fair compensation for the job and role you are applying to.

Be prepared with some questions to ask the interviewer that you want to know.

For example: What is the work culture like here? What tools/tech do you use for development (if it wasn't included in the job ad)?

Before the interview or phone call, ask what it will be like and see what details you get, as that might give you some additional ideas for preparation. Nowadays, post pandemic, there are a lot of remote interviews, so you might need to be prepared to have a computer, Internet connection, video conferencing software and camera, some software installed.

Portfolios

- Keep examples of screenshots and press of your previous work to show potential employers (if not confidential info).
- Keep information about all the products you worked on.
- If you worked on something that has a retail box, you could even bring one for display. For example, if you worked on the

software for Fitbit, you might bring one and show the software you wrote.

- If there were press articles that reviewed your software, keep them in your portfolio.
- References of people who will give you good reviews.
- LinkedIn recommendations from people you can include here.
- Keep both electronic and physical copies of your portfolio for backup.

Things You Should Do to Prep for the Interview

This could take you a couple of weeks to prepare, even if you have over 10 years of experience, because many places test you on things you never actually have to do in your job (or at least not without help from Google). If you have little experience, this might take you longer.

- Study the book *Cracking the Coding Interview* by Gayle Leaakmann McDowell.
- Understand Big O notation.
- Read up on the Fizz, Buzz problem, and understand the modulo operator.
- Practice string manipulation type interview problems.
- Practice writing data structures: Array, LinkedList, Binary Tree, parsing a string into a number.
- Know all of your data structures and their Big O notation for inserting, updating, sorting, and deleting items in them.
- Read up on some of the popular brain teasers or open questions asked in interviews.
- Practice reading/writing code in the language you will interview for.
- Be prepared for multithreading questions.

- Understand your framework/stack (e.g., .NET/ASP.NET/LAMP/WAMP, etc.).
- Be prepared to code something in the FULL tech stack you are interviewing for.
- Be prepared for some architecture/design questions and questions on your tech stack.
- Think about the types of work.

Think about the types of tasks they might do on the job there, and prepare for related questions. Remember, they want to know how well you understand the problems or the things they work on. They might understand that you don't know if their work is in a different industry than yours. It would still be a good idea to think about this to decide what sort of questions they could ask.

Some Example Interview Questions:

- What are you working on at your current or last job?
- What part of that did you specifically work on?
- What are some of your passions in software development, and why?
- Why do you want to leave your current job?

Things You Should Know:

- Computer science basic algorithms and data structures Big O notation for each of those.
- How to code review for your technology stack.

- How to write code for your technology stack.
- How to debug code and fix bugs for your technology stack.
- How to write unit tests.
- How to design algorithms and data structures to solve everyday computing problems in your technology stack.
- Understand networking related to your technology stack.
- Understand how to scale in your technology stack.
- Some details behind how your technology stack works (internals), message routing, order of calls, etc.

You should ideally spend a few weeks preparing for your interviews in general. Preparation should already be underway when you are applying for jobs. This way, whenever you get a request to come in for an interview, you are ready.

Sometimes, the interviews can be broken up into a few parts.

Recruiter Screening

Sometimes, your initial call discussion will be with a recruiter. They will be looking for keywords that were seen in your resume. They will ask general questions about why you are leaving your current job and how many years of experience you have with a particular technology. They are trying to see if it makes sense to pass your resume on to the company or hiring manager. They will likely also ask about the salary you are looking for. They might ask what you are making now (if the state allows that). You can just reply with what you are looking for. They are trying to determine if your salary is a fit for the position they are hiring for.

Initial Screening

This used to be called the phone screen. With all of the video conferencing now, it can be a little different. Similar to the recruiting call, you might be asked a little about your background and technology expertise. Some technical questions may be asked to gauge your level of experience relative to others, so you should be prepared to do some light coding or discussion of code on this call. This usually lasts an hour or less but can vary a little depending on the company.

Interview (the Main Event)

This is usually a multi-hour discussion and can be in person or over video conferencing. You should make sure you get plenty of rest the night before. Make sure you shower the day (at least if this is in person, please). First impressions can be everything. Make sure you are well prepared for the interview beforehand. You should have read up on the company to know what they do.

There will likely be multiple people, possibly one at a time, doing the interview, but sometimes more than one at a time.

Some example things you might be asked:

- Why are you leaving your current job?
- Why is there a gap in the timeline of experience on your resume?
- What technologies are you excited about? And why?
- Where do you see yourself in five years?
- What are your favorite things to work on?
- What exactly did you do for the jobs listed on your resume? Explain exactly the parts you did in addition to the whole project scope.
- Algorithm/and data structure questions.
- Implement a data structure (e.g., linked list, array, tree, etc.).

- Review some code.
- Write Code to do . . .
- Debug and fix this code.
- Unit test some code.
- Brain teaser problems. (These are a pain; hopefully, you don't get asked these. Search the Internet for examples of recent problems so you can be prepared.)
- What is the worst mistake you made? Be careful with this one. Offer something not too bad that you turned around and resolved quickly.

Answer the questions to the best of your ability. If you really don't know the answer to something, you can mention you are not sure about the answer but will give it a try.

If you clearly have to say you don't know the answer to something, think quickly to see if there is a reason to explain why you don't know it that would help your interviewer understand. Only provide this if it is something reasonable.

Here is an example that "might" be considered acceptable. If you were asked about a relatively standard framework API that you didn't know much about, your interviewer might be wondering why you wouldn't know that. If you elaborated and said something like, "At my current job, they have a wrapper framework that abstracts the lower level APIs so that we can run cross-platform easier. So we don't use the underlying APIs a lot." That response, in some ways, could put your interviewer at ease, since there is a reasonable explanation for the lack of knowledge there. But still, it could be a lack of knowledge in an area, so the explanation may or may not mitigate the interviewer's concern.

Interviewers are trying to judge if you have the skills and experience that matches what your resume says you have, what you say you have, and what they need for the job.

Keep your answers positive and the glass half full. Remember that you are being interviewed for both your technical skills and your interpersonal skills. The reality is that if someone doesn't like you, they are not going to want to hire you.

What are the interviewers evaluating?

- Are you able to answer the questions at the same level as other candidates (noting relative differences)?
- Would you work well with them, the company, and the team?
- Could you do the job the team requires?
- Do you appear to have knowledge and experience relative to your resume?
- Will you learn anything that you need to quickly enough to get up to speed as fast as possible?
- Are there any red flags? This includes gaps in time on the resume, mismatch between the resume and demonstrated experience/knowledge, or inability to complete questions many other candidates were able to complete. It could be almost anything else that is not what they normally see that might be concerning.

Don't get too nervous. If you pick the right technology stack, there are lots of jobs. Even if you don't do well in one interview, you will be learning for the next one. If you discover during the interview that you are not interested in the job, you have two choices: one option is to continue the interview anyway, so you get some experience and perhaps even a job offer to understand the market (and nothing beats having an offer); and your second option is to thank the interviewer for their time but explain that this particular job isn't one you will be interested in, and you don't want to waste any more of their time. In general, you should prefer continuing to get experience if you haven't had much interviewing. Interviewing is easier when you aren't really worried about getting the job at that point.

I've only stopped two interviews that I've been on. For one interview, as I was being walked in, I was walked down the halls of the building, and they had even the hallways crammed. Tables full of developers lined up and down the hallway. They explained they were overcrowded and were planning to move the building in maybe less than a year. Then we sat down, and the interviewer explained the position was for a 401k system. Given the overcrowding and working on a system that wasn't revenue generating, I told the interviewer, sorry, I'm not interested. I thanked him for his time.

I really should have found out more about the system I would be working on before coming in for the interview. That and the overcrowding just made that a no for me.

The second time I stopped an interview was, surprisingly, at a Microsoft interview. It was Microsoft consulting, though. The interview was going quite well. I really liked the idea of working for Microsoft. I realized, though, that dealing directly with client aspects of the consulting portion was just not what I was interested in doing. So I thanked the interviewers. They asked if I would consider working in Redmond. I wasn't interested in moving, so it also wouldn't have worked for me.

Salary

At this stage, research what jobs are paying, or know the pay you want based on the job you are currently in. Some states don't allow a company to ask about your previous salary. Even if it's not limited by law, you are often not required to provide that information. If they ask, you can just tell them what you are looking for. You should have researched reasonable salaries for the role by looking online to see what similar companies in similar industries are paying.

At this stage of interviewing, you should just be at the point of what you are asking for. If you believe your salary is a little low, you might ask for a higher salary closer to where you researched it should be. You don't want to be too high to scare the company off, but you don't want to come in low, either. That's why the phrase "I'm looking for around $XXX" can be useful, so they know you might be flexible, but that is what you are looking for. Or just ask them the range, and specify you are open at the moment, and you can indicate if the range is ok, if it is.

Sometimes, a good idea is to provide a range for a salary. Make the low end of the range something you would be fine with and the high end of the range something you would hope for. It should probably stay within a $5,000–10,000 range. This can be beneficial if you aren't sure if you are marketing yourself high enough. Companies generally don't want to give you more than what you are asking for, with some exceptions. If your salary is low, they might consider giving you a bit more. They would want to do this so you come in with a competitive salary. That way, you wouldn't leave right away if you found something higher. Giving a range, as suggested, makes the company think a little bit more about giving you the high end. If they want you to come in and have a competitive salary, it's sometimes easier to get a better salary upfront than it is to get it adjusted later. That's why, giving a range like that can help.

Often, this discussion should ideally be kept between you and the recruiter (ideally, not the hiring manager). Working through the recruiter creates a good separation, so the negotiation doesn't feel too personal with the hiring manager at this point in time. The idea is that you want to keep the relationship with the manager that you might work with friendly and not have to do hard negotiating directly with them.

You should consider the industry you are coming from and going to, as well as the location you are coming from and going to. For example, if you were moving jobs from a New Jersey job to a New York City job and wanted to just break even, you would need a salary increase probably just to pay for the additional commute costs and taxes. However, if you were doing the opposite and moving from a New York City job to a New Jersey job (depending on the area, if it isn't right near New York), you might expect perhaps less pay. Plus, you might have fewer commute costs, so lesser money may allow you to break even.

Also, remember that you don't know if benefits will cost more or less at the company. You probably don't need to be asking about benefits early in the conversation, but at some point, if they are interested and make you an offer, you might want to ask so that you can calculate that and see if you need more money or not.

If the benefits are more expensive, you could bring that up with the recruiter. Say: "I know I asked for this, but your benefits are more expensive than expected, so I would need this salary. Is that possible?" You can see what they say. If they disagree, you probably still have the original offer in hand and can still decide based on that.

CHAPTER 10

Starting a New Job

Usually, you will be given some information about your onboarding plan. It often involves some initial HR and benefits information and payroll paperwork. There may be an operations discussion about logging in for the first time and some support contact numbers. In a medium to large firm, there will often be many training courses to complete. The training will vary by the industry your company is in.

You will likely meet your manager and team and attend the team meetings. If you are working on a particular product, you will likely get training on how to use it.

After that, you might set up your development environment. You may undertake some architecture training and code walkthroughs to familiarize yourself with the code base. You might have to run it and fix a small bug to help understand and walk through the whole process, end to end.

Don't worry, everyone feels a little weird starting a new job. There are a lot of unfamiliar things, people, and processes. Sometimes, you start having doubts when switching jobs. That's typically normal and comes with change and dealing with it. If you were leaving your old job, there was a reason for it, and this new job was one you decided was going to be better. Don't second-guess yourself initially. Give yourself time to learn and settle in. It will probably take a few months or more to know if this is the best job for you.

If, after several months, it still doesn't seem right, you might need to make a choice. If it's very bad, you need to look for something else; otherwise, you should consider sticking with it for a year. Leaving jobs before even your first year could create a red flag on your resume for companies. Companies don't like to hire and train people who are just going to leave soon after, so doing so early could leave a bad reputation for you in the company you are leaving, and future companies seeing the short job time on your resume may ask why. There might be other options to switch groups internally, but those have risks as well. A company hires you for a reason. Switching very early may not be allowed by the company (they may have a three-month, six-month, or one-year policy of switching after just being hired).

Working with Others

Treat everyone with respect. Your safest way of thinking about this could be to treat everyone like they may one day become your boss/manager. Don't think it could happen? It could. It's happened in many scenarios, and sometimes, with some people you would never expect. If you wronged someone when they didn't have power, and now they finally do, how do you think you will be treated?

There are sometimes even crazy moves of people from groups you would never expect, like the head of marketing becoming the Vice President (VP) of development, or the head of product becoming the effective VP of development. It's happened. So you might think to yourself you can just tell this or that person that you can't help them . . . that is until one day, your organizational structure has changed. This might not be a common occurrence, but it happens a couple of times in a career, so don't be too surprised when it does. If you treat people right and with respect all the time, it will be less of an issue when it actually happens. Sometimes, the direction you were given could have caused a rift with others in groups within the company who can come back to bite you in scenarios like these through no fault of your own. So the best thing is to help folks out when you can.

Impressions

An impression of someone is the reality of someone to the person you made that impression on. That means if they think you did something wrong and you didn't, in their reality, you did. You might think this is a pointless argument, since you don't care what someone else thinks if they are wrong. However, this can matter a lot in your career, especially if the people who think you are wrong are in the management chain or end up there, or are just influential to people in or out of the management chain, or even just create the rumor mill. Then their reality becomes everyone's reality. So the impressions you make are pretty important. Strive to make good ones. For example, don't just say no to requests. If you say it too often, the impression of you will be that you don't want to do work or want to avoid work. You could have had a really valid reason. For example, you may be working on a high-priority project or may be going to be out on PTO. That doesn't matter if the other person doesn't know or understand all that. Perhaps even if they did, it wouldn't matter to them. You might think to yourself, "Well, my manager knows what is going on, so I will be fine." Your manager may not be there all the time, or might not have as much power or influence as you think. Make your manager's job easier by controlling the impressions you make.

- Don't just say no to something. Say, "Let me get back to you on that and see what we can do." If you won't have enough time/resources, check with your manager.

- Provide enough context if you suggest a different course of action for folks to know why you are suggesting something.
- Make sure you do work that you should do and not try to have it go to others. If there is a good reason, you still might say, "Let me get back to you." Talk to your manager first, or at least elaborate so they understand the reasons if that will work and is reasonable in your scenario.
- Try to be positive (see Positivity).

Development can be done individually on small projects or as small changes to a larger project. Large projects are often a team effort from conception through delivery. Something as simple as knowing whether an enhancement that is planned has positive value or even negative value can be important to move forward. It can sometimes be as simple as someone knowing the right person to ask the question. As a developer or a member of a development team, you will be relying on your team to help you when questions arise that you can't answer, and they will be relying on you to do a thorough job as well. You might even think you have thought of everything but still can't solve a requirements question, and your teammate may find the right person to ask, and you would get the answer you need to move forward.

What Does It Mean to Be a Good Team Member?

Help others out when they need help. Review the pull requests, help them test, and help them with ideas and design. Help them with critical support incidents, and so on. One day, it will be you who needs help, and you definitely want your team to want to help and support you when you are in need. So the best way to do that is to help them when they need it.

Developing Large Features or Software Products

These often require working very closely together with other people. One person might be right about the user interface web page code. The other person might be writing the back-end server code to support it. To make sure it fits together and works well, a discussion of the API/Calls that will be needed and used from the front end to the back end may need to take place. There needs to be an agreement on how to implement it from both sides. There could even be multiple people working on different user interface code and multiple people working on the back-end code, and everything needs to be integrated well for it to work. This can require quite a bit of discussion and coordination with your team members.

Mentor

Hopefully, when you just join a company, they will assign you a mentor, someone you can comfortably ask questions about various things to help you get started at your new firm and on your career path. If they haven't chosen someone for you, find someone on your team or elsewhere you seem to connect with, someone who has more experience with the company and can show you the ropes of the new job and the career path going forward.

A person like this at your organization will be enormously helpful in not just onboarding but also continuing to progress forward. As you decide to move along your career path at some point, find another mentor in the future, for example, if you want to go into management, and if your current mentor is not on that path.

A mentor can help you know who to talk with to fix your computer. They could help you set up or find someone to help you set up your development environment. They will likely know how to get any software licenses you may need. They can help you get used to the processes and systems your organization uses.

CHAPTER 11

Deadlines, Estimates, Communication, Notes

Early Career: Software Engineering Deadlines, Target Dates, and Estimates

You likely already know about deadlines. Throughout school, your teachers gave you deadlines/due dates for your homework, projects. Your parents told you to clean up your room now or else.

Throughout your career, you will probably have to deal with estimates, target dates, deadlines, or any other variation you can think of that your manager or company expects some work you need to do to be done by a certain time or day.

Throughout the history of software development, either teams/staff have been told they need to finish by a particular day or been asked for estimates of when it would be complete and then be held to making the "estimated" date.

Agile attempted to correct this issue by providing what they call story points to estimate stories. These points are basically just numbers the team makes up to correspond to story sizing. Often, though, they have some relationship with some time/portion of a sprint: a period of time to work on a story. For instance, 13 points might equal a sprint, and six points perhaps about half a sprint. By not having a direct, obvious correlation, anyone looking at the points on your stories won't be able to figure out how long something takes, only the team. That kind of works, but at some point, either your manager will interpret, or you will be asked when something will be done, and someone will have to do the work of either calculating team velocity or translating those points into time, which are roughly the same thing.

Agile should have helped if organizations would agree to realize that schedules need to shift and move based on discoveries or changes in work. If the team is kept on target daily through scrums and per sprint, then things should move in the direction the organization wants. Even relatively Agile organizations, at some point, want an estimated time frame for a feature or fix.

Of course, once you have an estimate or target date, someone will probably misinterpret that date as a hard date you will make, even if you put many disclaimers on your Powerpoint. Congrats, your estimate may have just become a deadline.

Unfortunately, Agile didn't solve this one, since people and teams will always get asked this question. It helped to keep people informed at least and follow directions and course correcting as needed, but still, the deadline issues linger.

What Should You Do About Estimates and Deadlines?

These Are Just Some General Guidelines

- Following Agile is a good start, as hopefully, most of the time, you won't be put into the position of hard targets with changing requirements/work.
- Provide ranges of time for estimates—estimate best case, average case, and worst case—and provide the range from best to worst.

- Make sure to include the calculation of what percentage of time a day you or the team can really focus on your tasks. If you get interrupted daily for support issues, include the time you may need for those in any of your time frames if you do the work.
- Include time off for you or other staff that will be part of the work.
- Make sure you have gone through the stories in enough detail to reduce the number of surprise elements you might find while working on it.
- Estimate in some slack time percentage based on the unknowns/knowns of your work. For example, maybe 20 percent of work increase over time if the risks/unknowns are limited, or perhaps larger based on the risks/unknowns in your project.
- Engineers can sometimes be overly optimistic, and many projects have been underestimated by significant amounts. Sometimes, as much as double the work or more might need to be done. Going through the stories to the point where you've reduced the chance of these types of surprises will help.
- Keep written records of the estimate ranges you state for the best and worst case so when someone says you missed your estimate, hopefully you can dig it out, and they will see it fall between your best and worst case estimates.
- On slides, be clear with your estimated ranges and disclaimers. They are estimates that may change as the project progresses.
- Make sure the padded estimates are documented to the parts you padded and why, at least for you to recall later.
- Make sure your padded estimates seem reasonable. If they sound quite large to you and other software engineers, think about them again a little and see if it makes real sense to stick with them. Then decrease or even increase if needed. Prepare for questions about why they are so large. A story breakdown

with detail can help others see the reasoning for the time frames once they know what is really involved. Many folks other than the developers may have a simplistic view of what needs to be done and think you should finish tomorrow and wonder why you are saying it will take three months.

- With Agile, you practice your estimating skills each sprint, so hopefully, you will get better and better over time. However, even people who have been estimating for years get it wrong or off, especially on large projects. Try to review your estimates when you complete the work to see how you did.
- Discuss with senior folks on the team. But if you are doing the task, think how long it would take you to do it if it's *your* task. If you are in your early career, it might take you longer than one of the senior folks, so their estimate should be considered from that perspective.

Will these things help you? Maybe not. They might help blunt the criticism when the estimate/deadline is not met.

Early Career: Team, Internal, External Conversations/ Messaging

Most companies want to control their external messaging for customers and others so they can adequately project the image and direction they want. They may have all sorts of guidance around social media use, PowerPoint, slide deck, templates, fonts, tone of your message, and more. Limiting the negative and accenting the positive can be a good start. Plus, limiting conversations around problematic topics.

In some companies or even at just various times in companies, you may find another want or need to even control the internal messaging to other teams within the organization (perhaps not to quite the extent as external, but still significant). For example, perhaps the sales team is expecting you will deliver feature Y by Q4 of this year, but your team does not know how that's even possible. You might be told to limit your conversations with external groups on the topic until your team can work up a plan of what they can or can't do.

I'm not sure how much organization size matters, but my experience has been that smaller organizations tend to be less political, but I'm sure that can depend on the specific organization. But sometimes, it can be important that the salespeople deliver a consistent message to customers until a plan can be worked out.

Personally, I prefer honest, direct communications. But sometimes, that can get you into trouble. When you tell the salesperson that you have no idea how that feature could be delivered when they just sold the customer that feature, they go and talk to their boss. This goes up the chain until you get a comment back from your boss that you should stop talking about this until there is a plan. So you can see things can get out of control fast, even internally. I'm not saying this is right or how it should be, but it can be a fact of life in many organizations, so you should just prepare for this.

Keep Track of What You Need To Do

Create a good system for keeping track of what you need to do. Your manager and your team will rely on you to keep track of things that need to be done. You will need a good system for keeping track of things and deliver what has been asked of you on time.

For Development Work

Usually, there is a ticket tracking system that, at least at a high level, will let you know what you are working on.

For Time-Based Deliverables

Put the information on a ticket in the tracking system, if that is related to what you are working on. Also, you can add a note to your calendar (Google calendar, Outlook calendar, etc.).

For General Notes

Use a directory structure on your computer or Google Drive or a work personal shared drive so you can have access to it when needed. Add text files, Word files, Excel sheets, or anything else needed.

You can also use OneNote, an app installed on many new windows computers for keeping track of information.

To-Do Apps

Trello can be like your personal scrum board.

Todoist is a nice to-do application available on many platforms.

Other Ways

Try using Post-it notes. Yes, they can stick great to the bottom of your monitor.

Keep Track of What You Learn

Inevitably, you will learn a lot of things on the job. Some things you might want or need to remember later. If you think something you learned might help others, you could possibly share it on an internal blog in your company. If it's just something useful for you, create a folder structure on your computer, OneNote, or Google Drive, and store text, Word, or other documents about things that you learn. This way, you can search for information when you need to find it again. I've been keeping track of information this way for years. I've collected an internal knowledge base of hundreds of articles and a personal one with at least as much. I've personally used them to find the information I needed countless times.

Occasionally, other people will find your articles and find a use for them.

CHAPTER 12

Working with Your Manager

What Does Your Manager Want?

One of the biggest links you have to the company you are working for is your manager, so it can be very important to understand what they are looking for from you. If you don't know, why not ask? Ask how much communication they want. Do they want daily or weekly status updates? Just updates when there might be risks to deliverables or issues possibly coming up or that have come up? How does your manager like to communicate? E-mail or some instant messages? What information is your manager looking for in communications? High level or detailed?

Determining what, when, and how communication is needed can help to avoid problems/concerns.

Every manager is a little different. Some might want or need to know everything that is going on at regular short time intervals. Others may just want the bigger picture.

Many managers might say they want their employees to be able to operate on their own, solve problems on their own, and only engage them if they have issues, questions/concerns that require/need their input. Sometimes, depending on a project's state can change expectations. If a project is at risk or might run late, a manager might want more frequent reporting/status so they can help mitigate risk, and also to stay informed, so that if questioned by their manager, they can respond.

Your manager will obviously want to know when you want or need to take off work. Some managers might want to know when you will be out for an hour and make sure you know to make up work or take PTO. Other companies/managers may have a mechanism to report needing to take an hour or so for a doctor appointment or something occasionally without needing to ask, with the expectation that you will make up the work later or take it as PTO.

Also, try to predict something your manager might want to know about. If your manager's manager asks you about something important, and you aren't sure your manager knows about it, then that is probably something you want to bring up. If you are invited to a meeting with senior executives above your manager, you might want to mention it to your manager to see if they ask to be added to the invite list. If some critical support issue comes up that could be escalated through a different path to your manager, then you should probably let your manager know. Keeping your manager abreast of activities that could be escalated to them is useful so they are prepped with information that they can respond with in case it happens.

When e-mailing your manager about an issue, it's often but not always best that you think through the issue and have an action plan on your own. Can say, "FYI, we found this issue. Plan to correct it this way." That way, you aren't always e-mailing your manager with a problem and expecting them to solve it for you. The idea is for you and the team to be as self-sufficient as possible. It's best to e-mail it and have a path forward, whenever possible. That way, your manager doesn't need to get involved if they like your path forward. If they don't like it, I'm sure they will bring it up. If you feel it is important for your manager to get involved, then, by all means, discuss it with them.

Take Control of Your Career

If you are looking to get promoted, find out what the requirements are. Work on progressing your career toward that goal. If it will require training, ask how you can get it or figure out how you can get it. Some companies may have internal training or even pay for training if needed.

Find out what you will need to get a promotion. There may be company requirements or expectations for each of the roles.

At each level, there are increasing expectations for demonstrating:

- Expertise
- Leadership
- Good decision-making
- Autonomy
- Implementation/coding/process
- Supporting the product
- Designing good solutions
- Good communications skills
- On-time delivery

Act Professional

Don't do non-work activities during work. That means don't watch random TikTok videos, and so on. Wear business-appropriate attire as required when in the office. Don't send too many non-work-related e-mails/messages during work. Minimize the number of personal calls during work.

Communicating with Upper Management

Keep your e-mails short and to the point. These folks may get a lot of e-mails and not have a lot of time or a deep understanding of the systems being worked on. If you really must provide detail, try to keep it less technical and as short as possible. Create a summary of what you are trying to describe and put that at the TOP of the e-mail. Add the detail in a section CLEARLY after the summary with a heading that makes it clear it's detailed, so they don't need to keep reading if they got enough info from the summary. This makes it more likely that your main points will be read and understood. It also allows the flexibility of upper management to dig into the details if they desire, or at least discuss it with their staff.

When communicating with upper management, it's important to know your audience. What might they be looking for or not looking for?

Managing Up

This term was coined and has since morphed to mean many things.

One of the earliest references seems to be by W. Turk in Defense AT&L (2007).

I prefer to think of it as creating an effective and efficient relationship and communication between you and your manager (or higher up the chain) to achieve your and the organization's set goals.

When you work with a manager, you should either figure out or ask about their communication style, and you should be able to determine how they like to communicate and the topics they are interested in.

For example, you might have one manager who just wants to see the big picture and know the important items that they need to take action on. If you tell your manager about the problems building a particular part of the software, they may assume they need to jump in and take action, when all you were looking to do was explain why things were taking a little longer. Perhaps instead of a simple statement, try saying, "The timelines are tight. I might need to get back to you, as we could hit something that would cause a problem for our timeline. I will let you know." That way, the manager knows they don't need to take action yet; they aren't bogged down in the details, and they know you will inform them if it looks like there is an issue.

You could then again have another manager who wants to know every detail before there is ever a problem, so if you neglected to tell that manager what was going on, you could have more serious ramifications.

Let's say, you are not working with a technical manager, and you have come to a scenario that requires a decision because it will affect the product release dates. This could mean you would need to be able to effectively communicate the pros and cons less technically so that your manager can understand the risks/benefits of each of the options available to you.

The Power of Taking Responsibility

Take responsibility for your actions and sometimes a team's actions if you are a lead developer or manager. At some point, either with your manager, other leaders, or even other staff, there will be a case where you may have done something that wasn't the most efficient or not quite right, or you may have missed something. You might be faced with someone yelling or blaming you for this. Sometimes, that can be a good time if you, in fact, were responsible and declared, "Yes, I did, sorry, and I will do my best to prevent or correct it."

Accepting responsibility can cut both ways. If it's terrible, folks could think poorly of you, but if it's not so bad, many folks see the power in accepting blame and correcting it. Many times, this is enough to stop or blunt the criticism being tossed your way. Sometimes, someone else is afraid they may get blamed for something, and once you take responsibility, it relieves some of this burden, or if they are venting, it sometimes cuts it short. As long as this is delivered honestly and sincerely under the right circumstances, it can be quite effective.

CHAPTER 13

Mindset and Psychology

Give credit for others' work whenever possible. I saw this in action at one of my early jobs, and it has stuck with me ever since. Everyone at this particular company made sure they gave credit to the people involved in the work at appropriate times and conversations when things came up.

Whenever you talk about work someone else did (presuming it would be perceived as good), bring up their name. The effect of this is others will probably do the same when talking about your work. People like to be given credit for the things that they have done. Have you ever been in a meeting where someone brought up the work you did, and people thought the work was something the person talking did? They didn't say it was their work, but when they talked about it, people naturally assumed it was. How did it make you feel?

If everyone followed the principle of always giving credit, it's sort of like advertising each other's good work in the company.

This sort of culture of giving credit to others has stuck with me since this early job, and I now try to make sure that when I talk about others' work in appropriate conversations, I give credit to those involved.

Think Like an Owner

Working for a company, when you need to make a decision, think as if you were the business owner. What would an owner do? Obviously, only make decisions within your realm of responsibilities. Even within those, thinking like an owner/manager can help you decide the best actions for the business. Managers and business owners like to see people think about the company this way. Everything you do should have this mindset within the limit of your responsibilities.

An obvious example is an urgent customer issue, where you devise a workaround to restore service quickly and then follow up to fix/prioritize the bug after. There are less obvious ones like not wasting the company's resources by leaving cloud virtual machines running when they don't need to be if it will cost the company money and not benefit the company.

Think about how you are building the software, the time, the expense, and the benefit to the customer. If the time to build a feature will cost significantly more than the benefit, perhaps discuss it with the team. See if your assumptions are correct, and if so, is there a different way to build it? If it is too costly to produce, decide with your Agile team if it should be built at all.

Really, this can be for anything, though. Don't waste company office supplies, for example. This mindset can help guide you into better paths or outcomes.

The Power of Positivity

One thing that you will find in many instances is that management expects positivity.

They don't want to hear you or the team can't do something; they want to know what you can do. Saying no to doing something, saying it's too hard, or saying there isn't enough time or resources (even when true) is often not what management and the business want to hear.

You might say to yourself they aren't being realistic . . . sort of. Management doesn't always expect the impossible, but they would much rather know what can be done rather than what can't. Be the glass half full rather than the glass half empty, and your career will go much further, much faster.

For example, someone asks you to do a task that will take weeks, and they want it in one week. Instead of saying no, say, "Hmm . . . Ok, I understand what you want. The timing sounds tricky. Let me talk to my manager about that and see what is possible." That way, you didn't say no. You told them you would discuss with your manager to see what's possible. You might talk to your manager, and maybe the ultimate answer is that it's not possible, or your manager or higher-level managers can assign more people to make it possible.

Rather than excuses, provide alternatives. For example, if a particular implementation is going to take too long, determine if some functionality could be dropped. Find out what is or is not required in the minimum viable product. Can additional people be brought in to assist? This way, rather than saying something can't be done, you provide methods for how it can be done. This helps keep conversations positive.

Impostor Syndrome

This likely happens in many fields of work, including software development. Impostor syndrome is the feeling that you don't know what you are doing, and you wonder if you should have even been hired for the job in the first place. It's the general feeling of lack of confidence in yourself or perhaps like you are faking it.

Know this: if you have gone to school for computer science or computer programming and/or have built up experience over years of development work, then realize it's a feeling that lots of people get.

For existing work that you have already done, most folks can get these feelings to subside pretty quickly, as you can reassure yourself that you have been doing this for a long time and worked on many projects, so it can be obvious to you and others that you know what you are doing.

This can be harder when you step into a new role outside your comfort zone and you aren't sure you have the skills to handle this. Just think about how and why you got there. People chose you for the role/assignment, likely because they thought or knew you could do it. Think about the skills you have exhibited so far, the projects you have completed, and how they prepared you for your new role. Just know, again, that this is a feeling a lot of others get from time to time. Don't let it bring you down.

Don't Be a Jerk

There was one person a development team didn't like to deal with. It was someone from the team who just was mean-spirited and deserving of much stronger language, let's say. He would constantly berate people as too slow and call them an idiot, saying to them they did not know what they were doing.

One time, he even berated a manager, saying the person on his staff was stupid and wondering why he had to be out or why we should have someone on our staff who was in the military and got called into service. From that conversation and others, many people started keeping a list of these conversations with the problematic person.

Other people came forward and mentioned similar things. In a large company, HR teams like to collect enough evidence before someone is fired for infractions like these. At the same time, there was an acquisition in progress of a large group of people from the firm that worked on a particular product that was being sold off to another company.

"Luckily," this person somehow got tagged as part of the sale of a group to another company.

So the moral of the story is, don't be a jerk.

Change—the Only Constant

You should be prepared for a change in all of its forms.

There is a saying that "the only constant is change." In business, that often seems to be true. Your management could change, and your job could change. When you don't have control over the change, your choices are to flee, fight, go with the flow, or embrace it. I would suggest leaning more toward the "go with the flow" mentality or embracing the change most of the time. Of course, every situation is different, and you will need to decide the right path for yourself. For example, management teams tend to change over the years, and when new management comes in, they sometimes wish to try to make some positive change in the org. They might shift managers and tasks and even exit some senior staff to bring in people they feel will bring about the change they desire. If you resist that change from the top, it's rather unlikely things will go well for you.

So if it makes sense, find the positives in the changes being made and see if you can navigate the change to provide the best outcome you can.

That doesn't mean always going with the flow. You will need to make the right decisions depending on the circumstance.

One Example

One day, your manager is replaced. You had a good working relationship. Now you need to start over with someone completely new. You accept the change, of course, and embrace it. Things are going ok initially but soon take a turn. This new manager is rubbing people the wrong way, and something you did seems to have annoyed him to the point he might want you to leave. A case like this is tricky. The best bet is to keep your head down out of the way of your manager's wrath and quietly search for internal or external opportunities. As it turned out, the manager ended up leaving not too long after, rubbing too many people the wrong way, perhaps.

A new manager replaced him, so now you're on your third manager. You decide to accept the change and embrace it, and hopefully, this manager will be much better. Luckily, the new manager is much better, and you are able to continue working in the job you desire.

CHAPTER 14

Continuous Learning

Programming Language

One of the ways that can be good to learn a new language is training. This could just be a self-paced video course, a book, or in-person training.

In-person training with a hands-on approach can be very useful to quickly learn some of the language details and get some confidence in the language. Since they are often only a week long, you definitely won't learn everything you need to know, but you will know at a high level how the language works and how to do some basic implementations.

Some of the most fun trainings I've been in was where they had three well-known book authors teaching the training. Usually, one of them taught the session from the front, and the others helped the students out hands-on. They added some fun exercises like needing to dig out secrets from a library with calls to it, which were clues on a scavenger hunt in the hotel we were in to get prizes. They covered a lot of material. The days were long but interesting.

It was a great experience meeting some popular authors of books and learning a lot about the language.

Constant Learning

In the field of software engineering, you should be open to constantly learning to stay current with the field. That doesn't mean you need to learn every new technology that comes out or be fluent in every language. Find a set of technologies to stay current on and follow deeply, which is likely the technology stack you are working with so that you stay marketable for your job. You should just keep reading to keep an eye on technologies that are coming out and may be starting to grow. Also, keep an eye on the technology stack you use to see if it is growing, shrinking, or staying the same. If the current technology/language you are working in is starting to disappear, it might be time to look at another technology/language that is more likely to keep you current for new work. You can often find language/technology surveys to help you determine what is hot and what is not.

The technological landscape of software engineering is so vast that there is no one person who can know everything in any depth. So you will need to decide on the technology to focus on where you can be marketable for your services. Use job boards to keep up to date with how many jobs exist for the tech stack you are using are in your area. Check on this once a year just to see. Are jobs drying up, or are they more plentiful? This can give you an idea of when you need to look for work, what your prospects might be like.

If you try to catch up in your field at least once a year, it should be enough to keep up with the technology changes. Most times, there's only a few language or framework changes a year, though it can depend on the language and framework.

Team Presentations

Team presentations—Collaboration with benefits:

It can take a bit of work to put together presentations for technical topics like new architectures or new features, so a lot of folks and teams perhaps don't do as many as they could or should.

Why should you?

- You can get valuable feedback from other developers that can shape your feature/design.
- It fosters a good team spirit of collaboration/sharing and mutual respect.
- Some folks could bring up legitimate concerns that you have not thought about.
- It provides valuable presentation skills for engineers.
- Software engineers like to know what's going on in other teams.
- It is good to let all the software engineering teams know about new features, so when they are finally delivered, they are easy for everyone to understand and support.
- This can provide great visibility for your career. Demonstrating confidence and expertise to other engineers is kind of like advertising.

Presentation skills can be valuable. What if your product was about to launch, and you knew of a critical flaw in the product but couldn't make a convincing case to management that the product would fail?

Data representation/visualization and presentation can be critical to getting your point across.

You might do some of this already if you are following Agile and doing reveals of new functionality. As long as those are shared, they can be very useful. Even making recordings that you can at least share if you have teams in other time zones that would want to watch could be very useful.

So think about anything about your team that might be worth sharing across teams. You may help fostering a great collaborative environment, knowledge sharing, and understanding among your teams.

CHAPTER 15

Getting a Promotion/ Raise

Job Titles

Throughout your career as a software engineer, developer, or programmer, you will see many organizations have many titles. Sometimes, this is done to make people feel special by giving them lofty titles, and other times, it's about aligning with the industry to make it easier for folks to see what a position maps to, making hiring easier. Other times, it could be the opposite reason, where a company doesn't want comparisons of their engineering levels to outside groups or just wants to be unique and make folks feel special.

I would encourage not concentrating on or worrying about titles too much unless, in your organization, it is tied to increasing salaries to a level you would like to seek. Years of experience required can vary by organization.

Software Engineer, Software Developer, Programmer (Sometimes Application Engineer or Associate Application Engineer)

These are usually starting titles given to software engineers at various organizations.

There can be even many variations of these, like just Engineer, Engineer II, etc. In some financial organizations, they might have an AVP or even a VP in front of these, even at these levels.

Senior Software Engineer (or Developer, or Engineer II)

This is usually the next level given to software engineers/developers, and many folks are in the range of 2–5 years' experience before they achieve this, depending on their organization, the economy, and skills. Again, there can be many variations of this. Financial companies may put a VP or SVP in front of these.

Lead Engineer, Staff Engineer, Tech Lead (Sometimes Senior Engineer II)

At this level, folks have likely demonstrated the ability to lead other developers and design significant solutions with little involvement of other management/architects for localized projects. Again, there can be many variations of these titles.

Senior Staff Engineer, Senior Lead Engineer

At this level, engineers in many organizations are near the top end of the technical path. Some organizations may use the term consultant or have a higher level for a consultant. Folks at this level are expected to be able to architect medium-scale solutions and lead small teams of developers to implement them.

Architect Track:
Architect/Application Architect
These folks would be called on to architect solutions for products and product areas.

Senior Architect
These folks would be called on to architect solutions for products, product areas, or entire product lines or suites of products.

Manager Career Track:
Manager, Development Manager, Engineering Manager
This is often an entry-level management position. Folks with this title may be beginning to start their management career or have 1–4 years of experience.

Senior Manager
Usually, after a couple of years of the previous level, managers will be promoted to senior manager. Usually, senior managers have over 3–5 years of experience. At this level, they might have other managers who report to them or not, depending on the organization. Promotions aren't based on just years; they must demonstrate a capability to lead. Senior manager levels can sometimes manage other managers.

Director, Engineering
Usually, at this level, folks would have over 6–8+ years of experience as an engineering manager and would have reporting managers (though not always). Financial organizations might have AVP, VP, and SVP before

a director of engineering. As with other jobs, years of experience can vary by organization.

VP, Engineering

Depending on the organization (for example, in financials), this position probably requires over 8–10+ years of development experience as a manager but can vary by an organization, often in charge of entire product lines or multiple products or even all the development activity at an organization depending on its size.

Chief Technology Officer (CTO)

Usually, there is only one of these for an entire company, but at some large organizations with many divisions, there could perhaps be more. Usually, all the development organizations would report to the CTO and possibly other areas.

What Purpose Do Job Titles Have?
Software Engineer
Senior Software Engineer
Lead Software Engineer
Senior Lead Software Engineer
Etc.

Would It Be Better for Everyone to Have No Title?

Not knowing if someone is in charge of an area or group might make it a little more difficult in some internal interactions. It could result in not knowing whom to trust. If someone is a VP or manager at the company, you might trust them more on particular prioritization or asks than perhaps someone with a lesser title. When communicating with customers, it's meaningful to them when they are communicating with senior leadership at a company. You could tell customers this person is in charge of 80 percent of the company's resources, though only to those who were at a meeting where that was explained. If someone saw CIO on the signature line of an e-mail, that definitely would have some meaning to the customer compared to software engineer or lead software engineer.

Titles mean something to people who hold those titles as well. Some people care about titles almost as much as money. Somewhat standardized titles across the industry also help with compensation when moving between companies. There are pay grades for different job titles. By having similar titles across the industry, developers might have an easier time getting at least a matching salary for their level.

Years of experience can be a proxy for the level of pay, but not always. Standardized titles also give developers a way to determine if they are paid fairly across their job roles by comparing salary survey data. While I personally don't think about titles much for myself, I can at least see the pros and cons here.

How Do You Get a Promotion/Raise?

If you are looking for a raise, my recommendation is to collect information, comparing your experience relative to what people are paid in your area. For example, if you are a software engineer, compare your years of experience with what others are paid in your region (like the New York metro area, for example). You should find salary survey information and match your experience with what others in a similar role are paid.

For each role, companies usually have a min, max, and average or midpoint for a particular role based on the salary surveys they use. If you have reputable information, you might be able to show you should be paid more. Your company may know it already, or maybe their salary survey shows you should be paid less. Sometimes, the key is that now at least your manager knows this is something that is important to you, so they can try to help you as best they can.

Just realize that it can sometimes be hard to get a big jump in pay, so sometimes managers have to work it over a couple of years. Sometimes, a large jump in pay is possible if you are significantly underpaid and the company's own salary surveys show this, which can make it easier. Not all companies have salary surveys where they track this, but it is pretty common, especially for mid to larger companies.

You should also create a list of things you did that were big and that created value for the company. Large projects that you played a significant role in completing and things of that sort can be useful to remind your manager and the higher-ups of your value.

The big projects that higher-ups would remember or know about can be important. Promotions are often decided higher up the chain, so having a list of high-profile projects that you can mention can be a great way to promote yourself. Ideally, you and your manager should be working on a list of projects or accomplishments that show you are ready for the next level of promotion. Keeping a sheet like this can make it easier for your manager to have a promotion discussion with his manager.

Also, think about whether there is a need for someone in a promoted role with your skills. For example, if the promotion is from senior software engineer to lead engineer, you might suggest that with a promotion, you would be ready to lead a particular project if your manager thought that was appropriate. You should really do some thinking about your capabilities and think about if you have demonstrated the skills of the new role to them to other people and your manager already. Often, people are promoted when they are already demonstrating the skills required for someone in that role.

Titles, Role, Responsibilities, Money

Some people are looking for better titles. Some want money. Some want the responsibility of managing more people or different things or some combination of those. In this author's view, titles alone don't carry a lot of benefit in most companies. Having held the title of Senior VP sounds lofty, but in financial firms, there are probably 50,000 of those in just one company. That can even hurt your prospects if it is on your resume, with other places thinking there is implied meaning there and not understanding title usage in other firms. Unless a title is needed to get the responsibilities or money you want, perhaps your energy should be focused on the latter.

Some folks are very career driven. Businesses seem to build this idea of a career path that you should always be progressing toward some next higher level.

Is that really what you want, though? Different responsibilities often come with higher levels and higher pay. For example, if you are currently a manager of developers being promoted to a middle manager, managing other managers may not be what you want. Staying technical and involved with day-to-day developer tasks might be more what you are interested in. As a developer, do you really want to be promoted to lead others? There are different expectations and responsibilities. Consider your strengths. Are you really a leader? There is a business principle called the Peter principle (Hull & Peter, n.d.), whereby you might continue to be promoted until you have no idea how to do your job at that level. You can probably learn, but you may have to learn very different skills for your responsibilities that you haven't had before. Is that really what you want?

Different organizations have different standards around promotions. Some organizations might only promote to a higher role if there exists the need for someone in that higher role. For example, if you normally only hire one lead developer per team, then the company may not promote any other folks to that position unless it opens up and is appropriate. Other companies may treat it as a progressing career track where developers have the ability to take on more and more responsibility.

Managers can't just decide who gets promoted on their own. Rather, managers can suggest or recommend people for promotion if they feel they are suitable. There might be guidance around this, like a person should have been in the current role for 1–2 years. Usually, to get a promotion, there is an agreement that your manager checks with the manager above your manager that a promotion is warranted. Even then, the suggestion/recommendation is sent high up the chain for review. There is usually a budget available for promotions, and that means a limited number of people can get promotions in a year, regardless of how many are recommended for it. If too many people are recommended for it, management may initiate discussions down the chain with the question of who should be prioritized for promotion, or might even have a verbal death match-like meeting. The meeting might have all the managers make a case for their recommended promotions so everyone can hear how their promotion stacks up against the others to determine who should get a promotion.

This means even if promotion is warranted, it might not be possible to promote someone for several years, depending on budget, economy, other promotion candidates, etc.

Be Introspective

Has your manager told you things that management wants to see more of before a promotion? Think hard about what you are doing and how you are doing it. Think about positive and negative interactions you have had and how you can learn from them. Learn the specific requirements for a promotion from your manager. Work with them on things you can do to meet those requirements. Just realize that sometimes, you need some opportunities to meet certain requirements. For example, if your manager wants you to show leadership but there haven't been opportunities to demonstrate it, then it may be hard to get a promotion. Sometimes, you can come up with your own ideas or ways to demonstrate leadership.

Find leadership opportunities that you do have. Volunteer for a project and deliver it with added value. Take ownership of the work handed to you and bring it up to another level in terms of solving it. Sometimes, opportunities don't get dropped on you. You need to make them.

References:

Hull, R., & Peter, Dr. L. J. (n.d.). *The Peter Principle: Why Things Always Go Wrong: As Featured on Radio 4.*

CHAPTER 16

Changing Jobs/Roles

When you want to change jobs while you are still working at your current job, you should do it carefully to not make your current employer suspicious. You will need to apply to jobs online, just like we went over in the finding a job section. But you should refrain from posting your resume online so that your current job doesn't find it and see you are looking for a job. You might ask, "Why don't I want my current job to know?" Well, because if they know, your life may change in ways you haven't foreseen yet. You might get excluded from meetings and events if they know you are looking for work elsewhere. You might get the work no one else wants to do. They could, of course, instead look for ways to keep you there. If they were planning layoffs, maybe you are in the first set to go. It could just be uncomfortable if your manager found out. Hopefully, that scared you enough to make sure they don't find out.

Once you find and interview for the job, make sure everything is fully set for a start date. If they do a background check and won't clear you till it's done, then you might want to avoid giving notice until that is done. Giving notice can be done directly to your manager, in an e-mail, or both. It can be simple and to the point. "Hi. As of today, I am giving my two-week notice. My last day will be XX/XX/XX. I am so appreciative of the opportunities you gave me, and I wish you and everyone the best of luck." You should realize that some companies may require you to give more than two-week notice, so you should have read your employee handbook to see the requirements. Financial companies sometimes have clauses that you can't leave for a certain time. Usually, those are only people at a high level and would have been specifically told that, so if you aren't, the likelihood is that you won't be affected by it.

Leave on Good Terms

When you are leaving, you should be very professional and do everything you can to help them wrap up anything you are working on. They may ask you to stay a little longer to help finish up work. You don't have to (unless you were one of those higher-level employees who needed to give more notice). If they were asking for maybe one more week and it didn't mess up your job offer, you could consider it. If you want to do it, make sure it is ok with the company you are going to. If not, then the answer is no, you need to leave in two weeks. The company you are joining won't wait for you, so you need to go.

You want to do the best you can to not leave a bad reputation when leaving. If you go out on bad terms, anyone involved may remember that. That might mean they would never consider rehiring you. It might mean you wouldn't get good references from people you worked with. Your reputation is important. You can even tell them just in case you run into any issues that they can e-mail you or give you a call if they have a question or need to find something. That's not required, but it can be a nice gesture.

Don't burn any bridges. If things go wrong at your new job, they might let you come back.

Make sure to get all of your colleagues to connect with you on LinkedIn. You can do that now or wait till you leave, depending on if you want your colleagues to know.

Counteroffers

Your current company might ask you what you want in terms of money and position. It would be awkward if you told everyone you were leaving and then decided to stay and take the counteroffer.

It can be tricky taking a counteroffer. Was money the only reason for your leaving, and did they solve that? Will your relationships be the same now that the management chain knows you want to leave? You will need to carefully gauge if it is what you want and if it is worth staying for a counteroffer. It would also really annoy the company you were supposed to join, so much that they might avoid hiring you if they see your name, to avoid going through that again.

Changing Teams

Sometimes, in a company, there comes a point where you don't want to stay with your current manager or team, so you decide to find an available open role on another team that interests you and can get the manager there to agree to take you for that team.

You think to yourself, "Great, that worked out well." Maybe, and possibly not yet.

Lots of firms, before they will let you move, will evaluate active projects and make sure you complete anything pending on your project before they let you go. This could last for the entire project, whatever length it is, which could be like a 1–6 month time period. Time and requirements may vary by firm or project (not all firms handle things this way, but a lot do). Some firms give the current manager the ability to cancel the trade. Others give the current manager up to a limited amount of time to make sure current projects have been completed.

If, for some reason, the other manager can't wait that long, they may have to find someone else. Then your position just evaporates, and you are now working for a manager who knows you want to leave. It's possible you might get the smaller, less interesting projects to avoid disruptions because the manager figures you might look to leave for a different place again.

Learn the rules about switching positions before you put yourself in that position. Your HR representative may be able to tell you, or your employee handbook or perhaps someone you know who moved can help you (but make sure it's in a similar group/division, as things can be different in different areas).

Also, if you do something like this around the time of layoffs, and it doesn't work out, you could easily be added to the layoff list if you were not already, on the presumption you were looking to leave, anyway.

Companies with more employee friendly policies have rules that have a limited max time allowed for the transition from the existing manager. A current manager can ask you to stay in a role to finish things up in a limited time. This way, the current manager can't be a blocker to team/division changes for too long. Figure this out early so you know what to prepare yourself for.

CHAPTER 17

Career

LinkedIn

Once you have your first job, when people leave, or you do, connect to everyone on LinkedIn. Over time, you can build a network of people you worked with to help you find jobs when you need them or perhaps hire people if you need them. Prior relationships are the easiest way for you to acquire future jobs, so keeping your contact list up to date is very important. With LinkedIn, people keep their contacts up to date, so you have access to their info in one place.

The best times to update can sometimes be when you meet people, when they join, or when they leave the company.

You can also ask coworkers you know or have known to write you a sort of blurb to describe how great it was working with you, if you think they would give you a good write-up to get good comments on your LinkedIn account.

LinkedIn has also become a great place to look for jobs. Be careful about your privacy when looking for a job while you currently have one.

I would recommend checking your privacy settings, so folks don't see updates when you are just changing your information. I also personally don't recommend that you put the name of the current job you are at on LinkedIn, only previous jobs. Just like you wouldn't put your home address all over the Internet, making your current company listed has similar risks.

LinkedIn also has a jobs section now that is very popular with recruiters, so keep that in mind when looking for your next job. Fill in details about your past work, projects you've been on, and so on. People can find you that way. You will occasionally get recruiters asking about jobs that you may or may not be interested in.

Making Money from Your Own Software

As a software developer, it's possible for you to write some code and perhaps make some money from it. Most folks probably don't make much of a living from it, but it is possible to make some side money or even a business from it if the idea/app is highly marketable.

Write an Android/IOS App, Websites, Desktop App

These platforms are very popular. It's possible to write an app where you can make money from people seeing ads on your app, so you can offer it for free (you probably won't make too much money with ads, but it's possible). You can also offer premium versions that people buy that have additional features worth paying for, perhaps. Or you can offer add-on purchases people could make for customizations, games, and games.

Similar things apply to websites and desktop apps. Websites, though, require hosting, so you will have to pay for that to support it. The key is having an app designed where users need to spend time using it so that more ads can be presented to them. An example of an app I made a long time ago was a Halloween soundboard to play spooky sounds. A game of some sort would have perhaps been even better.

Marketing

You will need a way for people to find your app/website. Perhaps through the Play Store, Google searches, or ads. You will need to figure out where your users would be and market to them effectively to get them to your site or to download/buy your app.

You can send links to your site or app to people in the media you know who review apps/sites of the type you wrote.

Find websites that review apps/sites like yours, and send them a professional sounding e-mail offering your app for an unbiased review.

You might consider search ads or ads on other sites to direct people to your app/site.

Publishing Your Software

If you want your software in stores, you might want to go through a publisher. Just like book publishers, there are software publishers that can help with everything from packaging to marketing, though it's best to have some plans on your own, as you probably know your users best. These days, though, getting into stores isn't really important other than the online stores.

Book Authoring

No one recommends writing a book to make a lot of money, since so few people actually do make significant money from it. Years ago, I was offered the opportunity to be one of several authors for a technical book. The pay was something like $25 per page. I instead gave a friend the reference to do it, and he did it instead. I had thought about it for a while but never got around to doing it. It can be hard to write a lot of information this way. It can be hard to find a publisher that would want to publish your book. Even if you could, would you want to, if the royalty percentage were only 10–15 percent net profit for most sales? The contracts are often for your entire life! That's right. Unless someone breaches the contract, you won't get out of it for your entire life. That's a lot of commitment. Most books supposedly don't earn more than the initial upfront payment.

Of course, you can self-publish, but that way, you have to manage everything on your own. You may need to hire editors, cover designers, book formatters, and index creators. That's not cheap. If you glance around the Internet, some people say sales might not equal what you put into it.

Your Company Has Been Bought—Now What?

If you had options/stock in the company being bought, you might stand to make some money from the deal. If it wasn't a startup, you might not make too much from the deal, though that can vary depending on the firm.

You should do some research into the acquiring firm to see how they typically operate. What usually happens to the firms they buy? How successful are they in taking a profit making business and continuing it or making it better? Some firms just buy businesses, lay off as many people as they can, and sell them to try to make a net profit on the deal to contribute to their bottom line. So by doing some research, you can learn more about what might be the fate of you and your firm.

If the founders of the firm were still in the company when it was bought, sometimes they are kicked out immediately or decide to leave, or sometimes they are asked to stay on for some multi-year deal to make sure the business is stable. If you are at a high enough level in the firm, you might also be offered some form of potential compensation to keep you on board if they are worried people might leave.

Usually, if the company buying your firm cares about the people and the product, they take a gentle approach to integration in the first year to give them time to learn the business and people better, mean-ing they would avoid making huge organizational changes and staff changes. If instead you see those things in the first year, you are in for a much different ride. Certainly, companies will look for areas that are redundant to integrate, like HR and accounting. so there can some-times be layoffs or integrations there first.

Thinking through these things should give you a better insight into how secure your job is and if you need to be looking at other opportunities. Think about your position in the firm and what is happening to other people in a similar position.

You might be wondering how often companies get bought. Most of the time, it would usually be a smaller company being bought by a bigger company, but sometimes, it can be a division of a large company being bought by another company. I've been through at least four acquisitions of companies or divisions being bought in my career so far. So if you are working for a small or mid-sized company or a segmented division of a larger company, you never know.

Avoiding Layoffs

This perhaps isn't the best title for this section, since layoffs are mostly out of your control and unavoidable. But if you are clued in, you can sometimes avoid them.

If you know your company or division has hard times, not making sales and revenue forecasts, and people with some insight are talking about layoffs, you need to ask yourself some questions and make some decisions. Where is this going to end up? Will it turn around? If I get laid off, will I be able to find a job right away? Might I get a layoff package and then be able to find a job right away? Is it better if I start looking for a job now?

First important question: Are there other groups/divisions in your current company you could transfer to that would not likely be part of any layoffs?

Before joining a company, you can ask if there have ever been any layoffs, when, and how many people. That way, you can get a feel for the company's history.

If layoffs are pending and your performance hasn't been good, there is a greater chance you would be on the layoff lists. You could try to improve your performance before then or get ahead of it by looking for a new job if you think that approach is the best for you.

None of these can guarantee you can avoid getting laid off someday, but sometimes, keeping a watchful eye for some clues can help. If the company starts having some layoffs and is cycling through groups, that's a pretty big clue. If there is a lot of talk (from reputable sources, not just random gossip) about your group, product, or division not making its numbers, that could be a clue that things are not going in the right direction. If bonuses have been reduced to nonexistent because of a bad year, that is certainly a clue. If you can't figure out how your company will make money, because customers are leaving for some significant known reasons, that can be an even bigger hint of pending concern. Significant management shakeups at the top to mid levels can also clue you into changes happening that should be a warning to keep an eye/ear out for more info.

If your company was purchased, and the new company starts making significant changes immediately within the same year, including management and staff, which is not usual in the first year after a merger (usually they wait till the second year or later for big changes), it should be a warning to keep an eye/ear out.

Suppose you see and get the direction that they are winding down business on your part of the product, that is definitely a clue to figure out what comes next. Don't wait around passively. Quietly collect information and figure out what the business plan is or what your plan should be on what happens next.

One Example of a Layoff

One day, I was at work at my cube, and everyone was at their desks. Through the entry door, swiftly walked a stream of 20–30 uniformed security guards. They each quickly walked to a very particular desk and told each person that they could collect what they could carry right now and would need to leave, escorted by the security guard. This isn't typical of layoffs that I've seen since then. This is why it stood out so much. Companies are worried that employees could sabotage some computer systems, so they exit them quickly. More typical in recent days, employees are asked one at a time to an odd meeting, told they are being laid off with the benefit details, and then escorted out. During that time, their computer account access is being removed.

CHAPTER 18

Process: Waterfall

PROCESS

In these process sections, we will cover waterfall and Agile processes from the beginning to the end of the software development lifecycle (SDLC). This covers requirements, source control, architecture/design, implementation, validation, deployment, production, support, and more.

Waterfall

Requirements:

- Design
- Construction/Implementation
- Testing
- Deployment
- Support

Waterfall might remind you of a tranquil place in a forest, or a loud, beautiful spray of something akin to Niagara falls, but nowadays at least in the software world, people don't think of Waterfall SDLC as something pretty.

Waterfall has fallen out of favor. Most shops are now interested in variations of Agile development.

What is the waterfall process? Waterfall SDLC process is when one activity must be completed before another can begin. Each phase of development is completed before the others. Requirements collection, followed by Architecture/Design, followed by Implementation/Construction, followed by Testing and Deployment.

When should you consider using waterfall?

- Possibly a large, highly regulated software development project (even many of those use Agile now, though).
- If large parts of the projects can't be decomposed into smaller parts to fit in sprints (two to three weeks).
- Won't have ready access to the customer/stakeholders during software construction.

Very few places use the waterfall process anymore. Most have moved toward some variation of Agile, so we will cover Agile in more detail.

Critiques against Waterfall

There were many failed waterfall projects. Some of these were blamed on analysis paralysis. That's where requirements continued to be analyzed deeper and deeper, and there seemed to be no end of new things that would be found that would keep the project from starting the next phase.

Formal testing used to wait until the end of the project before it was tested formally. Since that could be weeks, months, or even years past the time it was implemented, a lot may have been forgotten by the team. Even worse is that many of the product's capabilities may have been built on top of untested functionality. Waiting till the end often created a cascade of bugs found throughout the system. The project would inevitably be delayed by the "unexpected" number of bugs found at the end.

With Agile, testing happens along with the feature/enhancement, mitigating many of the late issues found. Also, Agile doesn't usually wait for requirements to be 100 percent complete. Agile usually waits for enough of the requirements to be defined so that the details can be left to the implementor. As long as nothing architectural significant was left unknown, Agile would continue.

CHAPTER 19

Process: Practical Agile with Scrum

Scrum in the Real World for Software Development

There are many development books on using Agile and Scrum, but few that offer more practical information, real-world usage, and advice. This section is an attempt at providing not just the outline of Agile and Scrum but also real-life usages. Many people and books seem to prescribe ways to do Agile and Scrum. The folks that came up with the concepts behind Agile and Scrum often point out that they are just frameworks, and you do not need to use them exactly as stated.

If you are someone who needs to follow all the "rules" for a process or system and cannot tolerate any variation from the mainstream, then this might not be the particular book for you. Some treat development processes like a religion that must be followed and believed in as exactly written (again, if you fall into this category, this is not the book for you). This book is based on my experiences with development processes, Agile, and Scrum, so I'm sure others have had different experiences and may come to different conclusions.

I'll include real-world examples that actually happened and were used as a part of our Scrum process. Some folks might find some good or some bad things in real-world examples. I find things are not always that black and white to fall into good or bad. Sometimes, what works is fine (that does not mean you cannot think about better ways in the future). So, ultimately, use these experiences and decide what works for your company/project and your team.

What is Agile?

Agile evolved over time. Some of the core concepts of iterative development were around long before the term Agile with respect to software development was thrown around.

The core values originally stated: (Beck et al., 2001) (*Manifesto for Agile Software Development*, 2001)

Individuals and interactions over processes and tools

Working software over comprehensive documentation

Customer collaboration over contract negotiation

Responding to change over following a plan

Generally, it is said that the values on the left are valued more than those on the right.

Practical Advice:

The heart of these values is in the right place. Understand that this is the spirit of Agile, not the law of the land. Agile is a set of values, principles, and a sort of framework that can be adjusted to fit your team and environment. It's suggested to try Agile with Scrum in the prescribed form first, working with someone who has the experience to act as a mentor, before trying to adjust it too much. It's good to really understand what works or doesn't work in your environment. Changing too much before you know what Agile/Scrum brings to the table (or doesn't) might cause you to veer away from some practices that could be helpful before you really try them.

Practical Advice (Continued):

If you follow the values, they can make your life a lot easier. For example, if your sales team could negotiate a collaboration over contracts, even if you aren't a contract developer, getting your product owners to agree not to commit to specifics that must be hit for a release to allow for collaboration could help deliver better features. So if you can make those happen, Agile can work better. If you can't convince sales/product folks, Agile still works, just perhaps not as ideally as its founders hoped.

Let's take, for example, the value "Responding to change over a plan." The reality is that if you are near the end of a release or contract, and you need to accept significant change late in the release, it can significantly affect your contract/release. If there is an unwillingness to change any item in the triangle of scope, time or quality of life can become difficult or impossible for the Agile team. If one or more of those items can change in a way to achieve your goals, then perhaps your team can meet those criteria. So you see where you want to try to live up to the spirit of the values but temper that with the reality of what your environment/business can handle.

The 12 Principles of Agile (Beck et al., 2001)

- Satisfy the customer through early and continuous delivery of valuable software.
- Welcome changing requirements, even late in development.

- Deliver working software frequently (weeks or months, preference for shorter time frame).
- Cooperation between business and technical staff.
- Build projects around motivated people. Trust them to implement.
- Face-to-face communication is the best communication method.
- Working software is the way to measure progress.
- Speed of development should be maintainable indefinitely.
- Continuous attention to technical excellence and good design.
- Self-organizing teams bring out the best designs, architecture and requirements.
- Simplicity.
- At regular intervals, the team reflects on the best ways to become more effective and tunes/adjusts behavior.

Practical Advice:

Again, these principles, like the values, are inspirational and sometimes aspirational parts of Agile. Do not point to all of them as law. Use them to provide direction, guide, and inspire. Temper them with practicality in relation to your company, team, product, and environment. If your team is all remote, you may notice the principle "Face-to-face communication is the best method" may not be applicable in your environment. But don't dismiss it too quickly, as even if your whole team was remote, perhaps you could use technology like Google Hangouts, Skype, or some other product to allow for a reasonable replacement of face-to-face communication when possible. I've worked with teams that almost exclusively used video chat, and it works reasonably well.

This doesn't mean you should ignore these principles. It means you should use these principles, common sense, and business environment to guide your decisions related to them in your implementation of an Agile process.

Agile Software Development Process Pros and Cons

Just what are the benefits of Agile software development versus the detriments.

First Some Background

Before we get into the pros and cons, let's cover where the Agile software development concept started. Agile was created in part due to many failed software projects. Agile is in opposition to what was a cumbersome waterfall software development process.

With Agile, it was viewed that software didn't need the kind of upfront design as civil engineering problems would, where failure would be a disaster. The software could deliver value sooner to customers and get feedback to improve it going forward.

It was also viewed that since there wasn't a specific language for requirements/design, there would always be a lack of clarity when trying to implement it, since some items will come up between a thought experiment and practical implementation.

Some precursors to Agile were Rapid Application Development (RAD) from James Martin. However, iterative/incremental development ideals existed as early as the 1960s (Kikama, 2010).

In the 1980s, some now well-known software thought leaders such as Grady Booch, Fred Brooks, and others wrote articles and books on incremental development. One article, Barry Boehm's "A Spiral Model of Software Development and Enhancement," was well known.

In the early 1990s, what's known as Scrum and the process were created. Later, it was presented at a 1995 conference for object-oriented software (Schwaber, 1990).

In 2001, the *Agile Manifesto* was written about the ideals of Agile from an approach and how it differs from other methodologies.

One of the culminations of Agile was the Rational Unified Process created by Rational Software Corporation. It appealed to a lot of different parties, the waterfall folks as they understood it, and the iterative development folks since it embraced that methodology, showing the phases of development could overlap with each other and didn't need to be executed purely sequentially like a waterfall. This may have brought large companies to consider embracing the process.

Agile Pros

- Reducing overhead (reduced work in the beginning, less need for encyclopedic-sized requirements/plans).
- Giving customers value sooner.
- Prioritizing business valuable items as conditions change.
- Accepting change and going with the flow.
- Faster feedback for customers and teams.
- Encouraging team members to help solve the problems for the team, so it encourages a good team self-sufficiency attitude.
- Allowing enough flexibility to change things that aren't working well.
- Keeping teams on track since there is a checkpoint at every sprint.

Agile Cons

- Teams with many different skills may not fit the original Agile definitions that expect a cross-functional team, with anyone being able to work on anything. This can make it difficult to do normal team activities like estimating together, since some folks won't know how to estimate a task. If you had, for example, a neurosurgeon and a marketing grad on the same team, it might be hard for the marketing grad to estimate how long neurosurgery would take. This can even be true for members that are part of a normal team, such as QA team members. Can they estimate the software implementation time frame? Can developers estimate the QA tasks? Agile often asks everyone to offer their equal estimate on the implementation time.

- Agile can be confusing to understand, since it's a framework and not a complete SDLC.
- Adoption concerns for companies not used to it or not trained to focus on the right things.
- Large teams. Agile works well with small team of four to maybe 10. As teams get bigger, it's hard to come to consensus or have meaningful scrum meetings together, so processes are needed to manage larger teams.
- Less predictability. Given the flexibility allowed in Agile planning into the future more than half a year can be hard and not as accurate. Development estimates were never that accurate over long periods of time. This can make organization planning for the year or more hard to accomplish, since Agile methodologies rarely plan that far out unless absolutely needed due to the likely inaccuracies the farther out you go.
- Teams are supposed to be self-contained to be able to deliver a solution. Many times, for large products/organizations, this isn't possible, with teams split into different functional areas.
- Even though Agile allows flexibility of process, some organizations may not allow enough flexibility in their process to allow for changes needed to reduce overhead.

- Agile often involves balancing the ideals of Agile with the ideals of the organization, which sometimes are the opposite of a truly Agile process but are needed by the business. This can cause some friction with Agile enthusiasts.
- For teams new to Agile, a lot of discussions/time get spent on questions about how something is not Agile and needs to be fixed.

Not all combinations of products/companies may be the best fit for Agile. For actual hardware engineering, for example, where things need to be precisely designed upfront before you make them, it's perhaps not the best fit. However, it's likely possible to add Agile aspects to those projects, like iterative design and teamwork.

That said, Agile can get used in a wide variety of even highly regulated industries like healthcare and finance. Agile is now sometimes used even outside the original scope of software.

Should You Use Agile?

So should you use Agile? If it seems like it makes sense for your project and organization, it's definitely worth trying. Agile has had a lot of successes. It's worth trying if you haven't yet. Most shops these days are doing some form of Agile, so if your organization is not doing it yet, it is probably time to try.

Mitigating the Cons of Agile

Teams with different skills: Teams naturally organize around the most appropriate team member working on the appropriate task. If possible, we can work on cross-training to have better skills among all of the participants. Different skills just mean the team isn't as efficient as the ideal Agile team. People could pair program to learn an area as well as cross-training.

The other part of this is estimating what areas can be done by the most appropriate team members. Developers could estimate their portion, and QA estimate their portion, and sum the fibs, story points, or hours as appropriate if QA or Dev doesn't have good ideas about each other's tasks. Team members will start asking the questions in their heads, "How long will development take, and how much time does that leave for QA in the sprint?" What often happens is the person with the subject matter experts might be asked to help with the estimate. Alternatively, the person who is expected to do the work might be asked if all of the team is not well versed in the areas being discussed.

Agile Confusion/Adoption: Either consider getting a consultant to help or have one or more members trained in the Agile process. Don't get too caught up about whether your process is correct yet, as long as you're making reasonable progress toward it. It's best to follow the practices as closely as reasonable where you can still accomplish your goals. Just remember, Agile is a framework and not a specific solution, so Agile could be what works for your organization. Sometimes, it takes some preparation for the org to move forward. Sometimes, it takes senior leadership buy-in to make an org move toward Agile. And then again, sometimes, just one team starting it catches on. Agile is so popular these days, it shouldn't be too hard for organizations to agree if they aren't doing it already.

Large teams: While Agile can get harder to scale for larger teams, it still works in many organizations. It's best when an Agile team is self-contained and can execute their stories themselves. If that's not possible for some or all items, it just requires some extra planning.

Track and manage dependencies, and plan to execute in an order that satisfies the dependencies. Plan at least a few sprints. Determine when other teams will pick up dependent tasks. That way, they don't get blocked.

Sometimes, companies will create a meeting called the scrum of scrums, where each team sends a representative. These don't need to be every day. They could be once a week, or every two weeks, based on need. They would cover progress, dependencies, and impediments.

Less predictability: This could be up to the team to avoid changing things too often. Or maybe management needs to get used to the lack of predictability. Or they should get used to that the team can only easily predict a few sprints out. It is possible to stay on track for longer times if a team has a history that can guide estimations. It also requires dedication to stay on the planned project path. Often, it also means leaving enough slack time in the planning to allow for changes. Don't book people to 100 percent capacity and plan on hitting that. When things change, your plan will definitely be affected. If, instead, you decide on a lower committed estimate of, say, 50–60 percent, it could give you room in your schedule for when some plans inevitably change.

A lower committed rate would be calculated like this. Let's say your team uses 5-point stories for one person for a two-week sprint. If four people are on the team, that would be 20 points per sprint. If you knew your release would be five sprints, that would be a total of 100 story points the team could do. Instead, though, only allow 60 percent of that to be committed, meaning only committing to features, enhancements, or bugs that are up to 60 percent of the total capacity. Also, work on all of those items first. That should leave plenty of time to almost guarantee they get in unless something major comes up.

Organization not allowing you to do some Agile processes: Let's say your organization mandates you to use hours instead of story points.

That's fine. Agile can work well with that. What if the company doesn't like having sprints? You could probably internally have sprints without bubbling that up to the organization. Say your team doesn't have a customer stakeholder. Just find the next best person who can act as a stakeholder for the customer and try to think the way your customer does. Even contact them to ask questions, if allowed.

A lot of discussions/time spent on questions about Agile: Some teams spend huge amounts of time trying to think about how to split a story so it fits in a sprint. Agile would prefer a functional deliverable unit be created for a story in a sprint. Sometimes, that is just not possible or doesn't make much sense, especially when organizations expect a ticket representing a story to be a deliverable unit.

Usually, there are ways to work around this. You could implement a portion of the story as a subtask and deliver that. Don't get too caught up on it being some usable feature. Sometimes, that's not possible. The actual key is trying to deliver the most value possible toward that checkpoint for the part that you can deliver.

Agile would like each part tested as part of the delivery. Sometimes, it's easier to break a story into a dev part and a test part. You'll need to find ways to make it work for your organization. Perfectly Agile, no, but this is the reality of Agile. It's not always a neat and clean story breakdown, depending on what you're working on. That doesn't mean you shouldn't at least think about what you plan to deliver to break it down further to see if you can.

While Agile isn't perfect, it is one of the best development methodologies we have today. While Agile doesn't require any tools to be Agile, I believe the tooling, if chosen wisely, and if it does not create too many unnecessary processes with them, can help improve development practices/processes for the future.

Agile Sprints/Iterations

Providing iterative small incremental updates to the software, using short time frames (i.e., weeks, often two to three weeks for an iteration), with the goal of having an available working release with the improvements after an iteration. If the iteration doesn't deliver enough value, it doesn't need to be released to customers but should be available for internal review (working software as a measure of progress).

Why are iterations/sprints typically two to three weeks? There is no requirement that they be that length. It's more about a comfortable amount of time to be able to deliver value in each sprint. Sometimes, that could be hard in a shorter time frame, like a week. You could set a sprint as a month if you wanted, but a month is kind of a long period of time to not get feedback on how your development for the sprint is doing. The idea is to have a time that is not too long so you get short feedback cycles and not too short that you can never finish anything. The teams I've typically worked with have used two weeks most of the time, with an occasional three-week sprint when there are a lot of holidays or people on vacation in December to allow enough time for people to complete some work.

Agile Is Not Waterfall

Agile is often compared to a waterfall SDLC. Waterfall methodology is when one phase must be complete before moving on to the next. All phases have to occur in order, and each step must be completed before moving on to the next. One often cited criticism of waterfall is that requirements analysis takes a long time. This is because many times, as different parts of the system are built, new information is learned that provides more detail about the requirements than could have otherwise been gathered (and sometimes analysis paralysis can occur). Also, if the requirements change in theory, that could mean going back to the requirements phase.

What Is Scrum?

Scrum can refer to the whole Scrum framework or potentially the daily Scrum that we will discuss next. Scrum provides a framework around Agile, with suggested particular roles that people are in: deliverables, processes, and events.

Scrum is kind of an add-on framework related to Agile. We'll describe in this section the processes related to the Scrum/Agile framework.

From scrum.org—What is Scrum?

(scrum.org, 2018 – https://www.scrum.org/resources/what-is-scrum/)

Daily Scrum

The daily Scrum meeting is a meeting where the team meets to discuss the previous and current days' work. You may hear this referred to as a stand-up meeting, that is, in person. The idea is to limit the discussion to 15 minutes so the team can get on with the sprint activities. The scrum master is responsible for running this meeting.

There are three questions asked of all the active participants:

- What did you do yesterday?
- What will you do today?
- Are there any impediments?

The meeting is not intended to be a status meeting for managers but more of a way for the team to understand what work has been accomplished, what still needs to be accomplished, and to adjust the team direction (though let's be honest with ourselves, it's kind of status meeting as well).

If there are any impediments blocking the team, the scrum master takes note, and their task will be to work on removing those impediments for the team or taking responsibility to find who can and make it happen.

If people repeat the same update as the day before (like "same as yesterday, and same today") and it's not informative, the Scrum master might ask, "Can you expand on that a little?"

Who should attend the daily Scrum: Product Owner, developers, QA, scrum master (other active team members). Others can attend, but in general, as long as it is not interference with Scrum.

Daily Scrum: Practical Advice

While this is intended to be an in-person stand-up meeting for 15 minutes every day, there are other options.

What time of day should you have the daily Scrum?

Presuming your company has normal hours of 8–5 or 9–6, my recommendation is to have this meeting in the morning, early enough in the day that there is still plenty of the day left to act on the information, but not so early as to cause grief or attendance issues. For example, 10:00 or 10:30 might do ok. Any earlier might force your team into certain life choices to make it that early.

Long Discussions

If someone launches into a discussion that will be too long for the 15-minute scrum (if you have five team members, each update should be less than around three minutes, for example), the scrum master should redirect them with something like, "Let's continue this discussion post Scrum." This way, we can get all the updates in the approximately 15-minute time frame.

Post Scrum

Teams I've worked on usually allow for a post-Scrum time after the initial Scrum of 15 minutes so that not everyone needs to be there, but some important conversations could happen for a few more minutes. We rarely let post Scrum go beyond another 15 minutes. If other conversations need to happen, we schedule separate meetings. Post-Scrum time can also be used for people who joined the Scrum but are not active, Agile team participants to ask a quick question or offer some information (briefly).

Post Scrum is not part of the normal Scrum process. I have found it fairly helpful if kept very brief, and if not all team members are needed, they are free to leave. We try not to let our meetings go over 30 minutes (15 minutes Scrum + max 15 minutes post Scrum, if needed).

Do You Have to Stand Up and Meet in Person

This is the recommended way to encourage briefness and good communication bandwidth. That said, I have worked in an environment where we almost entirely did Scrum via Google Hangouts/Webex or Zoom since the company had a flexible work-from-home policy, and we had team members at different office locations. It is about as effective as a good video chat system. Sometimes, we just post scrum updates into a group chat system like Slack when enough people have overlapping meetings and it would not make sense to have Scrum (sometimes, folks want to attend a reveal of another scrum team on our product that overlaps with our scrum).

Fun on Scrum

It's ok to have a little banter before or after scrum once in a while. Just keep it short. Having a little fun is good for team spirit. I can recall scrums where someone working from home joined in a superhero mask (we had scrums via Google Hangouts), or used the funny Google Hangouts hats (when they had that feature), and more recently, virtual backgrounds on Hangouts, WebEx, or Zoom, for example.

Does "Daily" Scrum Really Have to Happen Every Day?

Many scrum advocates would say yes. I would say daily ensures you stay on track, but if the time does not feel well used to your team, you might consider alternate times, though it depends on a lot of factors, including:

- The work your team does.
- How much they need to work together vs. independent work.
- Whether there are significant dependencies or impediments that can often come up.
- How well the team members can manage their work.

Under the right circumstances, with all independent, single-person work, no dependencies, low complexity tasks, and team members who can manage their time well, you could live without having it daily. I know some teams that only do Scrum two days a week, and it works for them. Those teams have very independent tasks. They are very self-managing and will talk with whomever they need on their own to continue the task.

Teams can be successful with adjustments and the right circumstances. I would say if you can try daily and if your team thinks you can scale back the days, try it a little at a time. It won't be a big impact on your project. If it doesn't work for you, then switch back. Different times of a release might be helped by having scrum every day, though, so be careful your project doesn't go off the rails.

On sprint planning, grooming, or reveal days, we will sometimes skip scrum. If it were a day we had sprint planning or grooming, we would add Scrum to the beginning of that meeting to reduce our meeting load a little.

More recently, we started not having Friday Scrum. This started from a corporate level for one summer, with no meeting Fridays. People liked it so much, they didn't want it to stop, so we got rid of Friday Scrum. If there was something urgent, we would have it, but if not, folks might just post updates in Slack.

Scrum Roles

Development Team

The development team consists of everyone who is part of the Agile team involved in delivering the features, fixes, or functionality. It likely includes developers, QA staff, product owners, and the scrum master. This can be a multidisciplinary team that can deliver end-to-end functionality.

The entire scrum team is responsible for delivering all items accepted into the sprint by the team. This means that if more testers than developers are needed at one point, developers might help test,.

The size of the team is considered ideal if it is seven or less.

The team should ideally be in the same location. If the team is spread across locations, it is recommended to have a team at each location. If that doesn't work, make sure you use video conferencing for your scrums and other Agile meanings. It can still work well enough virtually. In reality, one of the team Scrums we've had has been virtual for years (pre-pandemic; some people were in the office, some home, or some in a different office.

Development Team: Practical Advice

Sometimes in the meetings, more folks are considered part of the team. For instance, managers of the team members for developers and QA may be involved in Scrum. They may or may not participate in Scrum directly, though they can sometimes participate more actively in grooming and planning activities. Sometimes, there is a project manager as well.

The entire Scrum team is responsible for all items, though often, developers may be working on different stories during a sprint (though they can work on the same one if a story requires it).

Team size: Though seven is sometimes quoted as the ideal size, plus/ minus a couple, I've seen teams larger where development and QA together totaled about 14, and it was still effective. It may depend on the team, project, and tasks that need to be accomplished.

Multidisciplinary and full team: The recommendation is for the team to have dedicated members to be able to deliver all required functionality. I agree that is the most effective way to do it, but sometimes, it's not that simple. For example, imagine that the feature being implemented requires the operations team's involvement in the sprint. The operations team is a totally different team. The work involved only requires perhaps one day of work on the ops team to implement. You're not likely going to get the ops team member to be dedicated to your team for the sprint. Then their priorities on their team might end up taking precedence over your teams and really fudge things up. Or even worse, they don't have time to work on it this sprint at all, so it will have to be handled later. We will discuss how to manage scenarios like that later. For now, just a taste to help you think on team composition.

Co-location: While it is recommended to have everyone at the same location, and that is ideal, it is possible to still have a fairly effective team using technology to make up for the distance, like Google Hangouts or Webex for video chat/meetings. It is probably best to have folks within the same time zone to avoid any meeting time concerns. It is still possible to make things work even with different time zones, though it is usually less efficient. When we have folks working remotely in different time zones, we still ask them to make the scrum meetings so that we can stay in sync (this can be a significant burden to folks, depending on the time zone, so be careful if you should do this or not). Alternatively, sometimes virtual, Scrum updates via e-mail or a group chat posted during off hours can help, but the communication bandwidth is pretty narrow then and not as effective for keeping folks in sync.

Product Owner

This person owns the product backlog in terms of what will be worked on and in what priority order.

Scrum Master

The scrum master is ideally someone who is an expert on Scrum. They are responsible for helping the team maintain the process and scrum values and principles.

This person does not have particular authority but leads or facilitates the ceremonies like the daily Scrum, sprint planning, and backlog grooming. They are responsible for helping the team get unblocked if there are any obstacles encountered in the sprint.

Practical Advice

Who should be the Scrum master? It could be anyone who really knows enough about scrum. Project managers have been known to fill this role. Team members have been known to fill this role. A rotation through the team can work. Each sprint has a new team member take on the role. It's not usually a full-time role, unless one scrum master serves multiple teams. Managers of the team can also fill this role, though, in some Scrum books, this is not recommended, since managers have actual authority. Perhaps when the manager talks, it could stifle the information flow of the team and not allow them to be self-managing. I think some managers can handle this role, but it is probably best to have someone else be the one to handle it regularly for any of the ceremonies (daily Scrum, sprint planning, etc.). A team manager could jump in to help the Scrum master with impediments, for example, to help with some of these role activities. There is definite value in a self-managing team, so if someone on your team can fill in, using a rotating role could work well.

Planning, Grooming, Reveal and Retro

The Scrum Process, Artifacts, and Ceremonies

Stories, Bugs, and Tasks

Stories are typically enhancements/features, though they could be used for anything. Try to make sure these are discrete updates that deliver value for the sprint. Ideally, it should be a functional feature; if an actual functional feature isn't possible, then at least some testable code deliverable unit.

Ideal: A complete, functional, and testable unit

Practical: Sometimes, it's hard to have a testable unit in the sprint, so periodically, breaking the story into a dev story and a QA story and linking them together would work, sort of like a part 1, then part 2. It would be better if you could have a full portion of functionality, working and testable, but instead of that, you could separate dev from QA and create separate linked stories for each.

Sometimes, breaking the stories into testable layers can help, for example, perhaps UI being separate from the server side. Agile would prefer a fully functional story, but if that's just not doable, you could break the story into smaller parts or deliver layers at a time.

Why would you break stories in a weird way?

- A fully or partially functional story can't fit in a sprint.
- There is seemingly no logical/reasonable way to break the story into smaller functional testable units.

You should think hard if there is a way to split them such that it makes sense before choosing an alternate route.

Why go against what Agile says? Could you just make the sprint longer? Perhaps, but Agile likes regular intervals, not changing them all the time. Once you set that precedent, how much bigger could you make a sprint? It would be what they call a slippery slope, meaning it would be tempting to do it too often.

However you decide to split your stories, remember that one month is a long time for code to be developed without any testing, so it would be best if no code waits that long for testing if it can be avoided.

The main benefit of Agile is that it provides sprint-sized checkpoints of implementations to make sure the team stays on the right track of what the stakeholders desire and offers small time horizon checkpoints to allow stakeholders to adjust the course if needed. Thus, splitting stories isn't perfect if stakeholders can't see it.

Splitting stories and taking more time to deliver has some risks. You can mitigate the risk with perhaps dev unit tests, code reviews, and discussion with stakeholders on your implementation for the partial story.

An Example of Why to Split or Roll a Story

Many Agile books and articles describe a story as a feature or change that has value for the user. Some will describe it as a description of what the user wants from their perspective in their language. Some write-ups may mention that a user doesn't have to be a product user. The story should also include requirements. A story should be something you complete in a sprint.

Let's say your sprints are two weeks.

Great! Let's say we queue up the next feature for the sprint. We want to multithread some back-end code to make it faster. We pick the smallest part we can write up as a story, adding our database table structures needed to support new installs and upgrade installs. Unfortunately, the team decides that the estimate for this smallest piece will take more than a sprint to implement and test.

What do you do? Perhaps you split the implementation and the test into different stories. Alternatively, just let it roll to the next sprint. Why does it matter? It doesn't really, if there is no difference other than one story or two from a functional perspective. It does allow the developer to mark their work completed if split into two stories.

Depending on your release process, you might need to mark particular stories as not releasable until all parts are completed if split into multiple parts. If the story is not split and doesn't finish in a sprint, the team won't get the points from completing the story added toward their velocity for the sprint. Some companies track this information for all of their teams. Depending on your environment, you will need to decide what works better for your team.

Enhancements/Stories

One interesting thing to note is some companies track the number of work hours spent on significant enhancements, as some of the time spent may provide a tax advantage to some firms, so you might be asked to track that.

The Sprint

Limited duration

- Limit work in progress (WIP)
- Focus on idle work, not idle workers
- No significant changes to work in progress

The Definition of "Done"

It sounds silly, but what does "done" mean? Done with development? Done with testing? How much testing? Ideally, most stories should be done when development, unit testing, and testing are complete.

Sprint Planning

The first part of sprint planning is usually about closing out the previous sprint—figuring out any stories, tasks, or bugs that can be closed—then deciding if any remaining items will "roll" (a.k.a., be carried over) to the next sprint. Alternatively, they could be put in the backlog if something wasn't started yet.

For the story/bug/task that needs to roll, you could consider a different option for the ticket. Sometimes, what you could do instead is break the ticket up. If, for example, dev work is complete but not testing, you could make the first ticket a dev part 1 story and close that. Then create a QA part 2 story to finish the work for this sprint. That way, you get the velocity for the last sprint and don't have to keep carrying stories over.

Some folks might say splitting the story so that just the dev part is marked completed is not really a completed story. While that's true, it does make it easier to estimate the new point effort for the new sprint and track the velocity more evenly. It potentially gives a false impression of velocity, since not all of it is completed work. Your team will need to decide what works best for them. Some businesses track velocity very closely and question anomalies from the points level. Using that mechanism to keep a more even velocity might be helpful if your process allows it.

When that part is done, the sprint is closed, and if using a tool like Jira, it would calculate the team's velocity for that sprint and show a trend for the sprints of velocity. The number of story points of completed work for the sprint becomes the velocity for that sprint.

Looking at the velocity trend, the team can decide if it's consistent, faster, or slower than usual and perhaps think about why.

The next part of sprint planning is pulling in the tickets from the backlog for this new sprint.

If backlog grooming was done well, then sprint planning should be straightforward. Pulling in new stories for the next sprint, making sure no one person picks up too many points or too few points for the sprint. This meeting usually happens once a sprint, just prior to starting a sprint.

All the stories should have effort/story points on them at this point (completed in the grooming meeting). So, for example, if 13 points meant one sprint to your team, you would make sure no person generally had more than that number of points for a sprint. Everyone won't always perfectly have 13 points. Sometimes, they will have less and can help others when they are done or leave unallocated time to work on support issues.

When stories/bugs/tasks are carried over, they still likely carried the points they had from the last sprint to the current sprint. For those stories, when they are brought in, you should reevaluate the work effort to see if it was correct for the last sprint and should be left alone or perhaps increased to account for additional work beyond what was expected. For example, if a story with 13 points from the last sprint rolled to the current one, consider what the points should be. If the team estimates it will take three more points to complete this sprint, perhaps add the three to the 13 to get 16. That would be a correct accounting of the effort that was actually put into the story if you want story points to account for that in velocity. This is something to consider, at least, if your company tracks velocity closely.

As part of sprint planning, you might decide one or more people on a rotating basis over one or more sprints should work on support tickets. They would pull in tickets as they finish them and need more work for the sprint. They should put effort into the tickets after they complete them so that velocity remains good. You can try to gauge how many people you need based on the number of tickets that typically show up in a sprint and how many are waiting. If there is really no support work at the moment, they can perhaps be given less critical stories that aren't on the critical path. That way, if they get interrupted, it won't be a big deal.

The Reveal

A reveal is a presentation of the completed work for the sprint of stories. If it was a UI story, it might be an interactive walkthrough of the scenarios, so the stakeholders can ideally see if they like it and want changes or not.

Ideal Agile process states that the reveal should be mandatory to show stakeholders the product. This can be dependent on your environment, though. If your primary stakeholders are your local business analysts (product) and your teams are working with them every day, then a reveal of this information might be redundant. When there is a multi-team reveal, you can decide if the information is significant enough to reveal or not or would need feedback from other teams. Revealing technical architecture changes can be useful for multi-team reveals. If you needed to work with customers, and they were not involved daily, perhaps you would want to reveal. Often, some teams I've worked with skipped reveals, as the information was not significant and/or redundant for the team reveals. Only significant items were scheduled to reveal. This often eliminated many of these meetings or cut down on the presentation times significantly. It also reduced the number of times people felt they needed to prep for the reveals. Your teams can choose the most appropriate path for your organization.

The Retrospective (or just Retro)

In the retrospective, the intent is to review the sprint and list out what went well, what could have gone better, and how things can be improve. These retrospectives might go better without management in the room and with a small team creating these notes in an anonymous form. Each sprint can be a little different. Sometimes, things go so bad that it's easy for people to "criticize" the sprint. Make sure it is criticizing the sprint or the process, not people, to avoid interpersonal issues. If you have a lot of average sprints and you just asked people to put anything they like in one of the columns, they all might do nothing. This can be ok and can reduce stress, but it doesn't give any data about what went right or wrong.

A different way to run the retrospective is to make it a little playful. Use Trello.com with stickers or just colored sticky notes on a board. Tell everyone they can put something about anything that happened during the sprint on the board and that everyone should put at least one thing on the board. The benefit of this is that everyone is in the same boat. No one person feels singled out. People can just put something like "Great team lunch" or "We hit the date for the release" in the "What Went Well" column. Those aren't super informational, but it helps the team feel comfortable putting things on the board and should make it easier for them to add other things.

When people place the cards afterward, you can ask people to drop emoticons on each of the cards (in Trello, this is pretty easy. This gives you a read of how the team feels about each card). This could be easy for people to do remotely or even in person when using Trello if everyone brought their laptops, perhaps.

Make sure the Scrum master/project manager or manager notes any action and follows up on improvement ideas if possible or adds them to an appropriate list to work on.

This usually is scheduled at the end of a sprint. You might add it to the same meeting as sprint planning, or perhaps just before it.

Backlog Grooming

Estimating the effort of each story, break them down into sprint-sized stories so they fit in sprints. Fully define the requirements and acceptance criteria prior to estimating. If a sprint was two weeks, this meeting is often scheduled once a sprint, though it can be less if enough stories have already been groomed to work for the next sprint. Sometimes in the middle of a sprint, you can schedule just in-time grooming with the three amigos—Product, QA, and Development—involved in the story.

Many companies have a standard set of information they want to make sure is filled out for bugs and stories.

These templates have information like:

- User scenarios
- Requirements
- Does this require a documentation change
- Is there any hardware impact
- Is there a user interface impact
- Does this change impact the database
- What are the acceptance criteria for this change
- What is the risk/impact of this change.

Sometimes, these meetings can be pretty quick if most of the stories needed for the next couple of sprints have already been groomed, though other times, some of the work is so involved that it could take an hour to get through the details in one or two tickets. Some teams will book four hours for these meetings, while others may book an hour and a half or so. If you have many items to address, perhaps adding a few more meetings in the sprint to break up the time a little is another option, rather than having a crazy long meeting.

For each task for which you create requirements, you will need to ask the team to estimate. This will be hard to do as a new team. Agile would suggest using story points. Initially, the idea is to get the team to agree on points. For example, you might say 13 points are a sprint. Thus, 21 points are more than a sprint, and 8 points may be half a sprint. Yes, the numbers don't make exact sense. If 13 points is a sprint, how are 8 points a half? Part of this involves using the Fibonacci series: 1, 3, 5, 8, 13, 21, etc. This way, things don't get too granular. It just explains a general scale of the story. The team should think about what an example of a one-point story is on which we can agree. What is an example of a 3-point story on which we can agree? Sometimes, this can be hard to get an agreement, but as long as it is close, it's usually good enough. Otherwise, just use time as the agreement: 13 points is a sprint, and 8 is half. There just needs to be a general agreement on the relative scale to know how much of a sprint it is approximately.

The team would decide how many story points the story should be together. If they can't decide, they can vote on the points. Anybody higher or lower than the rest of the group should explain why they feel that way. Then everyone should vote again to see if there is any better agreement.

Scrum of Scrums

A scrum of scrums is a higher level of scrums where a representative of each of the scrum teams of a larger project or product attends.

It is similar to a scrum but is run less often, maybe once a week or once every two weeks, or whatever is appropriate for the project. A quick summary of the work completed and planned work is good. Any blockers that affect other teams or the project/release should be brought up.

Tracking Progress

Velocity

When stories/tasks are groomed, they are given story points. When the team completes those as part of a sprint, they are added together to determine the total number of story points for the sprint completed. That is considered the velocity. Velocity is monitored over time to see if things are executing well and to estimate completion based on average velocity per sprint and remaining work.

Burn-Down Charts

These show the number of points remaining, which should decrease over time with each sprint. If it's staying the same or increasing, there is potentially a problem of unexpected work coming into the team, or stories/tasks aren't being completed in the sprint.

Agile with Scrum How To

There are many situations that take place that are not always described well in the Agile and Scrum framework.

Teams

What to do when the team gets large?

Generally, 7–10 is the high end of a scrum team, but they can be bigger if it works for the team. If it gets too big, consider if splitting into separate teams makes sense.

The one downside of splitting teams is that the manager, product manager, project manager, etc. might now need to attend multiple Scrums, sprint planning, and grooming sessions, unless you can still combine some of those if they make sense. The managers, the team, and other folks will need to decide on the best way to handle this for your scenarios.

How do you have multiple Scrum teams to build a product/features?

Try to organize the work so the teams can mostly operate on their own, except for a few dependencies. If there are dependencies, make sure they are queued up for the teams that need to work on them and prioritized so the dependency won't block the dependent team.

If needed/wanted, a scrum of scrums can be run once a sprint or an appropriate time frame to handle the cross-team dependencies.

What do you do when part of the team is remote?

Use Internet conferencing software like Google Meet, Zoom, Webex, etc. Teams can be quite effective operating remotely using this technology.

Backlog Grooming

What do you do when a story doesn't fit in a sprint?

Figure out a way to break up a story, if at all possible, into smaller parts that can be completed. If that means it won't be testable by that time, break it into two parts: the first part for dev and the second part in the next sprint for the test. This isn't ideal, since a feature would basically not have been tested for two to four weeks if your sprint is two weeks.

How Can You Estimate Support/Bugs?

This can be hard to do. Sometimes, you might be able to if it was simple to groom. If not, what you can do is break it into parts. First, investigate the issue and devise a solution, and then fix the bug. In the first part, you won't know how long it will take, so fill the story points in when complete. The first part should have provided enough information to estimate the second part.

How to Manage the Backlog for Large Projects?

Keep the high-priority shortlist at the top of your backlog and the rest further down. If the tool you are using to maintain your stories/bugs allows, keep a separate list for the bugs that aren't presently being considered to work on.

Sprint Planning

Should you let a story roll to the next sprint if it did not get completed?

You could, though you should consider updating the points, so your velocity number accounts for this. Also, more than once can be risky, as it means something has been developed without a checkpoint in multiple weeks. You could split the story up to complete the first part and a follow-up part in the second sprint. Not ideal, but sometimes, this can be an option.

The Sprint

How to Handle Unplanned Work (E.g., Support)?

If you find unplanned work to be a very common occurrence, assign enough people to the unplanned work you typically have for a sprint.

For example, if your team has six people, and you know almost always need a certain number of people (or your support backlog has enough items), assign the people you need to that for the sprint. For example, two people could handle unplanned work (like support work), and four people could work on stories/bugs.

What does the team do if they complete items for the sprint before the end?

The team member who needs work could pick up something from the backlog if it fits in the sprint. Alternatively, the team members that free up could swarm to help other team members complete their tasks (known as swarming).

Daily Scrum

What to Do When Someone Has an Impediment?

The Scrum master and possibly the team manager should do everything in their power to help the team or guide them to unblock that impediment.

Release Time Frame/Delivery Schedules

What do you do when management asks when you can have a release out in a number of days, not story points?

Your team probably has a general idea of converting story points to days, so you could use that and calculate with your team's velocity. Just be sure to include a range, a best case, and a worst case. Make sure to include time off for team members and holidays in the calculations. Add some buffer percentage based on risks. Perhaps your team on a previous project saw point expansion for a feature in the 15–30 percent range. If so, perhaps you could use something in that range to add some padding to your worst-case estimate. Be clear that they are estimates. If the timeline looks tight for a release, let them know and see if they would consider planning for it or at least allow for it in the following release if it can't make the current one.

If they want it sooner, then your projection shows. See if there is scope that can be reduced. Consider if you could only keep stories you need as part of an MVP, or consider if they could/would add resources to decrease the time of the project.

You might hear a term known as the iron triangle: Resources, time, and scope are the edges. You can keep two of those fixed but not all three if the project is estimated to exceed its timeline. For example, if the release date needs to be kept, then consider changing resources or scope.

Agile Story Points: Let me tell you a long story

This section is just to provide some varied views on using Agile story points. I've used them for multiple teams, and they work fine enough for most projects. The key is knowing when they may not be the best way to present or use an estimate.

When you enter the Agile world of software development, you are bound to come across some magical buzzwords such as Agile story points, fibs, T-shirt size, and more. If a developer is new to Agile, they will ask why? What happened to hours/days/weeks?

Let's look at some of the top rated answers.

Answer #1 Summarized: ("Agile—Why Do We Use Story Points Instead of Man Days When Estimating User Stories?" *Software Engineering Stack Exchange*, n.d.)

Using story points provides an abstraction so that you can instead consider effort/complexity.

Thoughts on Answer #1:
First off, lots of folks, when talking about story points and fibs, say those numbers are all about complexity and not time. Story points should consider effort and complexity.

The second part of this response makes a good point about humans doing a better job of comparing two things rather than estimating. This is based on the concept that story points or fibs should have a base story that is used for comparison for some low point story. The idea is that everyone on the team would know that story and be able to use it as a base for comparison. So if that story is considered a 1, something twice its size would be a 2.

On a team of, say, 5–7 people, it's likely that one story was only worked on by 1–2 people, so only they know the real effort that was put into the base story. Others might know something about it and the time it took. Thus, the rest of the team probably has some slightly different opinions on the effort involved. Are comparisons and using that really effective in this case? If that base story was worked on a year ago, do comparisons get worse with time due to our memory of that story? Possibly.

Let's even ignore that for a moment and say the base story is about adding text to a screen and making a button work. Could you really compare that base story to a new story about creating a Windows service to handle inbound file download requests? How many stories that an Agile team works on are so similar that they are easy to compare? From my experience, it seems rare to have a story similar to the base story for comparison. Thus, comparisons don't really compare that well.

Some people make the argument that everyone should have some common reference to agree on the time. As mentioned earlier, though, there is no easy common standard of measurement for everyone. There is no common baseline story that will mean the same thing to everyone, since it is often that just one or two people out of the team who worked on the story really know what went into it. Plus, since stories are often so different from each other, it can be very hard to compare.

Part of the second-highest rated answer on stack exchange was this:

Answer #2 on stack exchange summarized: ("Agile—Why Do We Use Story Points Instead of Staff Days When Estimating User Stories?" *Software Engineering Stack Exchange*, n.d.)

Your business analyst will be able to convert from story points to time/hours to discuss with stakeholders.

Thoughts on Answer #2:

The second-highest rated answer mentions an actual mapping of story points/fibs to staff hours, which many Agile story point proponents say should not directly be the case.

In practice, we've found most of the people on the team, when using story points/fibs, calculate in their head from the number and map roughly to time. This is generally easier for folks to get a grasp on when it's hard to compare against a base story. Let's face it, anyone outside the main development team is going to think in hours/days/time and not fibs/story points. By definition, story points/fibs can't even cross development teams, so there needs to be a common language at some point.

Answer #3 Summarized: ("Agile–Why Do We Use Story Points Instead of Man Days When Estimating User Stories?" *Software Engineering Stack Exchange*, n.d.)

Story points abstract time so that the team can decide 13 points should mean more than a sprint rather than just a sprint.

Thoughts on Answer #3: This is an interesting one. If using story points/fibs in theory, calculating the team's velocity, and seeing how far estimates are typically off, that might help determine better estimates for the future. This relies on calculating the committed story points compared to what was completed each sprint, calculating the difference, and looking at averages.

This idea is an interesting one, as it actually keeps track of estimates compared to actual completed work, which many shops are not following or don't bother to do.

One downside is that this relies purely on calculation to improve the team's estimates, with usually no easy feedback loop for the team to improve their estimating abilities, since the story points/fibs are supposed to be abstract. They don't look at time.

Let's think for a moment about how we could provide a feedback loop to learn if our point estimates are consistent or not. It would be by looking at the "time" it took to execute them and trying to compare with time. Without that, there really is no feedback. What else would you compare with?

Let's say we compared it to a story that took three points. How do we know it took longer than expected? Well, that three point story took three days, and this one took seven. We could just say without time, it took longer than the three-point story. But how much longer? Closer to an eight-point story. But everyone is always comparing in their heads to the days it took. Otherwise, how do you know how long a story took if you can't use time? So, to make sense of these things, most folks are still translating to time in their heads.

Here is another question. What if, instead of story points, we just used hours/days? Couldn't we still calculate the same thing that way? The developer estimated five days, and it took 10, so 100 percent over. Do that across the team, calculating velocity using days. The answer is yes. Was that easier?

This way, if something was estimated at five days and it took 10, everyone on the team knows pretty clearly the estimate was off and by how much.

The only "downside" some would argue is we can no longer create the psychological barrier to using an estimate for actual time . . . but what is the point of an estimate without time?

I can hear the argument from some, "Well, you're not supposed to use it that way." Ok, but the story points/fibs are being used to determine how many can approximately fit in your X-week sprint. How did someone figure that number out? Answer: They saw your average amount of work completed in a certain amount of time and used that to create a mapping from story points/fibs to time. So if your management remembers any math from grade school, how much is that abstraction buying you?

Answer #4 Summarized: ("Agile—Why Do We Use Story Points Instead of Staff Days When Estimating User Stories?" *Software Engineering Stack Exchange*, n.d.)
If you provide an estimate as one day and it takes three, you are late. If it was one story point, and it took three days, no one can say it's late.

Thoughts on Answer #4: Again, the very interesting point is that a story point is abstract, so it can't be considered late, as it's just an estimate as part of the velocity. Only then can you calculate team averages. As we've discussed previously, someone is likely converting story points to time in their heads, so they would likely still consider it late. This answer probably embodies one of the core ideas of this behind Agile. Since Agile is iterative working with the customer, things aren't late, as they are only estimates. The idea is to work with the customer/stakeholders to improve each sprint and not to work based on fixed target dates in general. That was one of the original ideas of early Agile, before it had to be expanded/enhanced, because real projects have real dates/timeframes and expectations. Agile can't really estimate short time frames well with story points, which is rather just calculated for a full project with velocity over time/trending. Still, for the project level, the estimation and calculation of the actual work done provide a compelling view to better analyze estimates for a project.

However, if there is a dependency on tasks/resources, those average team velocities may not work very well to estimate a project schedule alone, especially when there may be only one specialized resource to do certain work, and others must wait for that to be done.

So Agile methodologies came up with an iteration/sprint plan. A sprint/iteration plan would plan the work for all the iterations ahead of time. This way, the work that needs to be done earlier due to a dependency is scheduled for an earlier iteration. Of course, this means all stories must have been created and groomed to have enough estimates to know how many iterations/sprints there are to know where they will go. However, if the team is grooming out stories as they go along, this can be trickier.

Other thoughts: Working with teams onboarding to Agile training/teaching staff to understand story points, fibs, how to use them, and why we use them takes quite a bit of time and effort may often keep questioning its use for some time, trying to understand/grasp it.

Another thing I noticed after this training period is that the team sometimes seems more willing to give estimates (story points) for things they may not know much about. There was a completely new API to use for a story. No one knew how to use it or how complicated it was, but everyone on the team happily gave some fib estimate. Should they have? It seems like there should have been an investigation for someone to understand it deeper before estimating, but even then, only that one person would know it and not the team. Taking the time for the whole team to learn it wouldn't make sense. So does estimation by the team help or hurt in these scenarios? Prior to Agile, a good management team had the most capable people who understood the problem and provided an estimate. You could say in Agile, the team is supposed to go over the story so they understand it, but can a team really learn a new computer language or large API set in a few hours' time?

Consulting and other work: One day, management asked us to estimate work for the team or for consultants to come in and do it. This, for Agile story points, works for the team to come up with high-level estimates with story points and velocity but doesn't really work if the new work is meant for a new team of consultants who would need to establish their own velocity. We could estimate it as if it was for our team, but that doesn't map to consultants' time. Also, management sometimes doesn't want to hear about fibs or story points; they need to know how many consultants they need and how long they need to be onboard to complete the job. In these cases, we have to fall back to time estimates, and the team is not really directly in practice of using time because they use story points. However, since most folks map story points/fibs in their head to time, they come up with close approximations.

So is it worth the effort for story points/fibs vs. using time?
From the above examples, story points don't offer a huge amount of benefit over time. It might offer some detriments in not allowing the team to learn to improve their estimates, but folks having a direct mapping to time and being able to do actual time comparisons is easier rather than relying on velocity calculations. When it comes to hiring new teams of consultants, most management teams are going to want time, not fibs/story points, to know how much they need

to pay. As we said, most folks translate in their heads story points/fibs to time anyway, so is the extra indirection really helping? Velocity could still be calculated if story points equaled time. So why not use that? The argument of, "well, the story point is a range of time, so we shouldn't be held to a specific time" is a nice idea when you aren't time-boxed, but when you are, someone is going to want to know the time. Instead, perhaps estimates could be given in a range, saying something would take five to seven days instead of committing to either five or seven days. If story points/fibs can be a time range anyway, why not just give a range for a story? Someone might hold you to that date, you ask? Well, yes, I suppose sometimes your manager may need something by a date, but as long as estimates are considered estimates, your manager should understand that and plan accordingly.

More thoughts: The original *Manifesto for Agile* was a nice idea. We should just really think about some of these ideas being added into the loose set of guidance around Agile to see if they are really helping individual companies and teams or not.

From this discussion, you might get the feeling I don't like Agile, but that's not true at all. Agile, I believe, is a host of different concepts and processes that can be used, including Scrum, story points, fibs, XP, etc. If your management team takes estimates too literally, maybe story points/fibs can abstract them from that habit. For the right teams/purpose, these things can have some positive impacts. I also like to think about (just like almost anything in life can have combinations of positive and negative impacts) what are both the positive and negative impacts and make sure the balance and process are right for the company/teams. Even if you don't abandon your point system and team estimation, at least use the thoughts presented here to think about things critically when you are estimating.

So How Should We Estimate?

When providing an estimate, provide a range (average case, worst case). Have developers most familiar with the task, language, or technology estimate in days for a high-level estimate or hours for a more detailed estimate. Estimates from developers or others not familiar with the task and not going to work on it should be taken with a grain of salt and not be used for the average side of an estimate.

Ideally, have the folks who will work on it estimate it. If they don't know, create a task they can do in place of it to figure out enough of what they need to do, so they can estimate it.

Have QA separately estimate the effort for their work for each story for the point.

If you are having trouble estimating, break the task down into smaller chunks and estimate those. The smaller you break the tasks, the easier they are to estimate.

If numbers need to be given to management, explain the range and that the estimates are approximations, so they may be off (they should know this, but it's ok for the reminders occasionally).

Reviewing Metrics

At the end of the sprint review, the actual time spent should be compared to the estimates. Metrics for individuals should be provided only to the individual to improve and not used as management criteria for anything else. Metrics for the team can be shared with the team.

The team can still calculate the velocity by using the estimates in days or hours and seeing how many of the estimates were completed. They can also use the average case time frames.

But Can You Live with Story Points?

Yes. Most folks just have an approximate mapping of them to days they use to gauge the time. Purists might say you shouldn't, but you do, because the reality is that you need to know what will fit in a sprint. Story points can just be thought of as a range of estimates rather than a specific number when you need to provide some external person with an actual time. Internally, you can have a story point number that maps to a sprint. That makes it easier for people to quantify if something will fit in a sprint.

Summary

So what should you do? Just use what is comfortable and appropriate for your team/org. Don't get too caught up on one or the other. Either can be made workable. I actually did a small comparison of estimating methodologies, Agile story points, hours, gut feel estimates, and old style RAD of counting inputs and outputs. Surprisingly, all the estimation methods came up pretty close in time. Once I saw that, I realized the estimation method might not matter as much, since the person behind it has an idea about it, and that will probably flow through whatever methodology is used.

If your organization tries to hold you to estimates, then story points might be a good way of recording data that abstracts it enough to confuse other folks trying to use it as timing (for a little while, at least). However, the team often has an idea of a mapping of points to time, so it should be fine for the team once they get the hang of it.

Agile While Managing New Features and Support

So you create the perfect sprint with all the new features you want, and everyone starts working on them. Then, of course, a support ticket comes in, and you have to pull someone off their work to work on that. Then another ticket and another person pulled off. Then it seems many of those planned items don't get done for the sprint. What can you do?

Potential Assigned Person(s) to Handle Support/Questions

For each sprint, if you start out with no support work, you could assign one or more people (rotated per sprint) to be the folks who would get pulled into the support work. This protects the other work from being interrupted. You could try to assign those folks lower priority tasks in case they get interrupted for support work.

I've seen some suggestions this could be done by day, but if your issues are complex, it may require a longer time commitment, so sprint might be better.

Specifically Assigned People Each Sprint Rotated for Support/ Questions

If you have a lot of support work, you can probably get a feel for how many people you need for the sprint to work on support and assign those folks up front to handle any support items while the others can focus on the feature work being done.

Sometimes, the rotation can be difficult if features require a specific person's expertise, and it makes them hard to pull off for the feature work or support work. For sets of features, it might be necessary to exclude certain folks from the support rotation for a while to complete a feature set. It should be done carefully, as the dev folks remaining on support probably don't want to be in that role for too long.

Teams would need to be of sufficient size to accommodate the support work and new features, along with other work that needs to be in flight.

Bug Teams and Support Work

You could create teams that only (or mostly) work on bugs and support work. This avoids support work interfering with new features. Bugs are often isolated and can often be worked on by one developer (it depends on your product, of course). Bugs are easier to pick up one at a time.

Rotate different people to handle different bugs. Rotating people through large feature sets is harder, because it can often require detailed knowledge of the implementation shared among a feature team. Thus, bug teams and support workers are a little easier to fit together, as often support work can lead to finding bugs.

As above, you can rotate people each sprint to the support work while the rest of the team can focus on specific bugs. Developers don't typically enjoy working on only bugs, though, so it can be hard to hire for a team that solely does this. It might be good to mix things up a bit. Perhaps rotating teams to work on new features for a release or bugs, depending on the features needed and expertise, of course, could be one option.

You Created Your Stories for Your Project, but Now You Need a Plan—Agile Project Plan

Yes, you can and sometimes do need to use Agile project plans. If you have been living the Agile life, you may not have had to deal with creating project plans with Gantt charts and all of that fun. Ideal Agile would allow you to reduce features, add resources, or add time if needed. Then Agile would use team velocity to estimate completion based on the number of story points remaining. But what if your project has fixed resources and a hard timeline, and very little flexibility on features?

If your project is big enough or the time horizon is very close, you might need an actual project plan. Velocity can be used to calculate a very rough estimate of time. Dividing the story points by velocity provides a rough number of sprints to complete. It does not take into account dependencies or bottlenecks that would prevent forward progress or reduce velocity. In that case, a project plan with a Gantt chart with dependencies can be very helpful. You can try to work it more simply using a sprint/iteration plan. You would need to map out each team's sprints and make sure each team is never blocked by another team's task.

Why Would You Need an Agile Project Plan?

Why, you ask. One example is, what if stories are very dependent on each other, can't be divided up evenly, and/or have different effort versus calendar time estimates?

An example is a task where you have to monitor or maintain an automation testing environment. Let's imagine the effort for someone is five points (the equivalent of half a sprint/one week or something like that), but let's imagine it will take 30 days to run the automation. So any dependent tasks would need to wait for 30 days, not just the time needed for the effort. So that person will have a percentage of their time consumed over 30 days (roughly 1.3 hours a day). The combination of varied effort/time, hard timeline, fixed resources, very tight timeline, and a large project would probably make this really difficult to track and commit to without a plan.

Let's also face it that these types of things come up in development often enough. In this case, in a Gantt chart project plan, you could allocate a percentage of a person's time as well as extend the timeline of a task and dependencies to allow your project plan to flow right in a Gantt chart.

You may have noticed that I needed to translate story points to a time in there to do my calculations. If you have a time commitment, we are going to have to get closer to days and hours to be able to calculate and present our estimates so that we can make a target date to upper management, who could care less about story points in this case.

Organizing Stories

Let's say you start creating your stories, and you now have 50 stories to work on for your release. To get them organized into a Gantt chart, you will need to figure out the dependencies and figure out the flow to help decide on how you can resource the project. It can be a bit overwhelming trying to order that many stories into a sequenced plan rather than just figuring out which story to work next, as you would normally do in Agile. Now we need to order everything.

Dependencies

The easiest way to start ordering your stories might be to figure out what story comes first, then for all other stories, start with just finding one story that that story is dependent on (if anything). That's typically how project plans flow by mapping the dependencies. Starting there will help you create your initial Gantt chart and then further refine it by finding more dependencies. That should help you figure out if you have parallel paths that can be worked or not and help you decide on your resource allocations.

Tracking against Your Plan

Once you have a project plan to guide you, you should track how the team or teams are doing against the plan and update if needed.

In the military, they have a saying that no plan survives contact with the enemy. This is true with software project plans as well. For software, it might be better phrased as no plan survives contact with reality. Track how the teams are executing and adjust the times if needed. Decide if resources need to be added, some scope can be dropped, or time can be extended to keep schedules.

Builds/Continuous Integration

In order to be sure the code that is in your source control works, it should run automated builds/testing at least once a day, or even more ideally, on every planned change (e.g., pull request). If the automation is too heavy for every pull request, perhaps just run unit tests there and save integration tests for an overnight build.

To be effective, the builds should be on a separate controlled build machine. Limited users should have access to change it, ideally owned by automation, a build team, or QA but could be managed by developers if done carefully. Depending on your environment, development ownership may not pass audit criteria of separation of duties. Those criteria are supposed to prevent a random developer from making a change in code or a build that could allow malicious code to be built.

Installation capabilities should also be deterministic/immutable and repeatable, without errors.

The environment where the code is deployed should also be immutable to allow for consistent builds.

A source code repository should be used to allow for repeating builds.

All code needed should be from source control or another versioned repository.

References:

"Agile—Why Do We Use Story Points Instead of Man Days When Estimating User Stories?" *Software Engineering Stack Exchange.* (n.d.). Retrieved September 17, 2022, from https://softwareengineering.stackexchange.com/questions/182057/why-do-we-use-story-points-instead-of-man-days-when-estimating-user-stories Licenses: https://creativecommons.org/licenses/by-sa/2.5/and https://creativecommons.org/licenses/by-sa/3.0/.

Agile Body Snatchers

(jk)

Agile reminds me of an old movie called *Invasion of the Body Snatchers,* where people were replaced with aliens that looked just like them.

It's almost like software engineers have been replaced with people thinking the exact opposite of the way they thought before.

Don't believe me? Before, Agile programmers hated meetings, and they probably only had one meeting a week or two, maybe less.

With Agile, programmers have now accepted not 1 meeting, not 2 meetings, but 13 meetings in two weeks! Like I said, it's like the opposite alien took over. You have your sprint planning, grooming, reveal, and oh, let's not forget the 10 scrum meetings.

Before Agile, developers hated being asked about their status. Of course, now, we have those 10 daily scrum meetings per sprint to solve that. I know, I know, they are not status meetings (wink). It's like the opposite people are inhabiting your bodies.

What do programmers do all day? You know. Sit and code. And what do they ask you to do in Scrum? Stand up! Still don't think opposite aliens have inhabited programmers yet? Still not enough evidence for you?

Before Agile, programmers hated deadlines. There would be a deadline once a release. Now, you have accepted deadlines every two weeks for sprints!

Before Agile, QA and development were more separated. Now, they work together. Even more opposites.

So if this is all made up, and it's not alien body snatchers, why did people related to the Agile process have to say it's friendly with the term the three amigos?

More opposites. A lot of developers, let's be honest, mostly just code and don't have time for sports. So what they do is steal the rugby term "scrum." There are more terms you have heard of, like "swarm," which may be taken from lacrosse.

So we are comparing this idea of people who are not who they once were, like aliens. If aliens were to have thought up this concept, what terms might they use? Hmm . . . Velocity and Burn-Down might come to mind. Coincidence?

Here, we are talking about having people basically cloned and, of course, what term do you hear with Agile? Pair programming. Coincidence?

It's almost like up doesn't mean up, down doesn't mean down . . . Oh wait, done doesn't mean done. Now, you have to say, "Done, done, done."

So you know if there were aliens, they would probably even play some alien games. You know, different from the rest of the human race. Oh, wait, you play Planning Poker. Hmm . . .

Still don't believe it? These body snatchers have made you liars. What do little kids get told at bedtime? Of course, stories. I know what you are thinking. Stories have more than one meaning. They could be fiction or non-fiction. But of course, they go and estimate them in another word for lies: fibs! So I know what they meant by stories.

Still don't believe me? Lots of villains, some aliens, liked to be called this. For example, in *Star Wars*, what did Darth Vader call the emperor? That's right, Master. And of course, we have Scrum Master in Agile. What does that make you?

So I know now that probably every one of you has been taken over.

You know, maybe it's not body snatchers or clones. Maybe they can take over your mind with just a thought that could explain all of this.

This reminds me. Before Agile, most projects were late, and now, not so much. So maybe this whole body snatcher, clone, mind-control thing isn't so bad.

Oh crap, I'm late for Scrum. Bye, amigos! And now, I'm "done done done."

CHAPTER 20

Process: Requirements

Requirements

Requirements are the documentation of the functionality a software implementation should achieve. Requirements can also cover technical details about the constraints or support it should have.

When coming up with requirements, it can be helpful to think about different types of users who might use the software. Consider their wants, environment, and needs. Also consider the wants, environments, and needs of the company a user using your software may work for (if that is appropriate for the software being written). Write all of that down, describing each type of user and their role. You can even give that persona a name. Make it as detailed as appropriate. Then think through how that user in that role would want to accomplish a task or set of tasks in the software and write that up as a user scenario.

User scenarios can help guide defining your requirements. Ideal Agile would recommend writing the user scenario in the user's language and perspective. I believe when they say this, it just means informal. User perspective and scenarios can be important. For example, at a bike shop, someone looking for mountain bikes may have some different wants and needs than someone looking for road bikes.

If we are designing a new interactive touch screen for an elevator, one user of the elevator might be a business person, while another might be someone delivering packages. The functionality of the elevator might be the same, but what if the touch screen is too sensitive to input when a delivery person is wheeling in large packages, and it triggers the elevator to go to random floors? It is important to think through user scenarios, implement them, and test them.

For example, the following could be a user persona: The user Jason is an avid biker and is interested in buying a bike. Jason is 23 years old. Jason is interested in mountain bikes.

Suppose we were making a website to sell bikes. We would start creating user scenarios for Jason.

- Scenario 1: Jason would like to view mountain bikes online.
- Scenario 2: Jason would like to compare multiple bikes features/stats.

From these, you could break it down into much more detailed requirements.

Scenario 1 basically requires having a website that can display bikes in a useful and pleasing way for Jason, so it would need many requirements.

- Would need to display bike pictures and descriptions of bikes in a store-like format.

From this, we realize we need:

- Another user persona and multiple scenarios
- A website owner or company
- An IT person for site setup

- An administrator would add bike information, pictures, details, and perhaps pricing.

This is just one methodology for figuring out requirements.

As part of the ticket for stories or bugs, capture:

- Requirements
- User scenarios
- Acceptance criteria (When do you consider the story done/tested? What tests are needed?)
- Additional support requirements
- Additional hardware requirements
- Any translation requirements?
- Is User Interface design needed?
- Is Architecture design needed?
- Estimated effort in story points or hours/days
- Risks/Impacted areas
- Are downstream systems impacted?
- Are there any dependencies?

Requirements Tracking (Stories, Bugs)

There are a variety of products available to help track stories and bugs. Jira is a popular web product, and Team Foundation Server, a product from Microsoft, has tight integration with Visual Studio.

CHAPTER 21

Process: Architecture/ Design

Architecture/Design

Architecture/design could be described as designing a system or systems in an organized way to meet the functional, performance/scaling, and business goals required and to handle the inevitable changes expected over many years.

One particular area of focus is where different systems, subsystems, and servers interact, considering the level of change that is likely to happen over 2–5 years. If you are asking how you can do that, you can look at your organization's history of its systems and see how similar systems or areas did over those time spans to measure the likelihood of change in those times. If change is likely, design a system that allows for that change/flexibility over time.

Consider how to build your architecture in phases rather than a big bang. What deliverable parts could be built that add value to the customer and your business, either now or in the future? It can often be difficult to fund/staff very large projects; instead, break it down into manageable chunks to deliver some value of the new architecture earlier.

Enterprise Architecture (EA) Frameworks

NIST EA diagram

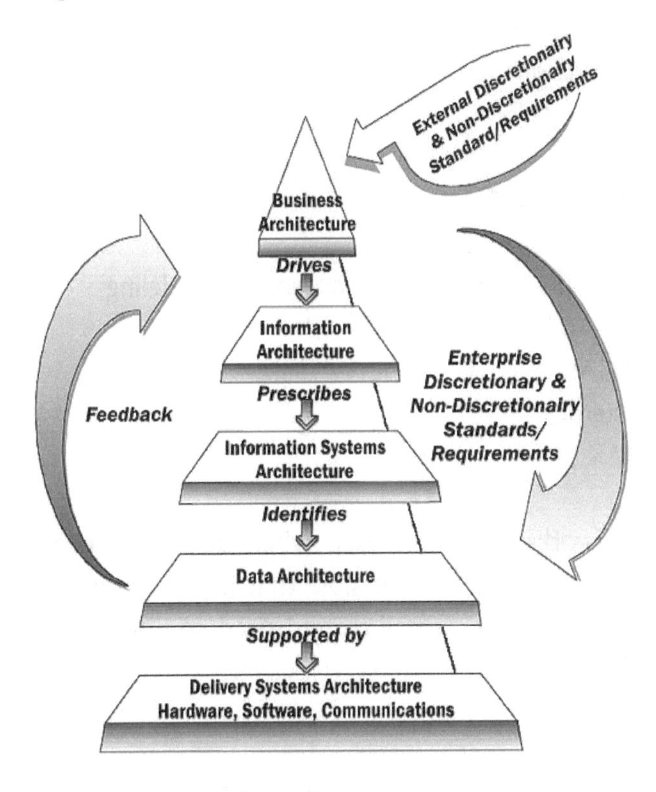

https://en.wikipedia.org/wiki/NIST_Enterprise_Architecture_Model

https://commons.wikimedia.org/wiki/File:NIST_Enterprise_Architecture_Model.jpg

(*File:NIST Enterprise Architecture Model.Jpg—Wikimedia Commons,* n.d.)

This is just a sample list of some of the EA frameworks.

The Open Group Architectural Framework (TOGAF)

This is considered a popular framework. From a quick survey of frameworks, this one popped to the top of the list. Some folks seem to recommend that, like Agile, it's a framework, and you should pick the parts that make the most sense for your organization. (TOGAF | *The Open Group Website*, n.d.)

Other EA Frameworks:

- ISO 19439 Framework for enterprise modeling
- Lean Architectural framework
- MEGAF
- Praxeme
- TRAK

These frameworks are often used when dealing with architectures across large enterprises. It's possible that if you are working on one product or team or in a small to mid-sized company, you will never encounter these.

Whole System Level Architecture Patterns

This is a sampling of some of the system level architecture patterns:

Client/Server: Early designs or simple designs can have one type of machine designated as a client and the other as a server that serves the client.

Multitier (N Tier): This can encompass client/server and beyond. Rather than just a client and a server, there can be multiple tiers of servers to support layers of functionality.

Domain driven design: In some senses, this is like object-oriented design of objects to fit the business domain they are to be used in and driving the whole architecture based on that.

Service oriented: Services are self-contained remote application, logic, or portions of the functionality. They can be composed of more services.

Architecture/Design: Audits

Artifacts:

- There should be a record of the design.
- There should be a record of the design decisions made and their reasoning.

Designing Resilient/Redundant Systems

All software/hardware of any sufficient size or complexity will eventually have an error or bug or will fail in some way. Handling those failures through software, process, or both can keep your system online and functional or allow them to recover in a timely fashion in most cases.

There are third-party products that work like the following: One system had a setup that every server used had a primary, warm secondary, and often warm tertiary server. On top of that, a disaster recovery (DR) site had an equivalent warm primary and warm secondary server. The primary server (or currently acting as a primary server), for each message sent downstream to the next server, is sent as a broadcast message so all the secondary, tertiary, and DR warm primary/secondary would be kept up to date. If a server encountered a problem due to hardware, memory, or execution, the secondary, tertiary, or DR servers could be promoted to primary and go from warm mode (keeping update state in memory) to hot active primary mode responding directly to messages.

Scaling, multiple server recovery options, were all considered in the design. With business applications, time is money, and millions of dollars can be lost in seconds, so being ready to reliably handle any possible failure is critical and sometimes even mandated in some ways by regulatory agencies.

Consider all the ways your system could likely fail. How you could recover in those circumstances and decide the level of redundancy, resiliency, and cost that makes sense for your business environment.

The acronym CORPS can help you remember some of the architectural considerations:

Change: Design for the expected change in the next 2–5 years based on changes of previous 2–5.

Resilience: Design for service/component failure where needed/appropriate.

Objective: Design for the required functionality.

Performance: Handle scaling for the desired load.

Supportability: The architecture should be supportable and maintainable.

Discussions

When coming up with new architecture, it is best to start with small groups comprising people you trust to have good architectural ideas and produce some suggestions for the architecture. Having people other architects also respect is a good idea. When you have larger meetings, it will help to have some people who agree with you to guide your discussion if you are looking to promote an idea. Make sure you've analyzed and discussed before presenting, and your odds of getting some kind of agreement will increase.

Sometimes, whiteboards can help to get the ideas flowing. If remote, use Visio, LucidDraw, whiteboard built into your video conferencing app, or even MS Paint, if you have to. Sometimes, it can go well even without any whiteboard if everyone involved understands the design well enough.

UX Design

Ideally, your company should have a team of UX designers who can help with creating these designs. Typically, the process starts with a discussion of user scenarios and requirements. Then the UX team will create wireframe designs for review with the stakeholders. There might be a few iterations, then it might be decided to just use it as designed, or if there are still questions, a proof-of-concept implementation of the wireframes might be done.

If you don't have your own team of UX designers, consider familiarizing yourself with UX design. Even though *Psychology of Everyday Things* by Donald Norman has nothing to do with software, the concepts it presents do translate. *About Face* by Alan Cooper is now a bit dated, but it goes into a lot of things that used to be wrong with the design. Things have improved but not as much as they should have.

Look at websites that work well for you and others. Look at websites that are bad for you and others, so you know what to avoid. Read more here.

A Simplistic Architecture Approach

A simplistic approach to architecture design when you don't want or need enterprise frameworks.

Definition

Define the problem or goal that you want to achieve. This means putting together the requirements or specifications in order to fully understand the problems and goals of the architecture.

High-Level Solution Proposals

Based on the definition of the problem and the goals, create a few solution proposals on how the problem can be solved. For example, one solution might use message-based streaming. Another solution might use a concurrent big data solution. Identify the risks to the different solutions. Understand the areas the teams don't know enough about without further research. Write up the solutions in enough detail so they can be discussed with appropriate stakeholders and teams to vet the underlying ideas and concepts.

Review the proposals and hear what everyone's thoughts are on the solutions. Record the pros and cons, plus concerns on each of the solutions. Identify either a clear winner or the need for more research.

Incremental Action Plan

From the identified architectures, if there are risks, decide if there is the need to build any proof-of-concept (POC) tests to determine if the solution will be viable or not.

Write up a plan that can incrementally move toward the architecture in phases, if possible, avoiding needing to build everything before releasing. Review the risky parts and iterate until you have reduced the risks within reason based on implementation, planning and proof of concepts.

References:

File:NIST Enterprise Architecture Model.jpg—Wikimedia Commons. (n.d.). Retrieved September 17, 2022, from https://commons.wikimedia.org/wiki/File:NIST_Enterprise_Architecture_Model.jpg.

CHAPTER 22

Process: Source Control Management

Source Control Management

You should always have some type of source control for your source code so that each change to files can be versioned, making it possible to track the reason for changes or revert back to older changes if needed. Some examples are Git, GitHub, Team Foundation Server, SVN, perforce, and many others.

Functionality and Workflow

Source control systems offer a variety of functionality and features. It is often best to match the workflow you need or desire with the functionality of your source control. This influences the way software is built, tested, and versions of the software managed. The structure/workflow can improve productivity if done right and impede it if done inadequately.

Sometimes, this workflow needs to be defined in conjunction with your software's hardware/deployment process, as machine type and cost could be an issue depending on the software you are building and the type of hardware it needs to run on. It also can be influenced by the business processes you have or want to have.

For example, let's say your test systems require so much hardware that you can only afford one test environment. Then you might need a branch structure and a workflow that allows multiple people to work on different things and perhaps be able to test them in the same environment, somehow (not ideal, but sometimes cost realities rein in idealism).

Git, for example, is designed for distributed version control. It was needed to maintain all the different variants of Linux and allow people to make quick changes in their local environments where they could have access to a massive amount of source code. Therefore, it excels at taking large branches of source code and having them independently worked on and merged back in.

Git works more with getting the code you need and making any changes you need to and committing them back to source control when ready. Git has a much more complex series of commands if you want to master it.

The Team Foundation Server (TFS) has integrated issue tracking into the Visual Studio IDE and doesn't quite have the same ability to branch and merge large repos of source code, but it is still quite powerful and well integrated.

TFS instead wants you to check out individual files when you intend to change them and check them back in when done to prevent or ease merging. TFS commands are relatively simple, with not a huge amount of options for the main functionality of source control.

Each of those systems has different pros and cons that may or may not fit the workflow you need.

Branch Plans

A branch plan is a structure you plan to use as you develop your repository.

There are some well-known ones like gitflow used on GitHub. That plan is more designed around Single Instance Multi-Tenant (SIMT) development, as it doesn't have plans for creating branches and maintaining old versions of your software in case hotfixes/service packs are needed.

Answer the Questions:

- What branch will the main development happen in?
- Where will feature branches (if needed) be created?
- When we want to create a release, when/where will that branch live, and for how long?
- How will we handle building a hotfix for the current production release of software while we will work on the next release—what branch will that be fixed in? What is the merge plan?
- What if not SIMT? How would you handle/what branch for hotfixes?

Some Examples of Branches that You Would Need to Consider:

- Master/Main branch
- Development
- Release branches
- Service/Hotfix branches

Also, you should consider how to use labels/tags in your source control system.

Typically, labels are used to identify a particular version of all the code that makes up a release of your software (a branch can also do this, but a branch could be changed by anyone committing changes. A label doesn't change unless explicitly changed).

These steps could apply to many software rollouts in general:

Step 1: Think of your tentative desired workflow/branch plan.
Step 2: Think through the workflow using the tools you plan to use.
Step 3: Do a proof of concept, trying parts of it with the tools you plan to use Source control/CI.
Step 4: Review these workflows with a group of developers to make sure there are no obvious issues. Make sure you have representation from all of your major projects if you plan this to eventually roll out to them to make sure you get feedback. Have a write-up of the workflow and presentation for them.
Step 5: Once everything looks good, trial a small project using your workflow to make sure everything works as you would hope.
Step 6: If all goes well, you can expand the usage of your workflow and tools to other teams slowly. Sometimes, things you missed are discovered during rollout.

Workflow and Branch Plans

These are interrelated, so it can sometimes be hard to choose which to think through first. Sometimes, starting with a known branch plan and then walking through using it as related to your workflow can help get the thought process going.

A common workflow is the GitHub workflow:

- Create your own fork
- Create a branch
- Make changes to the branch
- Create a pull request
- Review/Test and comment on the pull request
- Merge the pull request.

Gitflow Branching

Gitflow suggests that you have a main branch and a develop branch off that branch.

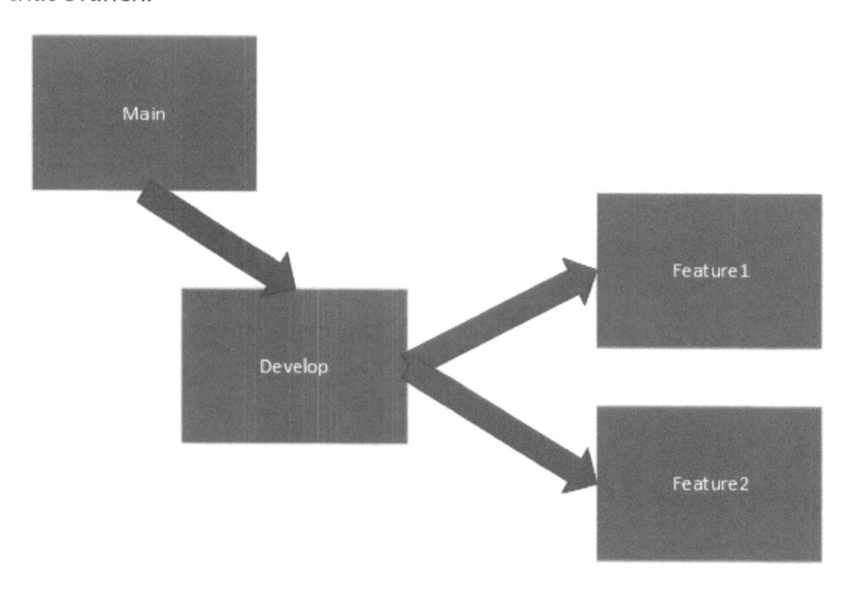

Main

Main->Develop

Main->Develop->Feature1

Main->Develop->Feature2

In practice, though, this is a lot more work for many environments needing to merge everything back to the main branch to track your production code. Git can track all of your versions via tagging just fine without needing to do that.

An easier branch structure is the following:

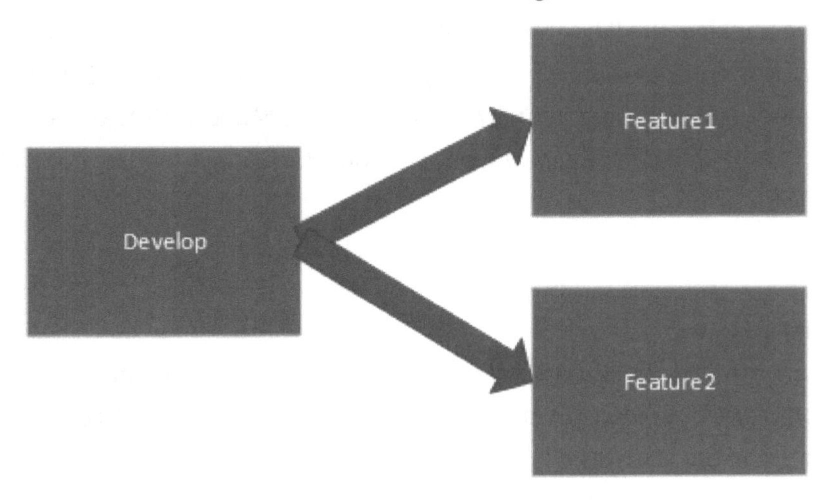

Develop

Develop->Feature1

Develop->Feature2

Develop->Release1.0

Develop->Release2.0

This works well when almost everyone is working on the next release in the develop branch. You can use tagging even in the develop branch rather than even using the release branch. You really only need the release branch if you need to create some sort of hotfix on that branch. If your software is cloud based and everyone is on the same version, it might make sense to just update that release branch directly.

If, instead, your software has individual hotfixes based on the version your customer is on, you might create another branch off the release branch: Develop->Release1.0->Release1.1.

Source Control Products

Team Foundation Server (TFS)

This is a relatively recent implementation by Microsoft that includes source control, ticket management, workflow, and more. It is well integrated with Visual Studio. Its positives are the tight integration with issue tracking, the IDE, and source control. The downsides are it doesn't perform quite as well for very large source control projects as it can handle. TFS can integrate with git now. Given Microsoft's takeover of GitHub, it kind of makes you wonder about the future of source control in TFS.

Git/Github

From the creator of Linux, Git was created to manage the massive repositories of Linux for distributed version control. Git is free. Can't beat that price. It was designed for managing large amounts of source code this way. Git isn't as easy to learn as TFS or some other source control products. There are UI tools that can help with basic git commands. Sometimes, you're required to go to the command line to do some more sophisticated commands. Git has an incredible amount of capability, which can make figuring out those sophisticated commands rather complex.

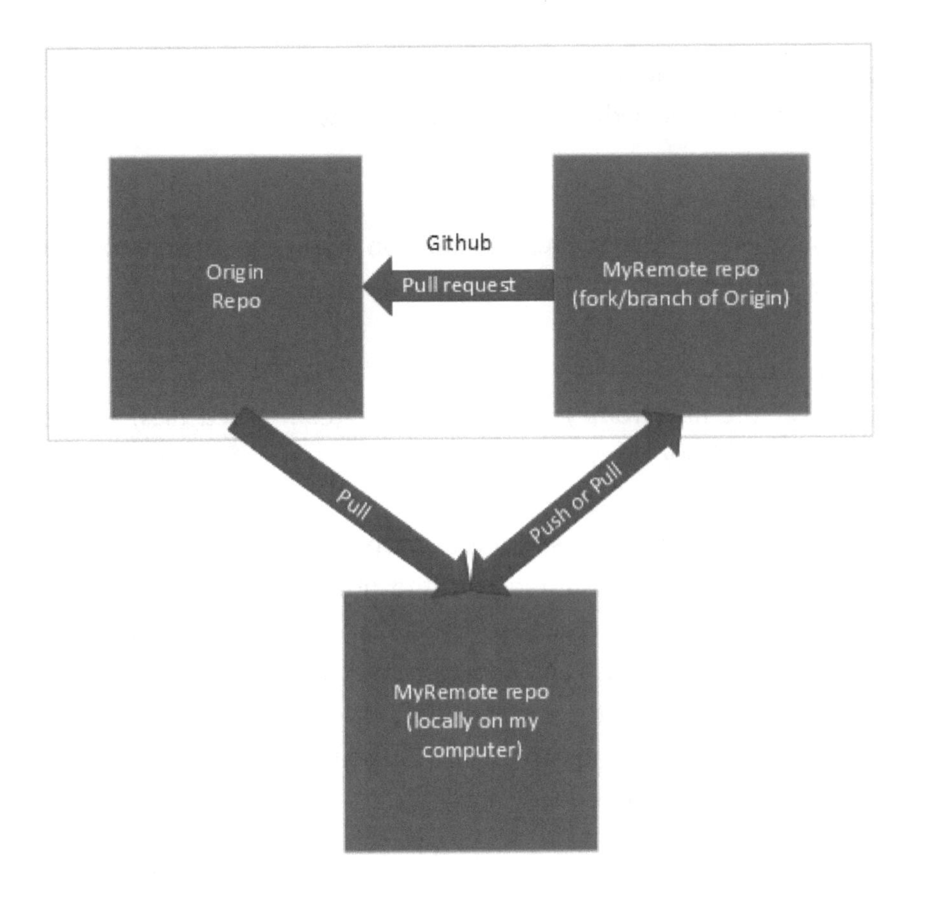

Some helpful git commands:

git diff
See what files have changed on your local.

git status
See the files that you have modified.

git log
See the history of changes.

git checkout [branch]

Make the specified branch your local copy.

git pull origin

Get the files from the remote location and merge them into your repository and local.

git push origin

Push the files from your repo branch (committed files) to the remote repository

GitHub is now Microsoft's server for git repos.

Many people like the pull requests and other features on this web/git-based service. Pull requests (PRs) allow showing the differences between a source branch and its target branch. It allows users to comment on the PR about the changes. PRs allow the ability to review and merge changes to the target branch. It is also possible to create a PR to revert the change if needed.

SVN

This is another popular open-source version control system, often used for Linux but can easily be used on Windows as well.

CHAPTER 23

Process: Implementation

Implementing a Feature/Bug Fix

Developers should code the feature and then the unit test. If it is a bug, developers should ideally reproduce the bug and then fix it. After implementation (or before if Test Driven Development [TDD]), a unit test should be developed. Sometimes, unit testing can be manual, but ideally, it is added to an automated test set so that it can be useful for regression testing. Most lessons about coding stops at implementation, but in the business world, many additional processes may be needed, depending on the regulatory environment the business operates in. Unit testing is a standard part of most development work, and testing in general is also a big part of development building automated regression tests as code is added or changed. Some businesses need to undergo audits of their process, so they require doing certain activities and collecting artifacts as proof of those activities.

How do you start coding? Where do you start? It's best to think about your design/requirements first. A fully groomed story is necessary. If you can break down the functionality into individual features/stories you can implement, it can be easier to understand what needs to be implemented. If you can break it down to the classes you need and what they do in a document or at least in your head, then you probably have enough to start.

Sometimes, developers might start with writing code (or a test) that uses the method they need and then implementing the missing methods that are needed to complete. Other times, developers will just code the underlying method for the class the way they believe it will be used. Once you know the input and outputs for your method, if it's simple enough, it's usually easy to work through coding the method you need. After a while, you won't even think about this consciously, and it just comes naturally.

Some people like to code a little, then try it through the debugger to make sure everything works, then keep coding. Other people like to code a full method first, then test it and/or run it through the debugger.

Unit Testing

Ideally, automated unit testing could focus on the API of a class or set of classes and the contractual surface between them. In some shops, there is a focus on 100 percent coverage. Ideally, new projects should be started this way and kept at 100 percent coverage. Sometimes, that can be tricky for legacy code. Developers can try to refactor over time to improve their code and add tests in legacy code bases. Using dependency injection when testing through the interface alone is hard to do but requires designing for dependency injection. There are some alternatives like accessing private methods using products like TestMock, but those aren't ideal. Do you need 100 percent coverage? Is testing properties of objects that are unlikely to fail useful? Is most software currently written achieving 100 coverage? Even if there was 100 percent code coverage, it's unlikely to cover 100 percent of all possible scenarios that could occur (100 percent coverage doesn't mean it's covered well). That doesn't mean it's not worth considering or doing, as lack of coverage means there is untested code. For new projects or projects where this is easy to maintain, it can be worth doing. In highly regulated industries, this might be required as well.

For example, as mentioned in their testing blog (https://testing.googleblog.com/2020/08/code-coverage-best-practices.html),

Google considers:

60% coverage = Acceptable

75% = Commendable

90% = Exemplary

(*Google Testing Blog: Code Coverage Best Practices*, 2020)

Be careful when implementing unit testing to try to implement it in the least brittle way possible. Test the contracts/interfaces that classes expose for use. If tons of tests break every time you try minor refactoring, you might want to look at the way your unit tests are testing your code.

Test Driven Development (TDD)

The idea of this process is to design the test first and implement the code to make it pass. This way, you can ensure testing meets the expected criteria. A recommendation is to design your code first, then implement tests, then write the code to make them pass to make sure you have a complete understanding of the test you need to write. This is a very different way to write code and might not be for everyone or every business organization. It can be hard with legacy code if test automation is difficult to create. Care should be used with this method that you think through your code design first, then write the tests. What can sometimes happen with test first is that you may implement your tests one way but find out later that you need to redesign your code and your test either because of the tests or because the design needed to be thought through differently.

When you get a chance with that caveat mentioned above, try it and see if you like it. It is a different thought process when developing. It can be refreshing, frustrating, and satisfying at various times. Give it a try and see what you think.

Pair Programming

Sometimes, you might want to have one or more programmers work together on something. In most shops, this isn't the norm, but sometimes, it can be surprisingly effective if they work well together. It's kind of like having an extra set of eyes checking or thinking about the code as you are coding it. It can be a little distracting at first. Usually, there is one person driving (on the keyboard) and another person watching and recommending changes when needed but not interrupting unnecessarily. It could be possible with today's tools for two developers to be coding different routines in the same file, perhaps; that hasn't been the norm to date, but that doesn't mean that might not happen.

Logging

Make sure your application does sufficient logging. Every log line, at a minimum, should have a date/time and indicate if it's an error, warning, or informational. Every instance of an exception code should be logged either in the method that was running or a higher-level method if that makes more sense.

If exceptions or errors occur, be sure to log the error and the method/stack trace. In your environment to view logs, you can use a log aggregator and search service like Sumologic (www.sumologic.com). Services like these let you search all of the logs in your environments, parse data, graph data, and more.

Think about whether you will need additional information to properly support your application. Is there enough log information to tell if your application is still working properly in reasonable time intervals (especially if your application is part of a cloud service)? Do you need more than error details to support your service? For example, if your app/service creates documents, should it report how long it took for it to complete a document? That way, you can measure if something is slowing down document creation.

If you are logging for an API, does it log the inbound request, outbound response, and error? Does it include the total time for the call and perhaps break the time down to data retrieval (database) vs. formatting?

Does your service log when users fail to log in/authenticate three times or more to make sure you can create security alerts if this is happening a lot and for the record of what took place?

If when supporting your application/service, is there a unique ID passed between services to indicate the request is part of some transaction you should be logging? You should consider if a unique ID like GUID makes sense on your logging as well. For example, when errors are returned in the application to the user, if it gave them a GUID, you could use that GUID to trace to the log file the error that occurred.

Here is some pseudo code example of logging:

```
log.Writeline(Info,"About to perform operation:"+operation);
    try
    {
      //Perform operation here
    log.Writeline(Info,"Completed operation:"+operation);
    }
    catch(Exception ex)
    {
```

```
        log.Writeline(Error,"Exception operation:"+operation);
        throw;
    }
    finally
    {
        //Cleanup code here
    }
```

Implementing Audits

Artifacts

- Auditors like to see traceability from changes to code.
- Have a link from your story/issue tracking to the code changes. Perhaps through integration or making sure that your issue track number is in your code commits.
- Evidence of unit testing, link to code, attached output of the unit test run to issue track system (or if using like GitHub and PRs, it could be automated unit test runs for each PR get attached to the PR and only allow merge if they pass, for example).

Traceability

Auditors like to be able to trace a change request to the code change in the code repository, who made the change, and unit tested the change (and next we will cover testing).

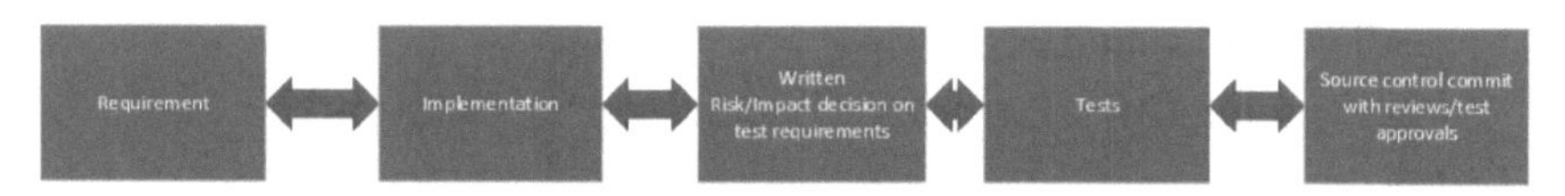

Testing a Feature/Bug Fix

Testing/Legacy Code

Old legacy code that doesn't have full regression test/coverage and often doesn't have complete written specifications can be tricky to enhance. Any changes would require either building a new automation test suite (which could take a very long time if it's a big area to test) or could require a large amount of manual testing if the change is large and the risk is large. If the area processes/uses large amounts of customer data to ensure it works well, you might have some alternative options such as parity tests. For some functionality, it might be possible to implement a parity test that compares the old functionality with the new functionality to ensure it is the same.

Let's say, for example, the area of code processes customer data and outputs in a different format. You could then, if you have access to that data, process it and compare it with the old algorithm and the new one. With enough data, it should be able to reduce the risk and can sometimes be automated and act as part of a regression suite, at least for a particular change or release.

Testing: Audits

Artifacts

- Changes should have a record of possible impacts
- There should be documentation about what was tested exactly

Builds/Continuous Integration

Ideally, every time someone creates a change, there would be an automated build and unit test run to check that it is ok. If using GitHub, a PR checker could be run via Jenkins or another build system to run your build and your unit tests. Your build should happen in minutes (ideally less than 15 minutes). If you have a very large build and automation process for unit tests, you could probably live with one build a day, but then you will have to figure out if someone broke the build each day and then fix it.

Continuous integration should run your system/integration tests. These should run ideally in an hour or at most again a day or somewhere in between. If it takes a long time to design the test to run in parallel so it can run faster, even if that means bringing up multiple copies of the system to test, it will probably be worth it.

Continuous Integration: Audits

Artifacts

- Have documentation in your SDLC that is required
- Have a record of builds to demonstrate to auditors if needed

Merging the Change

Usually, a PR has continuous integration run on it, so it includes unit tests and integration tests. The code should be reviewed, QA tested, and agreed to/approved by the stakeholder ideally before merging.

Artifacts for Merging

- A PR like on GitHub is a good record of change
- A record of someone, ideally more than one other developer reviewing (a comment saying so on a PR would work)

- A record of QA approval of a change—a comment on a PR would work
- Make sure the person that merges is not a person who contributed to the change or initiated the PR

Should You Comment Code—Write Them, How Much, or Not?

Hopefully, in this section, we can answer the question of whether you should comment code, what they should be, and how much or not.

The standard fare that tends to be recommended for comments is:

- You don't need them most of the time. Write self-documenting code.
- Write narrative-based comments.
- Write comments that give the thoughts behind why a method exists.
- Write as much as needed.

Another reason for not documenting code that seems to be given is that they are always out of date and useless, and the code should be self-documenting. Otherwise, a comment is a code smell.

Who is right? What is the answer?

Obviously, this is like one of those instances in programming where most folks have their belief and will tend to stick with it.

I would suggest that all the above ideas should be used for the right circumstance.

Let's take a simple example code. I'm going to give you a pricing algorithm for merchandise in a store, and I want you to describe in English what it does.

Imagine this is pseudo code for getting price:

if (DayOfWeek==Saturday) price = baseprice*1.2 else price = basePrice*1.4

if (DayOfWeek==Sunday) price=(Saturday base price)*0.6

if (DayOfWeek==Monday,Tuesday,Wednesday,Thursday,Friday) price=baseprice*1.0

The code is pretty clear in what it does, but what if your manager comes in and asks you why are the prices mostly lower during the week but lower on Sundays? What if there was a comment that said during the week, pricing was lowered to bring shoppers into the store and increased on Saturdays to get more money from the mall traffic on the weekends.

But why is the Sunday price lower? It turns out they lower the price to get rid of inventory before deliveries come in on Monday. Could you have written a self-documenting code for that? Maybe, but sometimes, comments can make clear the WHY of things. The code shows what things do but often doesn't explain why. You could say this should be in requirements, and that's correct, but how many companies have you worked in that have perfect, easy traceability to requirements? Instead, what happens is that you look at code, understand the code, and then ask why someone would write it that way.

If you are writing a prototype that is throw-away code, there isn't much reason to document, right? Not if your shop is one where prototypes get converted to the real deal, then perhaps one of the other options might make more sense.

You should try to write self-documenting code.

But the reality is that it is probably not enough to make code easy to understand. Don't believe me? Would you be happy if .NET, C++, or Windows SDK came with no documentation and made you read through the source code to figure out how to use a function?

I don't know about you, but I certainly wouldn't be as productive in that case. I know you are thinking to yourself, "That's a standard framework API from a big company that lots of people use that's different." Yes, it is somewhat different. The productivity benefits many more users, and with a lot more money to be made. Providing good win32 SDK documentation can help Microsoft sell more products.

Ah . . . so we have a motive. Fewer people would probably want to use the API if there were no documentation, and the company would make less money. Hopefully, you agree people "are" more productive using the APIs with good documentation.

You might be thinking that we write code for internal use, so we don't need to be that formal. Yes, that is correct. You don't "need" to be, though the cost of that decision is reduced productivity by people needing to read code to figure out what to do.

You might be thinking, "If I wrote self-documenting code, I wouldn't need to write documentation." Maybe, if you wrote a very simple function. But in a complex function that returns a value, wouldn't you rather just have a statement or two that say what the function does, what argument it takes, and what it returns? Do you really want to make someone dig to find out it's a null return on an error to the bottom of the function?

Self-documenting code is a nice idea, and I think it is something to aspire to, but I haven't yet seen production code with anything more than the simplest of methods ever reach the level that I could just glance at the method and know everything about it.

Even if I thought I wrote self-documenting code, it might be due to my contextual understanding. Someone else looking at the code still might not understand it.

So if you plan on remembering what your code does months from now or if someone else will need to maintain it, do them a favor:

- Try to write self-documenting code.
- Use well named methods and variables.

- Realize you probably didn't write it well enough to self-document.
- Document using as many comments as needed; not too much, nor too little for the method, parameters, and return values.
- Provide the reason for the existence of the method. Keep it simple.
- Fix tricky code if possible so it doesn't need comments. If you can't due to time or other reasons, comment it enough so someone would understand it.
- If you change the method, check your comments.

Decide how much documentation is appropriate. The next time you find yourself trying to figure out how to use a complex method with no comments, time how long it takes you to figure out how to use it, then write some quick, succinct comments for the method and answer for yourself. How long would it have taken if there were comments?

If the project is worth writing and maintaining, consider if comments might be worth writing as well.

Software Development Environment

This should be designed for the easiest possible developer setup. The ideal scenario is if a developer can pull the source code, build it, and run it using their IDE. If it's not that simple, it should ideally be made very simple steps that always work, or it should be automated, and there should be a helpful guide for solving issues where they can fail. If failures are common, then the automation should be fixed.

The longer it takes for environment setup, the longer the onboarding time, diagnostic, support, and even regular installation take.

How to Write Cleaner, More Understandable Code

Limit what each function or method does to one thing. Classes should have a single, well-defined purpose as well. Limit side effects from occurring where they might be unexpected. When you write code, think about what someone you don't know would think when reading the code. What would they not know or need to know that might not be obvious from the code? Write self-documenting code so it's highly readable and understandable, but still comment about why you are doing things and describe in comments the holistic purpose of how methods are used to give the reasoning and the bigger picture. If something in code is tricky, ideally make it NOT tricky. If that can't be done, make sure it is well commented.

Environments

The environments you might have and the order could be Development, QA, User Acceptance Test (UAT), and Production, in that order, so the release should be promoted in that sequence. Development builds and tests in the development environments (which includes QA testing also). Official QA, when it is started for a release, should be done on QA environments—clean and ideally not touched by developers. However, in practice, developers have access to help with issues, but this should be coordinated carefully with QA. Once QA is passed or sometimes at the same time as it goes into QA, it can go into the UAT environment. The UAT environment should be in an isolated production environment separate from regular production if you deploy to this before it has passed QA. If it's only deployed after QA is passed, then it can be in the regular production environment.

No code should get into the official production environment without being tested.

Dev-Ops

A term coined for the joining or rather collaboration between development and operations. If you look online, it will talk about tools, automation, feedback loops, and continuous improvement. It all boils down to working together from the beginning of the application life-cycle integrating operations not just at the end for deployment but into the entire process. This means collaborating to avoid silos. If you start designing/implementing a feature, make sure operations are invited to those meetings. You might ask yourselves, "Why?"

Well, your fancy new design just happens to require multicast UDP, and if you had not brought in the operations team, you might not know that your network hardware has a limitation for both performance and the number of supported multicast channels at once. Things like that are probably good to know ahead of time. You would be surprised at how often your operation teams think of things in their area related to a design that might be helpful to operations or development or both.

If your application is a very database centric database, administrators (DBAs) can be an excellent source of help to improve the performance of your stored procedures. They often have a very keen eye for performance issues and can read SQL plans in their sleep. They also often have optimization knowledge that complements developer knowledge to come up with great solutions for performance.

What Are the Main Correlating Factors to the Introduction of Bugs?

Lines of code created, changed, or the complexity. The more lines of code change or the more complex they are, the more likely you are to introduce bugs. A paper for an article called *Number of Faults per Line of Code* by M. Lipow in 1982 correlated the number of bugs related to the number of lines of code. From that, we can extrapolate that the more lines of code we change or introduce, the more likely we will introduce bugs. Bugs are often measured in bugs per thousand lines of code. So if there are a thousand lines of code changed, there is a pretty good chance there are a couple of bugs in there. An average software is considered to contain 15–30 bugs per thousand lines of code. In one company, I had heard that the expectations were about four bugs per thousand lines of code. It could be the code was of higher quality. It's possible it was somewhere in between. Some measures might consider this a part of code complexity, which is also a contributor to bugs.

Other factors can contribute to bugs, such as expertise in a particular code area. With complex code, there can be a lot of dependencies that aren't well defined and may not be obvious from the code itself. Someone fixing a bug in an area they are not familiar with might not know that another area of the code needs to be changed as well. This can be mitigated by learning as much about the functionality and the code area as possible.

CHAPTER 24

Process: Testing/Validation

Testing

On Agile teams, testing is done along with the implementation, both automated and—where needed—manual testing.

Automation Testing

It is often used for regression testing to make sure the existing functionality doesn't get broken. These days, developers are often asked to build automation testing. Years ago, this used to be handled by the QA team. Sometimes, SDETs (Software Developer Engineers in Test) will work on the automation. Often, some type of test framework is used, such as SpecFlow (https://specflow.org/).

Integration Testing

It brings together the systems to see how everything works together.

Fuzz Testing

It can be used for inputs to push the data boundaries to the extreme. There are often many data edge cases in certain software. Fuzz testing can use specific cases or random data to test boundary conditions on data entry and more.

Parity Testing

This can be used on a large scale to determine that nothing significant has changed in an application. Let's say, for example, for your application, all data changes go to the database. A new release has a huge performance change, but there aren't supposed to be any changes to functionality. Regression tests look good, but you don't have 100 percent code coverage. Parity testing can come to the rescue by comparing your changes to the old release and see if, after running any automation, the databases compare as equivalent. Sometimes, you will need to write specific comparison returns that ignore certain differences like ordering that might be expected due to the nature of automation runs.

Performance Testing

This typically is set up to test the performance of the system under specific scenarios to see how well it will perform under certain conditions. Variations in this testing might be considered load testing when applying a certain load to the system. For example, you might want to make sure the performance under a normal user load of, let's say, 500 users never takes longer than one second to return a web page. You might also want to make sure your site doesn't fail if there are 1500 users accessing it and the service just degrades in performance. You might also then want to see if your system could scale to handle the additional load.

Ideally, performance tests should be run as part of the normal CI process or at least once a day/week. This is because it can be extremely difficult to figure out from all the changes in a release what made the entire release slower. If instead this was run every day, it would be easy to see what changes caused the performance test to get slower.

Validation

This for formal testing processes might be called validation. It is testing regression and new features/enhancements or changes to ensure they function as documented. For a formal testing, this process is often documented. Automated test script outputs might be attached. Manual test script results, testing plans, risk assessments, and more are all documented to cover the bases for an audit.

Validation: Audits

Artifacts

- Documenting all features, enhancements, bugs/changes.
- Documenting the testing for all changes.
- List of who tested what.
- List of who made the changes to code.

Traceability

- All code changes should be traceable back to the issue tracking system as to why the change was being made.

CHAPTER 25

Process: Deployment

Deployment

Decide the best ways to deploy your software. If you build Android apps/iPhone apps, this is relatively easy if folks are auto-updating, but you would still want to deploy to small subsets, if possible, over time.

If you are a large cloud provider and have thousands of servers, it might be better to try to do slow rollouts rather than a big bang install to reduce the risk of an issue being found during deployments.

If your application is sharded in some way, you can perhaps install it on a single shard rather than all again to reduce risk.

Ideally, always have a way to roll back in case of issues. Hopefully, this should have been built in.

If there are large amounts of servers, hopefully, there is a significant amount of automation to reduce the time for rollouts.

If you have primary and secondary backup servers, perhaps roll out to only some primary servers first to limit the risk since they can always fail over to your secondary.

Old/New (A/B) Deployments

To reduce downtime, some cloud service providers or other software use a mechanism to deploy the new code while the old code is still running. This can be to different servers or to the same servers but in a different location. The benefit of this is reducing downtime. It can also potentially offer instant rollback in case some issues are found depending on your implementation.

Rollbacks

Ideally, your deployment mechanism would offer a rollback option. That way, in case of catastrophic issues, you could roll back the software. If your application involves both binary and database changes, this can be tricky, especially if the customer made changes with the new release, and now you need to roll back. The concern would be if the database changes made were incompatible with the old version. The idea is that if you can plan for this to make sure any changes made are both backward and forward compatible, then rollbacks become easy to do.

One way to do this on the database side is to keep different stored procedures for each release that are easy to roll back to. You could only change the name of the procedure changed and version it either by name or schema. In special cases, there might be releases with database changes so large that the teams could not easily handle the rollback scenarios. In those cases, more testing could be done on the release to reduce risk. On those releases, if issues arose, they would need to be fixed on top of the latest release.

Deployment: Audits

Artifacts

- There should be an unchangeable record of the request for all deployments.
- There should be a record of all executions of deployments.
- There should be a record of testing to make sure all deployed ok.

CHAPTER 26

Process: Production

Production

Production systems at most companies are not accessible directly to software engineers. If they are, they would likely be in some sort of limited time/access or read-only mode.

Production networks typically have firewalls between them and corporate networks and require small holes poked through them to allow connections to servers software engineers and operations folks can use (often called jump servers).

Production: Audits

Artifacts

- All changes to production should record the change was made, who made it, and at what time it was made to link to the code/configuration changed.

CHAPTER 27

Process: Support

Support

You build that great new feature, and you deploy it, only to discover you can't keep it running. How can you prepare and prevent situations like this? This is just an initial list of some high-level areas/pointers to help you start thinking about how you really can support your code. I'm sure there are other things folks can think of as well.

Coding, Testing

Make sure the code itself is well designed, reviewed, and well tested: unit tests, system tests, integration tests, etc. Make sure it's version controlled, using recent, supported versions of all used software.

Cost

Make sure all of your licensing, cloud provider service, or other services fit within a budget you are willing to live with the long haul.

Performance and Hardware

Don't neglect to check the performance of any new code and make sure you will have the machines, CPU, memory, and disk space to support your code.

Deployment

Make sure your code can be deployed with the minimum amount of manual effort. Make sure if the deployment fails, it leaves you in a recoverable state to either roll back or move forward. It's best when you can support a rollback to reduce the downtime you have in case issues are found during your initial deployments.

If possible, plan a slow rollout to sets of machines and servers to give the new code some time to run on some customers' machines rather than all at once. This gives you time to uncover things you were unaware of in your testing.

Logging

Be sure your code has enough logging support to help you find problems when they occur. Also, make sure you aren't hiding errors/exceptions. Make sure they get logged and you have a way to easily find them and diagnose. A lot of coding in school is written to produce a result, and then you are done. Code in a business may be running at customers' locations daily or 24/7 in a cloud service for your firm. When things go wrong, you need to be able to quickly figure out the cause of the problem and find a solution. Logging can help you do that. Learning to write production code means learning to write just the right amount of logging; not too much to flood the logs, and not too little to have no idea what is going on.

Deciding what to log can be tricky.

To start with:

- Log all errors that are truly errors with stack trace information.
- Log any security specific events, such as logon and logon failures. Include enough information to figure out the user ID, source IP if over the network.
- Log any time-consuming or CPU/memory-intensive operations' start/end so that you can track down performance concerns.
- If using a database, log stored procedure calls that took significantly longer than the usual or a fixed time defined by you.
- Log information about actions your users take and the time it takes to do them, especially long-running operations and any details around those. That way, you could compare if things got slower recently.

There are likely lots more things you might consider logging, but that should help you get started.

Make sure they are appropriately marked with categories such as critical, error, warning, and information. Also, make sure there is enough information in your log so that someone monitoring knows what to do.

At a financial company for trading software, one day, someone from the app support team came running over to the development group. "Hey . . . What's this critical error? DOOMSDAY WARNING!!! Only 1000000 left!!!"

Developers quickly looked through the code and found the warning. "Oh, sh*t, we are about to hit the limit on a 32-bit integer for order IDs!"

It might have been nice if the log actually said that! Luckily, the limit wasn't hit that day, and the order IDs were updated to support 64 bit by the next day (things move fast when money is on the line at a financial firm).

Tracing

If you have multiple services that can be involved in a messaging path, make sure there is some unique ID like a GUID that can be sent with the message all the way down the line so you can trace what happened in each step of the message. Also, be sure you can determine the source of the message/host and service that called the current service you are tracing.

Time Syncing

Sync all your servers to the same date/time within a second or less of each other using UTC time. This will help with your logging/tracing analysis.

Network/Application Tracing

Sometimes, you need low latency server to server information tracing your packets between multiple machines to determine where there was a slowdown or something got dropped. Doing this often needs a central appliance to collect packet and application data and/or a coordinated time source. These appliances can trace packets from machine to machine at microseconds or better, tracking even individual application requests out and responses. These can be essential in areas like low latency stock-trading scenarios, where order times are measured in microseconds.

Monitoring

It's great that you have logging, but if you are in a software as a service environment, who is monitoring the logs to find issues before your customers do? This means your logging has to have been built with monitoring in mind, or there must be other ways to monitor your software for conditions that would be a concern: Resources CPU, Memory, Disk space, network bandwidth, and others. Applications like SolarWinds are often used to monitor those.

There are some great application monitoring services available, like NewRelic, that can instrument your web applications to tell you about slow network calls, database calls, and even slow regions of the world due to Internet performance. They can be expensive, though.

Alerting

Excellent, you have logging and monitoring, but what happens when your monitoring finds something that folks would need to know about preventing an issue or an outage? That's right, alerting—basically notifying a group of folks that there is an issue that needs to be investigated. Decide which groups/teams need to be alerted. This could be through e-mail, text messages, app notifications, and others. Make sure not to have too many that are meaningless or where nothing can be done with them; otherwise, they will end up being ignored. Sumologic.com can monitor your logs and set up alerts as well.

Standard Operating Procedure (SOP) or Runbook

Ok, you've got logging, monitoring, and alerting, but what should happen when you get an alert? When the alert goes out, what should the team do? Are there diagnostics steps they should take, actions that should happen, and other groups that should be notified for certain conditions? Come up with a plan and write it down. Make it available to the teams that need it.

Training

Ok, you've done everything else, but if you don't train people in the different diagnostic procedures from your Tier 1 support to operations to engineering on how your new feature functions and how you diagnose issues, what will you do when things inevitably go wrong? Complex features likely need some training to handle when failures happen to figure out what is going wrong. This is especially the case when the logic involves messaging that goes between many services.

Escalation Process for Critical Incidents

Have a good support escalation process in place, from taking initial customer calls to escalating to an internal support group/operations, all the way to escalating to development. Make sure you have reasonable ways and processes to get in touch with the people who will be needed at any time of day.

Using automation to call people can be useful. Make sure this is sustainable from a people's perspective (your staff likely doesn't want to be on call 24 hours a day, 7 days a week, 365 days a year). Staff appropriately to allow for normal or time-shifted work weeks as needed. Staff teams to cover the hours a day needed. If not staffed fully, and if you need to escalate to on call, make sure it's a sustainable rotation that isn't too frequent and not overwhelming.

Operational Impact

In addition to the above items for each of those areas, think about whether your software changes will have an operational impact on people. For example, does it require more manual work to deploy the software for the operations team? Will customer support get more calls due to a confusing feature or thinking something is not working when it is? Something as simple as changing your password reset process for your users could greatly increase or decrease calls to customer support, which impacts their time/money. Do consider that if you can add a new feature and just make a back-end flag for your operations team to turn on, it adds a little additional work for your company's personnel. It doesn't sound like much, but all of those little things add up, and sometimes, it will surprise you.

We did something like this for a flag, but we also had a migration script that could run for many hours to enable it. We figured our ops team could handle it, since this shouldn't happen too and may happen for only a few customers here and there. That was until we found out a customer who was a reseller supported hundreds of other customers, and they wanted this feature turned on for hundreds of customer apps that we had this manual process for. Think about the impact your software decisions have.

All of these items and more are part of making sure your software is supportable.

How to Handle Support with Agile Scrum Teams

Often, you will have a backlog of investigations/support tickets. Pick a certain number of developers to keep working on the backlog of investigation/support items by default. If the backlog starts to get too big or some items are more urgent, prioritize work for them. If that still isn't enough, then you might have to pull in additional folks in the sprint to work on items and pull them off other work. Ideally, you would have enough people assigned to the support role by default to avoid those situations from happening often. If it does happen, try to select people to pull in who would have the least impact on other work.

For example, if there are seven people on the team, you might rotate two people every sprint to work on support/investigations by default.

The ideal number of people on support work per sprint is based on your continuous backlog, so that regular work scheduled doesn't get interrupted by support work.

The rotation can get hard if the team is working on complicated features/stories with tight timelines. Ideally, just build support time into your feature schedule. If it doesn't allow for that, you could exclude some people from the rotation for a while. You generally want to make sure all developers get to work on actual development, though, not just support work. On average, most developers don't want to work only on support work, so to avoid attrition of your team, the best bet is to find a way to rotate folks into some coding tasks within a reasonable amount of time on a regular basis.

If the investigation results in a bug, correlate the bug ticket to the investigation to keep track.

Support teams working on investigations and bugs could be split from the teams doing features. This has pros and cons, though. One positive is enabling feature teams to work uninterrupted by support work can help them make greater progress. A pro for the support investigation team is that it's often easier to rotate investigation research within a team only handling bugs or investigations. Bugs, often the smaller type, don't usually take more than a sprint or two. The cons, though, are that the support or bug teams might not be experts on the new features or functionality implemented. Also, having feature teams cause bugs and not have to fix them isn't ideal from a learning perspective.

An alternative idea is just allocating a percentage of each team/product to fix bugs. This can be adjusted based on the support issues the product is experiencing. Rotation to bugs and investigations can still be tricky. It can be too impactful to have people working on multi-sprint features rotated off a feature in the middle. Larger teams might have enough smaller features to make sure this isn't an issue, so it might depend on the product, team, features, and release cycle and how well it goes.

Splitting the support team off does avoid this, but as mentioned before, a lot of developers don't like to be just working on only bugs without working on new features as well at some point.

Prioritizing Investigations/Escalation Process for Noncritical Incidents

A customer support team will inevitably escalate many issues to the development team to be investigated and solved. Customer support teams are usually scaled (have lots more people) to handle many simultaneous issues from customers. Development teams don't usually have nearly as many people, and the investigations escalated to them are usually harder, being issues that take longer to solve/research. This means the process needs to be designed to handle as many tickets at the customer support level as possible before escalating.

A usual way this is done is to have Level 1 Customer Support handle simple questions about known issues or just product questions. If they can't answer, it's escalated to Level 2 Customer Support (sometimes called technical support).

Level 2 Customer Support can handle much deeper issues for product corrections. Some of the folks in Level 2 sometimes even have some basic coding experience or deep knowledge of the product, like internal database schema. Level 2 sometimes is tasked with being able to even run data correction scripts or simple corrective scripts (often, customer support is never allowed to change product code, though Level 2 can sometimes debug down to product code).

Level 3 is usually the main development team (though rarely this can be a separate development team just for support issues).

How should support issues be prioritized for Level 3 (Development/Engineering)? Hopefully, Level 1 and 2 have provided some level of organization to help bucket these issues into at least urgent, high, medium, and low and sometimes have a time target that can help drive prioritization of these tickets. We could then try to keep items in a queue of buckets of severity, such as urgent at the top, then high, medium, and low, adding each new item to the bottom of that category when they come in as a default.

It's possible that may not work so well in reality though, since there might be so many mediums that they will overwhelm the lows, resulting in lows never getting worked. Therefore, it might be easier to lump mediums and lows together and keep them in time order as they come in, avoiding starvation of low items. Of course, if you get too many urgent and high items, the same starvation of medium/lows could happen, so the process needs to be thought through holistically to appropriately mark items with a proper severity. If you get too many urgent/high, make sure you believe your rules around prioritizing those are appropriate or if they should be revised, or even if there are some solutions that can be pushed from engineering to Level 1 or 2 to handle if it is within their capabilities to reduce escalations to Level 3.

Be warned that some of this process can be as much an art form as a science, because often, many business factors can come into play in this prioritization, such as size of customer/contract, upcoming contract renewal, aggrieved customer getting senior management attention recently, upcoming customer commitment timelines for projects/regulatory filings needed. Make sure this has at least some semblance of process to it so it's not always the customer or the internal representative who screams the loudest. It might be good to consider a committee for review of lead customer support, technical account manager lead, engineering lead, and business analyst to meet weekly to prioritize and to meet/chat ad hoc for urgent requests to see if they really outrank other items in the queue.

CHAPTER 28

Process: Audits

Audits in Highly Regulated Environments

A lot of processes don't go into the details of how you make your process auditable and able to pass various types of audits. You might need to do this if you are in a regulated industry like medical or financial, or it might be required by your customers/company itself, or some combinations of those.

What is the goal of a software process/software audit? This depends on the industry, sometimes. In general, it wants to make sure there is a reasonable, documented process that has written records or methodology to be audited to ensure the software is written, tested, deployed, maintained, and tracked in a controllable, secure fashion that follows industry norms.

In general, the following points can be audited (make sure to check your industry standards if there are any):

- Requirements/changes documented and matched with code check-ins/merges.
- Appropriate testing of each change is a documented unit test and some form of system/integration test (generally, the person

who writes the code should not be the only person who tests the code—separation of duties).

- There is a well-documented and defined process for making and documenting changes to the software (e.g., recorded in a tool like Jira, etc.), and changes can be traced to the actual lines of code changed.
- Reasonable testing should be documented and performed, such as unit testing, system/integration testing, and performance testing. If testing won't be performed, it is best to record the reasons why some testing was selected but not others. Sometimes, they like screenshots or automated test output files.
- Some places check for documented code reviews, or at least something to indicate it happened.
- Builds generally should happen on isolated, controlled machines that have limited access other than to run the builds (e.g., Jenkins) to ensure any changes for production code were generated from a controlled set of source.
- Developers should not have write access to production.
- Proper access is granted to source control.
- Only production ready and fully tested code is deployed to production and should require some sort of approval different from the person requesting the deployment/change.
- Sometimes, auditors ask for verification to confirm the code that was built is the code that was deployed, for example by recording and verifying binary hash values of the built binaries.
- In general, there are appropriate access controls and approvals of the systems like source control, build box, production deployments, etc.
- If your software is cloud based, they might want to see audits around your process of updates to your software/deployment

and policies around that when there are urgent updates and regular updates.

The above items can often be accomplished slightly differently in each organization, but in general, there are obvious similarities.

Preparing for an Audit

You should know the following:

- What is in scope of the audit material and time frame?
- What is out of scope of the audit material and time frame?
- What materials are the auditors allowed to see or not?
- What general area of questions and information will the auditors ask?
- What relevant policies will the auditors ask for?
- Where are the policies or other data that they will be asking for?
- Who is the point person to answer questions for each area?

Usually, a person or team acts like your lawyer(s) to keep questions relevant and in scope, and often is the internal person who sets up the meeting.

When answering auditors' questions, make sure you understand the question first. Don't answer outside the scope. Limit your answer to only the question (don't expand or add to it). If it's outside of your area, don't answer, or say that it is outside of your area of expertise. It's ok if you don't know. Just say that you don't know or you're not sure and that you would get back to them on that.

Prepare a private chat channel with your internal team so folks can ask questions or point out things to the internal team during the audit.

What Should You Expect during an Audit?

The auditors will ask questions about each area of your process. Often, they will want to see the documents that define your process to make sure there is written documentation of it. They will also want to see written evidence of all aspects of your process. Sometimes, they will want one or a couple of examples. Sometimes, they will want a statistical sampling of each of the artifacts.

The following are common examples:

- They might want to see evidence that they write down the requirements.
- They may want copies of the issue track information that shows that you record it.
- They may ask for evidence of unit testing and evidence of reviews.
- They may want to understand how you restrict access to your source to make sure only approved items get into your source control repository.
- They will probably want to see evidence of QA testing and more.
- They may want to see how you make sure what you tested is the exact binary that makes it into production.

CHAPTER 29

General Development

Languages

Note: Most developers develop opinions about languages. The following information is laced with many opinions and is not necessarily true for everyone. Language usage changes over time, so search for jobs with the language in your area to get a feel for the relative usage at present in your area.

Visual Basic

This language is pretty dated but is still in limited use in various forms today. You can identify it by its ".VBS" extension.

C (*Chistory*, n.d.)

The C language is still around after many years. Over 50 years. This was one of the first programming languages I learned. It is very powerful and needs to be used very carefully to avoid memory leaks, writing to wrong memory locations with pointers, and so on. This language was one of the first deemed powerful enough to implement all of the low-level access to hardware in a more readable way with good performance. This is a compiled language originally notable for its ability to run on multiple platforms. It is good for device drivers and hardware access.

C++

C++ has all the power of C but with object-oriented programming abilities. This is a compiled language as well. It's possible to write low-level software to access hardware with great performance as well. This used to be one of the main ways to write Windows apps (earlier, it was just C). Now, it can still be used for Windows apps, but more likely, it would just be used for areas of the software that need higher performance or where APIs for some third-party functionality gain easier access from it. I've seen some jobs that suggest it is used in game programming. It is used in financial software for low latency trading applications and related data. It could also be used for hardware drivers.

It uses a concept called header files for one file/class to know about declarations of another (which seems antiquated now when you have other languages like Java and C# that don't need this).

C++ compilation seems a lot slower than the compilation for something like C#. At one company where I was working, our build would take about six to eight hours at one point. We optimized it and put SSDs in the build server, multithreaded it, and got it down to two to four hours or so. That was many years ago, now. Not sure if it has improved with newer versions. With header file processing, it might be hard, though.

Java

A nice cross-platform managed language. You will find this used for web server backends, Android apps, and much more. A very straightforward object-oriented language. A very popular language.

C#

C# has all the goodness of Java plus more. It is also a managed language (garbage collection). It is very well supported in the Microsoft tools and popular in the Microsoft tech stack. I've worked with many different languages, and this one is my current preference. It is fast, flexible, easy, and has cross-platform support. It's well supported and is getting new updates relatively often to continue to improve the language. Similar to Java, you don't need to worry about freeing memory like C++, given the garbage collection. You don't have to worry about corrupting memory with bad pointer references that could happen in C++. It's still powerful enough to run soft real-time applications. It is used in some trading systems where low latency isn't a major requirement. It can still deliver reasonable performance when coded correctly. Java is used in similar ways as well.

Javascript

Probably one of the most used languages in browsers to control web pages, it's also used in many other places. A type-safe version called Typescript is available to use to get some type of safety. This language is everywhere, given the ubiquitous web pages. It is very flexible in doing this job. It is a very flexible language, even used on some gaming platforms and elsewhere. It is generally interpreted on the fly. It can be a little more painful to debug, given the way it's used in browsers, but the debugging has gotten better over the years.

The language is so flexible that it's almost too flexible. It does not really have a great way to identify types, so they use a methodology called duck typing. If it looks, walks, and quacks like a duck, it's a duck, meaning if they support the same methods, you could say it's the same.

Extremely flexible and powerful to do certain things. Coming from object-oriented programming languages, though, the lack of requiring types just feels wrong. Typescript can help with some of that.

PHP

A scripting language used on many websites. This was and may still be one of the most popular website languages. (*Historical Yearly Trends in the Usage Statistics of Server-Side Programming Languages for Websites W3techs.Ashx (1504×555)*, n.d.) It started to fall out of favor several years back, but it was used so widely that there are many websites that still use this. The job data (*Job Search | Indeed*, n.d.) in my area didn't show a lot of jobs compared to other languages.

Python

A very popular scripting language used for a variety of reasons.

Rust

This language has gotten a lot of press, but at least at present, in my area, there are very few jobs (*Job Search | Indeed*, n.d.) for this language. Known for its concurrency safety.

(*Fearless Concurrency—The Rust Programming Language*, n.d.)

Ruby

This is an object-oriented scripting language used for some web development and more. Based on current job data, it doesn't seem as popular as other languages. (*About Ruby*, n.d.)

SQL

SQL as a language has variations that are similar but different between various databases. It is a database-specific language not designed for general use but instead designed for writing or retrieving sets of data from a database. It is well designed for this and makes managing data easier than it would be in many general-purpose languages.

PowerShell

A scripting language on Windows, designed to be more powerful than the original batch language in the native command prompt shell. It has the specific purpose of running batch-like commands from the command line.

bash

This is more like the Linux version of command-line scripting, though I'm more used to Windows. On Windows, the Unix/Linux command-like shell was originally called bash, I believe. I've used this name to mean the same thing for Unix/Linux, but it really depends on the shell used for Linux as to which scripting language it will use.

There are probably hundreds more programming languages out there, some general purpose and some with a particular purpose in mind.

Perl

It was initially used by most folks as a great special-purpose language to do text parsing. It can do much more now, though it is probably still most used for text processing. General-purpose languages aren't usually bad at text processing, nowadays. The processing gets built into the core language, Java/C#. Looking at job listings, it's not as popular as the general-purpose languages, but it had a lot more jobs (*Job Search | Indeed*, n.d.) mentioning it than I expected.

Algorithms/Data Structures

Algorithms are ordered sets of actions to solve a well-defined problem. It can have the information you put into it and should have the information you get out of it. The same data in must produce the same data out.

Algorithms are trying to teach you how to solve problems and how to estimate the amount of work an algorithm will need to do based on the way it operates. Knowing this type of information helps you compare algorithms to select the right one for the job.

Here is a video on algorithms and data structures video: Algorithms and Data Structures Tutorial – Full Course for Beginners (https://www.youtube.com/watch?v=8hly31xKli0).

Note: I didn't watch this entire video but checked the outlines and segments. It looks like it would be a good free reference.

Typically, algorithms have to balance memory and time. Sometimes, when comparing two algorithms, it's good to compare the worst-case scenarios of one algorithm with another.

Constant Time

If we do the same number of operations regardless of how many items there are, that is considered the constant time or O(1). For example, we sort an array in memory (don't worry about the sort part), but let's say after it's sorted, we want to know the time it will take to get the first smallest item. Since I always need to access just one item in an array regardless of whether there is one item or a million, even if I need to do a lot of actual operations, if that doesn't change significantly based on the number of items in the data structure, it would still be constant time O(1).

Linear Time

Imagine someone dropped a deck of playing cards such that all the cards were spread out all over your room, and you have to pick them up one at a time. You would have to pick up 52 cards. What if someone dropped two decks, you would have to pick up 104 cards. So the comparison is relative to the number of items there are. How many times do you need to do something with them? In this case, it's one time for each card. This is considered linear. Big O notation considers this O(N), as you need to operate on the items N times (N is either 52 or 104 in these cases).

Imagine if, instead of cards, you had to pick up 10 bars of super slippery soap. It is so slippery that with each one you pick up; you end up dropping it and have to pick it up again, resulting in you having to pick up the bars 20 times. So the Big O notation, in this case, you would think would be O(2*N), since you need to operate on the items twice. But even with that number, we still simplify it to O(N), since it's linear (1*N, 2*N, 3*N, etc., are all linear).

Data structures

Data structure	Insert	Find	Memory
Linked List	O(1), O(n)	O(n)	Nonsequential
Array	O(n)	O(n)	Sequential
Binary Tree	O(Log(n))	O(Log(n))	Nonsequential
Hashtable	O(1)	O(1)	Nonsequential

Linked Lists

You can add or remove linked list nodes to the beginning or end of the list in constant time O(1). Inserting or finding in the middle, though, will take O(n) time, so if you just need to insert and remove from the ends of the list, the performance can be very good. Linked lists nodes are often allocated one at a time from heap memory, so they are not sequential in memory.

Array

An array is a sequential area of memory, with each element the size of what the array type is made from. So if it is an array of 32-bit integers, each element will have that size. Inserting into the array (O(n)) is costly, since memory needs to be allocated, and elements need to be shifted in the array. Finding items in the array is also an O(n) operation.

Binary Trees

Each node of the tree can go to child elements, usually arranged so that the left node child node should be less than the parent node, and the node on the right child node should be greater than the parent node. Insert and find operations are O(log(n)). Memory is not sequential, since each node is often allocated from the heap.

Hashtables

Hashtables are made up of buckets of where items would hash to. If there are enough buckets, insert and find operations are fast, on the order of O(1), same as constant time. To make finds fast, a hash is made of the item, and then hashes can be found and looked up in the buckets quickly.

Naming Classes, Methods, Properties, and so on.

As a developer, you will have to name probably thousands, tens of thousands, or more things over your career. This sounds pretty easy, right? Just give it a name. Though for those of you who are parents now, was it easy to give your baby a name? You wanted something that had meaning. It can sometimes be this way with code, though usually not quite that hard. You probably won't be naming your code after your parents or grandparents. ;)

Use names that are descriptive of the class, method, or action. Make sure its name is honest and complete and fits the coding standards of what developers expect of a method named that. For example, if you called a method "Add" and it removed, that would be a very bad method name.

Or what if you had a property called "IsTurnedOn," and when read, it removed something? Here, not only did it tell you something was turned on, it removed something in the class. First, you should never do that. Second, the name would obviously have been bad. If you really needed to do that, it should be a method like "CheckIfTurnedOnAndRemoveValue." It still is bad to combine two things like that, but at least the name is much more honest and obvious if someone were to use it.

For naming, many languages have coding standards. You should follow them or the standard for your company.

Pascal Case: MyClassName
Notice how each letter in the name is capitalized.

Camel Case: myClass
Notice how the first letter of the class is lowercase, but the second word in the name is upper cased.

Hungarian Notation: iCount
Not really used much anymore, but the idea is to indicate in lowercase the variable type in some way. An "i," for example, could be an integer, then the name. This was used before editors were really good at showing the defined types when you hovered over them.

Snake Case: My_Class
Snake Case is not used as much anymore (Pascal or Camel Case are more common). This came about because names for methods and variables can't have spaces. It uses underscores instead.

Classes: LinkedList, Array, Hashmap
Those are examples of both data structures and names of classes. A class doesn't need to be a data structure.

Your name should be clear to someone who would use it, and it should be clear what that class is, and how it might work or what it might do. Those names should give folks who understand the data structures expectations of how they will work.

Files that contain classes often are given the same name or a higher-level name of a set of similar classes that they contain.

Methods/Functions: Add, Remove
Add and Remove are pretty clear about what they do. Especially if they were in an Array class, make your names descriptive, clear, and obvious what they will do to when they are used in the context of your class.

Variables: threadCount, returnValue
Use variable names that are clear about what they are so that it is easy to read the code. Too short is probably not good, and too long is probably not ideal, so find a happy medium of descriptive with a reasonable length.

Properties: IsUppercaseOnly
This property is telling you something about the class being uppercase only, probably a Boolean the way that it is named. Properties should just set or return the value and nothing else and be named so that it is obvious what you should expect of them.

How do you put this together in a style guide?
A simple way is to show a very small, concise class with all the proper naming conventions used for each of the elements so it's easy for someone referring to them.

Servers
For production or lab names, you might come up with naming conventions that indicate its production or lab, the customer name, URL, number, or database name. You should have some kind of convention. Just plan for the future so it covers the scenarios you need.

A long time ago in a galaxy, well, actually, pretty close to here, when servers/machines were not in racks, there was one company that used to name all of their servers after Disney characters. To make sure you could easily find the server in the lab, people purchased figurines of those characters and put them by the machine/keyboard to make them easier to find.

There are probably lots more things you will eventually need to name, so just plan for the future to have a convention that is standard, makes sense, and is consistent to make your life and the lives of folks who may join the company after you easier.

Even More Naming

At some point in your future, you will spend an hour discussing a name for something. At that point, you might realize how important naming is to people. A name can have an implied meaning that can either convey something correctly or incorrectly. Imagine having a button on a UI that says "Delete." Will it be obvious from the context of the UI what they are deleting? Should the button say something more specific about what it's going to delete?

Building Software to Reduce Risks and Handle/ Recover from Errors

Imagine you are building software for a financial company.

Their software needs to operate every day on time for the stock market.

You need to deploy software weekly to handle the new features or fixes for your product, sometimes needing to deploy overnight in emergencies.

How can you make sure deploying software never puts you out of business for more than a few seconds or minutes?

- Make sure your deployments are backward compatible and your software supports rolling back fast to the previous version.
- If rolling back fast isn't an option, use hot/warm server setups where one server is in live production with your latest software version and your warm server gets all the same messages and keeps the same state as your hot server but runs on the previous version of your software. That way, you can fall back to your old version by switching off your hot server and making your warm server the hot live server with your previous version running.

- Have the ability to roll out software into production on low-use servers or production test servers first to see how they do and give them time to burn in using live data. The Nasdaq stock market always had test symbols (made up symbols to use for testing). Often, trading firms have test servers that can trade the production test symbols, providing the chance to test with real data in production.
- Build monitoring to detect issues fast and tools to identify and recover from the issues quickly.
- Imagine a scenario where your trading software fails in the middle of the day, totally crashes, and dies—trading software might require all of the day's data to be processed to recover. If you built a tool that can restart, recover, and reprocess on the fly, you might just save the day.

All software that has any significant level of complexity likely has bugs. You should definitely do all the standard practice stuff, like having continuous unit/integration testing automation with good coverage and test cases. There will always be something that slips through. Having truly reliable software means having a great software and testing process AND having great monitoring, identifying, and recovery software and process. This means building your software to handle the inevitable errors even when you don't know what they specifically will be.

Even recovery will never be 100 percent perfect, but if you really have taken the time to think through all the possible failure scenarios and create procedures, scripts, and tools to recover from them, you'll end up with great software, great reliability, and great uptime.

Reducing Time and Risk for Your Enhancements

Imagine you need to make a performance improvement to one of your software's algorithms (it's a big one). The change is complex, so you will need to test the correctness and performance impact of these changes on all of your customer databases to be sure it won't slow them down (which would take a year or more for the performance test). The best alternative you can think of is to performance test a statistically significant subset of customer data to have enough confidence to be able to release, but even testing a small percentage would take months. You have an automation test framework for performance, but it can't possibly test all the data scenarios your customers actually have.

One alternative to those hard answers is one that developers tend not to want to consider, since it might involve changing your architecture and supporting old code. If you keep your old algorithm as a fallback just in case performance isn't better in a customer environment, your risk has gone way down. Then, you can concentrate on making sure your data is accurate and limit the performance testing to a much smaller subset by just realizing that if you have an issue in production, you have the option to roll back.

No one wants to use old code or support it if that happens. Still, if the cost for the testing is too high and your rollback is designed well, it should be painless and seamless. Hopefully, it costs less than the extensive testing effort or risk required. With the statistically significant sampling, since only testing a subset would not have eliminated the risk, you could find a set of customer data that performs worse. Rollback in this scenario might be the least bad option to have to allow you to deliver enhancements to your customers faster, with less cost and less risk. Ideal? Maybe not. But a good business decision? Probably yes.

These still can be very difficult calls to make, because doing this may not be free and can sometimes add significant cost/effort, so that should be weighed against the testing time/cost or risk that you might otherwise take to see what is right in your scenario.

Also, your organization should build and pay for the redundancy/resiliency your business needs. Financial companies such as trading systems might have two backup servers for each primary server in the primary data center and a primary and backup server in the backup data center.

Code Performance and Improving

Don't Pre-optimize Unless Required

It's a common refrain these days that you shouldn't spend time trying to optimize code for performance unless you need to. What that leaves out, though, is initially choosing the proper design, algorithms, and data structures for the data set and use cases you will be operating with. Once you've done that, you can check to see if it handles your worst-case scenarios.

This doesn't mean you should never optimize. You definitely should when needed. If your requirements need a certain level of performance, of course, you should optimize for that.

See this ACM article about the background of the preoptimization discussion: *The Fallacy of Premature Optimization*, n.d. (ACM https://ubiquity.acm.org/article.cfm?id=1513451).

Scaling/Planning for Performance

What usually happens in a business as it grows is that you hit scalability issues you never theorized would occur. Now, you are faced with performance issues under pressure to solve them. The ways to head scalability issues off were to analyze your worst-case growth rates for 2–3 years. In the financial sector, one of the targets we used was three times our max volume per day for stock trading. There should be multiple variations of these stats at different time scales, most likely depending on your use case. We measured burst order rates per second, total per day, bursts by server, by partition, and more. Let's say our max burst was 10,000 orders per second. We would then plan to make sure our system capacity could handle at least 30,000 orders per second, and if one day we hit 15,000 orders per second, we would start planning for scaling to 45,000 order per second, etc., trying to always keep ahead. This, of course, presumes your system can scale well.

At some point, you will probably hit a hard performance issue that will take a lot of time to optimize. You might even think based on having your experts work on the issue for 6 months and still hit its limits that it's time for a complete re-architecture. One more thing to try before going that route is to add more people who know the area a little (or sometimes even not much) and are good in the performance areas you need. Adding new people to the mix can sometimes produce surprising new approaches that just were not thought of before.

We had one case recently where we thought we couldn't improve significantly without a huge effort and brought some new folks in, and one of them came up with an idea that within days was showing 10–20 times improvement! It was a method no one else who had been working on previous improvement projects thought would be viable. Surprisingly, the results were stunning. Not every scenario got that improvement, so it might not be the complete solution we need in the end, but for a shorter-term improvement that can help customers. Fresh ideas into the mix for a team can be good.

Don't Just Assume; Measure

You may think you chose the right data structure, such as a linked list instead of an array because you insert and delete often. Then you decide to measure and tune performance and find out if you keep a fixed-sized array that doesn't need to be too big, adding/deleting items is actually faster in the array than in the linked list! You might ask yourself how this is possible. On Intel processors, many have high-speed cache memory, and if your usage pattern keeps the memory small enough to fit in your L1, L2, L3 Cache (see Cache in Understanding Hardware), then the performance can be amazing compared to using a linked list, where memory can be all over the place, causing it to access or exceed limits for multiple areas of cache memory.

Performance Issue Scenario

We had built an app that performed pretty well, until one day, a new operating system was released that our customer installed and noticed that our application that used to use 50 percent CPU was now using 100 percent CPU. We analyzed the issue and couldn't find a difference in our app. The OS vendor reviewed the issue and said they found the change that caused it. They had switched by default to a multi-CPU kernel rather than a single-core designed kernel the old OS used. This added significant overhead for some multithreaded workloads. We had someone on our team spend about three months optimizing the app to get it back to the performance it had before the OS upgrade.

Strings of Numbers

If you are comparing numbers as strings, you might be able to get higher performance by converting them to specific number types. Strings often require processing each byte separately for comparisons, requiring more CPU instructions. Numeric compare can usually compare 32 bit or 64 bit values in a single CPU instruction.

Reusing Similar Strings

If you are comparing strings all over your code, it's possible you could benefit from reusing similar strings if there is a lot that is similar. Using hash codes (integers) for string comparisons can help. Comparing integers rather than entire strings can be much faster. Also, just having to go through repeats of the same string can sometimes slow things down. Storing the same string only once could perhaps improve your performance (sometimes called string interning, hashing, or atomization).

Data Structure Performance

If there are performance issues and you measure slow performance accessing an array or other O(N) data structure, consider if there is an O(log(N)) or O(1) data structure that would improve your performance. For example, if you have a large array and are trying to find strings in that array, perhaps a binary tree or a hash table data structure might make more sense to improve your performance.

Exceptions

Keep an eye out for throwing too many exceptions in a short time. Exceptions typically are more expensive to execute than regular program flow.

Language-specific Performance

In C#, creating and firing lots of events might be slower than, for example, calling an interface on an object alternatively. Anything where there are finalizable objects can add to the slowness of object creation. This is very important, since some of this information can depend on changes in the .NET JIT or runtime. They are not guaranteed to hold true in the future.

Performance Optimization Areas

Architecture: Choose the right design, algorithms, and data structures to achieve your desired performance.

Implementation: Optimize your implementation so that it functions at its best, given the design.

Compilation: Optimize compilation to improve the performance of your code even further.

JIT: For languages that support just-in-time compilation, optimize the performance of the code with JIT, if possible.

Runtime: Optimize the performance of your runtime if your language has one.

Below are some examples of performance differences in various scenarios with C#.NET. Optimizing to this level is usually not necessary, as it's for more extreme cases. Some of this data is a little dated, but it should be relative.

Comparing a method with a simple operation and try catch

- Public void Method() { count ++}
- Public void Method() { try { } catch { }}

- Try catch adds nearly 25 percent overhead to an empty method.
- Comparison of 10 million method calls ~15 ms (~1.5 ns/call) (no exception handling) vs. 20 ms (with exception handling) (~2 ns/call)

	Total (ms)	(ns)/Call
No try catch	15	1.5
With try catch	20	2

Comparing Exception Use vs. Object Allocations

Exceptions are very time consuming:

Compare 1 million object allocations at 3 ms (3 ns/call) vs. 1 million exceptions at 10343 ms (10343 ns/call). Ok, not really a fair test, but just a relative comparison.

Rethrowing exceptions is slightly more expensive than throwing:

	Total(ms)	(ns)/call
No exceptions	3	3
Exceptions	10343	10343

Comparing Boxing vs. Not Boxing

In .NET, it's considered boxing when you convert a value type to an object and unboxing when you convert from an object to a value type. Converting adds overhead.

Boxing can be 10–20 times or more slower than an assignment.

100M iterations:

	Total(ms)	(ns)/Call
No boxing	25	0.25
Boxing	265	2.65

That is a 91 percent difference.

Avoid boxing whenever possible. Sometimes, boxing isn't obvious—you can check the Intermediate Language (IL) code itself for performance sensitive areas, as there is a box instruction, so it is easy to tell from the IL.

Object Pooling

When you have lots of objects, object pooling can improve your performance by avoiding garbage collection. Object pooling means when an object is allocated, add it to a list; when it's used, remove it from the list; and when it is no longer used, add it back to the list. Alternately, the list can just keep track of what is allocated or not. Avoiding too many garbage collections can be beneficial if your application is very performance sensitive.

Foreach vs. For Loop

Foreach is roughly half as fast as for loop iterations, so if you need ultra-high performance, for loops are generally faster.

Private Static Readonly Bool

Using this set of options preceding your Boolean value and initializing it once in the constructor, when used in the code, can optimize in or out calls the first time the JIT is run. For example, if the bool was debugFlag and you defaulted to false and had code that said "if (debugFlag) {/* do debug code */}", it would even optimize out the IF check, since the JIT would know it could never be true once it was initialized.

Inlining

Methods that are less than approximately 32 bytes of IL can potentially be inlined. This basically means a copy of the code is inserted when it is used rather than jumping to the different methods' code location and jumping back. Avoiding jumping to different code locations in memory can improve performance. There are options to inline larger methods.

If any of the method params are structs, it won't be inlined. If you include exception handling in the method, it doesn't get inlined. If there are a lot of control statements (if's or switch statements, etc.), it won't be inlined.

The relative speed of method calls from fastest to slowest.

Interface:

- Non-virtual
- Static (Almost twice as slow as non-virtual)
- Virtual (3 times slower than a static method)
- Delegate
- Dynamic (as much as 90 times slower than delegate)

Finalizers

Objects with finalizers are about 70 times slower than objects without related to being created.

Synchronization Mechanism Performance

Fastest to slowest:

lock

ManualResetEventSlim

ReaderWriterLockSlim
SemamaphoreSlim
Mutex/Semaphore/AutoResetEvent

InterlockedIncrement vs. Lock
InterlockedIncrement is roughly three times faster

Local Variables
Methods with large numbers of local variables may be less optimized than smaller methods. JIT can enregister some variables into superfast CPU registers, but there is a limited number of them. If there are too many variables, more than registers, it can give up on that optimization of additional variables for your method.

JIT Ordering
Code gets generated in the order it's called for the first time, so if it's possible through the code to make sure the first time it will be called the way it will more often be called during normal usage, that could improve your performance. This is because code that runs in sequence with fewer jumps keeps more of the code you need in the cache, and that can help it run faster.

Conditional Attributes
C# has attributes that can be applied to methods such that the method will only be called if that condition (a compiler flag) is true. Otherwise, it won't be called at all. This can be useful for things like debug trace calls.

Cache Coherency

If there is a lot of memory or objects that will be used together, try to allocate them together. Keeping objects together improves caching of the memory and can improve performance.

Virtual Methods and Override Sealed Keywords

If you derive a class and override a virtual method plus mark it sealed, it will allow inlining of the method.

Code Reviews

If you are a new software engineer, you might not have done a lot of code reviews in college. In the working world, having your work reviewed and critiqued is a regular occurrence. This can take a little getting used to.

Some folks can get defensive when their code is critiqued. Just remember, when your code is reviewed, or you are reviewing others' code, you are not your code, and neither are they.

Some of the things you do for code reviews may be specific to your particular company's requirements.

When reviewing code, there are different levels of understanding:

- Do I understand what a method is doing and what is its purpose?
- Do I understand what the class is doing and its purpose?
- Do I understand how the code being reviewed fits in with the program/service being reviewed?

Those things sound obvious, but sometimes, they are not so obvious. For example, if you saw a method "int Add(int a, int b)" you could probably understand what it is doing. But if I told you this was a method in a program that e-mails people, you might immediately ask why that method exists. Couldn't someone have just done "int c=a+b;"?

Understanding the whys of the method can be important. Why does a method exist?

Code, by its very nature, tells you what it is doing, but it doesn't explain directly WHY it is doing it. Sometimes, you can figure that out, but other times, it can be a mystery without some explanation from the developer.

Think about that when you are coding something, and if it won't be obvious to someone reading the code as to why something exists or does something, explain it with comments or use better naming to explain it if possible.

Most code reviews look for:

- Correct functioning of the code: Does it work?
- Bugs: Are there any bugs or edge cases hidden in the code?
- Will the code perform well under the circumstances it is intended?
- Does the code conform to the style guidelines and coding conventions expected by your company?
- Are there better ways the code could be refactored to reduce redundancy?
- Is the code unit tested and designed to be tested well?
- Does the code have any potential security issues/vulnerabilities?
- Does the code have any privacy concerns (e.g., not using customer private information correctly or protecting it reasonably)?
- Does the code log correctly and handle errors properly?
- Can the code be monitored and supported well if/when necessary?
- Avoid using globals. They create a shared state that is easy to mess up, especially with multiple threads.

- Hard-coded strings and magic unknown numbers:
  - Hard-coded strings/numbers are bad, since if they are reused and need to be typed again, they could be mistyped.
  - Magic numbers in code like 1387329 with no explanation would leave you scratching your head. But if someone used "const int RANDOM_MAX_DEFAULT_VALUE= 1387329;" you might have some idea what they did, and its purpose.

When you are leaving comments for other people's code:

- Try to review the whole thing and to not leave piecemeal comments, so if this is on something like a GitHub PR, they will know you are done.
- Be respectful and comment on the code not the person. Keep all comments constructive.
- Focus on the bugs first: Make sure the feature works to match requirements, no bugs or unexpected operation, no architectural issues/flaws.
- If your company has coding style guidelines that are mandated, comment on those as well.
- If you leave comments, clarify if something you believe should be fixed before release vs. something nice to have.

MOUSES

With everyone creating acronyms, I decided to try my hand at it.

Remember what you should be looking for in a code review. Don't let MOUSES run around in your code.

Maintainability: Is the code maintainable/supportable?
Objective: Does the code properly implement the feature/purpose?

Unit Testing: Does the change include proper unit testing?
Speed: Are there any performance issues with the code?
Errors: Are there any bugs in the code?
Standards: Does the code adhere to coding standards?

Getting Pull Requests/Changes Reviewed

This can be tricky sometimes if you don't have a formal process. You could create a formal process to always assign one or two people at the start of a sprint for reviews so they know who should be looking at it. This can sometimes be tricky too.

In lieu of that, consider making your PR as easy to review as possible. Keep them as small as possible (small number of files and small number of changes).

Involve some key reviewers early in the changes so they understand what is going on before you need a review. Reviewers with context can do the reviews better/faster and easier.

Promote your PR through e-mail or group chat for review.

For large PRs, or if not getting traction, another way is to schedule a meeting with reviewers to walk them through your PR to be able to get a review from them.

How to Deal With Comments on Your Pull Request (PR) at the Last Minute

If they are critical, you can decide to fix them now. Or you can open another bug if the functionality works, but it is something you want to fix but isn't critical to the feature. If it's a minor improvement, you could open a story and mention any of these scenarios as a reply to the comment so the commenter knows you took their comments seriously and created an action plan to resolve them later.

Principles

There are all sorts of acronyms and principles that are created over time that become popular and sometimes fade when new principles and acronyms are proposed.

The SOLID Principle (Martin, 2000):

> **Single responsibility:** This just means there should be one main purpose/function of a class. It shouldn't be trying to do everything.
>
> **Open-Closed**: Open for extension but closed for modification. In terms of objected-oriented language, you could think of this as providing a base class that can be derived from to extend the functionality.
>
> **Liskov Substitution**: Allow the use of derived classes (without needing to know they are derived).
>
> **Interface Segregation**: Small, specific interfaces rather than one large generic interface.
>
> **Dependency inversion**: Rely on the abstraction (e.g., interface, etc.) rather than a concrete implementation.

With all of the above, these are good principles to consider when implementing code. It doesn't mean you have to take it to the extreme unless you need to, though. For example, you implement your code to only access everything through interfaces everywhere. In one particular code base, this could be extremely useful, but in others, it might be an abstraction with little reason. If, for example, you never had multiple implementations of an interface and never foresee the need for a class, adding additional abstractions could be overkill and make debugging/ support more difficult with a little extra benefit.

DRY Principle:

This one is simple: Don't Repeat Yourself.

The idea is from *The Pragmatic Programmer* (Thomas & Hunt, 2019). A very popular book, worth reading.

Changing one area of the system shouldn't have an impact on other unrelated areas. The principle can be applied to everything. Most folks interpret this as also meaning you shouldn't have duplicated code in other locations.

DUH Principle (made up acronym):

Don't Use Hard-coded values. Hard-coded values that are repeated or have the potential to be repeated are bad. It would be better to describe the value as the name of a constant. Otherwise, in retyping it, someone could make a mistake and insert bugs due to that.

DUG Principle (made up acronym):

Don't Use Globals. Globals that aren't constants are basically shared states. A shared state is asking for trouble when you have thousands of lines of codes and hundreds of classes that could operate on and change global values that can impact all code in the application.

If you see a global, you should think about whether it should be removed. There are some exceptions to this rule, like a global singleton logger, for example, so think if any changes of shared state would be an issue or not.

References:

Thomas, D., & Hunt, A. (2019). *The Pragmatic Programmer, 20th anniversary edition: Journey to Mastery* (Second edition). Addison-Wesley.

Getting in the Zone

You know the zone. You are so focused on cranking out code fast that you have all the context in your head. Nothing else is seeping into your mind except the code. Then someone interrupts you, or you have a meeting, and you lose all of it . . . sigh . . .

So what can you do?

- Organize your day, if possible, to give you the largest amount of consecutive hours without interruption. That might mean scheduling all meetings at the beginning or end of the day.
- Some people choose to use headphones to block out external sound if that seems to be distracting them. Bose noise-canceling headphones are great. Maybe on with no sound at all, just noise canceling on. Some people can listen to music. It might be better if the music has either no words, like classical or instrumental track, or a vocal track in a language you don't understand so as to not cause your brain to try to pay attention to the music too much. Since your brain doesn't understand the language, it can be less disruptive than native language vocals. Perhaps just the sound of the ocean might be calming. Find something that works for you.

- Take notes so that if you fall out of the zone, you have enough notes to get you back in more quickly.
- Make sure you have everything you need nearby. Coffee works for me in the morning.
- Open offices have their challenges with distractions. Distractions can be everywhere. Try to find a way to block your vision of other things going on in the office by keeping your eyes focused on the screen or finding things to block your view on the sides. Hopefully, you have a cube that's high enough to do that or your own office (or nowadays, working from home or remotely can perhaps be even better).

Windows Debugging

Production

Make sure your production binaries always have PDBs generated so that you can debug your release binary executables. Make sure you keep all of your PDBs for all versions of your application so that you can debug them.

Save Time Debugging

One most infrequently used debugging technique is to set a conditional breakpoint so that the debugger breaks when that condition happens. If you can pick the right condition to break on, it keeps you from having to step through hundreds of lines of code many times. If you have a loop that always fails on the 100th try, set a breakpoint on the loop count when it equals 100.

Dump Files

For production, sometimes, you can't debug, but you can get dump files that can help you determine what is going on. For example, let's say a process has a high CPU or memory, and you don't know why. You get a dump file (right-click on the EXE in Task Manager and select create dump) and load it into Visual Studio. With that, you can see the call stacks of all the threads and the current memory usage.

If the Change Was Recently Reproduced:

You could try reverting some recent changes to see if that fixes a newly introduced issue.

If you don't know where to start, revert to a version that didn't have the issue. Then use a binary search pattern to find where it was introduced, helping you isolate the issue if it's hard to find in the debugger, perhaps due to it only happening sporadically.

Check Everything; Don't Just Guess

Guessing rather than confirming can make you spend a lot more time looking for things, so make sure you check directly for evidence of anything you should check.

Be the Terminator

Of software bugs, I mean! You might know how it would not stop, no matter what, until it got its target. Sometimes, it really does take that level of determination to find the bug. Your target is that bug, and you will need to use every tool in your arsenal to find and eliminate it!

Overengineering

When you are beginning your career, you may have a tendency to overengineer your implementations. Starting out, we all like technical challenges, and we all want to impress our colleagues, so we tend to design complex implementations to solve what might be otherwise simpler problems.

It's important to remember that you are writing code for other people: users who will use your program, and other developers who will eventually need to maintain your code. In order to do that, you need to control complexity. Keep things simple, easy, and understandable. Your implementation should look like code everyone has seen before. Unique and novel are usually not good selling points for code, as the maintenance of such things is harder.

An example of this is an early career developer (who may or may not have been the author) who needed to implement a file format that could store icon locations, program information, and window positions. While the junior developer could have implemented an easy to read and decipher file format, he instead chose to implement one that tried to save bits everywhere, so he used binary and reduced space and size as much as possible.

The developer was quite proud of himself. That was until about three months later, when he needed to maintain this monstrosity, and deciphering all the crazy binary bits was a nightmare. Don't try to be "clever" with your implementation. There was no requirement to save that space. There was no need at all. This added a huge amount of complexity to the code for no reason at all. Don't do things like this. Make sure implementations/code are simple, easy to maintain, and understandable. You and your colleagues will appreciate this when maintenance is required.

Minimum Viable Product (MVP)

You might have heard this term introduced by Frank Robinson in 2001. Originally, it had a kind of profound meaning, and now it has started to be maligned. However, the core principle is very useful to keep in mind.

Software engineers enjoy writing code and making things. The focus is often on coding, as they like to build and see things work. You need to remember the business is usually there for one primary purpose: to make it and its shareholders money.

Time, as they say, is money. If the time spent developing is delaying getting a product into the hands of customers, it might be delaying the business from making money, unless the additional items being worked on offset the money that could have been made in the lost time, perhaps.

Thus, the idea of MVP came up. The idea is to come up with the minimal features/functionality needed for your customers to be able to achieve their goals and for your business to get money from the customers who are now able to achieve their goals.

When you are building things, think if what you are doing is really necessary or not to achieve the minimum viable product/timeline goals to be able to deliver value for the firm.

Some people don't like this, because they believe it means never doing anything else.

For example, addressing tech debt. It doesn't mean that. Improving tech debt should still be done. You should just be careful to consider and prioritize. What is the value of working on something for your company and working with your product team to decide what is really needed or not?

Think like a business owner AND a software engineer, and come up with the best implementation/prioritization that makes sense, using the least time but good benefits/rewards.

MVP thinking can be very effective in the startup stages of a company to make sure you build the minimum needed product in time to be profitable, and it still has its place in larger firms if it's used with care and balance.

Ideally, the MVP is defined upfront. Sometimes, it gets defined when a feature is running late and everyone is rethinking what the MVP functionality is needed for the delivery of a useful feature on time for the release, so it can be used in narrow areas as well as product scope.

Thinking Like Your Customer

To develop better software, it helps to really know what your customer wants and needs.

In the early days of software, a kid helping out a shoe store owner asked him what he needed. He said he just needed something a little like Lotus 123 (an old spreadsheet program for a TRS-80), but he couldn't afford it. "Can you make me something like that?" he asked. "But I just need this limited functionality."

"Sure," the kid said, and he created it and included support for saving and loading data from old cassette tape players. When you want to save data, you press the record button and the play button. It would often take a few minutes to save or load data from tape (that was the fastest speed that could be supported on the tape and was very fast for the time).

The software was delivered to the shoe store owner, and he said it worked, but the loading and saving are kind of slow. The kid, knowing the save was as fast as anything you could do on the machine at that time, asked, "Does it really matter that it takes 1–3 minutes?"

The answer was, "Well, it makes my thumb hurt."

"What?!"

"Yes," he said. "My tape player is broken, so I have to hold the button down the whole time it's loading, or it won't work."

Now, obviously, you probably won't cater to everything your customer wants, but some of the limitations or environmental factors they have that can impact the usage of your software might surprise you. So sometimes, the only way to get some answers is through having customers provide feedback for you.

Make sure you understand their exact usage scenario. How, when, and why are they using the software? What is the environment they are using it in? What is the hardware they will be using? Are there more than one person or types of roles of people that might use your software? If so, write the role and the scenarios they would encounter in detail, so you can use that to guide you on the development of functionality that makes their usage scenario work well.

Solving Hard Critical Support Issues

There is nothing more stressful than a production issue. Your customer has major problems, you are exceeding your service level agreements, and now it's going to cost your company money in paybacks to your customer per hour until the issue is resolved.

Of course, you happen to be on call when this issue happens. It's some sort of performance issue for the whole site. All you have are your logs to look at, and they aren't providing performance data.

You don't know where to start . . . What do you do?

- Collect as much information about the actual problem as you can (sometimes, a customer says it's a performance issue, and it's really something else, something very isolated rather than a general issue). Take inventory of all the areas you can look at (e.g., logs, dump files, database, network, disk, etc.).

- The first thing to think about is whether there is anything that is worth quickly trying or having done that could potentially restore service that would be acceptable/reasonable to try (create a list of possible things from most probable to least along with their downtime). Decide on the order of the actions that are worth trying. Decide if there is any diagnostic information you would like to collect before taking any of those actions (balance the considerations of restoring service ASAP or collecting a little info to help find the problem later). An example of an action for a web server might be to recycle IIS (Internet information service) on Windows, or restart Apache service on Linux, for example.
- If none of the actions to quickly restore service worked, either in your head, on paper, or online, draw a system diagram of all the parts of the system.
- Based on the data you collected on the actual problem, are there areas that you suspect (circle them), or are there some you can exclude with certainty?
- Based on the areas identified, rank them from the most probable to the least probable.
- For each system area in the most probable order first, think about the best way you will either be able to collect data to determine if the issue is there and what the precise problem is and/or reproduce the issue to confirm it.
- Think about what that system area does. For performance issues, is the problem CPU bound, I/O bound, memory bound, or some combination of the above?
- Think about all the different sets of data you have for that area and think about the most probable tools/data that will be able to determine the cause.

- Think about if there might be ways you could reproduce the issue in a dev environment alternatively (whichever method will be faster to find the cause).
- Does your product allow any programmatic customizations? (If so, could they be the cause?)
- Consider if it makes sense to call in other involved people or teams to investigate. For example, if you suspect a database, the operations DBA team, for example, might be able to help narrow the issue down. If you suspect networking, if you have an operations networking team, perhaps they could help. Think about an appropriate set of groups/people to call in to investigate areas of the problem.
- If you get stuck, go back to the beginning and the big diagram. Bring in other appropriate folks you think can help.
- If you find error messages, Google them to see what other people's solutions to similar errors were.
- On Windows, if appropriate, don't forget to check the event logs for your scenario—a sometimes forgotten location for error information.
- For performance issues that are more CPU/Memory bound, you might consider running tools like the Windows Performance Recorder/Analyzer that collects all the event trace data for Windows.
- Don't forget, for Windows systems, the Windows Sysinternals tools can be a great method of finding what is happening on a system and tracking down errors.
- Don't cause more harm. Make sure you test any changes you plan to make in a test environment, if it is at all possible that anything else is a risk. Easily reversible changes that won't cause any significant or permanent harm could be considered a calculated risk. For example, changing a timeout for a database

connection is easily reversible and probably won't cause significant permanent harm (it can have an impact though, positive or negative, so consider the risks).

Avoid Duplicating Code

This was mentioned in other sections in this book, but it is worth mentioning again. (Yes, my editor pointed out the irony.)

If code will be duplicated, it's often better to refactor or redesign than duplicate large amounts of code.

There could be small exceptions to this rule. For example, to ensure backward compatibility and due to time constraints, you may need to duplicate one method to make a date, and you could fix it correctly later. There are always some exceptions, sure.

On the whole, you should think long and hard about the cost of maintaining duplicate code. This is especially painful when large portions of a code base are duplicated so you can create a "brand new version" of your product, and you don't want to worry about that "old legacy code." If you still need to support and maintain the old code, how much will it cost to port fixes to the old code into the new code? Merging costs will increase with time as the code bases diverge. At some point, the cost could double or more in time/testing. If you don't need to support the legacy code and port changes, this could be fine. Committing to do that until you have definitely stopped supporting the old code is not recommended. If you have an ironclad commitment to stop support for less than six months, maybe you could start it. It is recommended to wait to duplicate code until the end of support of the legacy code, as plans often fall through, "legacy" customers complain, and then you need to port fixes.

One possible exception is if the business MUST accelerate massive changes on a new version, and the old architecture would cause enough delay to cause a significant lost opportunity cost to the business (e.g., miss out on a multimillion-dollar contract, perhaps). Even then, the business should perhaps be prepared to as much as double the team size or more to support both the old legacy code and new code. It may not need to be double, but that is perhaps a worse (perhaps not worst) case possibility. Some percentage more will probably be needed to keep up the same velocity and even more to increase it.

Improving Testing

Most folks in the industry would consider automated testing as the way to go. Most would recommend the standard test pyramid. The test pyramid means it is typical to have more low-level unit tests than high-level integration tests.

UI could, in some cases, be just integration tests or API tests perhaps if there is no UI.

Don't get too hung up on the pyramid for its general guidance. The key is that if you can have proper tests at the lower levels, as long as other things don't cause side effects outside of your unit tests, it might need fewer tests overall to test at the lower levels than if you tried to test all the possible combinations of the functions that might be called at the higher levels. An API or a UI might call hundreds of underlying functions in varying combinations, so it would be nearly impossible to come up with all the combinations of testing needed at that level to test all the underlying functions properly at that level. If, instead, each of the hundred underlying calls could really be designed and unit tested in isolation, you don't have to worry about all of those combinations that might occur at the higher levels of the pyramid as much.

Most automated testing uses specific values to test happy path (sunny day) scenarios where everything works and includes some of the "known" edge cases.

What can happen in a lot of software is that different data can hit other unknown edge cases, but your automated testing will never find them, since it replays the same data over and over, leaving it to manual testers to hopefully find them.

Instead, what if the automation could send random data for the data types needed that conforms to a possible correct input but is random enough to find unexpected issues (for example, Unicode issues)? Consider fuzz testing or fuzzing methods to try multiple edge case inputs to find issues with the software.

Finding a Balanced Way to Test

If you aren't careful with the way you build testing, your tests might be too brittle, causing little changes that could require large refactoring of your testing. For example, for an API, if it is possible to get full coverage just by calling the public interface of the API that needs to remain the same, the tests would not be very brittle, since the API would have to continue as is, and the underlying changes should not impact the testing.

The alternative would be if you tested every little private function individually but all of those had to change due to a refactor that resulted in no change to the actual functionality in the API. Then all of your internal tests might need to be rewritten too. But if you had written against the public interfaces, that wouldn't change, and then the internal refactor wouldn't require refactoring your tests.

You will need to decide the right balance of where to test your APIs to get the coverage you need without potentially needing to redo all of your internal tests if you end up needing to refactor internals at some future point in time.

User Interfaces

User interfaces are the way software allows users to see or do things with it.

- User interfaces should be clear.
- User interfaces should be concise.
- User interfaces should perform actions as the users expect.
- User interfaces should be responsive.
- User interfaces should allow entering in a way users are comfortable.
- User interfaces should not lose the user's work.

Think of it this way. You walk to your front door, then turn the knob, and then pull the door open. After that, you walk through the door and pull the knob to close it.

What just happened there was you, as a user of the door, easily understood you needed to turn the knob, then pull it open. Then you walked through and pulled the knob on the other side to close. Simple, right? You do that probably every day, not even thinking about it. If you can design your software to work in a similar way, your users will be pretty happy.

So how did you know what to do? There are parts of your environment that you learn about, and there are parts of your environment that are obvious in what to do.

With a doorknob, you learned to open a door. You need to turn the knob so that the latching mechanism will open for you to be able to pull it. The doorknob has a natural affordance that is shaped in a way that makes it easy to pull (and the learned behavior to turn it). An affordance is a way something looks or even feels that can give you clues about how you should use it.

User interfaces already use these learned behaviors and environmental factors to make it easy for users to know what to do. For example, if you saw an obvious button on a wall, you would know you could press it. If that button was big and red on the wall and it read, "Fire Alarm," you would know not to press it unless there was a fire.

If you think of another type of door that has no knob but a plate on it, it might be obvious to most people that you can't pull it and would have to push it. To make it even more obvious, many doors have the text "Push" written across them.

There are objects all around you that are obvious about how to use them, or you have learned to use them. You use them daily, probably without even a conscious thought going through your head.

There is an excellent book that describes all of this, originally titled *The Psychology of Everyday Things* by Donald Norman (Norman, 1988).

Understand Your Users

When building a user interface, you should understand your users. You might want to break down the different types of personas/roles that might use your application and how they might use them. Think about an ATM. Some users just want to get some money out of the machine. Other users want to deposit money in the machine. Also, don't forget that someone needs to add money to the ATM for customers, and someone else may need to diagnose issues with the machine.

So you can break those down into the different types of users and how they might use the machine. Sometimes, someone might even combine getting money and depositing at the same time, so there could be a combination of scenarios you want to support.

Think about it—there are probably hundreds of thousands of ATMs in the US alone. You could probably walk up to any one of the ATMs and, in about a minute, get money out, and you didn't need to learn about each different machine. Even though many have slightly different interfaces, they are all typically similar enough so you know what to do.

This example shows a very simplistic user interface for the average user where getting money is easy enough, and they never have to learn anything new. If you can design your interface for your software this way, your users will have an easy time using it.

Think about some of the other scenarios, though, like someone diagnosing an issue with an ATM. Your average user would have no clue what to do with all the information it would likely provide or the diagnostic steps or areas it would need to go through to analyze itself. That type of user is going to be more advanced and will probably need to have learned something about the user interface in order to know how to use things properly. Since this is someone working with an ATM probably all day every day, that is probably ok. It's not the same as someone who probably only spends one minute at an ATM once a week.

Thus, expected experience level of users can help guide you on the complexity of your user interface and how well your users will be able to cope with the complexity.

Think about the Environment of Your Users

Let's say you are designing a software system to either turn off systems or turn on cooling systems in case of an emergency in a high-radiation environment for a nuclear reactor. Your users might be in heavy radiation protective suits. If you use a touch screen, you better give large spaces for their gloved fingers to work. Also, the system should be simple to understand and might need confirmation to make sure accidental touches don't cause a nuclear meltdown.

The environment of your users and the way they use your software can make a huge difference in how you design your interfaces and the software and hardware required.

Data Entry

Allow a natural, expected flow of information. For example, when entering an address, users expect to enter a name, street address/name, town, state, and zip. How would it seem to the user if that entry was out of sequence? It would seem awkward and weird. There are expectations for certain types of data and entry, so it's best to follow the expected patterns of entry your users expect.

Pressing the tab button should often go to the next logical field for the user to enter data. Shift-tab should go back through the field order.

Allow users to enter data in any order they feel comfortable. Don't block them from doing it. You can highlight it in a way to indicate you need the information, but don't prevent them from moving around the screen.

You should not require users to enter data that doesn't make sense to them. This is especially true for privacy-sensitive data, because if the users don't understand why it's needed, they will probably abandon your data entry form. If on a shopping site you required the user to enter their social security number, you probably wouldn't get any orders, as everyone would think you are a scammer site for requesting that type of private data.

In many western languages and locales with left-to-right reading, users' eyes will initially be drawn to the left-top of a page/form and work down if it's a single column. If it's more, the organization, layout, and spacing can influence where the user's eyes are drawn next.

Standards

You may have noticed a lot of websites operate in a similar way, even though there are differences. Some of this is due to there being standard controls that all websites use. Other parts of it are sites that use standard ways of entering data or navigating so that it is easy for users to understand what to do. Using common, standard behaviors is a good way to increase the usability and ease of use of your website or application. Find and modify, as appropriate, a standard to use for all of your apps at your company. Make your software look and feel similar across products.

Colors

Colors can be used to enhance and brand your user interfaces. They can be used to indicate errors, particular conditions of concern, and more. You should know that colors that have one meaning to you might have different meanings in different cultures. If you design a red emergency button to not press in case of an emergency, that may be obvious in one culture but not in another. Know your environments/culture and allow customizations so that your user interface can adapt appropriately. Also, remember that there is a significant portion of the population that is color-blind or sees colors a little differently, so take that into account when designing your interfaces so that those users will still be able to distinguish items in your user interface, not just by color.

Find Good Examples of User Interfaces

Look at applications you find easy to use, understand what makes them easy to use, and when you build your interfaces, model your interfaces/interactions off those ideals.

Number of Clicks or Key Presses, or Mouse Distance Movements

To reduce your users' workload, count the number of clicks, key presses, and mouse movements it takes to get through your user interface. Try to do things that reduce the number to keep the workload of your user to a minimum to accomplish the tasks they need.

Usability Testing

There could be an entire book covering this. The idea is to have actual users test your product and you, with their knowledge record, watch what they do. Sometimes, you can learn a lot from how your users use your software. By watching them, you can see that maybe they paused because they were confused or needed to repeat operations that were clumsy at your interface. Using screen capture software and a video camera to capture the actual user so you can sync the two together can help determine what the user was doing while using your software. An alternative is to use user knowledge to capture their interactions with your UI to learn from their usage that way.

After the test, you can talk to your users and ask them about what they are doing. You should try not to interrupt them during their actual usage to avoid impacting their flow or making them self-conscious.

Short-Term Memory and Information

Don't make your users have to remember something from one screen to put on the next screen. Your users, being human, have a limited amount of short-term memory. They likely remember things they need to use fairly often, like their phone number and street address, but they are less likely to know what the city or county lot code for the house is. Seven digits are about the maximum most folks can remember for a short time (yep, the same number as a phone number without the area code). Also, humans are likely to make mistakes by copying things manually, so don't make them copy. Computers are good at that sort of thing.

Languages and Internationalization (I18N)

Internationalization is sometimes shortened to I18N, because it's an "I," and then 18 letters followed by an "N." Yes, it's a long word.

Remember, if your user interface needs to be used at different places in the world, your interface must have strings that change based on the language. Languages around the world are read from left to right, but some languages go right to the left. This means when you create strings that have parameters in them that need to be replaced with values, your implementation should allow for changing their order in some cultures.

This means if you really want to be friendly to those languages and cultures, you might need to even change the data entry order for certain things.

Also, realize that dates, numbers, and money are formatted differently in different cultures, so you should support the formatting for the languages/cultures your application will support. Even sorting order can be impacted by the language and culture, so be sure to test that as well.

Layout/Spacing

How close you put things together or perhaps if you put a box around them can either help relate fields/buttons together or make them appear unrelated. If, in an address field, you put the name, then a huge number of vertical spaces, then the street address, and a huge number of vertical spaces, then the city-state, people might not understand the field usage and be rather confused. So consider how your fields are organized on your page. Be mindful of how close or far explanatory text is from the related fields.

Alignment

If you have columns, make sure the fields in those columns make sense. If there is organization, make sure the text for those fields and the fields themselves are aligned so that the fields look organized. Not having them aligned can slow down the user, as it takes more effort to read the fields/text. Text is often better left aligned so that it keeps a straight column of the text that looks pleasing to the eye and is easier to read.

Sounds

Windows sometimes use sounds to indicate when there is an error, such as when you can't type in a location. Sometimes, it can make sense for a user interface to have sound, for example when you leave your key in the ignition after you turn the car off with the door open or leave the driver's seatbelt off when you start driving.

There might be times when some sound could help alert the user to something they may have forgotten or didn't realize and should be alerted to.

Try to make the sounds appropriate. Sometimes, sounds can be cultural. Also, know that sometimes the lack of sound can be used to indicate an issue if the sound is used for other things. When you close a car door, sometimes you can hear it didn't close at all or didn't close right. If you try to start your car and don't hear any noise, you know there is a problem. Consider the environment your user is in to determine if the sound is appropriate. A library probably doesn't want loud sounds, and if your software is for checking out books, perhaps sounds are not the best option.

Visualizing Data

Computers can have access to a lot of data, so much data that humans can't possibly look at all of it or understand all of it. Part of being a software engineer or user interface or experience specialist is creating visualizations of data to users in ways that can present the data that users need in easily understandable ways. Poor visualization can make the data being misinterpreted or just not understood. If that visualization/graph of the data was supposed to give an operator of dangerous machinery like a nuclear reactor enough information to keep it operating safely, that could be incredibly important. Think carefully about the best way to present data, test it with users, and make sure they can easily understand what you are presenting.

Model View Controller (MVC), Model View Presenter (MVP), or Model View View Model (MVVM)

("Model View Controller—What Is the Difference between MVC and MVVM?" *Stack Overflow*, n.d.) (Krasner & Pope, 1988)

This is an architectural interface pattern used for various types of interfaces. A model can be thought of as dealing with the data. Sometimes, this could just be a class with only data properties. The view would be the presentation of the data for display. The controller would be performing actions with the view based on input.

To help me keep the separation of logic in my head, one way I thought of this is to consider it this way: You might have different views that could use the same controller. Imagine if the view was a dialog. If one customer wanted a custom dialog, it would be cool if it could still act like a view that could work with the controller. A typical way of handling this is to create an interface for the Model, an interface for the view, and an interface for the controller. So to mimic any of those, you just need to implement the interface. Model, View, View Model, and Model View Presenter are basically the same with different names. There are some differences in the way they were used in reality. MVVM is a well-known pattern for Microsoft WPF applications. In WPF, the view has bindings to the View Model by name. Other patterns and implementations might not have as tight a binding.

You will hear different suggestions about how there are subtle differences in these patterns. To me, though, it is still a mix of separation of concerns. There are even some suggestions online that you could use a controller with MVVM, which would potentially be plausible to get a better separation of concerns.

Cognitive Load

When designing user interfaces, you have to remember that there are humans who will be using them. The humans who are using it make mistakes. They don't like repetitive actions. They can only focus on one thing at a time for the most part. Can you remember an entire phone number without reading it from somewhere or repeating it to yourself a few times? Most people can't remember more than about seven digits or so in short-term memory. With long-term memory, you obviously can remember your home phone number because you've had to repeat it so much. Don't make your user copy numbers from one place to another or remember too much information.

You need to think whether your user interface is designed for beginners, intermediates, or experts. How proficient will they be using your software? For example, you can walk up to any ATM machine and use it, even though their interfaces are a little different. They are simple and similar enough that it works out ok. You can pretty much get into any car and drive it because of a similarly easy-to-use interface. Now imagine a nuclear reactor interface. There is probably no way you are designing that for someone who doesn't know something about what they are doing. At the same time, you would want to make it easy enough that critical information and alerts are available when they need it. Those specifics are all very different in the information they provide. They work for different levels of users. Thus, consider your level of user in your designs and their knowledge plus cognitive load.

Reference:

"Model View Controller—What Is the Difference between MVC and MVVM?" *Stack Overflow*. (n.d.). Retrieved September 17, 2022, from https://stackoverflow.com/questions/667781/what-is-the-difference-between-mvc-and-mvvm. License: https://creativecommons.org/licenses/by-sa/2.5/and https://creativecommons.org/licenses/by-sa/3.0/

Technical Disagreements

At some point, you will get into a disagreement about how to implement a particular architecture or feature. If two or more sides are arguing passionately, there might be very good reasons on both sides. If it gets heated, say that you would like to take some time to think about their recommendations. Take a couple of days to think through this more to make sure you're thinking about this the right way. Don't go crazy on an argument. Leave yourself an out, as technical discussions can be very complex and multifaceted and can be hard to grasp completely in the heat of the moment.

Very likely, there are pros and cons and costs to each of the options. There are probably even more options that aren't being discussed. Make a spreadsheet that color codes the pros, cons, and unknowns, so it's easy to visualize which option gives the best set of pros and cons.

If some of the cons have very small risks or vice versa, maybe break those out to a different table, so you are comparing something closer, like apples to apples.

Or make a chart highlighting color and size for the pros and cons.

You might discover a compromise scenario that works better, or you may realize you have been looking at what others have been suggesting, the wrong way.

Once you can really understand the core of each side's argument better, you might be able to formulate a better plan.

You may even need to go back and say, "Look, sorry, I agree. I think with the core idea of what you want to accomplish. I think I just had this concern that I could use your ideas on how to solve."

Then, rather than them being an opposing idea, they can help you solve the concerns that you have.

An example: There was a disagreement about a change for an API. One group of folks recommended using the same ID used presently so that consumers of the API don't see any change in ID or representation; otherwise, it could break downstream consumers. The other side wanted the ID to change, as the parsing code needed to change to parse out the data for display, and the ID would effectively act as a version. In this scenario, a possible compromise solution would allow some internal representation to change, but we would also map it internally so the external API users wouldn't see a change, avoiding breaking the consumers' systems. Or even using just a new ID with a completely new but similar meaning in addition to the existing ID would be a potential compromise.

Here is another idea that can help. Sometimes, people will come up with objections because of things they think are wrong with a solution, but you don't think they are significant issues. You should carefully assess if they are significant issues or not and think if there might be ways to address them. But one way to get the conversation back from a "you vs. them" discussion is saying WE/US. Say to them, "I hear your concerns. I know WE can solve this. Let's think creatively. Are those showstoppers? Are there ways around them? Let US think about this together and come up with a solution. I know WE can."

Sometimes, getting out of the "you vs. them" mentality can bring them back to the table, at least considering what you are talking about.

Deciding If You Should Fix a Bug Now

I know most of you read the title and are probably thinking, "Um, it's a bug, of course we should fix it." The key, though, is when.

Questions to Ask:

Was the bug in earlier versions of the product? If so, how long?
If the bug preexisted, why wasn't it fixed earlier?

Was the bug only present in the last version, or a couple of versions (i.e., newly introduced)?
If it was, you might consider it a higher priority, as customers haven't seen it before and could hit it as they upgrade.

Is There a Reasonable Workaround to Use?
Notice the word "reasonable." It should be something customers are willing to do (that doesn't mean they want to do it, but you can convince them to).

Does This Bug Cause Data Corruption/Inconsistency/Significant Misperception?

Would this bug stop a user/customer from a primary workflow/usage scenario or significantly degrade the workflow to the point customers would consider it unacceptable?

This can be a judgment call if you don't have customer input.

What Is the Effort to Fix This Bug?

If this would take one year to fix and there is a workaround, even if it's unreasonable, you would now need to seriously consider if you should spend the effort to fix the bug or use the workaround in terms of your business costs/customer costs. Effort to fix the bug needs to be weighed against the negatives of the bug.

Is there any other cost to fixing or not fixing the bug?

For example, a customer not renewing a contract.

There may, of course, be more criteria that you might use to decide this. If a customer wanted a bug fixed for a multimillion-dollar contract, someone might really want that as a priority. This should at least give you some basics to start thinking about these types of scenarios.

Testing Private Methods

To summarize some thoughts on how you could test a class that has private methods:

- Test the public interface—confirm that you can cover all of the private methods by calling the public methods.
- Consider a friend class to test.
- Dependency injection might be an option.

- Not ideal, as they have problems, but you could use a tool like Type mock to help if this is a common scenario (Perhaps legacy code, where refactoring all the code may be too costly at the moment).
- Make them public. I know, this is the opposite of a private method, but do they need to be private?
- Use a compiler flag for a special test version to make them public for only that specific test build.

There is no one right answer on how to do this. Pick the most appropriate one for your scenario if you need to test the private methods directly. It would be best to be able to test through the public interface if that is reasonable to do.

Coupling/Decoupling

Coupling is when two or more things have been tied together. This can be via code referencing other code. It can be through references to a shared library. It can even be a higher level of reliance, where an API could potentially be coupling.

The issues caused by coupling can be:

- Hard to maintain.
- Hard to debug.
- Hard to use.
- Brittle; can break easily.

The reverse of this can be called decoupling or breaking these bonds to avoid coupling.

It's always best to avoid coupling when possible and avoid deep coupling whenever possible as well. Doing this can make your app much easier to manage/maintain.

Dependency Injection to the Rescue

Dependency injection comes in a few varied forms, but the general idea is that interfaces can be used to retrieve an underlying object that can service that interface.

When instantiating an object, it can automatically be injected with known objects that support the interfaces it needs. This can avoid direct coupling of one object to another, but it does link them to an interface that an object needs to support.

Dependency Injection Can Help You

- Prevent direct coupling of objects.
- Provide alternative functionality for an interface where needed.
- Automatically instantiate objects with all the related object/ interfaces they need to function.
- Instantiation can be configured to create, or use a singleton, or instantiate new objects per request or other types of lifetimes of objects, if desired.
- Setting up classes to support accepting interfaces to replace some functionality it uses can help with testing, because it makes it easy to mock a class implementing the interface to support your test scenarios.

Dependency Injection Cons

- There is still an indirect coupling of objects that need to come together properly for it to work.
- Configuration needs to be provided in a file, problematically, or both, to make it work.
- Debugging missing injected interfaces can be a pain in the *$#@*!

Imagine a Class:

```
Class WriteMessage {
    public WriteMessage(Iwriter writer) { ... }
    //...
    }
```

You could tell your dependency injector anytime you see an Iwriter interface inject it with a class that supports it as a singleton that writes a log file. Or later, you could change the configuration to have it be a writer that goes to the database.

Thus, dependency injection offers a lot of flexibility, even at the level of configuring completely different output targets.

Root Cause Analysis

Examine a Bug/Process Failure (Root Cause Analysis)

When a problem/bug occurs, you should examine the cause to determine what failures in the process allowed it to occur and to determine corrective actions.

For example, imagine a scenario where a change broke deployments. After examining the issue, it was determined that the original change was made by a team member who didn't understand the rules of one of the deployment files and therefore did not follow standard procedures. Next, it was determined that the change was not tested for all deployment scenarios. On top of that, code reviews missed the issue in the deployment file.

This should be approached by default as a process failure, not an individual fault. There could be more training on the deployment file to ensure anyone making changes knows the rules to follow. Testing should ensure that the code was tested from officially deployed environments and all scenarios tested. Code reviewers can receive additional training and recommendations for scrutiny of deployment file changes.

Avoiding the blame game on individuals focuses on process solutions that impact more than just individuals but help get all the teams on board to find preventive actions and mitigation techniques to prevent future problems.

To really and fully examine the failure for the root cause, you can use methods like the 5 WHYs (Ōno, 1988; Ries, 2010), an idea developed by Taiichi Ohno. Ask why up to five times or more to try to get to the root cause of the issue.

Imagine in our scenario a code change broke deployments:

- Why did the change break deployments?
  - The code didn't set permissions on the file correctly.
- Why didn't the code set permissions correctly?
  - Misunderstanding of the permissions required.
- Why didn't our test automation catch the issue?
  - Our test automation doesn't cover deployments.
- Why doesn't our test automation cover deployments?
  - It's been technical debt that costs a lot to implement.
- Why does deployment automation cost a lot to implement?

- o We don't have an automation framework to help with deployments.

The idea is to ask enough questions to try to get to the root cause of the problem and what you should do about it.

More Detailed Examinations of Failures

- Clearly define the problem in a comprehensive definition.
- Collect facts/evidence as appropriate based on the error (e.g., errors, logs, screen shots, CPU, Memory, Network, Disk, and other related resource utilization, etc.).
- Decide which of the facts/evidence might be irrelevant, symptoms, or root cause.
- The Five WHYs can help you ask questions into the right areas.
- If not clear, brainstorm possible causes/hypothesis:
    - o Come up with ways to test your hypothesis.
    - o Run tests. If you reproduced, move on to the next step, or test and come up with other hypothesis.
    - o If you still can't resolve, consider what you would need to do to figure this out if it happens again (e.g., more logging).
- Create stories/bugs to fix the underlying root cause bug or process issues or to implement additional information collection to find the problem in the future.

You should consider the scientific method when programming, especially think about it when considering how to reproduce bugs.

Formulate your problem statement.

Think about the facts that you know are true or aren't sure about.

Form a hypothesis (basically an idea) of something to try to answer a question about the data you don't know or an attempt to reproduce based on the things that you do know. Change one variable at a time to test. Try it, and if it doesn't work, reevaluate and form another hypothesis to test.

The software can be very complex with many variables. You will need to be systematic about your approach to problem-solving. Use the things you know to guide you to the right test to find the right solution. The great majority of the time, it will be enough to help you find the problem.

If you aren't able to figure it out or reproduce it, think about if you can add logging into a future release to help you find the problem.

When you have run out of ideas, ask your coworkers for help. Sometimes, the answer was right in front of you, but you just couldn't see it. Other times, just talking about the problem might point you in the direction of something to try that can help find the solution.

If you have still run out of ideas, consider if it's a third-party product, and if it makes sense to get support from them. Also, consider more logging or even debugging tools that can capture information when the problem occurs.

Out-of-Memory Issues

When this happens, create a dump file of the program that you can look at in a debugger. If you find out the type of data that is using up memory, it can give you a clue as to where the issue is and how to solve it.

Random Crashes

Microsoft has some tools that can attach to a process and wait for the program to crash and exit. It can capture the memory and stack trace at the time of the crash and create a dump file. You can load the dump file into the debugger and check the call stack to find clues as to the underlying cause.

DebugDiag: https://www.microsoft.com/en-us/download/details.aspx?id=58210

Random Performance Issues

When the app has a high CPU usage, and you don't know why, you can create several memory dump files in a row and examine them to see what methods are being used on the call stack to determine what is using up CPU time. Microsoft has some tools that can record Windows event tracing and tell you what exactly is happening on each CPU and each context switch to each thread so you can diagnose what is happening in your process, even in production. Windows Performance Recorder and Windows Performance Analyzer can help you track down random performance issues on Windows.

Understanding Hardware

Understanding more about the hardware your software can run on can benefit your understanding of how things will work and how they will perform. This can be critical when working on something like a driver for a network card or video card. This can be less important for general development, like web development. But even in general development, sometimes understanding aspects of the hardware environment that is running the software can be beneficial.

CPUs

For example, if you needed to process data using multiple threads, and you randomly decided 10 threads would be good, and they are very CPU intensive threads, and you find out your software will only run on a single CPU machine, then that may not be very efficient. If each thread needs the full CPU time, the computer will be at 100 percent CPU capacity till all threads are done. It could even make the OS slow while processing.

Many home computers have 2–16 processors. Business computers can have 2–128 processors, sometimes more. At the moment, 16–32 core is more common in servers but can be scaled down or up, depending on what is needed.

Many modern CPUs can speed up and slow down based on need.

CPUs are the brain of the machine. Without it, nothing would work. It is what reads instructions that tell it what to do with the machine. Instructions for a CPU could be one byte or more to instruct the CPU on what to do. Many of the instructions for the CPU are very simple, such as loading a value into a register (an area in the CPU that acts like a variable but in very fast memory); writing a value to memory; incrementing a value in a register or in memory; if a register equals a value, jumping to a different place in memory (sort of like a simple form of IF statement in higher-level languages).

Memory

A computer your software is running on may only have a limited amount of memory. If your software requires more memory than the computer has, then it will probably stop working. You should design the software for the environment. It will run on defined hardware based on your software's need, depending on your business requirements.

Most modern home computers have 8–64 GB of memory, depending on cost/configuration. Business servers can have hundreds of GB of memory, depending on the need, cost, and configuration.

Random Access Memory (RAM) at its lowest level is just a bit, which is just a 1 or 0 value. It's hard to believe that everything in your computer is working because of the equivalent of billions of light switches that can turn the memory either on (1) or off (0). A byte of memory is 8 bits. A WORD in memory is 16 bits. A double word or DWORD is 32 bits. RAM is faster than hard disks by a lot. It's faster than an SSD too.

Memory is used to store everything your computer needs to use or execute/run. In order to run a program, the binary code is loaded from the disk/SSD into memory. If there was data included with the program, it is loaded into memory as well. RAM will only store data while power is on. If you turn the computer off, RAM will lose all of its information. This is why you should never just turn off a computer while it's in the middle of doing something. If you do, the RAM will lose all of its information. Suppose that information was important to you, like something you were typing, and it wasn't saved to disk, then that information would disappear.

NUMA Memory (Non-Uniform Memory Access)

Usually, in server machines support, certain banks of memory are faster to access for one processor than another. Normally, the OS is designed to allocate memory for the processor requesting it. It's slower for a processor to access memory in a different bank. There are often APIs on the OS to allocate the faster NUMA memory for the processor currently running.

Disk

You need to design software to stay within and use a reasonable amount of disk space for your business needs.

There are two main types of disks today. Hard Disks have spinning platters and read/write heads that need to move to different parts of the platter to read or write data. Sometimes, these platters are stacked, and there are read/write heads on each platter. These can hold 12 TB of data or more but are relatively slow compared to SSDs.

SSDs have no moving parts and are more like memory. They are much faster than disks with spinning platters. Hard disks have higher latency to read and write data than SSDs, caused by both the need to move the read/write head and to need to wait for spinning platters to bring data to the heads.

SSDs have write limits to a part of it and are basically used up over time (but last long enough that most users won't hit these limits). If one part of the disk is written to more than that limit, it will no longer be able to write to it. To mitigate this issue and handle the failure of cells, early SSDs can map to a still working cell internally. SSDs also have some extra internal capacity to make up for some failures. They also spread writes across its memory to avoid hitting the write limit on any one area.

Also, many SSD technologies need to clear the flash memory before it can write to it again. Some are designed to clear unused areas in a background process to make writing faster by clearing it before it is needed. SSDs also have some interesting technology limitations: When a cell is written, it can impact the surrounding cells a little each time, sometimes to the point of causing data loss at some time between three months to a year or more, depending on the memory technology being used. To mitigate this, a background process will often rewrite old data that has been touched and rewrite nearby cells after certain periods of time to avoid data loss.

You would think with all the SSD limitations, no one would want to use them, but they are just so fast, and most of those limitations end up not being an issue for most users.

Networking

Home-based networking, if hard-wired, is 100 Mb–1 Gb/sec. If Wi-Fi, it can be highly variable and can range based on the distance to the router, around 5 Mb–9.6 Gbps/sec or more, depending on Wi-Fi technology and range.

Internet connections at home can range from 1–2 Mb/sec to as much as ~1 Gb/sec for some cable or fiber connections.

Business networking can be faster for hard-wired fiber from 1–10 Gb to even 40 Gb or more, depending on configuration/bonded connections or more.

Cache Memory

Regular memory, compared to processor speeds, is rather slow. To help compensate for that, there can be three levels of cache memory from fastest to slowest (and often from the smallest size to the larger size): L1, L2, L3. They usually range in size from 1 MB to 10s of MB. This means code that accesses smaller amounts of memory can run faster than if it's reading and writing large amounts of memory. Cache memory is often allocated in cache lines that can be different on different hardware. On some Intel hardware, it can be around 128 bytes. This knowledge can be useful in multithreading, as accessing the same area of memory within the same cache line from multiple threads can make memory access slower (especially when one is writing to the memory). This can force flushing the cache line to regular, slower DRAM memory. When this is purposely done, it helps keep memory in sync. But two threads accessing close in memory (within the same cache line/size) can cause slowness for access to that memory. This is known as "false sharing" of memory, since the hardware is acting like it's being shared and requiring slower memory access to sync.

Most development isn't that performance sensitive and doesn't need to worry about these concerns/limits. If you are trying to push computing speed to the maximum, then perhaps this type of information can be useful.

Sound Cards

Sound Cards give you a way to play audio output. It could be playing sound for a video, music, game sounds, or more. Many sound cards can handle MIDI so that you can load instrument samples such as piano, guitar, and others, and have it play the music you program yourself. Sound can even overlap, so you can have more than one sound playing at once (which is obviously useful for things like games).

Graphics Cards

Graphics cards enable a visualization of data as output in the computer. Simple modes can adjust to your monitor for the right horizontal/vertical resolution and refresh rate supported by your monitor and card. Drawing internal can control the colors and brightness of each of the pixels in the supported resolution. Many graphics cards today can support multiple monitors, allowing you to see more data on the screen at once, which can be very useful. Graphics cards have high-speed video memory onboard and a GPU (Graphics Processing Unit). Many mid-level GPUs have hundreds of processing units, giving them the ability to process many graphics calculations at once. GPUs are very good with array/vector/vertices in terms of math processing. They can process many types of math operations concurrently up to the number of processing units supported on the card. This functionality is great for 3D graphic rendering. It can also sometimes be really good for crypto-mining and machine learning use cases. ("What Is a GPU? Graphics Processing Units Defined," n.d.)

FPGAs (Field Programmable Gate Arrays)

You can think of these like a programmable parallel processor. Depending on the hardware implementation, you can do simplistic processing of data simultaneously on multiple bytes of data. With the right hardware, you could parse a million bytes of data simultaneously. While these are not close to quantum computers, they might be the closest thing available now, so much so that some quantum computer simulators use FPGAs. Companies in the financial industry were experimenting with using these to reduce the latency of trading data.

This isn't a normal part of most computers, but it is present in some of the Intel server hardware, and you can buy these separately.

Networking

Networking is the way computers communicate with each other, either locally like on your local Wi-Fi or corporate network, or remotely over the Internet.

Ethernet Network Interface Cards (NIC)/Wi-Fi

Computers often come with network cards built in. The network cards create the ability to send bits over wires from the computer to usually switches and routers that can send the information to other networks, then computers. Wi-Fi can send bits over radio waves instead of a network cable.

Data Transmission

If you wanted to send data, you would likely use one of the standard protocols available (Hunt, n.d.) (HTTP, SMTP, TELNET, FTP). Underneath those protocols, use the TCP protocol; other protocols can use UDP. The most common protocols being used today are likely HTTP, TCP, or UDP, though the others are still rather common.

If you just want to send data from one local computer to another, you might use the TCP protocol. If you want to send 100,000 bytes of data, you will open a connection to the other computer (IP address and port) that must be listening for that connection. Then you would send the data. The TCP protocol would then break your data into packets that can send packets of different sizes. Let's say it was 1500 bytes. This isn't just your data being sent. It includes additional information needed to route the packet to the right computer and more. There is a header set of bytes that has additional information. The header contains at least the size of the packet, a checksum to check for packet errors, a sequence number to make sure packets get assembled into the right order, an IP address of the source and destination computers, and a source and destination port number on the target computer. At the lower level, packets can be broken into frames of bits (0s and 1s).

Switches

Switches allow computers and devices on the same network to communicate. Let's say your switch has four ports to plug in an Ethernet cable. The switch could take a frame going from the computer on plug 1 to the computer on plug number 4.

Routers

Routers help get the frames/packets to other computers, potentially on other local networks or remote networks like the Internet. Computers on the local network often know the router as the default gateway and will send packets through it if they are connecting to a computer not on the local network/switch.

Networking Wire and Latency

You would think the data you send would arrive at the speed of light/ electricity to the other computer. While in some ways that is true, the reality is that the data you send will arrive much slower than that. To send the information, your data has to be converted to 0s and 1s on the wire through electrical states on the wires.

Let's say 1 is 2 volts, and zero is 0 volts. This transition from 2 volts to 0 volts and back can only happen so fast, as the networking hardware is designed for only a certain speed. If that speed were 100 megabits per second, and you divided it by 1, 000 milliseconds, you get about 100,000 bits per millisecond. If we divide it by 10 (8 bits plus – 2 bits of estimated frame overhead per byte), we get roughly 10,000 bytes per millisecond.

Usually, there is protocol overhead on top of that, and it does not account for errors. If you needed to send 50,000 bytes of data over a 100 Mbps link, you have a nearly guaranteed latency of at least 5 ms for the full amount of data to get there. If this were a Gigabit link, it would be much better at 0.5 ms. This can be important for games, stock market trading, video/audio links, and more. This is similar, though often much worse, over Wi-Fi based on the link speed, interference, distance, and more.

TCP vs. UDP

TCP protocol requires a specific connection to another computer. TCP also will resend packets that had errors and reassemble them in the correct order. UDP doesn't require a specific connection and can broadcast channels to multiple devices on the network at the same time (multicast). For the protocol, UDP does not automatically rebroadcast any packets with errors, so the program using it will be required to do that. UDP can be very efficient and fast if the application using it can handle the error scenarios. For example, low latency applications can often benefit from UDP. Even voice or video could benefit if the protocol can prefer a slight degradation in quality due to a lost packet rather than a delay in data due to a slower, lossless protocol, like TCP (Hunt, n.d.).

TIP: For UDP, make sure the networking hardware that will be used can support all the multicast channels you need.

File Systems

Operating systems often support several types of file systems. There are some legacy file systems around that can still be in use, such as FAT or FAT32. Some of the older systems could easily become corrupted, such that the file is no longer organized correctly or doesn't have the proper contents anymore. Newer filesystems like NTFS tend to handle software and some hardware failures better, such that the file systems are less likely to become corrupted. Older file systems had much smaller limits on the disk sizes and file sizes they could support.

There are many other types of file systems: NFS, EXT2, EXT3, XFS, FAT (*Filesystems*, n.d.)

Certain file systems have additional built-in features like the ability to compress or encrypt files or add permissions. Some file systems are designed to scale better than others.

File systems usually live within a disk partition. Disks can be partitioned into continuous areas to allow placing multiple of the same or different file systems on a disk.

File systems obviously handle files, plus directories. They often have a place on the disk, or multiple places on the disk, where they keep track of the files and directory information for that disk.

A file can live at different portions of the disk. It might not be a contiguous area of the hard drive or SSD. File systems can become fragmented over time. To keep track of which part of the disk has been used for a file, the private internal directory management location can keep track of areas of the disk that were used for a file, so it knows where to go to get the parts of the file.

File systems usually provide tools that you can run to defragment the file system to improve the performance of reading and writing files by having them be in contiguous locations (more of an issue for hard disks than SSDs). Hard disks are often organized into tracks (a circular area of the disk) and sectors (a part of the circular track). The size in bytes of those areas can depend on what the hard disk supports. Even though SSDs don't have a disk, they are often formatted in the same way as if they did.

XML/HTML/CSS

There are many technologies that make up what you see on the Internet. Here are some of the main ones.

XML

Extensible Markup Language (XML) is a type of generic language used for formatting textual format types of documents that can be used for a variety of purposes to store or transmit data. This was designed to be readable by people and computers, so it was possible to understand the organization and data.

The benefits are that people can read it to understand it so that, in theory, it is easier for people, developers and others, to use. This is a common format used for the entire Internet and APIs.

The downside is that it uses more data/space than a binary format to store or interpret, so it can take longer to process. Usually, it's fast enough, though, that the readable format outweighs any additional processing time. That may not be the case for every scenario or usage. (*Extensible Markup Language (XML) 1.0 (Fifth Edition)*, n.d.)

A very simple xml document:

```
<?xml version="1.0">
<mydoc>
</mydoc>
```

There is the header which will have something like <?xml version""1."">.

This is followed by the open tag (Element), in this case <mydoc>, but that name can be anything. There should be a closing tag (Element) for the document </mydoc>. Notice the first line has a VERSION that is an attribute, and it has a value of""1."".

XML elements can be nested to allow you to create a hierarchy:

```
<yourdoc>
<Email From="me@me.com"
To="you@you.com">
<Subject>Hi</Subject>
</Email>
</yourdoc>
```

You can use different element and attribute names. There are variants of XML that define the elements and attributes you should use. You might have heard of Hypertext Markup Language (HTML).

HTML

(*HTML Standard,* n.d.)

HTML is what the Internet is built using. The browser receives this from web servers and uses it to render what you see as a web page.

(*HTML Basic,* n.d.)

HTML Document below:

```
<!DOCTYPE html>
    <html>
    <body>
    Hi
    </body>
    </html>
```

The above is a very simple web page. You might notice it fits the requirements of XML with opening and closing elements. It supports attributes as well. HTML expects specific elements to display in a web browser. All web pages of any complexity will use this. Other technologies are used as well.

CSS

Cascading Style Sheets (CSS) is used to apply different styles to elements. That could be color, fonts.

```
<style>
h1 {
color: blue;
}
</style>
```

This would change all of the h1 elements to the color blue on the page.

JavaScript

JavaScript can also be used on a web page to make the pages more interactive, even actively changing the page without needing to make requests to the server. Most browsers support JavaScript.

Web Servers

Two of some of the most popular web servers are:

- Apache is an open-source web server that can run on many operating systems.
- Internet information server (Microsoft's web server service) can run on Windows and some other OS.

Common Web Programming languages

There are many programming languages used on servers and browsers to create web pages. These include:

- HTML/CSS
- JavaScript
- PHP

- Java
- C#
- Ruby
- Python
- SQL

References:

Extensible Markup Language (XML) 1.0 (Fifth Edition). (n.d.). Retrieved September 26, 2022, from https://www.w3.org/TR/REC-xml/

HTML Standard. (n.d.). Retrieved September 26, 2022, from https://html.spec.whatwg.org/multipage/#toc-dom

HTML Basic. (n.d.). Retrieved September 17, 2022, from https://www.w3schools.com/html/html_basic.asp

Resource Utilization

CPU Utilization

At some point, you will want to measure the CPU utilization of your code and of other things running while your code is running. Most of the time, the operating system provided metrics will show you a good approximation of the CPU usage. In some extreme cases, it may not. Some OS resource monitoring happens at intervals. For the CPU, it may wake up every millisecond and check to see if a CPU is busy (1, 000 times a second). Over the course of one second, if 500 of the 1, 000 times it woke up and checked it was busy, it would calculate the CPU is 50 percent utilized (500/1, 000). But what if there was code using the same system clock waking up every one millisecond, then running for a few millionths of a second and going back to sleep? If it woke up at the same time the CPU utilization check was run, the CPU would appear to be 100 percent utilized, when in fact, it's a much smaller amount.

If OS had a better way to measure CPU utilization, like CPU clock time used per thread, and to calculate at intervals, it might not calculate it this way. On Windows, it does not, so it can sometimes show a misrepresentation of CPU utilization. The same could be true for other resources if they are measured in a similar way, which depends on the resources as to whether it's just checking for activity compared to how much activity when it wakes up to check resource utilization.

Prototyping

Prototyping can be a great way to test out changes, architectural design, and more.

Usually, these are quick and dirty implementations that include the main functionality and architecture. They might be used for testing basic performance or other characteristics of the design/implementation to determine its suitability for a particular task. Make sure folks know this will very likely be throw-away code and will just prove the basics of the design but not necessarily the correctness of an implementation.

A prototype might sufficiently mimic the functionality, possibly even in different languages, as long as a result is deemed similar enough to determine a course of action. Imagine you have a piece of SQL code, and you want multiple threads of it to run. You could simulate that right in SQL. However, in the real code, you plan to use multiple C# threads to run it. The SQL code may be good enough for the prototype to determine the performance and suitability since it should run equivalently when the launching is moved to C#.

Windowing Systems

All major operating systems have some type of windowing system that comes with them. Windows, Android, iOS, Linux, Mac, and Unix all have a type of windowing system.

Browser implementation of HTML could probably be considered a type of windowing system (though limited to the browser window).

You have most certainly used these systems if you use Windows, Android, iOS, etc. It is what allows you to see and input data on the screen.

If you have never tried developing user interfaces before, it can take a bit of getting used to if you've just been writing more simplistic sequential programs. Windowing systems often employ events everywhere to handle various different UI conditions, such as a focus event where a text control gets focus.

Getting used to processing code by events, compared to sequential code for some folks, can take some time.

You should take care not to interrupt/interfere with the flow of events to controls. Follow the well-established patterns closely to avoid causing control or other event issues.

Also, in UI, event-driven programming testing can be more difficult, because there are so many events that are making your program work correctly. If you think about the number of events going through the system and the potential combinations of events fired, you can see why it might be hard to uncover all the bugs.

To test, you will likely need to find a third-party product to send commands to the UI so you can test your UI as it is. You could build your own or use some hybrid with some open-source code, if absolutely needed. For instance, Selenium is great for helping with browser testing.

Care needs to be taken when building automation for UIs. If not careful, it is easy to cause many tests to fail with slight changes to the interface. Having the test code find UI elements by a specific element name rather than location could prevent some types of failures. For example, some browser test automation might allow the recording of user input to be played back for testing. Depending on the method the recording uses to determine the next action, it might not work if the UI is altered slightly. Let's imagine if the recording found a web element by the label name, but later that label needed to be renamed slightly or due to translations appeared with an altered name; here, the test would fail.

Multithreading

Many windowing systems are single threaded and typically run on the main UI thread. This means if you need some blocking or long-running activity, you would need to have that work done on a background thread to avoid the user interface being hung waiting on that activity.

It is dangerous for another thread to directly call or interact with a UI element/thread, as it can interrupt the flow of events being sent to them, and the UI itself is not designed to handle multiple threads calling it.

There are two primary ways for a user interface to retrieve information from a background thread. The first is a shared variable or memory area that is protected by a thread synchronization object (e.g., critical section, monitor, mutex). The user interface could then poll the shared variable for information when needed. It shouldn't do this in a tight loop, as it would block the user interface. In Windows, for example, you could use a UI timer that triggers a certain number of milliseconds to poll the background information (C# Time Class System.Windows.Forms as one example).

UI timers are different from other timers. They are designed to post a message on the main UI thread so that the handling of the timer can happen on the UI thread. That allows the manipulation of UI components from the timer event. From the UI timer event, you can poll the shared variable.

In the second way, if you just want a notification when something happens from a background thread, that requires using specific methods for a thread to post an event to the main UI thread from another thread. Then the main UI thread processes that message later and usually calls a method to handle the action on the UI thread so that it can safely update UI controls. Windows forms, for instance, have Control.Invoke that can be called from a background thread with a delegate (a reference to a method that will be called on the UI thread).

Double Check Locking

The need for volatile with the double-check locking pattern for C#

There have been many articles written about double-check locking. Such as whether it is safe to use on .NET or other platforms/compilers/languages and if the volatile keyword is needed.

Double-check locking is safe on the .NET platform running on x86 hardware (if implemented correctly), though it may not be in other languages/platforms/hardware due to their memory models.

Below is an example of the traditional style of double-checked locking.

```
Public class Singleton {
private static volatile Singleton _instance = null; //does this need to be volatile? Best answer is Yes.
private static Object _locker = new Object();
public static Singleton GetValue()
{
  if (_instance == null)
  {
    lock(_locker)
    {
      if (_instance == null)
      { _ instance = new Singleton(); }
    }
```

```
        }
        return _instance;
    }
```

Volatile avoids some compiler-level optimizations, so it will access the variable directly in memory. This hints to the compiler the variable is used on multiple threads. You would in most cases not need to use this if the variable use was inside a synchronization objects protection.

As you'll see in this article ("Understand the Impact of Low-Lock Techniques in Multithreaded Apps"), technically, if you are running on an x86 machine with the Microsoft version of .NET, this would "work" without using volatile: ("Understanding Low-Lock Techniques in Multithreaded Apps" | *Microsoft Learn*, n.d.) https://msdn.microsoft.com/en-us/magazine/cc163715.aspx#S10.

The basic explanation of why it "works" in specific cases without volatile is that the x86 memory model and the .NET memory model allow it to work at the moment with the current implementations of x86 CPUs and .NET compiler/JIT. Many people point to this article as proof that volatile is not needed since it seems to be from a very authoritative source—Vance Morrison, a lead on the Microsoft JIT team.

In this article, he even shows a way to completely remove locks from a typical double-check locking implementation but does note that you could end up with multiple objects that way for a singleton (he doesn't mention that would mean that your singleton shouldn't maintain any state if it is used that way, since it could lose some information for other instances of the singleton get lost/collected).

At the end of the article, Vance Morrison makes these general low-lock techniques and volatile usage more clear and suggests the use of volatile:

If you need more convincing, for non-MS implementations, if you want to follow the ECMA spec and be sure this will work for all memory models/hardware that follow it, it is best to add the volatile keyword.

("C#—The C# Memory Model in Theory and Practice" | *Microsoft Learn*, n.d.) https://msdn.microsoft.com/en-us/magazine/jj863136.aspx

The ECMA group wrote up a spec that allows for a more flexible memory model than Microsoft, presently implemented to allow for more optimizations on different platforms. If you follow the guidelines for the ECMA spec and use volatile, you are much more likely to be able to work across more platforms and be future-proof to some extent.

If you need any further convincing, in a more recent article, volatile usage gets clarified that while it may work on x86 and Itanium at the moment, it doesn't work on ARM and may not work in x86/Itanium or other architectures in the future ("C#—The C# Memory Model in Theory and Practice"; "C#—The C# Memory Model in Theory and Practice, Part 2" | *Microsoft Learn*, n.d.)

https://msdn.microsoft.com/en-us/magazine/jj883956.aspx

Summary: Recommendation for Old Style Double-Check Locking: If you are going to use this older style of double-check locking, either use the volatile keyword or use the VolatileRead and VolatileWrite functions for any access done outside of a lock/synchronization construct.

There are a few reasons:

1. It's the safest standard thing to do, as this will match that ECMA spec to allow running on a wider variety of hardware/platforms if you might ever need that (e.g., Mono).
2. Many of the articles (except "The C# Memory Model in Theory and Practice") don't take into account other factors like if the field was touched elsewhere and if the JIT/Compiler does start to support enregistration of class fields (putting them into CPU registers as an optimization; this is currently done for local variables and it is suggested in the future they might do it for fields). Will Microsoft ever change this? Hard to say. I suspect

much multithreaded code would break if fields were allowed to be put in CPU registers without some really intelligent compiler implementations. But we know on some platforms, just the nature of the hardware platform can make this tricky, so better safe than sorry, use the volatile keyword or appropriate volatile read/write functions.

The New way:

Here is an alternative example using the lazy init provided by the .NET framework to avoid having to worry about possible issues with double-check locking.

Microsoft decided to make it easier for people trying to implement the lazy initialization pattern by using the new Lazy<T>, so that they do not need to worry about the internals that make it happen.

```
public class MySingleton
{
    private static readonly Lazy<MySingleton> _myInstance
      = new Lazy<MySingleton>(() => new MySingleton());
   private MySingleton()
   {
   }
    public static MySingleton MyInstance
    {
      get
      {
        return _myInstance.Value;
      }
    }
}
```

Unicode

Most modern computing started with the English ASCII character set. Most of the characters that were standard were in the 0 to 127 range. This is what many developers in the English/Western world learn. It's pretty easy. One character fits in one byte. Moving through strings is easy in code, one byte at a time.

Unicode was invented because software needs to support every character on the planet, and left-to-right and right-to-left character sets, and sorting can be quite a bit more complex. Unicode can be thought of as a numerical representation of a character in a language/culture. Something like UTF-8 is the way to encode that Unicode value to be used.

There are many variations of encodings. These are just some of them:

("The Absolute Minimum Every Software Developer Absolutely, Positively Must Know About Unicode and Character Sets (No Excuses!)," *Joel on Software*, n.d.)

Encoding	Min size (bytes)	Max size(bytes)
UTF-8	1	6
UTF-16	2	4
UCS-2	2	2
UCS-4	4	4

There are other encodings like UTF-7 (high bit is zero), UTF-32, and more. The most common by far today are UTF-8 and UTF-16. UTF-8 is pretty efficient for English-like languages that can use the same number of bytes as ASCII for normal ASCII encodings. You should know UCS can be in big-endian and little-endian variants.

In this international world today, most strings should take into account Unicode to allow for language/character differences.

String Manipulation

If you are manipulating strings, you can't just go through strings byte by byte without taking into account the encoding of the string (if you were using a fixed byte encoding, you perhaps could go 2 or 4 bytes at a time). For variable byte encodings, though, you can only go forward, not backward, through strings to manipulate them and handle the encoding correctly. Some usages of string manipulation may require a collation as well. Some SQL usages might require it, for example. There might not be one collation that works well. To parse properly, it may require the actual locale the data is in. Either knowing and storing it or perhaps detecting it.

Sorting

Unicode and related encodings are sorted differently from normal ASCII. The collation/sorting culture will need to be used to compare/sort strings. It is best to use the built-in capabilities of your language if it has them.

Fonts

In some ways, in the Windows world, you just need to make sure the fonts support the Unicode characters you need. Rarely is it that easy, though, as many fonts provided offer just one culture and may not even cover all characters. So a font for Chinese is often a specific dialect of Chinese, and you need another font for others. This can make finding fonts for Unicode support quite challenging, as selecting one font will work for some characters, and another font will work for others. You will need to find the right set to support the ones likely needing to be used by your users of the software. Given how varied that can be, that can be quite difficult.

Google offers some public domain fonts (https://developers.google.com/fonts). You can check and see if those help. If you didn't know already, fonts are protected just like software, so you can't just use a random font you find in your software unless it's public domain; otherwise, you might need to license it.

("The Absolute Minimum Every Software Developer Absolutely, Positively Must Know About Unicode and Character Sets (No Excuses!)," *Joel on Software*, n.d.)

Notes

Microsoft SQL server nchar nvarchar use UCS-2 often by default, newer versions of SQL server can support UTF-8. ("Collation and Unicode Support—SQL Server" | *Microsoft Learn*, n.d.)

Security

Security is essential for today's software systems.

Think carefully about both what authenticated and unauthenticated threats can do to or with your software. This means threats can come from outside or inside. An insider who previously worked at your firm could leak information that grants an attacker enough information to succeed in an attack.

Make sure you consider the supply chain as a vector for possible attacks against your systems. Any software you use for your firm will need to be protected and, if possible, isolated from other systems or at least monitored.

An example of this was the well-known SolarWinds attack that compromised their systems to allow the installation of malicious code onto hundreds if not thousands of other companies, including some government sites. SolarWinds was often given very high permissions to run on whatever server/machine they accessed, so they had the ability to do almost anything.

Such examples show that update systems can not only be used to keep your system secure but also as an attack vector.

- Check the third-party systems you are trusting on your network; isolate them if you can.
- Make sure to encrypt any passwords in your system using password-safe hash algorithms. These are more involved than regular hash algorithms and usually take longer to run, making it harder for brute force password attacks of the hash.
- Build your systems with security in mind. Don't let unauthenticated, unauthorized, unprotected activity run actions they should not.
- Encrypt data at rest whenever possible.
- Use encrypted connections between any external systems and ideally even internal systems.
- Don't try to invent your own encryption or crypto safe hashes. Trust the APIs the industry uses for current best practice and use those. Encryption is hard, and even experts can get it wrong, so non-experts are unlikely to do better than existing algorithms and are likely to do worse.
- Protect against the OWASP top 10 security risks (https://owasp.org/).

Privacy

Privacy is becoming more and more important when building software systems. As more and more of our life is now digitally online, there is a greater risk of significant harm and invasion of privacy than ever before.

Digital ads keep track of everything you do online. What if you had health problems that were tracked, and health insurers started to deny coverage to people based on the risk of what you have been searching for?

What if your digital life could be rated online, and your rating was used to deny you the use of taxis, planes, trains, where you could live, and what you could buy? It sounds far-fetched, like the *Black Mirror* episode, but things like this are already happening in some countries. Think about it, this happens nearly every day, even in the US.

Recently, we tried to book a home rental online through a very well-known travel site, and the person renting didn't trust us because we didn't have a rating yet on the site since we hadn't used it before. Uber already said that a low rating by a rider might prevent them from getting rides.

There are definitely positives and negatives from that, but what happens when you are rated unfairly? What do you do?

What happens if your location is leaked online and someone who saw you had a really nice watch tracked you and followed you home?

There are all sorts of risks to potentially your life and your privacy.

When designing software systems, consider all of these. Protect your users' right to privacy. Don't collect the information you don't need. Don't use the information for a purpose that is not needed for the core functionality the user wants from your product. Tell your users what you will use that information for. Let users opt out of permissions, and allow your app to keep functioning as much as possible with the lesser permissions.

There are many privacy requirements by law from EU countries now. Make sure you follow them and even do more to protect your customers' data/privacy.

Even if you need some data for certain feature use, consider if it would be possible and reasonable to allow your users to opt out and use the feature in a different way. For example, a lot of apps ask to enable your location to find local restaurants, but many also offer the option to type in a city, state, or zip code.

Consider supporting eff.org. They help support individuals' digital privacy and rights.

Public Key Crypto Systems

Public Key Crypto Systems

Public key systems underlay the security that you use every day to browse the web. The https (TLS) secure web links you use every day use public key cryptography to be able to exchange encrypted information.

Traditional symmetric encryption requires a shared key that both parties that need to communicate know. If, let's say, we took a stupid simple cipher of adding 1 to everything, then the person on the receiving side would need to know to subtract 1. That means 1 is your shared secret.

To share that private secret, you needed to give the other person that number securely, either in person or via some secure, trusted communication channel that you know would not be intercepted.

Public key works differently. There is no shared secret, which means two people don't need to meet and don't initially need a secure communication channel to exchange a shared secret. For each user, there is a private key used to decrypt things encrypted with that user's public key.

Imagine users A and B:

A freely gives public key and posts it on the Internet for anyone to use.

B freely gives public key and posts it on the Internet for anyone to use.

A wants to send a message to B.
A encrypts a message with B's public key.
B decrypts the message with B's private key.

B wants to send a message to A.
B encrypts a message with A's public key.
A decrypts the message with A's private key.

So, in this case, public keys can be posted for anyone to use, and the only person who can read messages encrypted with the public key is the person who holds the private key.

This has been an incredible leap for secure communications, allowing the setup of a secure way to communicate with anyone without the need to share a private secret.

Luckily, math came to the rescue to create this for us. It's really not too complicated for a lot of folks to understand.

The process:

Choose prime numbers p and q

N = p * q

Z = (p-1) * (q-1)

Pick a random number e where 1 < e < z and e has no common factors with z

Find d where ((e*d)-1) is evenly divisible by z

Note: In my testing, I also needed to add (and e!=d)

Public key is (n,e)

Private Key is (n,d)

M = Message to encrypt

Encrypted Message (EM) = M^e mod n (uses public key values to encrypt)

Decrypted Message = (EM) ^d mod n (uses private key values to decrypt)

Example code below shows the relatively basic math that underlies public key systems that form the foundation of web security. To simplify the code to make it easier to understand, less than optimal algorithms were chosen, so this won't work for a large prime. Also, for secure encryption, additional things are done to make the encryption harder to crack. This sample is just to show the core logic principles that make public/private key encryption work.

```
Random random = new Random();   //Not suitable for actual
encryption. Use crypto random.
int p = 229, q = 107;           //pick two prime numbers (obviously
MUCH bigger than these for
                                //real use. Small numbers used to focus
on the code.)

int n = p * q;  //n= number to use with modulo operator

int z = (p - 1) * (q - 1);  // computer one higher than the limit of e
(z=72)

// 1 < e < z  Find an e (pick a random number that matches the
criteria
//Also has no common factors with z - I used IsPrime to enforce this
but it really only
//needs to avoid common factors - Don't ever use this random
number generator for real
// encryption (use a cryptographic random number generator)
int e = random.Next(2, z - 1);

while (!IsPrime(e))  //This IsPrime is too slow for large prime's ok
for tiny
    e=random.Next(2, z - 1);
```

```
//find a good d where (e*d)-1 % z=0 (evenly divisible by z)
// This is probably not the best way to find a d that works
// But a quick dirty algo that seemed to work (Too slow for large prime's don't use)
// Some writeups say d < z
int d;
for (d=1; d < z; d++)
{
  if ((((e * d) - 1) % z) == 0 && e!=d)
    break; //d is good
}

//visualize our key pairs
var publicKey = (n, e);
var privateKey = (n, d);

//We will encrypt the letter A which is 65
BigInteger messageToEncrypt = 'A';

//Encrypt our message (umm well character in this case)
BigInteger encryptedMessage = BigInteger.ModPow(messageToEncrypt, publicKey.e, publicKey.n);

//Decrypt our message - result will be 65 'A'
BigInteger decryptedMessage = BigInteger.ModPow(encryptedMessage, privateKey.d, privateKey.n);
```

//IsPrime(n) is from Wikipedia (*Primality Test—Wikipedia*, n.d.) https://en.wikipedia.org/wiki/Primality_test

Thanks to this website (*One Big Fluke › Simplest Explanation of the Math behind Public Key Cryptography*, n.d.) (https://www.onebigfluke.

com/2013/11/public-key-crypto-math-explained.html) for explaining the math.

Don't use this code anywhere near production. It was just a quick and dirty way to demonstrate at a low level the basic math/variables needed for public key. It doesn't use cryptographic random number generation or other items.

Also note that with low prime numbers like shown here in testing, overlap and issues with encrypting values in the message were higher than those components.

Signatures

Public key signatures are a brilliant way to confirm who wrote/created something digital. It's created by the owner encrypting information or a time stamp and owner information with their own private key. By doing that, someone who sees the users' public key only has to decrypt the signature with their publicly available key and can thus prove the creator was the owner of that public key (and obviously the corresponding private key, which is considered signed).

Certificates

These are usually issued from an issuing authority (or can be self-issued). They have a bit more information in them like website/URL, owner, expiration dates, and issuing authority, and they are signed by the issuing authority. They also includes the public key to whom the certificate was issued. In addition, there is a corresponding private key kept by the owner of that certificate.

Exception Handling

```
try
    {
      ... // Code that might throw exception here
    }
    catch (Exception e)
    {
     // Be sure to add logging here for any failures
    }
    finally
    {
      //make sure code that executes here is unlikely to cause further
exceptions
      ...
    }
```

Exception handling should be used for exceptional circumstances. That means exception handling shouldn't be used as just a method of flow control in your program. Exceptional should also mean it does not happen very often.

Why does this matter? First, because exceptions, at least in C# and other languages, are a lot slower than other types of scenarios of just returning an error value, so if it happens often, you could significantly slow down your code.

Second, other developers will expect exceptions to only happen in exceptional circumstances, so they likely won't follow the flow. It can also be harder to figure out where things went depending on how far up the exception handling has to bubble up.

Third, there is an expectation wherever there is an exception. It gets logged. If this happened often, there would be too many logs, or if you didn't log in because it was usual, someone might have a misconception about what the code is doing and "fix" it (thus breaking it).

For example, if you are parsing a field that can contain a number or a string, you wouldn't want that parsing code to throw an exception all the time, since it's normal for users to type different things into a field.

The "finally" block is typically used to make sure to close/dispose of any resources you were using.

In exception code, you should decide how to put the code into the most stable state possible. If the code was in the middle of a database transaction, that might roll it back. If it was a calculation, decide what the safest thing to do might be.

Sometimes, if your code has no possible way to recover or it's an unknown exception case, the safest thing to do is nothing other than log or alert your support team that an error occurred and exit. Don't continue with bad data that would cause more corruption. Think through the recovery scenarios whether that is a likely one you should be able to handle.

For example, there could be a way to retry a database transaction if it failed due to a timeout. However, if the code failed due to another error converting a value of a string to an int, it might not be recoverable in the transaction, so retries may not be possible.

Every method that is written should consider these things.

Proof of Concept (POC)

A POC implementation can be a great way to prototype a concept quicker than you could normally to see if it meets certain criteria that would be required of it. Depending on what is being built, you can ignore certain aspects of the development process, like testing, even performance, aesthetics, or anything you aren't concerned about for the test purpose of a POC. You might build it just to test the look and feel; then performance might matter less. Or you might build it to test performance; then UI might not matter. Using this method can get quick answers to questions.

The concern many folks have with building POCs is that it sometimes looks so good, people say, "Great! Let's ship it now!" However, it was built ignoring areas of best practice in the implementation to get answers to questions about the design earlier, so these should be considered possibly throw-away code and not usable in the final implementation.

Sometimes, even before starting a POC, it might be worth taking a step back to see if there is some initial testing you could do to simulate the functionality as early as possible. That way, you can be more sure the effort you put into it will be worthwhile, since they can still take time to build. For example, you may have had a process running two threads, and you were planning to enhance it with some new functionality, but it required four threads. One question in your mind might be if the load on the server might be too high with more threads. If the POC might take a month to build, would there be a way to simulate the load sooner? In our case, it turned out we could tune our existing application to more threads to see the load. It wouldn't perfectly mimic the new functionality, but it would be a close enough proxy. That way, if the load of data looks good, we could have more confidence building the POC.

Object-Oriented Languages

Object-oriented languages are considered one of the great foundations of a language, allowing a great amount of flexibility for the reuse of code and organizing code in ways that make sense.

Derived Classes

Object-oriented languages allow creating derived classes.

Class Animal { Eat(); Sleep(); ...}

Class Dog : Animal { ... }

Since a dog can eat, sleep and do many base things an animal can do, it makes sense to derive a Dog from Animal that allows a dog to inherit the base functionality that an Animal can do.

Many languages can handle deriving from multiple base objects to further code reuse.

Polymorphism

Object-oriented languages allow polymorphism: You can make a derived method of the same name do something different from the base if you desire.

So you could have an Animal object with a function where FavoriteFood() returns nothing. But when a Dog object is derived from it, then it overrides FavoriteFood() and returns "kibble" or something like that. The ability to make a function with the same name do the appropriate thing for the object is polymorphism.

Criticism

Some of the recent concerns about object-oriented languages are that they are complex and hard to maintain when you have many levels of derivation and overriding of base functionality.

Overly complex derivation and overriding can make things harder to debug and understand. The best suggestion is to just balance these to keep them as understandable as possible and keep the depth only to the level that is needed, leaving it as shallow as you can.

Doing that should help mitigate some of the concerns about object-oriented languages.

Software Patterns

There are lots of patterns in software. There are some standard patterns of coding that were discovered to repeat themselves over time. Those patterns were documented (Gamma, 1995).

Here are some popular ones:

Creational Patterns

Singleton

This is pretty simple, instantiating one class that is used by multiple classes. Sometimes, the singleton is lazy initialized during the first time it is accessed.

Factory

Instead of creating a class like:

MyClass class= new MyClass();

Often, you would create an interface that can implement what is needed:

IAutomobile car= AutomobileFactory.CreateCar("Jeep");

This way, your factory can create different types of cars that you can use.

Others

Abstract factory: Multiple object factories for creating different groups of objects

Builder: Think of this as a pattern for a class to build multiple parts of a complex object.

–Prototype: Just think of this as the ability to clone an object that would be too expensive to create a new one in the normal way.

Object.clone();

Structural Patterns

Adapter

You can think of adapter pattern as just a way to change one API to match another.

It could be as simple as, let's say, you have two devices and the current drives/API differ in how you call them.

```
Class Device1 {
Void WriteData(string data) { //...
                                                  }
}

Class Device2 {
  Void Write(byte[] bytes) { //...
                                   }
}
```

We want to create a standard way to easily use either device.

```
interface IDevice {
    Void Write(string data);
}

Class StandardDevice1 : Device1, IDevice {
```

```
    Public void Write(string data) {
                    WriteData(data);
            }
}


Class StandardDevice2 : Device2, IDevices
{
        Public void Write(string data) {
                    //convert data to byte[] bytes...
                    Write(bytes);
            }
}
```

This way, you can just have:

IDevice device=new StandardDevice1();

And whoever is using the IDevice only needs to know to call device. Write the same way, and it should work the same for any device. You could also have a factory pattern to create the StandardDevice class with the appropriate interface for you.

Others

- Bridge
- Composite
- Decorator
- Facade
- Flyweight
- Proxy

Behavioral

- Chain of responsibility
- Command
- Interpreter
- Iterator
- Mediator
- Memento
- Observer
- State
- Strategy
- Template Method
- Visitor

To learn more about other patterns, visit here.
https://en.wikipedia.org/wiki/Design_Patterns

References:

Gamma, E. (Ed.). (1995). *Design patterns: Elements of reusable object-oriented software.* Addison-Wesley.

Upgrade Path

When you are developing applications that have an existing user base, you should always think about an upgrade path.

Inevitably, some reason will come along, and folks will think we don't need an upgrade path. People can just start anew on our new and improved version.

Usually, that decision proves to be a very bad one. The reason this is bad is that you have an installed user base of paying customers. If you make an upgrade easy, you likely have a continued loyal customer. If you make an upgrade impossible or hard, then your customer has to think, "Should we just go to a competitor since we don't have an upgrade path? Or stay on the old version till either we go to a competitor or the new version, eventually."

None of these scenarios are good for a business that desires money, and I would think most businesses do.

This has been seen at multiple companies for different products. One company built a client-server product that had no direct upgrade path, leaving customers in the dust, allowing competitors to creep in and making new sales difficult. They eventually tried to make an upgrade tool, but it was too little too late.

Another company was switching from individual customer solutions to shared solutions with no upgrade path. It eventually realized this was a problem for the company and tried to make an upgrade path, but at that stage, architectural decisions had already been made that prevented an easy upgrade path. Therefore, of the thousands of customers who wanted to upgrade, less than maybe a few or so did or tried, as it was too difficult an upgrade path due to its limitations. If it is possible to start some new projects your customers have, this could be an upgrade path. However, it may take much longer for that to happen.

Not having an upgrade path for your customers is a recipe for lost revenue. Don't do it if you can avoid it. Figure out a way to have a good, supported, easy upgrade path for customers so you can keep your customers paying you and not your competitors. This is a very costly mistake that could be fatal for a business.

If I Have a Hammer, Everything Looks Like a Nail

If you were a carpenter and you only had a hammer as a tool, you would probably start trying to use it in ways it was never intended. Maybe to pull up carpets, to hammer in screws (it kind of works but not really).

You should be careful of this when you are developing solutions so that the chosen language you know doesn't become the hammer that makes everything look like a nail.

I know an example of a scenario where someone we believe knew SQL and very little C# was asked to create a process that would denormalize views of data for reporting. So presumably, he created a launcher running in a C# service to launch a never-ending stored procedure that would run forever and denormalize data as new data was found.

That's a pretty odd way to call a stored procedure in C# that never ends. In testing or, more likely, production, it was discovered that it was leaking memory when it does that, and it was taking down the whole service (doing irregular things can expose irregular bugs).

So then, rather than just directly calling the stored procedure, it outputs a .exe on the fly and writes it out onto the disk. The code inside it would launch the never-ending stored procedure from the C# service; that way, if it ran out of memory, it was only the new .exe that it spit out and not the service itself. And, of course, memory leaks still happened in that, which would cause it to fail occasionally but not bring down the whole service.

So make sure you are using the right capabilities for the right task. Don't do irregular things, as you may possibly encounter irregular problems as well. If you need, either call in other developers with the right skills to help, or learn the technology to make things work more normally.

Fail Early

When developing code, nearly everything you do can result in some type of error condition. You will need to decide which conditions are normal, which conditions you can handle, and in which conditions you should terminate the program.

If a user enters a letter in a numeric field, humans make mistakes, so this is normal. Handle this condition with an error indicator for the field.

If the user enters a valid value but it's not valid for a later business calculation, again, this can be normal. Your code should handle it with appropriate error messages and actions.

If the program is running, and the data you receive does not match any expectations you have that should be valid, you need to decide if this is a local error, and if you should just abort this transaction. Or is the application's internal state potentially corrupt at this point and it would be safer to crash than to continue to propagate bad data that the user or other automation may act on?

Asserts

If you want code to be super protective of inputs to validate everything to make sure all parameters are within bounds, you could explicitly code or use assertions.

You could set it up so assertions only run during debugging to find things early and not slow production code. Or you could leave assertions on in production to find issues even there and throw exceptions.

```
Double Divide(int a, int b)  // a divided by b
    {
        Debug.Assert(b!=0); // confirm b is not zero. This would just catch it in the debugger earlier in this case

        Return (a/b);  //if not debugging, it would still throw an exception here.
    }
```

This case is perhaps not the best example, since it would just throw an exception later, anyway. But there could be other things you want to assert that would not, and you could find where the parameters have unexpected values before things go horribly wrong.

When not running in debugging, the assertion would not exist. You could write your own assert to use for debug/production that would take action, regardless.

Microsoft Foundation Classes (MFC), an early window framework for Windows apps in C++, originally seemed a little buggy, but a lot of the time, it was developers who passed bad information to the libraries. So Microsoft added asserts everywhere, and it did find some issues with MFC, but also, lots of developers would see these failures in the framework much earlier due to the problematic parameters, so it was then a bit easier to find where things were going wrong.

Make sure your asserts are correct. If not, you will have a lot of errors show up when you least expect them. If there are conditions, the parameters are supposed to have other values you didn't expect for valid reasons.

Contracts

You might hear the term contract or design by contract. You can think of it pretty simply as a defined, documented API that you tell someone about. The idea behind it is that you create a contract (API) that others can write to implement the functionality they need, and you handle everything else internally behind the scenes, so users of the contract/API don't need to know about those details.

Operating Systems

What do operating systems do for you? How do they work?

- Load the system and device drivers for the hardware in the computer.
- Provide a method to display some form of user interface graphics or text (not a requirement, but most do).
- Provide a user interface or command line for the user to run programs/applications.
- Load programs into memory and run them.
- Support allocating memory for the programs.
- Support the ability to run on multiple CPUs, applications/programs/threads, and manage the CPU time of each thread/program to try to share the resources.
- Provide a file system to read and write data to various devices (e.g., Hard disk/SSDs), I/O.
- Protect programs from each other. Protect the operating system from the user-level programs, such that, generally, one program won't directly interfere with another (not a guarantee of no interface; just some basic protections of the memory of that program from being directly interacted with by other programs).
- Allow the user to use various hardware, such as keyboards, mice, printers, and monitors.
- Support connecting to a network to connect to the Internet.
- Provide basic applications a user will need to navigate running programs or looking at the file system.
- Provide APIs that programs can use to access the GPU/monitor, CPU, memory, network, disk, devices, and more.

These, of course, are just some very high-level areas that operating systems deal with. There are probably hundreds, if not thousands, of little things operating systems do for you under the covers that you don't generally have to think much about.

Without an operating system to load, your computer will use just the BIOS bootloader to get to the point that it would try to load an operating system from the disk and stop. Your computer wouldn't be so useful that way. You can install multiple operating systems on the computer (e.g., Linux and Windows) in different disk partitions, and you can boot to one or the other if you desire.

Databases

There are lots of databases on the market. From a high level, they fall into two kinds: SQL and NoSQL. This section will discuss SQL databases.

Databases, at their core, seem pretty simple. They need to support Create, Read, Update, and Delete (CRUD) operations in a transactional way.

Performance

In reality, though, databases end up being quite complex, and it can be difficult to have them perform well in all of the scenarios all of the time for any type of complex application.

When multiple operations are occurring in a database, some rows, pages, or entire tables might need to be locked in read or write operations. Obviously, that could impact the performance of other ongoing operations.

Since there is a lot of data in large databases, SQL uses statistics to calculate the best query plan it can use to try to retrieve the data being requested in a high-performance way. Sometimes, that can cause a query to execute well, and other times, the statics might change a plan that was working well to a plan that performs horribly. Then the query might need hints or indexes that help it retrieve data in a higher performance manner. Sometimes, it might require redesigning the entire query to operate in different ways.

So how do you make sure it will always work well? The best you can try to do is test in scenarios with small, medium, and large databases with a variety of data and hardware to see how the system performs. If it doesn't perform well, try to optimize the queries. Pull in database administrators to help as needed, as they are often experts at reading and optimizing query plans. Also, analyze the hardware in use to determine if the CPU, memory, and disk are enough for the scenarios you need to run to optimize it.

SSD disks can greatly improve the performance of SQL servers, since almost all operations have some component of disk involved.

Many times, queries can be optimized without a huge effort. But sometimes, significant query redesign is needed, which often then requires a lot of testing.

There are some good production database analyzer products. One example is SolarWinds Database Performance Analyzer. It can show you what is using or blocking resources on the SQL server over the course of days, even down to the SQL text, and plan if it has a significant impact for the server. They can be costly, but if you don't have other ways to monitor database activity, they can be worth it.

In general, it's obvious that the more joins you have, the slower things will be. You can denormalize data to improve performance significantly for certain scenarios.

The number one issue we see with database code is very often some sort of performance issue. Another issue we see not as often is code that didn't expect some type of data like null, for instance. Some of the databases, when they are quite large, can have a large variety of data. Sometimes, bugs in code introduce unexpected data values, which can cause problems with other code.

Read *Pro SQL Server Internals* by Dimitri Korotkevitvh. It can help your understanding of how Microsoft SQL server works if you are using MSSQL.

Scaling

Think about scaling from the beginning of any application that will eventually need to scale at the server level. At the very least, consider some sort of partitioning or sharding by default. Find a way to distribute your usage across multiple databases in a logical way. Have a way for your server components to find the right database the needed item is in. Too many applications don't consider scaling. Then they get too far down the road, so there is so much code that needs to be changed that the cost is very high.

It's tempting to ignore scaling. Since it's your initial version, you won't have many users, and the need to scale may be nonexistent. Instead, if you plan to use a standard SQL database like Microsoft SQL, consider at least putting a database access class in place. Have that class support sharding. That is the ability to go to a different database based on some specific criteria. Include the concept of a master database internally that can find the right shard based on the value you decide to shard on. Internally, that class can just go to the same database right now. Make sure you build all of your code with sharding in mind, but at the moment, it's the equivalent of one shard. Later, you will be glad you used that data access class everywhere, since it will make sharding your data much easier.

Testing with Production Data

Testing with production data can sometimes be the best thing to do. With data privacy concerns and GDPR, you may not be allowed to move production databases to places where you can easily use them for testing. You can use data masking products to remove sensitive data from databases so you can use them whenever and wherever needed.

https://www.red-gate.com/products/dba/data-masker/

Normalization (Codd, 1970)

The information that follows is from "A Relational Model of Data for Large Shared Data Banks," defined by Codd (1970), in an ACM Paper. Information below is summarized/paraphrased.

It is the process of organizing database data in a particular way. There are variations: first normal form, second normal form, third normal form, etc. While there are higher forms, most databases stick with something like the third normal form when normalizing data. It's generally a process of organizing data into a relational database model so that data doesn't get duplicated and queries can return data in a reasonable way.

First Normal Form

Every column must only have one value in it. Don't try to stuff multiple values into the same column. Create a different column or table. To link the multiple values stored in a different table, there would be a key reference to the other table.

Usertable for a grocery store:

Username	GroceryListID
John	10
Michael	11

Username GroceryListID
John 10
Michael 11

GroceryList table

GroceryListID	Item
10	Apple
10	Bread
11	Coffee
12	Milk
13	Sugar

GroceryListID	Item
10	Apple
10	Bread
11	Coffee
12	Milk
13	Sugar

A breakdown in the above way would satisfy the first normal form.

Second Normal Form

This is satisfied if each table has just one column that can be used as the primary key. If multiple columns are needed, it would not necessarily satisfy the second normal form.

In the above tables, Usertable would satisfy it if the Username was the primary key.

Third Normal Form

A simple way to say this is to make sure only the data columns that are related directly to the row you are storing should be in the table. Don't mix different types of things together. Break logical things up into different tables.

For example, if you wanted to have a table of films:

Films table:

Name	Producer
Film1	John Doe
Filme3	John Doe

Name	Producer
Film1	John Doe
Film2	John Doe

Instead of doing this, create a new table called Producers, and have a key ProducerID and store that in the Films table rather than duplicate the producer name each time.

Database Denormalization

The opposite of this process is flattening the data structure into one table. Why would you want to do this? Joining the different tables together can make the performance of inserting and reading the data slower. If you need to generate reports quickly off the data without impacting your transactional database as much, denormalizing your data into a different table or, ideally, a database could benefit your system if the performance isn't enough when it's normalized.

How big a difference can this make? In one scenario with normalized data, we could pull only a few million rows an hour. With the denormalized table, we could pull tens of millions of rows per hour.

Data Science

Data Science (Dhar, 2013) seems like a relatively new field. However, some articles trace it back almost 50 years. It really seems to have taken huge steps forward with cloud computing power. People or companies can use tens, hundreds, or even thousands of machines or more to collect, analyze, or process data.

There are various software products that can distribute the processing of data across computers, such as Hadoop, BigQuery, Snowflake, and more.

The amount of data being collected today is massive. With software that can distribute and analyze large amounts of data quickly, science and business can generate new insights that would not have been possible before.

Companies may be able to analyze old data to find new products their customers might be interested in.

Statistics can be a part of data science. Analyzing large amounts of data may need to rely on it to find statistically significant data. Machine learning could also be used to predict things based on previous data.

Part of data science can be visualizing data in a way that can bring about value for science or business.

Dependency Injection

Dependency injection can help you decouple explicit implementations of objects/classes. If you wrote a service called configuration service, you would then have to explicitly call that object for the service whenever you needed it. Let's imagine you were initially storing the data on a disk, but you would like an option to store data as needed in the database.

One approach is that you could add to your current configuration service to have an option to go to a file or to the database. Then, you would need flags everywhere throughout the code to replace the code of the current method with the flagged version checks. If, instead, you wanted to go to a NoSQL database in the future, you would need to add another flag again.

What if, instead, you just have an interface called IConfiguration, and you call a factory service to create an object that supports the type of configuration you desire (file, database, NoSQL, etc.)? That way, each of those different concrete implementations of the IConfiguration interface wouldn't need flags for the different types of storage. They could care about just one type of storage each. That is pretty cool, but what if we took this one step further? I run a service where I can request any type of class I want, and if it happens to have an IConfiguration interface needed on it, it will be auto-populated with an object that supports that (this is a basic dependency injection).

Now, all of that is pretty cool, but let's say I take it one more step. I want to make it such that I can supply a configuration file that can configure which objects are associated with which interfaces and the lifetime of those objects (e.g., singleton, or create an instance each time, etc.). This is offered by many dependency injection libraries.

Dependency injection has positives in terms of decoupling things. However, it can also make configuration and debugging very complex.

Time Use for Event Ordering

What We Will Cover:

- What time should we use?
- How else can you get an accurate common time in a distributed system?
- Can we use time for event ordering?
- Are there other ways to sequence events with distributed time clocks?
- Can we compare times accurately?
- Can we use times for diagnosing data/message flow between distributed systems?

What Time Should We Use?

In distributed systems, it is often ideal when there can be a single source of time, so that time comparisons can more easily be made for support.

As an example: Using time recording on a single central database server can be useful since at least all times recorded are from one machine (in a SQL server scenario). On multi-machine databases then, this may not be quite as easy to get a single central time source.

For many server applications, for example, all server times are synced to GMT for the data center (and we often use the DB time).

How else can you get an accurate common time in a distributed system?

When using standard time synchronization sources such as Network Time Protocol (NTP), the time accuracy you get may only be within one second accuracy between machines, that is assuming it is functioning correctly all the time. Unless this is monitored closely, it is easy for machines to have discrepancies.

One second is a long time in computer terms, though, so if you had 100–1,000 events or more within the same second, you wouldn't be able to order events within that time frame with just time alone.

There are alternative software protocols/products on the market to help achieve more accurate resolution between machines, possibly down to a 1–15 ms or so.

Not specifically recommending but an example: DomainTime.

To achieve even higher resolution, using a time appliance and network/software or direct connections can achieve time coordination at the nanosecond level for analyzing the network or if the time source is used directly.

Example: Tipoff can have direct hardware connections with low latency to the single time source for all servers or be the central source for network packet trace times.

Can We Compare Times Accurately?

Yes, and no. This can depend on the use case required and the type of time source you are using to sync your distributed system's time and resolution required.

Can We Use Times for Event Ordering?

If you are using a central database time, and you want to display to the user the log of things that happened based on how they were added to a log or audit trail, you can order by time. Will this work so that it is accurately ordered by the operations as they happened?

In this case, the answer is maybe or no. For SQL server, for example, time stamps only have a resolution to the millisecond level. If multiple operations happened within the same millisecond, there would be no way to guarantee the correct sequence the order of operations. If you know your application is so slow that two operations can NEVER happen sequentially within the resolution of your time recording (i.e., 1–2 ms), then perhaps you could use this method. But what happens when you upgrade to the next faster computers and disks? Will it be fast enough to then have multiple operations with the same time stamp (same millisecond)?

Thus, it is rarely a good way to use time alone as a way to uniquely provide a guaranteed sequence of event ordering in a distributed system.

A better way might be to use a sequence number like a unique incrementing ID from SQL to order the operations. This can be thought of as an implementation variation of the logical Lamport clocks. (Sarkar, n.d.)

Even this may not work completely, depending on SQL/DB server isolation level/usages/locking because, due to request timing, sequence number 103 may actually be committed before 102 (if there were concurrent transactions, and the one that started later just happened to complete first, both within the same millisecond so time would not guarantee it either). Only an application or SQL sequence number with appropriate locking/ordering could make a guarantee to use for ordering.

Are there other ways to sequence events with distributed time clocks?

Yes, sort of. Again, this is based on the application and the resolution needed. Read up more on Lamport clocks and algorithms. Lamport clocks talk about using a sequence number for a machine or task and/or knowing the order of operations of your application's process. For example, if you know message A from server 1 must happen before message B on server 2, even if the timestamps are off, you can infer the order and times to some extent based on your knowledge of the ordering.

Can we use times for diagnosing data/message flow between distributed systems?

Yes, but we need to realize that time alone may not be sufficient to help you understand the order of operations. As mentioned earlier, machine time sync could be slightly different, and even if SQL DB time is used, concurrent transactions—unless exclusive locking guarantees order—could result in times not being in quite the expected sequence.

Often, understanding the system's message passing can help determine likely ordering even when time doesn't agree exactly. If your application is using server time from each machine, then the resolution may only be within one second. A lot of messages can be sent by a computer in one second. Application usage/slowness may mitigate this concern. If you know your process is so slow that it will always take more than a second, then that time resolution may be ok for support and perhaps this is less of a concern.

Again, this is rarely a good idea if exact sequencing is required. Sequences or Lamport clocks/algorithms would be better.

If you are using disparate times on servers, is there any way to compare times between machines?

This is presuming at least you are using NTP or ideally something a bit more high resolution.

If servers are recording disparate times, one thing you can do to try to determine the time difference is compare logged event times where you know a message is passed through two or more of the machines in question with very little processing overhead, and it's logged. Look at typical historical time differences for messages to get an approximate mapping of time from one machine to another. It may be possible to subtract network latency if there is a significant latency. Hopefully, most of the time, it's less than 1 ms, so it might be possible to ignore depending on your application. If there is processing overhead, we could calculate and average that to help determine a time difference between servers, if needed.

A shared logging mechanism that can record events at the time logged can help get times closer to more accurate on a single server. An even better method would be to have a shared high-resolution time source between servers. There are appliances and software that are sold to help with this.

Some Additional Reading on This Topic:

https://www.inf.ed.ac.uk/teaching/courses/ds/slides1718/time2.pptx.pdf

Sarkar, R. (n.d.). *Distributed Systems Clocks, Ordering of Events*. 30. https://www.ida.liu.se/~TDDD25/lectures/lect5.pdf

Garg, V. K., & Mittal, N. (n.d.). *Time and State in Distributed Systems*. 9. https://www.cs.rice.edu/~druschel/comp413/lectures/algorithms.html

COS-418, Fall 2016: Distributed Systems. (n.d.). Retrieved September 17, 2022, from https://www.cs.princeton.edu/courses/archive/fall16/cos418/ /and https://www.cs.princeton.edu/courses/archive/fall16/cos418/docs/L4-time.pptx

http://lass.cs.umass.edu/~shenoy/courses/spring17/lectures/Lec13.pdf

How to Handle Tech Debt

Tech debt is the bane of every developer's existence—the likely useful but hard to maintain code left around from needing to implement in a less than ideal way. It possibly did offer some value in reducing time to get some functionality or change out, but it drags on the software like dragging an anchor behind a boat. It might be that you didn't have time to make an automated way to enable something in the code and now requires manual work, or it could be the performance of an area isn't very good, and it will eventually be a problem as customer data grows. There are myriads of ways tech debt can cause problems for an application in the future.

Why not just fix it? That is the problem. Typically, the tech debt isn't visible. The product looks perfectly fine to the business, business analysts, and customers until it isn't. Because of this, until there is an issue that is obvious to them and causing problems, it often isn't prioritized. If it's not making or costing the company obvious money, it gets ignored.

Make tech debt visible and create tickets in your issue tracker for all of the tech debt. Make sure to indicate not just the technical reasons but also the business reasons that it should be fixed. Don't just say the architecture sucks so it needs to be fixed. Mention the architecture will cause performance degradation as customer files grow bigger. Based on data estimates, the software may be unusable in a certain amount of time at the current growth rate (provide the data to back it up). If you can demonstrate the issue, even better.

Try to make resolving tech debt a part of normal business. If you are doing Agile and calculate that you could fit roughly 300 story points of effort into your release, discuss with the business a standard arrangement that 10 percent of those should be toward tech debt items to keep them under control. Keeping the percentage low can make it palatable to business folks. If you have something bigger and more urgent, if it can be shown as having a potentially significant impact on the business, you can discuss getting an agreement for more resourcing. When possible, provide business justifications for the tech debt to help get agreement and priority.

If you are touching an area of code with tech debt for a new feature, consider including resolving the tech debt as part of the feature implementation. Obviously, there is a need to balance the effort for that and the effort needed for the feature and discuss it with your stakeholders.

Open Source Software

Open-source software is one of the great gifts some developers have given to the world. One of the prime examples is Linux, a free open-source operating system that beats out Unix, macOS, and even Windows for some use cases.

There are many thousands more open-source projects out there.

Should you use open source?

Consider These Items:

- Is it actively supported and maintained?
- Does it have a licensing agreement you and your company can live with?
  - Some licensing agreements require you to give out the source code for anything you make with it! Or not use it

for commercial software. Double check this depending on your use case.

- Is it known to have lots of bugs or security issues?
- Is open-source support really fast enough and good enough for your needs?

Many companies that use Linux, for example, don't want to get caught waiting for an open-source developer to help them or fix things, so they end up using Red Hat Linux rather than the open-source/free variety and then pay for support.

In that case, it turns out that there is not a lot of savings compared to Windows, so the need to decide the purpose or benefit of using it is really worth it.

Many companies use software to scan their source code for the use of open source to verify the license agreements are compatible with what the company desires. Many companies also have policies around using open source, so make sure you check your company's policy before just using an open-source library/product for your work.

Internal Open Source

It can be a benefit to allow internal organizations to change each other's products, treating them like open source. Open-source products have rules around code submission, so you can as well. You can allow submission to your product by other internal groups, as long as they follow the rules with proper testing and work in agreement with the product and engineering teams that the changes make sense for the product. This way, integrating products can control their integration with other products.

Data Pipelines

This is often referred to in relation to big data or something possibly related to an Extract, Transform, Load (ETL) process. This doesn't just have to apply directly to that but can be used in other scenarios. This is a type of data processing pattern.

For example, networking has different layers that form a pipeline of responsibility for the handling of data being sent or received on the network.

In its simplest form, think of it as a way to process data and do different processing in each step, perhaps one type of processing right after the other or even in parallel.

This could be implemented as simply as one class calling another class. To abstract it, you might do it through interfaces, delegates, or events. It could even be handled using streaming technology, passing messages between components/steps in a pipeline of data processing.

Context and Notetaking

Write down any contextual information you are keeping in your head.

If you need to add code somewhere later, add a comment like "// TODO: Finish this method." Maybe even throw in some non-compilable code if you are worried about accidentally leaving it in that state.

Take notes about the things you need to do. Take notes if you were in the middle of debugging. Find an app you are comfortable taking notes in, or even use a paper notebook and post it if you need more in-your-face reminders.

If you are worried about losing files with git, you could stash your changes to save them if you need to switch context for something else.

Managed Languages

Managed languages/frameworks like Java, C# or .NET have some differences from other languages.

Pros

- You don't need to manage pointers, as the language/framework does it for you.
- You don't need to manage cleaning up memory, as it is handled for you.
- Can be dynamically compiled when you run it for .NET/C# to work better on the platform it is run.

Cons

- Cleanup of memory is not quite deterministic.
- Garbage collection has some consequences.
- It might stop all threads to clean up memory.
- It takes time to clean up lots of memory at a time, which can impact application with low latency requirements.
- It can take time to compile the app on the first run C#/.NET.

I'm a C/C++ programmer originally, but as you have probably noticed, my favorite language preference, when it makes sense to use it, is C#. Header files in C++ often require a degree of maintenance and management that is not needed in the C# world (similar to Java).

Floating Point Numbers

Floating point numbers sometimes don't behave.

You would think that 1/7 added seven times would equal 1. In normal math, it would, but with double floating point math, computers use no.

(1.0/7.0) + (1.0/7.0) + (1.0/7.0) + (1.0/7.0) + (1.0/7.0) + (1.0/7.0) + (1.0/7.0) == 1.0

That comparison done with double variables in C# would not be equal.

That's because adding 1/7 together seven times equals 0.99999999999999978.

With floating point math, there is the opportunity to accumulate errors in the least significant bits of the double type.

The best thing to do in these instances is to decide the precision you need and truncate to within the supported precision and round if desired.

```
if (Math.Round(((1.0 / 7.0) + (1.0 / 7.0) + (1.0 / 7.0) + (1.0 / 7.0) +
(1.0 / 7.0) + (1.0 / 7.0) + (1.0 / 7.0)), 15)==1.0)
        Console.WriteLine("Equal");  //would be equal
    else
        Console.WriteLine("Not Equal");
```

An accepted answer on StackOverflow for comparing Equal:

```
bool CloseToEqual(double a, double b) {
  double epsilon1 = Math.Max(Math.Abs(a), Math.Abs(b)) * 1E-15;
  return Math.Abs(a - b) <= epsilon1;
}
```

Note: Method/variable names were changed. See "C#—Double.Epsilon for Equality, Greater than, Less than, Less than or Equal to, Greater than or Equal to," *Stack Overflow*, n.d.)

References:
"C#—Double.Epsilon for Equality, Greater than, Less than, Less than or Equal to, Greater than or Equal to"—*Stack Overflow*. (n.d.). Retrieved September 17, 2022, from https://stackoverflow.com/questions/2411392/double-epsilon-for-equality-greater-than-less-than-less-than-or-equal-to-gre. License:https://creativecommons.org/licenses/by-sa/2.5/ and https://creativecommons.org/licenses/by-sa/3.0/)

NP_Complete Problems

This topic can be a little complicated. NP-Complete means non-deterministic polynomial, which describes the amount of time that it would take to find the solution to a problem.

There is a class of problems in computer science that, as they get bigger, become nearly impossible to solve with the computing power of today. Often, algorithms can be devised to find a reasonable solution to the problem but not necessarily the actual solution to the problem.

An example of this type of problem is called the traveling salesman problem. Imagine a salesman who must travel to every major city in the country, and you want to calculate the shortest possible path that will take him to all cities at one time. Today's current algorithms can find an approximated shortest path solution but not the path that is definitely the shortest of all possible available paths. As the number of cities is increased, the computing power needed to try every possible path gets to the point where computing time might require hundreds of years or more. In 2020, the best they could solve this problem for was a mere 22 cities. (*Traveling Salesman Problem | Solve the Traveling Salesman Problem*, n.d.) (see this article https://www.popularmechanics.com/science/a30655520/scientists-solve-traveling-salesman-problem/).

Because this is basically a large graph with many paths between nodes, the combinations quickly get out of control. Understanding this type of problem is important. That way, if you are ever asked to solve something similar, you would know that you might be able to find an approximated solution but not a definitive solution to the problem when the numbers get too large for current processing power.

C# Using Var

C# var vs. strongly typed

This can be one of those developer holy wars to avoid, but here is an opinion on this one.

Using var seems to be the rage today for reducing redundancy. Mostly, var is pretty benign or helpful, but perhaps it shouldn't be used all the time, as there are possible problems that it could cause, even adding confusion or code misunderstandings in some cases, making code harder to read, or causing bugs.

One possible example of a problem scenario for using var (there could be more):

The only problem is var could hide the type in the code so that you don't know what is returned, and the actions on the code could not work as expected.

Let's Say You Wrote Your Own Type Comparison:

```
int Compare(int,int);//compares ints
int Compare(string,string);//does comparison of strings in alphabetical order
return 0 if equal, -1 if parameter 1 is less than parameter 2, 1 if parameter 2 is greater than parameter 1.
```

Let's say GetValue originally looked like this:

```
int GetValue(string);
```

You wrote code like:

```
var myvalue1=GetValue("## 10 ##");  //GetValue parses out 10
var myvalue2=GetValue("## 100 ##"); //GetValue parses out 100
```

```
if (Compare(myvalue1,myvalue2)>0)
//do something.
```

In this case, if GetValue was modified either purposely or accidentally to return strings, the comparison would not compare correctly in all cases, but if int was returned from what was parsed, then it would compare correctly.

If the code had instead been written as below using int instead of var, *compilation would have failed* if GetValue return value was changed to string:

```
int myvalue1=GetValue("## 10 ##"); //GetValue parses out 10
int myvalue2=GetValue("## 100 ##"); //GetValue parses out 100
```

You could say this isn't something that would happen, but something very similar to this did happen with production code (it was VBScript, which had dynamic typing; in the above scenario, var acts somewhat like that, but instead allowing compilation to happen for something you might not have intended).

Summary:

I think it is safer to only use var when the types are obvious (or a few other scenarios that make sense).

Microsoft's guidelines for var: ("C# Coding Conventions"—*Microsoft Learn*, n.d.)

Use var when it's easy to tell the type of the variable being assigned.

You shouldn't use var when it's not easy to determine the type visually.

(Microsoft Reference: https://docs.microsoft.com/en-us/dotnet/csharp/fundamentals/coding-style/coding-conventions).

My Recommendations for Guidelines for Var Usage:

- Use var for anonymous types.
- Use var with linq.
- As Microsoft says, you can use var if the type is obvious. I say obvious means WITHOUT using IntelliSense (GitHub doesn't have IntelliSense when reviewing code), with the caveat of if it makes things simpler; but if not, it shouldn't be a requirement.
- You "can" use var if the types are crazy complicated and muddle the code (though that is probably a smell itself and ideally avoided).
- Use explicit types otherwise.

Reference Articles:
Some Other Viewpoints on Using Var:

- Uses and misuses of implicit typing – Fabulous Adventures In Coding – Site Home – MSDN Blogs
- Department of Declaration Redundancy Department

Microsoft Coding Guidelines:
https://msdn.microsoft.com/en-us/library/ff926074.aspx

Perceived Speed

Perception is sometimes everything, and sometimes, it's possible to change the perception of speed without actually changing the speed of the operation. There was a UI that we were creating, and it needed to send updates to a third-party system that was slow. This made the whole interface seem slow. Our competitors' interfaces were slow as well, because they were using the same third-party system. To improve the perception of users, rather than having the UI wait for the third party to respond, it would batch updates and send them asynchronously so the user could keep pressing keys without waiting. The UI was also changed to have an indication of when the third-party system had caught up to the user's input key presses. It was a subtle UI change, but the users loved it. They no longer felt like the interface was slow, even though the speed of updates to the third-party server had not really changed.

Holy Wars

Ok, not really religious, but some developers treat them like they are. That means the belief that their way is the best regardless of any data. But many of these are in the gray area, so there is data to support things from both sides.

So the best bet is don't get into these debates. Just pick one.

Tabs vs. Spaces

Some folks are starting to believe spaces are superior since they work the same no matter which editor you are in, even across platforms between Windows and Linux. Sometimes the argument is, tabs are more efficient. While true in this day and age, the amount of extra storage is not likely to break the bank.

The best bet is to pick an option and ask everyone to stick with it so that it is easier to compare code when doing reviews. Or use tooling to help auto-format it with the selected option.

Where Should Curly Braces Go?

```
Function1 { }
    Function2
    {
    }
    If (val==1) {
    }
    If (val==2)
    {
    }
```

This one hardly seems worth arguing over. Let folks use what they want or define particular scenarios where one might be chosen over the other as a standard and stick with it.

VI vs. Emacs

Originally Unix based tools are now passed on to Linux and are available on pretty much every platform. Let folks use the editors they like as long as it can still produce coding style compliant code if you have a style (which it should).

Comparing OS, Languages, Frameworks

Examples: LAMP vs. WAMP, Android vs. iOS, Java vs. C# vs. Ruby,.

Languages should be chosen if they are often used to solve the types of problems you are trying to solve, if your staff knows them well, or everyone agrees to learn it because it is needed. This is similar to operating systems, since if the business makes money selling Mac software, it makes sense to have Macs. For the most part, though, if the tools can be used in a reasonable way to create the software you need, it should be fine.

Surprisingly, there have even been Windows-based .NET projects where perhaps half the developers are using Macs and running VMs on them to debug/run code. That's even with laptops in use that are often half to a third the power of desktops, then adding VMs that are often at best 75–95 percent of the underlying hardware, depending on usage. However, they still get work done in an environment they are comfortable with, apparently, so I guess let it be if your shop is into that.

Coding Style

It's possible to have software without a coding style, but there probably should be some base coding style to make it easier to compare code changes. For example, the naming of class member variables vs. function names vs. parameters is a common standard in C#.

Don't get too strict on every little curly brace unless you are going to have some automated tools do all the formatting for you. Otherwise, code reviews will drive folks nuts.

C# var vs. specific type, like int

Var a=1; OR int a=1;

In some cases, like linq usage, you have no choice but to use var. But lots of folks are using this for everything now, and it was never really intended for that, even as per Microsoft.

Most of the time, you will be ok if the types are obvious. If they aren't, it can be hard to read and even very slightly risky in some cases.

Message Streaming

Streaming message products like Kafka, Kinesis, etc. can offer ways to make an application that uses a database processing thousands of transactions per second to instead handle tens of thousands or even millions of transactions. This can take applications that had high latency and change them to something with very low latency when implemented well.

Instead of transactions being processed in a single database if the application is split up, that transaction processing is handled in machine memory, and processing is sharded such that each server only handles a configurable shard/partition of data, instead of the database being the mechanism for persistence, processing in memory, and writing a persistent stream of messages that are written to either high-performance file systems or NoSQL databases.

Transaction processing in memory is very fast, and sharding the processing across multiple servers allows scaling.

This methodology is used for many types of very scalable systems.

Imagine a web server selling books. See the diagram below. If the large arrows are all message streams that can send back and forth to the appropriate server based on the title of the book, the processing is sharded. It's processed in memory, the transaction is written to a high-performance disk message store, and the transaction information is returned to the web server. NoSQL could be used as the persistence or potentially even sharded databases that are written lazily from the message stored to disk, or NoSQL should perform well enough.

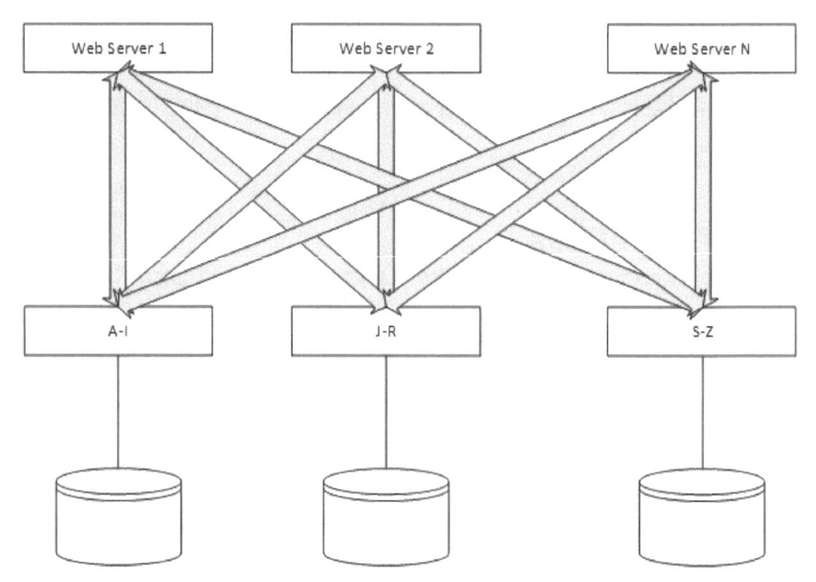

Should You Learn Assembly Language?

Should you learn assembly language? If you are programming with languages like C++ or C, then at least a little can be helpful sometimes. It still can be useful for everyone else as well. Assembly language is about as close to the CPU as you can get. At that level, you can understand how the CPU and your code really work. Once you know assembly, you understand what your high-level language gets translated into.

Assembly language really isn't that hard. It's actually very simple. The instructions are a little more cryptic than you might be used to in languages like Java/C#/C++.

The other part of understanding it is how high-level language maps to assembly language. Once you know that, you can understand what your language is doing for you under the covers at the lowest levels. You might think if you are writing in a high-level language like Java or C#, you don't need to know about assembly as much. Occasionally, you might. Even with C#, you sometimes are using components or even drivers that could end up causing some type of error. Having a little knowledge of assembly when you get a dump file can be useful in those cases. Just getting comfortable reading raw dump files and the related stacks can help you solve Windows blue screen errors by finding the driver most likely causing the issue.

Writing Apps for Profit and Fun

Below, you can find some detail on a few of the applications I created, two with some help from a friend.

TBBS Add-on

I was probably around 13 or 14. I had been running a bulletin board system off my TRS-80 Model 3 computer. Originally, I wrote my own BBS in BASIC, even before I had an auto-answer modem. If I heard the phone ring, I would just flip the switch manually to turn it on.

Later, I was able to get one of the best modems at the time, a 300 bps Hayes modem that had the auto-answer feature. For folks who don't remember 300 bps, that was only about 30 characters per second, so you could watch the text slowly fill your screen from the data coming over the modem.

When I had saved up enough money, I also bought TBBS software to run a BBS that was much better than the basic BBS I had written. It had configurable menus to have message board systems and download areas. When people would dial into my computer, you couldn't tell who was on it until after they logged out. You would literally see the text of the person who was dialed in on the screen.

I decided to write multiple add-ons from TBBS in Z80 assembly language. One of them could figure out the logged-in user and display it in the corner of the screen while they were logged in. I published this as one of the downloads on my site as shareware and posted it to other sites. That was probably one of my first shareware products. I don't think I made much money from it. I did get a call from someone who said they were a navy sub commander and used my software for their TBBS system. At maybe 14 years old, that's pretty exciting.

I was running on my TBBS system with four double-sided floppy disk drives. The disks were wearing out, and I didn't have the money to buy more. One of the users of my BBS bought me some disks and dropped them by my house so that we could keep the BBS running. We had a small community of users who liked using the system.

A Mini Spreadsheet

In the early days of software, a kid helping out a shoe store owner asked him what he needed. He said, "I just need something a little like Lotus 123 (an old spreadsheet program for a TRS-80), but I can't afford it. Can you make me something like that?"

"Sure," the kid said, and he created it and included support for saving and loading data from the old cassette tape players. When you needed to save data, you would press the play button to load the data, and press the record button to save the data. It would often take a few minutes to save or load data from tape (that was the fastest speed that could be supported on the tape and was very fast for the time).

The software was delivered to the shoe store owner, and he said it worked, but the loading and saving are kind of slow. The kid, knowing the save was as fast as anything he could do on the machine at that time, asked, "Does it really matter that it takes 1–3 minutes?"

The answer was, "Well, it makes my thumb hurt."

"What?!"

"Yes," he said, "my tape player is broken, so I have to hold the button down the whole time it's loading, or it won't work."

Yes, this was copied from the thinking like your customer section, and you probably figured out that kid was me. I was probably 15 or 16 years old. Probably my first paid software job that wasn't a shareware product.

SCOPY Super Copy Utility

I finally bought an IBM PC-compatible computer at perhaps 17 or 18 years old, preparing for college. I had been playing some games on it. Games at the time had various types of copy protection. They would make the floppy disks they gave you uncopiable by normal means. They did this by using larger or smaller than normal sectors on various tracks on the disk, sometimes even going beyond the track's expected limit for the drive. I was always afraid my disks would go bad and I would lose my games, so I decided to write a copy utility that could copy these game disks to back them up. At the time, things like this were allowed. With the current laws like DMCA, I don't know if things like that are allowed anymore.

There were some other options to copy disks at the time. There was some hardware and software you could buy called the option board, and it could copy nearly any disk. That was expensive, though, and required hardware. There was another software package that was very good at copying disks with just software but didn't always work. It didn't have many options to make things work; it either did or didn't.

So I decided to write an app that had flexibility in options to try to copy more disks than the currently available software-only solutions. It was written in C and used a DOS windowing-like system to have different information displayed at the same time. I don't think many people chose to send money for it, but I did get a few people writing to me once in a while over the years about it.

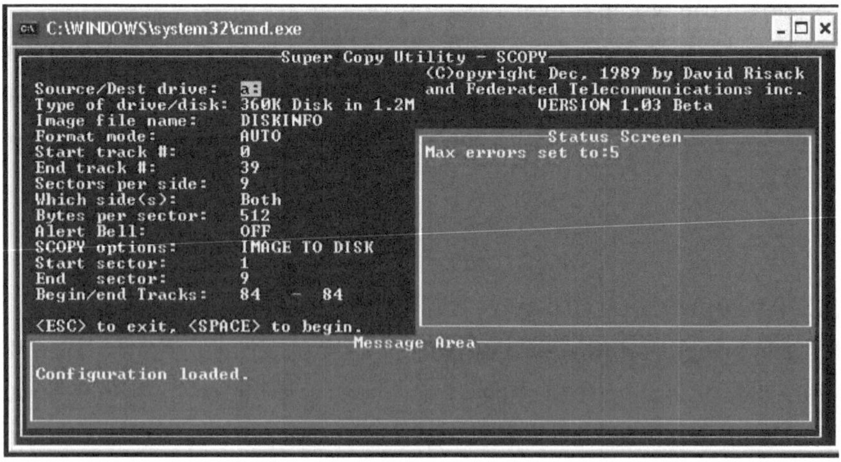

```
C:\WINDOWS\system32\cmd.exe
                    Super Copy Utility - SCOPY
                              (C)opyright Dec. 1989 by David Risack
Source/Dest drive:   a:       and Federated Telecommunications inc.
Type of drive/disk:  360K Disk in 1.2M          VERSION 1.03 Beta
Image file name:     DISKINFO
Format mode:         AUTO                  Status Screen
Start track #:       0              Max errors set to:5
End track #:         39
Sectors per side:    9
Which side(s):       Both
Bytes per sector:    512
Alert Bell:          OFF
SCOPY options:       IMAGE TO DISK
Start sector:        1
End   sector:        9
Begin/end Tracks:    84   -  84

<ESC> to exit, <SPACE> to begin.
                         Message Area
Configuration loaded.
```

HyperFont and Debugging Assistant

I wrote these two products with two coworkers. We were working on executive user interfaces created with HyperPAD. It was a HyperCard like development environment but in DOS. The thing with DOS was that you could only use the DOS font characters. HyperFont allowed creating your own DOS fonts, so you could essentially create graphics if you designed your fonts the right way. Debugging Assistant made it easier to debug HyperCARD code. Both of those were add-ons to HyperPAD. We were able to convince the company that made Hyper-PAD to include a flier for our products in the box.

Unfortunately, these products didn't sell too well. HyperPAD, being a DOS product, was on its way out with Windows taking over. When you create products, you should know your technology and whether the need for it is expanding or decreasing to gauge how many buyers there would be.

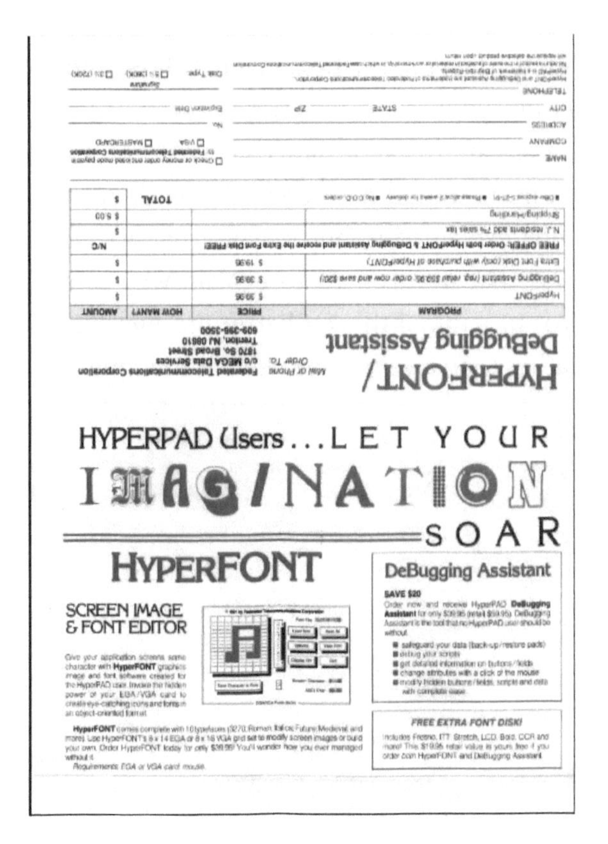

Virtual Monitors

I was thinking, I wish I had more space to lay out my applications on-screen on Windows 3.1. I decided to try to create a program that would simulate multiple monitors, switching between them with a key press on the numeric pad or the application icon. I asked my coworker who I worked with on the HyperPAD work to help create all the visuals and icons in the application, plus documentation. I initially called one of the people responsible for acquiring software in the company Egghead Software. That was a company with many retail stores selling software. I sent a copy of the application to them; they liked it. They recommended we work with a company called Baseline Publishing that could help us publish it. They did the box, manual, disks, and more. We got a lump sum of money for selling it to the stores.

Unfortunately, after that, it didn't sell well, and I wondered why. I think our box front should have been clearer about the benefit. The back of our box explained it, but maybe it wasn't clear enough. The other issue was that it was hard to explain why someone needed a virtual monitor program. I think a better product would have filled a larger need rather than a very niche need at the time.

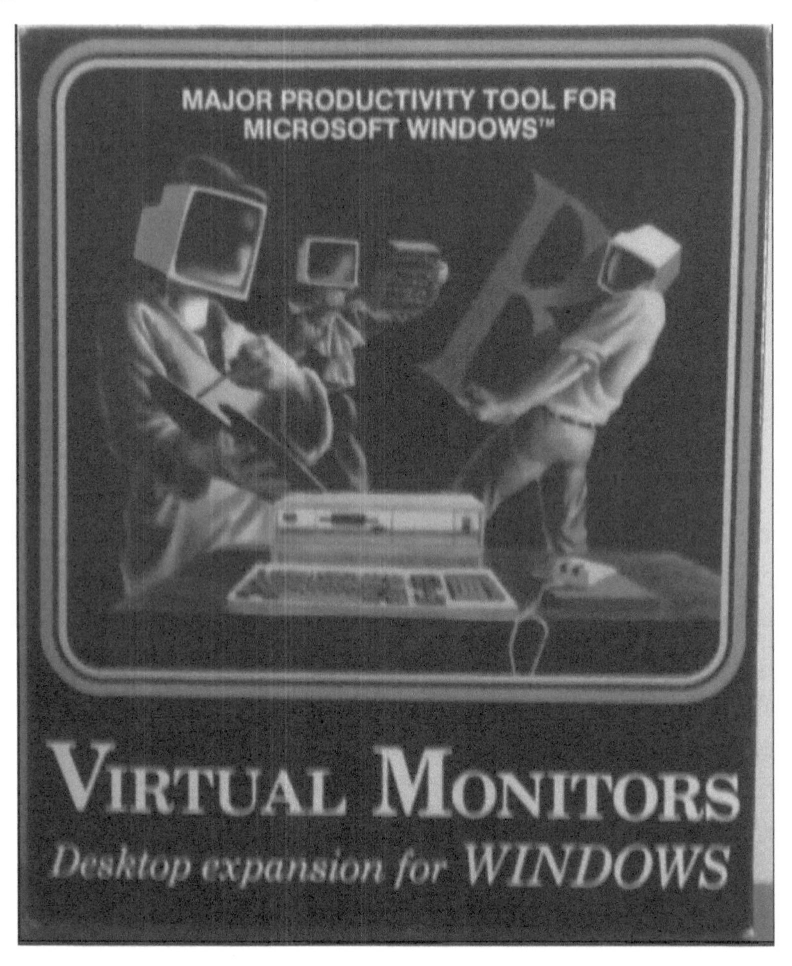

QuotesNow!

At the time, I had been interested in charting stocks. I wanted to use charting software like MetaStock, but I didn't want to pay the subscription rates for stock quotes when I knew there were free quotes on the Internet. I decided to write an app that could track a stock portfolio and pull current data from various sites on the Internet. It could also download the data into MetaStock format. MetaStock format was a proprietary format, and there were few ways to write it. I found someone who described the file layout online and wrote code to output that format. The app was designed to allow me to auto-update some of the detection logic for scraping quotes from the Internet just in case websites changed.

I bought a third-party package that protected software to make it a 30-day trial and required generating a code to unlock it after the trial expired.

I uploaded copies of my applications to all the major download sites. I created a website where people could pay online. I found one of the few credit card processors at the time that would allow taking online orders called Teleflora. They had a simple DOS app that allowed processing credit cards that I did manually at the time.

To my surprise, it started getting some downloads and purchases. I was getting 10–30 orders a month. The stock market was going up at the time, which I am sure contributed to the interest. Having the right product at the right time can be critical. QuotesNow! got reviewed by a major publication, *Barron's*, which is a well-known financial paper.

It was reviewed by other publishers as well, including in other languages, even though the app only worked in English.

Over time, as the stock market started to go down, so did the orders. It was a fun project while it lasted, though.

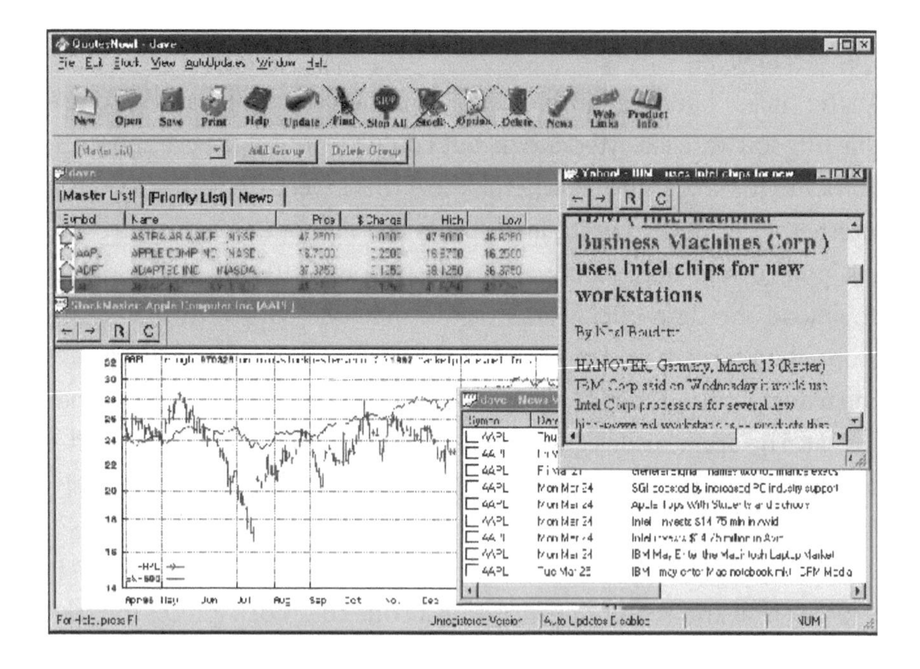

Android Apps

Just as Android started to get popular, I decided to write some Android apps. This was before there were even actual apps for things like Facebook on there. I created several ad-supported applications. One was to create unique passwords automatically from the password you supplied and the website name. Some launcher apps auto-launched a browser to popular sites like Facebook. The apps were getting millions of ad views a day. Over time, as there was more and more competition, the ad views got less and less.

Will AI Replace Software Engineers

What will the future hold for software development?

Tooling

Software development tooling will continue to get better. It will incorporate machine learning to help us with tasks. Visual Studio 2022 is already an example of this and shows how much better IntelliSense can be with machine learning.

Machine Learning to Replace Software Engineers

It's possible that AI or machine learning may be able to generate software for some limited use case scenarios, sort of like the code generators of past years and low-code or no-code type scenarios. It could and already has reduced the need for software developers in those scenarios. Will it replace them entirely? Not likely anytime soon. Think about all the code generated that way. It can only work in limited scenarios. Most code generators were generated once, and then you can't really enhance any of it. Users always like improvements, and generated code is pretty static in the same way. If they come up with ways to regenerate the same code with improved interfaces, that could help. It would also have to handle the upgrading of databases. But how many code generators do you know who could handle all the potential upgrade scenarios in a cloud-based environment?

Software engineering will probably remain in demand given so much coding is needed for the Internet.

Highly Regulated Environments

Software engineering in a highly regulated environment is pretty similar to most other environments.

The differences typically are:

- **More Process:** The SDLC is followed more rigorously, and segregation of environments and personnel duties is also sometimes needed.
- **More Testing:** It sometimes takes three times the development time, with focus on automation testing whenever possible.
- **Auditing:** Regulated environments usually have one or more audits a year.

Unregulated environments may or may not have regular audits. Regulated environments are typically guaranteed to have multiple audits a year, so everything they do as part of the process must be tracked and documented, so there is proof of the process and the decisions made.

There needs to be a clear process of design, security, and privacy checks that are documented.

Authorized developers should, for the most part, be the only ones with write access to source control. No one developer alone should be able to commit a change to the source control system (at least as part of the process). There should always be one or more developers who are documented as having reviewed the changes. There should be documented unit tests.

There must be evidence of what was tested for QA testing. Testing should not happen just on a developer's machine.

There must be evidence of a decision/risk assessment if performance testing is needed or not for individual changes and the release as a whole.

There should be a way to trace source control changes to the enhancements/bugs that document why the changes were made.

Before the code is merged, unit tests should be run. It is great if this is built into the system, so that merge is not allowed until the code is verified to work with unit tests.

When testing the release, all changes made to the release must be documented and tested. Performance/Load testing should happen if a documented risk assessment indicates it should happen.

Recursion

Recursion is a way of programmatically writing a function/method that calls itself to implement an algorithm or solve a problem. Sometimes, recursive functions can be written in less code than iteratively. It can sometimes be easier to read and write that way.

This isn't too common but comes up when working with things like file systems that can have folders/files within subfolders. It can come up when processing anything that has a hierarchy to its structure, like XML or a binary tree.

Recursion can have a downside in that when each function call is made and has not been returned yet, it may take up space on a program's stack (which typically has a more limited amount of space than the main area of the program's memory). Plus, any variables on the stack used by the program for each level of recursion take up space. It's possible that if it goes too deep, the program could get an exception that it ran out of stack space. There can sometimes be a way to prevent running out of space with something called tail recursion. When the recursive function call is the last operation executed, some compilers can optimize the usage to avoid using the extra stack space (that sometimes is not obvious to implement; be careful if you try and test). Given this, recursion needs to be used with care to not go so deep, as it could run out of stack space, or confirm your implementation and compiler allow for the tail recursion optimization.

Any function you can write recursively can be written iteratively. It can be more code. If your recursion is deep, iterative would avoid the concern about running out of stack space.

If you can't think how to implement iteratively, think about using a linked list/stack. Push things on and pop them off just like a stack. Sometimes, that is a simple way to convert a recursive solution to an iterative one.

See the example functions below that demonstrate a simple algorithm implemented recursively and also iteratively.

```
/// <summary>
    /// Recursive
    /// Calculate val*val + (val-1)*(val-1) + (val-2)*(val-2) continu-
ing until val-N==1 includes that then stops
    ///
    /// So val=3 would be (3*3)+(2*2)+(1*1)=14
    /// if val<=0 return 0
    /// </summary>
    public static int CalculateRecursive(int val)
    {
            if (val == 1)
        return 1;

            if (val <= 0)
        return (0);

            return (val * val) + CalculateRecursive(val - 1);

              }

    /// <summary>
    /// Iterative
    ///
```

```
/// Calculate val*val + (val-1)*(val-1) + (val-2)*(val-2) continu-
ing until val-N==1 includes that then stops
 /// So val=3 would be (3*3)+(2*2)+(1*1)=14
/// if val<=0 return 0
/// </summary>
/// <param name="val"></param>
/// <returns></returns>
public static int CalculateIterative(int val)
{
    if (val <= 0)
  return (0);

        if (val == 1)
  return 1;

        int total = 0;

    while (val >=1)
    {
    total = total + (val * val);
    val = val - 1;
    }

    return total;

     }
```

Cross-Platform Development

Luckily, there are many ways to do cross-platform development. Sometimes, this work can be done with little or no change to the code between one platform and another if the code is using basic built-in language functionality. Otherwise, more complex code would need to build platform-specific implementations or layers. For languages that use interfaces, you could provide an interface to abstract the platform-specific functionality. Then, on each platform, you would replace the underlying implementation for the interface with one appropriate for the platform.

C/C++ requires recompiling code on a different platform (e.g., Windows, Linux, Mac, etc.), and it will output binary code for that platform.

C#/Java work a little bit differently. C#, for example, compiles to IL, and then that can on run any platform where .NET core CLR has been installed on. When run, the JIT creates the final machine code needed to run for that platform.

Perhaps the ultimate cross-platform environment is a user's browser, since HTML/CSS/Javascript running there run on any environment where the browser supports those.

Rate Limiting Algorithms

There are many times when implementing server APIs, you might want to limit the number of requests that can come in at one time or within a time period. The reason is to try and prevent overloading of the server or monopolizing of the server by a particular API at least.

Token Bucket

(*Announcing Rate Limiting for .NET—.NET Blog*, n.d.) Let's say we wanted to allow only 30 requests per minute. Imagine that for each minute. We have a bucket that can hold a maximum of 30 tokens. When a call to the API comes in, it takes one token from the bucket. If a call comes in and the bucket is empty, we could make the request wait until the bucket has tokens, or we could refuse the request and, in effect, say try again later.

Let's say every two seconds, we add one token (refill rate 30 per minute). We start out with 30 tokens in the bucket in the beginning. If our refill rate was the same as our bucket size, it would be possible to use 30 near the end of our one minute time slot and another 30 when it is refilled at the beginning of the next. With the refill rate only one every two seconds, it reduces that bursty behavior.

If you wanted to avoid bursts in even smaller time periods, like not more than 15 per second, you could change your bucket time and refill rates to shorter time frames to reduce short quick bursts. The bucket size could be a maximum of 15, and the refill rate could still be one token every two seconds to make sure we don't go over 30 per minute. That would prevent more than 15 calls in a single second and make sure we limit our per-minute rate. ("Rate-Limiting Strategies and Techniques" | *Cloud Architecture Center* | *Google Cloud*, n.d.) ("Algorithm—Token – Bucket vs Fixed Window (Traffic Burst)," *Stack Overflow*, n.d.)

Concurrent Calls

(*Announcing Rate Limiting for .NET— .NET Blog*, n.d.) This is another type of algorithm to prevent too many calls at the same time. Usually, this refers to active calls still processing at the same time. Where the token method counts everything that happened during the time period, the concurrent calls algorithm wouldn't let more calls happen while the other calls are still processing and have not been completed yet. Suppose we only wanted to allow two concurrent calls. If one came in and was completed, then two more came in immediately after that, those two would be allowed. But if one call came in and was still processing, and then two more came in, the last call would not be allowed in, since at that point in time, it would already have two concurrent and would either wait till one completes to let the other in or return a notification to the caller that it's busy; try again later. It's usually safer to tell the caller to try again later to avoid holding any server resources that could make the load on the server worse.

Client Retry Logic

It would be important in the case where clients are told they will need to retry if the server is busy that they implement a reasonable retry logic, such that the server is not constantly sent retry requests. There is a well-known methodology to insert increasing wait times between retries up to a maximum limit of retries. That allows the server time for the load to finish without hammering it with retry requests. That type of logic should really be used for any type of intermittent type issues where a retry is needed (e.g., network errors, timeouts, etc.).

There are several more varieties of these algorithms, such as fixed, sliding window, and more.

Shared Rate Limit Distributed Limit on Rate

If a rate limit is implemented on just one server, then the aggregate of the total number of servers would be the actual limit of requests/calls that could happen. If you wanted to control that limit so that it was a maximum among all servers, you would need a way to share the state of any rate limit between all the servers. One potential way to do this would be with a shared distributed cache. A database would also be possible, or perhaps a service handling the requests.

Plugin Framework

Plug-in frameworks have been around for a long time. This is basically a mechanism to add functionality to your program by dropping in a library that implements a class that supports an interface that can load or handle the events required to add or enhance the functionality in your application. A great example of this that you are probably familiar with is the Chrome browser. You have probably used some form of Chrome extension (a plug-in) that adds functionality to your browser.

Plug-ins allow developers to add useful functionality to the application. They might also give you a really nice way for internal groups within your company to build extensions for your application without having to coordinate too much with the main development team, since the plug-in framework contract is well defined. You should just think about would anyone really want or need to use it before you build it to make sure your company or your application has enough developer support that people would be interested in creating plug-ins for your application.

This can be a form of dependency injection and is available in some frameworks.

Discrete Math

Discrete Math or Discrete Structures often cover many different areas such as binomial coefficients, probability, random, conditional probability, standard deviation, Boolean math, and more.

I'm only going to cover one small part of Boolean logic, the most useful thing I still can't recall using from discrete math in college.

Imagine you have an if condition.

```
bool A,B;

If (A && B)
```

```
Dothis();
```

The logic table is:
(Presume 0=false 1=True, &&=And, ||=OR)

A B	Output
0 0	0
0 1	0
1 0	0
1 1	1

So it's only true when both A and B are true.

But let's say you needed the opposite of this.
"

```
If !(A && B)
  Dothis();
```

Notice the "!" symbol means NOT, which inverts the value returned. True would become false, and false would become true.

A B	Output
0 0	1
0 1	1
1 0	1
1 1	0

Notice that it reversed our logic table, so not is only false when both A and B are true.

So is there a simpler way to write that?

!(A && B) = (A || B)

So the NOT of A and B is the same as A or B. So the NOT of an AND condition converts it to an OR condition. And, of course, the inverse is true. A NOT of an OR condition would become an AND condition.

Finite-State Machine

Finite-state machines are a complex way to have a mapping of our current state to a new state based on particular inputs or changes.

Imagine you have one of those touch lamps, and it has two buttons. One button is the "off" button. The other button is the "on" button. If you press the "on" button more than once, it increases the brightness of the light. If it is at its brightest, the next press of the "on" button will set the light to its lowest light settings. So the "on" button can cycle low light, medium light, and high light settings.

If you wrote a program to do this, you might write something like: (Pseudo code below)

```
if (off button pressed)
 LightLevel=0; //off


if (on button pressed)
{
  if (LightLevel==0)
     LightLevel=1; //low light
  else
  if (LightLevel==1)
     LightLevel=2; // medium light
 else
 if (LightLevel==2)
     LightLevel=3; // high light
```

```
    else
    if (LightLevel==3)
      LightLevel=1; // low light
  }
```

While the above would work, if you wanted to add levels, change settings, or add more light levels, you would need custom code.

What if, instead, you made a two-dimensional array to drive our state changes?

So we check the current lamp setting and see which button is pressed to determine what we set the light level to next.

Current Lamp setting	0	1	2	3
Press off button	0	0	0	0
Press light on button	1	2	3	1

Current Lamp setting	0	1	2	3
Press off button	0	0	0	0
Press light on button	1	2	3	1

StateTable[x,y] contains the two-dimensional array.

```
CURRENTSTATE=0;
OFFBUTTON=1;
ONBUTTON=2;
```

Once that is set up, I think you will agree that this pseudo code is much simpler than the earlier code. Technically, we didn't need the current lamp state in the array, but I just did that so you could visualize it easier.

```
//button would equal 1 for the off button and 2 for the "on" button.
    Int GetNewLightLevel(int button)
    {
     return StateTable[LightLevel,button];
    }
```

You can use state tables like this, or even for parsing strings or streams of data to change your internal program state based on the input.

Compiler/Interpreter Design

You should know that this is a bit of a specialized field. Most folks don't write full compilers and interpreters. At some point, you may want or need to write a simple interpreter in order to act on some file you input or the user types. If it's a relatively simple grammar or language, you might be able to code it by hand. When it gets as complex as a language like C#/C++,. you would probably want to use additional tools to help generate the parser/scanners for a language to generate code that can parse the language for you. Complex compilers/interpreters often have different phases in a pipeline of processing the language.

This is not common for most software engineers to do, and entire books have been written on this topic alone.

An interesting list comparing parsers:

"Comparison of parser generators" — https://en.wikipedia.org/wiki/Comparison_of_parser_generators

Deterministic Disposal at End of Function Scope

This book is mostly about practical applications of code. Sometimes, you might write some novel code that's kind of cool, but you probably shouldn't use it anywhere. This is one of those examples.

NET automatically cleans up memory at some future point in time, but not at the end of the function scope, and it doesn't call dispose for you to clean up unmanaged resources as early as possible.

This code will allow a pattern:

```
void MyMethod()
    {
      MyClass c=new MyClass()
      //...
    } //c.Dispose() will get automatically called at the end of the method.
```

This sample code demonstrates how you can have your IDisposable objects disposed of automatically at the termination of the function scope.

Clearly, this implementation isn't suitable for every need due to the requirement to derive from ContextBoundObject for the outer class whose method scope you want to have to cause the disposal of disposable objects (and the performance potential concerns, if in a performance-intensive area).

It is, however, an interesting pattern that might be usable in some circumstances.

The basic concept is that by intercepting method calls through the ContextBoundObject and using our supplied classes, you can create a much cleaner method of cleanup for your disposable objects. The key is that for this to work, you want your function scope to cause the disposal to happen in the outer class containing that member function that needs to be derived from ContextBoundObject. You also need to apply the custom attribute [DeterministicDisposal()] to the class.

When this class gets instantiated, the CLR knows because it is derived from ContextBoundObject to look for the custom attributes. When it finds the custom attribute, it will make sure to use the proxy class specified to call with the constructor. The constructor of the proxy class creates the object and returns a proxy instead of the actual underlying object. This allows the proxy class to intercept any method calls.

When the proxy class is called the first time, it adds a stack to the context that the object is bound to (a context is just a related set of stored values). Normal objects that are not context bound can be executed in any context; ContextBound objects, when instantiated, are bound to a specific context. Because it is bound to this set of data, we create a stack type to use anytime we are in this context.

When a method is called, our proxy gets the first crack at it. We then store the current top of the stack, so we know where we were before we call the method. The method on the underlying object is then called. In the method for the object, the user may instantiate classes derived from our base class (DeterministicDisposableObject) or pass IDispsable objects to this class in the constructor, so they are protected for the scope of the method.

The DeterministicDisposableObject class adds itself to the stack that was created (in our proxy) for the context the ContextBound object is in.

When the function exits, we are back in our proxy after the method call. We would then get the current stack top and call dispose on all the items added to the stack during the method by our DeterministicDisposableObject class.

The proxy is then exited.

Again, I point out the object is a bit heavy given the proxy and therefore not always suitable. Care needs to be taken to only use the DeterministicDisposableObject within a METHOD of a class derived from ContextBoundObject that has our attribute [DeterministicDisposal()] applied to it.

You can find the source code here: https://github.com/DavesApps/AutoDisposal

```
using System;
    using System.Collections;
    using System.Diagnostics;
    using System.Runtime.InteropServices;
    using System.Runtime.Remoting;
    using System.Runtime.Remoting.Proxies;
    using System.Runtime.Remoting.Contexts;
    using System.Runtime.Remoting.Activation;
    using System.Runtime.Remoting.Messaging;
    using System.Runtime.Remoting.Services;

namespace AutoDisposal
    {
        /// <summary>
        /// Used to store constant for internal name used for call context properties or other deterministic disposal
        /// constants
        /// </summary>
        internal class DeterministicConstants
        {
                internal const string DETERMINISTIC_DISPOSAL_PROPERTY_NAME="__DeterministicDisposal";

        }

        /// <summary>
```

```
    /// This proxy class is used to be interjected between a context-bound object so that we can
    /// intercept the method calls to track disposable items and dispose of the object when completed
    /// </summary>
    internal class DeterministicDisposalProxy : RealProxy
    {
        readonly MarshalByRefObject target;    // used to store the target of the proxy

        /// <summary>
        /// Constructor of the proxy used to instatiate with the target object and type
        /// </summary>
        /// <param name="target"></param>
        /// <param name="type"></param>
        public DeterministicDisposalProxy(MarshalByRefObject target, Type type)
            : base(type)
        {
            this.target=target;

            //Get our stack object from the call context if it is there
            object obj=CallContext.GetData(DeterministicConstants.DETERMINISTIC_DISPOSAL_PROPERTY_NAME);

            if (null==obj)
            {
                //if the stack object is not already in the call context create it
```

```
                                        CallContext.SetData(Deterministic
Constants.DETERMINISTIC_DISPOSAL_PROPERTY_NAME,new
Stack());
                        }
                }

                /// <summary>
                /// The Invoke method will be called for each function
call on our contextbound object where our attribute was applied
                /// </summary>
                /// <param name="request">Information about the
method request</param>
                /// <returns></returns>
                public override IMessage Invoke(IMessage request)
                {
                        IMessage response = null;
                        IMethodCallMessage call = (IMethodCallMes-
sage)request;
                        IConstructionCallMessage ctor= call as
IConstructionCallMessage;

                        //Get the stack object that was created in our
constructor for the proxy
                        //So we can get the current high watermark of
the stack so we know the objects
                        //to dispose of after the method call returns
                        object obj=CallContext.GetData(Deterministic
Constants.DETERMINISTIC_DISPOSAL_PROPERTY_NAME);
                        Stack DisposalStack=(Stack)obj;
```

```
            //stack was not created if this fails
            Debug.Assert(obj!=null);

            //Get our current high watermark for the stack
            int BeforeCallStackTop=DisposalStack.Count;

            //see if this is the constructor call
            if (ctor!=null)
            {
                //We need to create and return our
proxy here to return it instead of the actual contextbound object
                //itself
                RealProxy defaultProxy = RemotingSer-
vices.GetRealProxy(target);
                defaultProxy.InitializeServerObject
(ctor);
                MarshalByRefObject tp = (MarshalBy-
RefObject)this.GetTransparentProxy();
                response = EnterpriseServicesHelper.
CreateConstructionReturnMessage(ctor,tp);
            }
            else
            {
                //Execute the method call
                response = RemotingServices.Execute
Message(target, call);
            }

            //Get the stacks current high water mark so we
know how many items to pop off for disposal
```

```
int ItemsToPopOffStack=DisposalStack.
Count-BeforeCallStackTop;
Debug.Assert(ItemsToPopOffStack>=0);

//If there were new items added that need to
be disposed of then
if (ItemsToPopOffStack>0)
{
//Loop to pop all of the new items off
the stack for Deterministic Disposal
for (int i=0; i<ItemsToPopOffStack;
i++)
{
IDeterministicDispose id=
(IDeterministicDispose)DisposalStack.Pop();
try
{
//Call our interface
which in turn will call the standard IDisposable interface

id.DeterministicDispose();
}
catch
{
Trace.WriteLine("Deter
ministicDisposalProxy exception - object may have already been final-
ized or destroyed");
Debug.Assert(false); //
check to see if this actually happens remove for production code
}
}
```

```
                }

                return response;

            }


        }

        /// <summary>
        /// DeterministicDisposalAttribute is the attribute that must
be applied to contextbound derived classes
        /// in order to take advantage of using the DeterministicDis-
posableObject base class (or as an object)
        /// This attribute causes our proxy to be injected between the
contextbound object and callers
        /// </summary>
        [AttributeUsage(AttributeTargets.Class)]
        internal class DeterministicDisposalAttribute : ProxyAttribute
//, IContextAttribute
        {

            public DeterministicDisposalAttribute()
            {
            }

            /// <summary>
            /// CreateInstance used to create our real proxy and
return it to the caller
            /// </summary>
            /// <param name="t"></param>
```

```
            /// <returns></returns>
            public override MarshalByRefObject
CreateInstance(Type t)
            {
                MarshalByRefObject target=base.
CreateInstance(t);
                RealProxy pp= (RealProxy)new DeterministicDi
sposalProxy(target, t);
                return (MarshalByRefObject)
pp.GetTransparentProxy();
            }


            /// <summary>
            /// IsContextOK just indicates to use the same context
for this new object by returning true
            /// </summary>
            /// <param name="ctx"></param>
            /// <param name="msg"></param>
            /// <returns></returns>
            new public bool IsContextOK(Context ctx, IConstruc-
tionCallMessage msg)
            {
                return true;
            }


        }

        /// <summary>
```

```
/// IDeterministicDispose our internal interface to be called for deterministic disposal
/// </summary>
internal interface IDeterministicDispose
{
        void DeterministicDispose();
}

/// <summary>
/// DeterministicDisposableObject this object can be used as a base class or just to pass an object to protect
/// by passing the object to the constructor.  Should be used within a method only.
/// The class that uses this in a method should have been derived from ContextBoundObject for it
/// to be deterministically disposed.  Should not be used in a non-contextbound object as call context would be saved
/// and would not be cleaned up, plus the objects would never get destroyed
/// </summary>
public class DeterministicDisposableObject : IDisposable, IDeterministicDispose
{
        /// <summary>
        /// Default constructor puts our object in the callcontext stack so we will get disposed when the method call is done
        /// </summary>
        public DeterministicDisposableObject()
        {
```

```
                    Stack                    DisposableStack=(Stack)
CallContext.GetData(DeterministicConstants.
DETERMINISTIC_DISPOSAL_PROPERTY_NAME);
                    Debug.Assert(DisposableStack!=null);
                    DisposableStack.Push(this);
            }

            /// <summary>
            /// Constructor used to pass an object that is IDisposable
            /// </summary>
            /// <param name="o"></param>
            public DeterministicDisposableObject(IDisposable o)
            {
                    //Save reference to our object so we can call its
dispose later
                    ReferencedObject_=o;

                    Stack                    DisposableStack=(Stack)
CallContext.GetData(DeterministicConstants.
DETERMINISTIC_DISPOSAL_PROPERTY_NAME);
                    Debug.Assert(DisposableStack!=null);
                    DisposableStack.Push(this);
            }

            /// <summary>
            /// virtual Dispose function can be override by a derived
class to implement objects own dispose
            /// </summary>
            public virtual void Dispose() { }
```

```
/// <summary>
/// internal DeterministicDispose dispose function calls
dispose on referenced object, this object
/// and frees interop handles to allow for garbage
collection
/// </summary>
public void DeterministicDispose()
{
    if (null!=ReferencedObject_)
    {
        try
        {
            ReferencedObject_.Dispose();
        }
        catch
        {
            Trace.WriteLine("Disposable
Object.DeterministicDispose Exception while calling passed objects
Dispose.");
        }

    }

    try
    {
        //call our virtual member function. It
may have been overridden so we should protect
        //from failure
        Dispose();
    }
    catch
```

```
                    {
                            Trace.WriteLine("DisposableObject.
DeterministicDispose Exception while calling passed objects Dispose.");
                    }

            }

            //Class members
            private IDisposable ReferencedObject_;          //used
for passed in object

        }


    }
```

Class1.cs:

```
using System;
    using AutoDisposal;

namespace DeterministicDisposalTest
    {

        /// <summary>
        /// Test class that implements IDisposable
        /// </summary>
        public class MyTestDisposableClass : IDisposable
        {
            public virtual void Dispose() { Console.WriteLine("MyT
estDisposableClass.Dispose called"); }
```

```
    }

    /// <summary>
    /// Test class derived from DeterministicDisposableObject to
show how disposal works
    /// </summary>
    public class MyTestDerivedDisposableClass :
DeterministicDisposableObject
    {
        public override void Dispose() { Console.WriteLine("M
yTestDerivedDisposableClass.Dispose called"); }
    }


    /// <summary>
    /// Test class for DeterministicDisposal. A Contextbound class
must be used with our attribute applied to
    /// it in order for deterministic disposal to work correctly.
    /// </summary>
    [DeterministicDisposal()]
    public class TestDeterministicDisposal : ContextBoundObject
    {
        public TestDeterministicDisposal()
        {
        }

        /// <summary>
        /// Test function to simulate some objects that need
disposal
        /// </summary>
        public void DoWork()
```

```
                {
                        //test of a derived deterministic disposable
object
                        //to be disposed at the end of this function
                        MyTestDerivedDisposableClass        dobj=new
MyTestDerivedDisposableClass();

                        //test of protecting a standard disposable
object to be cleaned up at the end of this function
                        MyTestDisposableClass               obj2=new
MyTestDisposableClass();
                        DeterministicDisposableObject      dobj2=new
DeterministicDisposableObject(obj2);

                }

        }


        /// <summary>
        /// Summary description for Class1.
        /// </summary>
        class Class1
        {
                /// <summary>
                /// The main entry point for the application.
                /// </summary>
                [STAThread]
                static void Main(string[] args)
                {
```

```
                    TestDeterministicDisposal tdd=new Test
DeterministicDisposal();
                    tdd.DoWork();

                    // note the console output shows the dispose
methods on both variables allocated in
                    // tdd.DoWork() were disposed

            }
        }
    }
```

Data Objects

Imagine if you could write classes where you almost never have to pass more than one parameter. You could create components that would implement logic to transform data to what you needed. You could chain a pipeline together to create new algorithms from existing ones.

The concept of componentized software came up a long time ago. The problem was that components were always different. You always needed new parameters of data and new classes that worked a little differently. There was no way to just connect one component to another and make it work.

This idea was part of a concept that a colleague/friend showed me many years back. It became the basis of the implementation of a UI and client API framework we built.

Imagine if you create a class called a data object that could hold multiple variables mapping a string name/type (pseudo code below). Data Object is somewhat similar to a database row. There are varying solutions to support something similar.

```
DataObject do=new DataObject();

    do["IsBegin"]=(bool)true;
    do["IsEnd"]=(bool)false;

    do["NumberOfCars"]=(double)1000000;
    do["NumberOfBoats"]=(double)2000000;

    // IsBegin changes from 1(true) to string "true"// IsEnd changes
from 0(false) to string "false"
    TranslateBooleansToStrings(do);

    // NumberOfCars changes from 1000000 to "1,000,000"
    //NumberOfBoats changes from 2000000 to "2,000,000"
    FormatIntegers(do);
```

Imagine if you had a class that could chain those calls together for you:

```
    Processor processor=new Processor(TranslateBooleansToStrings,F
ormatIntegers);

    //Does the same thing as calling TranslateBooleansToStrings
    //and FormatIntegers
    Processor.Execute(do);
```

If all of your information was passed around as data objects rather than individual, hard-coded typed variables, you have ways to operate on your data that were difficult before.

There are some things in C# that now allow you to deal with regular classes like data, such as LINQ. You might think you could use regular classes and wouldn't need a DataObject. The issue with LINQ is that it really wasn't designed for you to go through and update values. It certainly won't let you easily change or add types on an existing strongly typed object (unless it was designed to allow such things). There are likely third-party implementations that might make it possible to design objects to support operations like this, sort of like a data object mentioned above.

Think about the benefits of sending data around everywhere this way. You don't need to write specific code with hard-coded parameters anymore.

The benefit of sending data around this way is that you can write generic processing algorithms that don't need to be coupled with specific hard-coded properties/types.

You could even design multithreaded pipelines to handle transformations of data such that the transformation code can be written as if it were a single thread, but you could distribute data through multiple pipelines to scale if you like.

Imagine if you had servers you called, and all of the client APIs could return the same type of data object so that all of your standard components that work with data objects generically could work the same way.

Now imagine if you could connect either a desktop UI or web interface to the data object such that changes to the data object can affect the UI or UI changes can affect the data object, basically being bound to the UI. If you write logic that can modify data objects for a certain purpose, they could potentially be used in background processing or even connected to the UI processing. This means the things you write can be a lot more generalized than they are if you need to hard code types, properties, and classes.

The downside of this method is that data objects might be a bit heavier than a hard-coded specific type. But you could design an IDataObject interface and use that instead of the data object directly.

Then you could write hard-coded specific types that mimic the functionality needed for the data object but with much higher performance and potentially lighter weight.

This type of solution could be useful when you know you will be passing around a lot of data similar to a database row.

.NET Source Code

Did you know that if you are working with .NET, C#, or other .NET languages, if you would like to view the source code to better understand how things are working, you can.

.NET source code can be found here: https://github.com/dotnet

If you want, you can find tools that will let you debug even into the Microsoft source so you can see exactly what is happening. Redgate Reflector is one example (https://www.red-gate.com/products/dotnet-development/reflector/).

You probably won't need to do this very often, but it is great to know it is there. It is also great to see examples of production code used by millions of people. So if you want to see how it's done, you can peruse the source to take a look.

CHAPTER 30

Multithreading

Multithreading

Most programming languages themselves, at their core, are designed to run code sequentially, and by default, they don't directly take into account what needs to be done for multiple threads in the generated assembly language. Many languages support using multiple threads and leave it to the software engineers to handle the complexity of threads.

Multithreading Can Make Things Both Faster and Slower

Imagine a scenario where you need to write a document, and you know it will take you two hours. You realize your manager needs this document in less than two hours, so you ask a colleague to help you write it, figuring if you split the work in half, it should only take one hour for the both of you to complete. Both of you are sharing the same documents, editing at the same time in Google Docs. Each of you finishes in an hour and a half. So if you added both of your times together, it would equal three hours rather than the two hours it should have taken. You didn't finish the document in one hour. It took an hour and a half.

Multithreading can be very much like this. If you consider each of the people above as a thread, originally, one thread took two hours, and when you split the work into two, then two threads took an hour and a half each for a three-hour total. The two threads were still completed in less than what it would have taken to sequentially do the work, but you were expecting the time to be half of what it took before for each thread. It's still nice that the total amount of work completes in less than two hours.

What is happening here is that the work isn't exactly being divided by two. Multithreading adds a little overhead when a CPU needs to switch from one thread to another thread. In addition, resources are shared, like CPU, memory, disk, network, etc. Sometimes, two operations to the same memory, disk, or network can't happen at precisely the same time, so one thread is blocked for very small amounts of time while the other proceeds. That amount of blocking doesn't sound like much, but if there are hundreds of thousands of operations like that where there is blocking, it starts to add up.

Another scenario is where you have only one CPU. Imagine the same scenario, and you split up the work. It originally took two hours to complete with one thread, and with two threads, now it's taking two and a half hours! What happened? If your workload is entirely CPU bound, meaning it only needs the CPU, there really isn't any opportunity for two threads to do better than the original thread with only one CPU.

Imagine you had a project where you had to cut wood to make a shed. The cutting would take you two hours on your own, so you figure to ask a friend to help. The only problem is that you only have one saw. Thus, each person needs to wait for the other to finish with the saw before they can do any work. Sharing one CPU is kind of like that. It can result in slower times if the workload for the threads is running 100 percent on the CPU busy all of the time.

Let's rethink the above scenario, though, imagining the saw as the CPU. We imagined everything that needed to be done required the CPU (saw). But in reality, there is some benefit to your friend helping you saw. Your friend can get the pieces of wood set up to saw, so it may take a little less time. This can be similar to some thread workloads. If the workload you are processing wasn't waiting on the CPU 100 percent of the time and instead had to wait on the disk or networking, the multithreading could offer similar benefits to our above scenario.

Synchronization Objects

Most languages have thread synchronization objects that control the execution of threads. Critical sections/mutex are often used to protect access to variables/data by preventing more than one thread from being running at a time within the section of code it is protecting. By doing this, if a variable is read or written to, it can be assured to only be touched by one thread. This prevents what is called race conditions, where variables can be read from or written to at the same time other threads are reading/or writing, making the value that it writes or reads unpredictable.

Semaphores often have a count associated with them and are used to protect a certain number of resources (so that threads can be made to wait when it runs out of the resource it is protecting). They are typically slower than a critical section or mutex.

A hybrid synchronization object is a ReaderWriterLock, allowing your code to take a read lock or a write lock when accessing a resource (sometimes even allowing upgrading from a read lock to a write lock while it is holding a read lock). This can be useful for resources that are read more than they are written to, allowing many threads to read but only one to write. They are typically slower than critical sections or mutex.

Spin locks are an optimized synchronization object for a resource being accessed very often, and we'd like to get some better performance, not waiting as long for the resource. Instead, it polls a certain number of times before falling back to a critical section or mutex. Spinning, of course, uses up CPU for threads while it may be doing nothing other than waiting, so it is not necessarily the most efficient use of a thread, but it can depend on the circumstances.

Lock-Free Synchronization

Locks cause threads to be suspended and wait until they can acquire a synchronization object and proceed. Lock-free implementations typically poll in a way that is thread safe or can detect multiple threads at a point to allow or prevent access to a region of code. Lock free is typically faster. It's best not to try to implement these yourself and use a well-known and tested implementation, as lock-free synchronization can be very tricky and hard to know if you have implemented a safe pattern. If you really decide to try this on your own, you have a lot of reading and testing to do first. Great understanding of CPUs' memory barriers, atomic operations, volatile variables, and more are required before attempting to do this yourself, which is not recommended.

Memory Barriers

In order to improve performance, the processor/compiler can allow, in some cases, a read to be read from the cache without going to the actual memory location. Some processors could even allow a write to do that. Memory barriers are a way of telling the processor/compiler not to let that happen. There are both read and write barriers when both are used. It's called a full barrier.

Volatile

In C, C++, and C#, volatile typically means to not store the value of a variable in a CPU register and instead read or write directly to memory. It also usually means to use a full barrier for that variable when it is accessed. This alone does not make access to the variable safe to do from multiple threads without a synchronization object. It just means the value will be read/written to memory immediately rather than perhaps waiting till later for a variable that has been assigned to a CPU register to be put into actual memory. This can be useful because, in some cases, a compiler for speed might put a variable in a CPU register that is only visible to the local thread and not any other threads. Using volatile ensures writing or reading to the variable will be visible to other threads.

Interlocked Increment

Some processors have a lock-free way to increment and decrement values. Under certain circumstances, this can be used to update values and even implement lock-free synchronization algorithms.

Cache Lines/False Sharing

See cache lines under General Development Understanding Hardware.

Disruptor Pattern

The disruptor pattern, invented by the company LMAX, is a brilliant mix of software using the hardware to its maximum benefit. It provides low latency and high throughput of queuing items to send to another thread or threads. It brilliantly avoids false sharing situations or even sharing in some cases. It also benefits from reusing the same memory to keep it all in high-speed cache. It uses a ring buffer to keep updating the same memory while another thread reads. If the data is high speed, the writer stays ahead of the reader, and the threads avoid touching near the same memory at the same time, which greatly improves the performance of the solution. It is a lock-free implementation that uses the functionality of the Intel processors to the maximum benefit.

The downside of the solution is that to achieve this level of performance, only one thread can publish into the ring buffer. Many threads can read, though. This means it can't function as a normal multithreaded data structure like an array or a linked list that is protected by a synchronization object; it can only have one thread publish to the ring buffer to achieve this performance. Also, the buffer has to be sized such that the reader does not catch up to the writer too quickly. Hence, not all workloads may benefit from this pattern, but those that do like, low latency trading, can achieve incredible performance.

OpenMP, Task Parallel Library, and Other Threading Language Enhancements

These enhancements can be useful to parallelize code better. Some of these have ways to even execute a for loop with many threads. The downside of these methods is that they don't have great ways to automatically control the limits to the number of threads created based on the number of cores on a machine. They also don't really work well with other threads doing the same thing and leave it up to the developer to figure this out to manage things well. This can lead to creating loads of threads that overwhelm a computer, OS, or more. Often, it can be better to have logically controlled levels of parallelism in your applications.

How Many Threads Should You Use?

This depends on what the threads are doing and if they are CPU bound or I/O bound. If they are CPU bound using 100 percent CPU, it's probably best to use one less thread than there are processors to allow the OS to still have a processor to use. If the threads do very little other than wait on disk I/O, network, or other I/O, perhaps there can be lots more threads than CPUs, so this will be very workload dependent.

Why/When Should You Use Thread?

- Improve performance throughput with concurrency.
- Background tasks.
- Asynchronous to avoid the current thread waiting to improve response times/latency.
- Improve responsiveness of a UI.

Considerations

- An individual task being a well-defined set with not too much interaction with other threads is ideal.
- It's ideal when data does not need to be shared between threads at the same time. Keeping cross thread data access to a minimum will improve performance and make things easier to build and test.

When to Use Case Creating Threads

- Avoid threads when tasks are too small, so the cost to spin up a task/thread doesn't cost as much or more than the work it will do.
- Avoid too many threads if CPU bound, as more threads than cores may decrease performance and increase time to process; if I/O bound, the number of threads can be higher but will need to be tuned for your workload/machine.

- If possible, avoid complex ordering of locked resources to avoid deadlocks.
- Consider the impacts one thread will have on another thread.

When Memory Needs or Doesn't Need Locks/Synchronization

- When memory can only be accessed by one thread, no locks are needed.
- If memory that is shared by two or more threads is read-only, then no locking should be needed (volatile might be needed).
- Memory that is changed from multiple threads will require locks/synchronization.
- There are some special scenarios where updates can be done with non-blocking locks (sometimes called lock free) (Should only be used when performance reasons are worth it).

Resources can often be considered in a similar way to memory (e.g., file handle, GDI object, etc.)

However, in some resources, even reading can change their state, like file position, so consider the effects of any operations that happen on a resource and consider the level of locking that is appropriate.

Check out this site for some detailed C# info:
https://www.albahari.com/threading/

Recommendations

Make your intentions clear about which variables are being protected by which synchronization objects.

For example, see:
ThreadGuard (https://github.com/DavesApps/ThreadGuard). C#

This code is based on an idea recommended for C#. This could be done better at the C# and compiler level in some cases (GuardedBy feature)

.dotnet/csharplang#892

Multithreaded code is easy to get wrong. A couple of the main concerns are:

1. Race conditions due to unprotected variable access are easy to introduce/hard to detect
2. Deadlocks due to lock ordering
3. Live locks, lock contention

This code addresses some areas of problem #1. It does this by helping to make multithreading clear/defined about which synchronization objects are protecting which code elements are more visible. Currently, when using locks, developers reading others, code needs to infer what variables are to be protected and by which synchronization objects by looking at all the variables accessed in a code block between acquiring and release of a lock. If we can make this more visible in code, it will be easier to tell what variables/objects should be protected and by which synchronization objects. Also, this code has the ability to detect when unprotected access to variables/objects is attempted to catch when these problems happen.

Goals

- Make it easy to visualize protected and unprotected variable access
- Detect unprotected variable access

This isn't a new idea. Java already has something similar.

It's easy to make your multithreaded variable decisions visible and protect your variables from access without the synchronization object being acquired.

Example of creating a Monitor (standard C# lock) and using it to protect a bool variable (you can protect as many variables as you want):

```
MonitorGuard _mgc = new MonitorGuard();
GuardedVar<bool> _tcv = new GuardedVar<bool> (_mgc); // this variable is guarded by the _mgc monitor/lock.
```

Example of using the variable after acquiring the lock

```
using (mgc.Acquire ())
{
        _tcv.Value = true;

}
```

If you use the guarded variable without acquiring the lock first, it will throw a configurable exception by default, that is GuardFailureException.

With that code, it's easy to tell which of your variables needs multi-threading protection, and it will throw an exception when used unprotected. These are very lightweight checks, so performance should not be impacted.

ThreadGuard also lets you encode your intentions for a lock-free variable accessing via Volatile.Read and Volatile.Write methods. Normally when you do this, in many cases, you can only have one thread writing to the variable, and other threads can read. Sometimes you only use variables like this to tell a thread to exit—typically, the only safe usage is, for example, defaulting a bool to false like IsDone and setting it to true (ideally from one thread- though other variants exist).

You can encode your intentions as follows.

```
GuardedVolatileVarBool _tgvvIsDone = new
                                    GuardedVolatileVarBool(true);
_tgvvIsDone.Value = false;


    Thread thread1 = new Thread(() =>
    {
      while (!_tgvvIsDone.Value)
      { //do something here
      }
    });
    thread1.Start();
    //do something
    _tgvvIsDone.Value = true; // cause thread to exit.
thread1.Join();
```

So with this example, it's easy to see variable _tgvvIsDone is protected, and if it's used inappropriately, like writing to the value from multiple threads, it will throw an exception. It is also best practice (in some cases required) to use volatile for variable access, which it does in that class. It will even prevent changing the value to something different if you desire (only allowing one to write to the value; i.e., a one shot flag is often the safest way to use).

Summary

Thus, in the above code, you can:

- Make your intentions clear about the protected variables.
- Clarify which synchronization objects are protecting which variables.

- Detect improper access of variables without proper synch object acquisition.
- Clarify the intentions of volatile variable access and ensure use in a safer way.

In the compiler, they could use keywords instead of needing these classes. It may also be able to detect some improper use at compile time for some cases. In the meantime, consider using something like these ideas to make your multithreaded code safer.

If you like the ThreadGuard idea, please vote here:
https://github.com/dotnet/csharplang/discussions/892

Threading Synchronization Primitives

Threading Synchronization Primitives

These examples are all from C#, but have similar options in most modern languages.

Lock (Monitor): Used for synchronization of access within a process.

AutoResetEvent: Allows signaling the release of one thread at a time.

ManualResetEvent: Allows signaling and can release all threads until manual reset.

ManualResetEventSlim: Lighter weight Manual Reset Event.

Mutex: Used for cross process synchronization.

Semaphore: Allows for a certain number of threads to access a resource

SemaphoreSlim: Lighter weight semaphore.

SpinLock: When little contention may be beneficial as compared to lock.

ReaderWriterLock: Allows single-writer multiple readers.

ReaderWriterLockSlim: Lighter weight ReaderWriterLock.

Spinlock: Useful for low contention areas for reduced latency.

Exclusive Lock

One of the most common ways to protect variables/resources to allow only one thread in at a time. Lock/monitor is one of the fastest synchronization mechanisms in C#.

```
private object _lock = new Object();
    Private int count=0;
    public int Increment (decimal amount)
    {
       lock (_lock) {
        return count++;
    }
    }
    //NOTE: Avoid lock(this), as it can expose the possibility of
deadlock.
```

Lock/Monitor

Same as lock. Basically, lock is syntactic sugar for this.

```
bool _locked= false;
    var _lockObj = new object();
    try {
    Monitor.Enter(_lockObj, ref _locked);
     //... code to do something here...
    }
    finally
    {
     if (_locked) Monitor.Exit(_lockObj);
    }
```

Mutex

Similar to lock but also allows cross process locking via a named mutex.

The overhead for this type of object is significantly more than lock, so it really should only be used if cross process capability is needed.

It only allows one thread at a time to enter.

```
private readonly Mutex m = new Mutex (false,"GlobalNameHere");
public void Method()
{
    m.WaitOne();
    try { /* code here */ }
    finally { m.ReleaseMutex(); }
}
```

AutoResetEvent

Allows one thread at a time to enter when signaled. Signaled state allows one thread to proceed, which is triggered by the Set() call. Significantly higher overhead. Use when signaling to allow one thread to run/wake up is needed and the rest remain blocked until signaled again.

```
class AutoResetEventTest
    {
        static AutoResetEvent _autoresetEvent = new
AutoResetEvent(false);
        static void MainThread()
        {
            new Thread(WaitOnAutoResetEvent).Start();
            Thread.Sleep(3000);         // delay a bit
            _autoresetEvent.Set();      // notify the other thread
        }

    static void WaitOnAutoResetEvent()
        {
            Console.WriteLine("Waiting for Set() to be called...");
            _autoresetEvent.WaitOne();          // Wait for notification
            Console.WriteLine("Signaled and running...");
        }
    }
```

ManualResetEvent/ManualResetEventSlim

Manual reset events work similar to AutoResetEvents EXCEPT, when signaled (Set()), they let all the threads waiting in until it is Reset() (not signaled). Use the slim version for reduced uncontended overhead. Use when you need to signal it's ok for multiple threads to run/block.

Semaphore

Allows multiple threads to enter up to a configured count. Control number of threads access to a resource.

```
class HazardChecker  {
      static SemaphoreSlim _semaphore = new SemaphoreSlim (5);   //
5 People allowed in
       static void Main()
       {
          for (int i = 1; i <= 7; i++) new Thread (Enter).Start (i);
       }
       static void Enter (object id)  {
        Console.WriteLine ("Person ID: "+id + " would like to enter.");
        _semaphore.Wait();
         Console.WriteLine ("Person ID:"+id + " ID is in!");          // Only
five threads
        Thread.Sleep (500 * (int) id);            // sit down for a while up to
500*id milliseconds
        Console.WriteLine ("Person ID:"+id + " is leaving soon.");
        _semaphore.Release();
        Console.WriteLine ("Person ID:"+id + " has left now.");
       }
     }
```

ReaderWriterLock

ReaderWriter locks should be used when reading happens more frequently than writing and writes are short.

Richter's *CLR via C#* points out that this class is slower than using monitor/lock itself for both .NET 1.1 and .NET 2.0 (though the slim version available now might be worth comparing that to).

His book offers a reference to a class he implemented that outperforms the .NET variant significantly.

The single-writer multi-reader lock supports lock upgrades and downgrades.

The original ReaderWriterLock (not the slim version) is flawed. A common mistake with the original version in the process to acquire a read lock, loop through a collection to find an item to remove, then call upgrade to a writer lock, then remove the item and downgrade/unlock.

In the above scenario, when an upgrade is called, the reader and writer lock is freed, allowing another writer to potentially remove, modify, or add elements which could cause deleting or changing the wrong item.

The newer slim version is said to have corrected this.

If you will be doing more writing than reading multi-reader single-writer locks could perform poorly.

Spinlocks

Spinlocks are designed to be faster than regular locks when contention is low and locks are held for short time periods (can also reduce latency by avoiding entering the kernel). Spinlocks do a busy wait for the lock to free up, consuming CPU time for a short time period while the lock is being used by another thread. It does this with the assumption that the lock should be released quickly enough to avoid the thread being put to sleep and avoiding a context switch. By avoiding context switching or, in some cases, kernel transition, performance can be increased with the right implementation for certain lock workloads and scenarios. As in all threading implementations, testing is needed to determine how it performs for you for the scenario and workload required. Spinlocks are widely used in the Windows kernel, SQL server, and more.

Important factors: Contention, length of time lock held (i.e., workload), latency requirements.

- Reduced overhead compared to lock when uncontended.
- Busy waits for a short period to see if it can acquire the lock.
- Can avoid context switches if it can acquire lock during the busy/wait.
- Good for locks that won't be held long and require low overhead time, and can live with burning CPU for the busy wait period.

Thread Safe Collections (.NET)
Be careful about using them.

Sometimes, these are best avoided in most cases for the standard collections, as they are typically implemented by a wrapper around the collection.

Sometimes, you will need synchronization at a higher level anyway to allow for testing something in the collection and then doing an action on it.

MethodImplOptions.Synchronized attribute C#
[MethodImplAttribute(MethodImplOptions.Synchronized)]

Public void Test() //locks on the instance if applied to this method

Static public void Test() //locks on the type if applied to this method

[ThreadStatic]
public class MyClass {

```
[ThreadStatic] static double first = 1.0;   //first thread initializes, later threads get default
[ThreadStatic] double second=2.0; //Each thread gets the initialized value
}
```

Thread static will create a new instance of this variable on each thread. Note that this means for the life of the thread, the value/object will exist.

ThreadLocal<T>

```
ThreadLocal<string> MyThreadName = new ThreadLocal<string>(() =>
    { return "Thread id:" + Thread.CurrentThread.ManagedThreadId; });

MyThreadName.Dispose();
```

Similar to ThreadStatic, except can solve the problem of initialization for each new thread with the lambda. This form should be disposed of when done using for the current thread.

BeginThreadAffinity, EndThreadAffinity

```
[SecurityPermission(SecurityAction.Demand, Flags=SecurityPermissionFlag.ControlThread)]
    public class WrapperClassForThreadAffinity {
    [SecurityPermission(SecurityAction.Demand, Flags=SecurityPermissionFlag.ControlThread)]
    public void PerformMyTask() {

// Code that does not have thread affinity goes here.
```

```
    Thread.BeginThreadAffinity();
    // Code that has a thread affinity goes here.
    Thread.EndThreadAffinity();
    // And More code that doesn't have a thread affinity.
    }
    }
```

If your C# code relies on the underlying operating system thread not being changed this method calls will help your thread keep that OS thread affinity.

BeginCriticalRegion

```
public void DoMyWork() {
    // Code here can be aborted without affecting  other work
    Thread.BeginCriticalRegion();
    // Protected code here
    Thread.EndCriticalRegion();
    }
```

Provides a way to notify the CLR that a section of code is critical and might want to be handled differently if a thread abort/exception happens.

Named Data Slots

```
int slotData = randomGenerator.Next(1, 10000); int threadId = Thread.
CurrentThread.ManagedThreadId;
    Thread.SetData(Thread.GetNamedDataSlot("MyRandomValue"),
slotData);
```

This is another way to store thread specific data, though not as fast as [ThreadStatic]/Threadlocal methods.

Threading Topics

Compiler/JIT

- Can reorder writes/reads.
- Can store variables in registers where changes won't be visible to other threads.
- Can optimize out code if it doesn't appear to be used by the current single thread.

The Compiler and JIT can have an impact on your multithreaded code.

The compiler and JIT can reorder variable accesses and even not access variables when you would think it should.

The Compiler/JIT can optimize out code it doesn't think you need.

The key is that the compiler/JIT by default optimizes things under the presumption that there is only one thread running the code.

Therefore, if you read a variable A, modify variable B, and read variable A again, the compiler/JIT may completely optimize out the second read of A, since from a single thread point of view, it shouldn't recognize any difference.

However, if your code were multithreaded and that second read mattered, your code will see the old value rather than a potential new value.

Why would they do that?! Answer coming up soon.

CPU/Registers/Cache/Memory

Registers are very high-speed memory on the CPU separate and not directly related to the rest of the memory.

A Few More Details on CPU/Cores:

A CPU core can execute multiple operations at once, up to 5–8+ on many modern processors.

They can read ahead in execution and even predict which path your code may take and execute ahead!

Reads, writes, and executions of several instructions can happen out-of-order due to the speculative execution!

Again, the CPU executes code with the default assumption of the point of view of one thread, so it assumes that as long as the point of view of one thread won't notice the difference, it is fine.

How do we deal with the compiler/JIT/CPU to handle multithreading?

If you use synchronization objects like lock, monitor, semaphore, etc., all of those will ensure that you don't have to worry about compiler/JIT/CPU issues of not reading memory or reordering reads and writes.

If you stick with using standard synchronization objects, they are built to avoid many of the concerns. However, if you access memory from multiple threads without synchronization using non-blocking or lock-free methods, then things get much trickier

Volatile Keyword

Summarized facts from ("Volatile," *C# Reference* | *Microsoft Learn*, n.d.):

When you use volatile, it tells the compiler to assume other threads/processors/hardware could be updating the variable. Usually, when you do this, the compiler will read or write the value directly from the memory location where it is stored. It will avoid storing the value in some temp location, like a CPU register. This way, all threads are reading or writing the location of the value of the variable directly. If this wasn't done, it might be possible to not see updates to the variable in another thread.

See Microsoft reference:
http://msdn.microsoft.com/en-us/library/x13ttww7.aspx.

Note: This is ONLY true for same value/memory location sequencing. The volatile modifier is usually used for a field that is accessed by multiple threads without using the lock statement to serialize access. This may be ok if one thread writes and the other just reads.

In .NET, volatile forces the compiler/JIT to make sure writes/reads from a variable are requested directly to and from memory rather than to CPU registers and provide ordered atomics for lock-free programming. This effectively results in a half fence or full fence. Full fence on writes and read fence for reads. Compiler/CPU optimizations are also limited for the variables used before/after a volatile is used.

Acquire and Release Semantics

Some paraphrased facts from the Microsoft docs ("Acquire and Release Semantics," *Windows Drivers | Microsoft Learn*, n.d.).

You can think of "acquire" semantics as a way of preventing the reordering of operations and "release" semantics as a way to prevent certain reordering of operations related to writing a specific memory location.

Trying to make use of this knowledge for lock-free algorithms and data structures can be fraught with risk. Care needs to be taken if the code is intended to work cross-platform, since different hardware platforms may have different behaviors.

From Microsoft Docs:

http://msdn.microsoft.com/en-us/library/windows/hardware/ff540496(v=vs.85).aspx

Notes: Volatile has these effects on x86 not because the compiler/ JIT adds anything but just because that's the way x86 processors work when you read from a memory location or write to a memory location.

Memory Barrier (a.k.a. Fence)

Thread.MemoryBarrier() (a.k.a. Full fence read/write)

Synchronizes memory access as follows: The processor executing the current thread cannot reorder instructions in such a way that memory accesses prior to the call to MemoryBarrier execute after memory accesses that follow the call to MemoryBarrier.

Some people online suggest VolatileRead/Write just uses full fence memory barrier.

Thread.VolatileRead()

Reads the value of a field. The value is the latest written by any processor on a computer, regardless of the number of processors or the state of the processor cache.

Thread.VolatileWrite()

Writes a value to a field. On systems that require it, insert a memory barrier that prevents a read or write operation from being reordered after this call.

Implicit Memory Barriers/Fence

Standard synchronization classes are expected to create memory barriers/fences (e.g., lock, Monitor.Enter/Exit, Interlocked class, non-inlined functions, etc.).

Volatile Methods

Thread.VolatileRead/Thread.VolatileWrite

These methods perhaps should be avoided. There is some user community suggestion that they don't seem like they guarantee atomic operations and insert a full fence (mfence) rather than using acquire and release semantics.

Volatile.Read/Volatile.Write

These methods appear to guarantee atomic operations and use acquire/ release semantics.

.NET Volatile Keyword Compiler/JIT C#

Volatile keyword indicates to the compiler to ensure that reads and writes must be in order and the field should not be cached (as in stored in a register).

Volatile acquires fences (read or write).

When reasonable, use interlocked methods or higher-level lock mechanisms to avoid volatile keyword usage since this enforces all accesses to a field to be uncached.

If you can't avoid using volatile, perhaps using Volatile.Read and Volatile.Write methods provided by .NET may be better, as it does not require the above semantics for all field access.

By default, on the .NET platform, reads can be done out of sequence and writes must be in order.

Note: On x86 platforms, volatile prevents only compiler optimization, as the x86 memory model ensures acquire semantics on reads, release semantics on writes.

Quick Summary

Volatile affects the compiler/JIT so that variables won't be stored in a register, and thus that reads and writes happen to memory.

In .NET, it also insures acquire/release semantics, preventing certain memory reordering (technically on x86 platforms, .NET doesn't have to do anything for that, since the CPU supports this; in theory, on other platforms that don't have those semantics, it would need to enforce them).

By using the volatile keyword, you tell the compiler/JIT to never cache. It might be better to use the Volatile.Read and write calls if you need to allow some caching sometimes.

CPU x86 (Memory Model)

- Reads will not change order with other reads.
- Writes will not change order with earlier reads.
- Writes will not change order with other writes (with some exceptions for specific processor instructions).
- Writes will not change order CLFLUSH operation.
- Reads may change order with earlier writes to other memory addresses.
- Reads or writes will not change order with locked or I/O operations.

See the Intel developers manual for even more detail.

Intel® 64 and IA-32 Architectures Software Developer's Manual Combined Volumes: 1, 2A, 2B, 2C, 2D, 3A, 3B, 3C, 3D, and 4

See section: 8.2.2 Memory Ordering in P6 and More Recent Processor Families https://www.intel.com/content/www/us/en/developer/articles/technical/intel-sdm.html

(*Intel® 64 and IA-32 Architectures Software Developer Manuals*, n.d.).

CPU x86 Not Guaranteed

Reads may change ordering with older writes for other memory addresses.

Thread 1

```
a=1;
m1=a
```

Thread 2

```
b=1;
m2=b;
```

Running thread 1 and 2 on different cores can yield m1 == 0 and m2 == 0, because it is a change of order between a read and a write to different memory locations.

Reference: (*Intel® 64 and IA-32 Architectures Software Developer Manuals*, n.d.).

Modified example from section: Example 8-3. Loads May be Reordered with Older Stores.

Intel® 64 and IA-32 Architectures Software Developer's Manual Combined Volumes: 1, 2A, 2B, 2C, 2D, 3A, 3B, 3C, 3D, and 4.

https://www.intel.com/content/www/us/en/developer/articles/technical/intel-sdm.html

(*Intel® 64 and IA-32 Architectures Software Developer Manuals*, n.d.).

As I alluded to before, there are some things that are not guaranteed.

In this example, you might expect that you might see results of [1,1],[1,0],[0,1], but believe it or not, it is possible that you could run the instructions on both threads and end up with [m1=0,m2=0].

This is because of the reordering of instructions and potentially delayed writes can be cached (even if you used volatile). They can be cached at the CPU/core level.

We already saw how to solve this issue, though, using Memory Barriers (or synchronization objects/classes).

Atomic Operations

An atomic operation is an operation that can execute either completely or not. By default, any sequence of two or more machine instructions isn't atomic, since the operating system may suspend the execution of the current sequence of operations in favor of another task.

Access to 32 bit values/object references on 32 bit platform can be atomic.

Access to 32 bit and 64 bit values/objects on a 64 bit platform can be atomic.

(This only means Read or Write operations, not Read-> Modify->Write).

Interlocked operations (can do read/modify/write operations atomically).

Note: Atomics rely on memory alignment on 32/64 bit boundaries which .NET does by default for 32 bit variables on 32 bit platforms and 32/64 bit variables on 64 bit platforms.

("ECMA-335," *Ecma International*, n.d.).

See reference:
http://www.ecma-international.org/publications/standards/Ecma-335.htm

- Writing a 32 bit value is atomic.
- Reading a 32 bit value is atomic.
- Incrementing a 32 bit value is not atomic with normal instructions since it has to read first, then write.
- On 64 bit platforms, 32 bit or 64 bit reads/writes are atomic.
- Interlocked operations are atomic (like Interlocked Increment).

Atomic operations rely on alignment on 32 bit/64 bit boundaries in memory, which is the default way memory is allocated.

.NET Threads/OS Threads

.NET threads may not map to OS threads directly.

- This means don't rely on native thread API calls for thread control/information.
- This is mostly true for thread pool threads, though MS has not excluded this from happening for other threads.
- If you are manually creating your own new thread, it may actually map to an OS thread, but you shouldn't rely on that.

.NET threads may not map directly to OS threads, so avoid using native thread APIs.

This is mostly the case for thread pool threads.

Threading Performance/NUMA

Preallocating memory can be useful with object pools to avoid GCs, though consider NUMA.

For NUMA systems, accessing memory allocated in one thread/core and using on another thread/core can have some negative performance impacts on NUMA systems.

With NUMA, specific memory is associated with specific processors. Accessing memory from one processor on another processors NUMA node/memory results in additional overhead for each access.

NUMA stands for Non-Uniform Memory Access, which basically just means some memory accesses can be faster or slower than others. NUMA memory is associated with particular CPU sockets, so if you have two CPUs with four cores each, depending on the hardware, that might be two NUMA nodes.

The ideal usage is when you use memory from your NUMA node from a CPU standpoint and don't access memory from other NUMA nodes.

This is easier to take advantage of from C++ using direct Windows APIs to control allocation.

From a .NET perspective, you can assume if you allocate memory on a NUMA system, it likely will come from your NUMA node. So a less performant design would allocate all memory on one thread and use it from more threads than there are on a NUMA node.

A more performant design might be to make sure to allocate the required memory from a set of threads that will run on one NUMA node.

CPUs

NUMA memory is associated with processor packages (sometimes now just called processor). With NUMA, node refers to the set of processors and their related memory. Usually, the memory maps to a processor package (which has some number of cores).

Hyperthreading: Be careful with hyper-threaded processors. The number of cores can be misleading. It can show eight logical cores, but it is really four physical cores and four virtual cores. Often with multithreading in the past, it has been useful to not completely treat the machine like it has eight cores but instead only four in terms of deciding how many threads to create. Sometimes, hyperthreading can make multithreading performance worse. A virtual core and a physical core share the same execution resources (e.g., caches, bus, execution engine, etc.), so consider these things when using a hyper-threaded processor.

Hyperthreading works by duplicating the registers we talked about earlier for a CPU core and making it appear like there is a separate real CPU core (but it's actually a virtual core that shares the speculative execution resources that we looked at earlier and the L1 cache).

Hyperthreading is something to consider when multithreading, as in some scenarios, was found to decrease performance. The key is to test with real or close to real workloads with and without hyperthreading enabled (which can usually be configured in the machine BIOS).

With hyperthreading enabled, two threads are really executing on one CPU core, sharing certain resource CPU resources that in the past had some cases that were less efficient. There are claims that things are better now, but it would still be a very good idea to test those claims, since sharing resources creates potential for an impact.

Async/Await

Async and await keywords provide a very simple way to wait and continue running after an asynchronous task is run (returning to the function to continue when the task is complete.).

This can allow starting the async task and continuing work up until the point where you must await and will actually return to the caller but later continue at await. This simplifies some asynchronous programming.

```
private static async Task DelayAsync()
    { await Task.Delay(1000); }
```

Thread Priorities

Thread priorities must be used carefully. Real-time priorities can prevent even certain operating system functions from doing their jobs. Don't use up all cores with higher than normal priority threads. Don't mismatch thread priorities, as that can result in starvation or effective livelock or effective deadlock.

In Windows, OS threads have priorities. On the low-priority side, there is idle priority, which only runs when nothing else is running, and the highest user mode priority is real time.

It can be dangerous to run threads at real-time priority without thoroughly testing them. Real-time thread priority can be higher than some OS functionality, so it could have impacts throughout the OS.

Also, be careful not to run one thread at high priority and another at a lower priority when they share resources, as that can result in starvation or livelock. We'll cover that a little later.

Threading Issues

Thread Fairness

Threading in .NET is not fair ("Concurrent Affairs: Build a Richer Thread Synchronization Lock" | *Microsoft Learn*, n.d.) due to garbage collection, causing threads to be suspended, and due to .NET threads reusing operation system threads fairness is not similar to Windows threads.

Cause

When threads are interrupted, the lock queue order they were in when they were waiting is interrupted, and when resumed, the original order is not guaranteed.

Operating systems are generally designed to try to be fair to threads at the same priority, giving threads appropriate time to run and making sure they treat all threads fairly when contended on synchronization objects.

The implementation in the .NET framework prevents some fairness. In the case of waiting on locks, in many cases due to garbage collection suspending threads and then running them again, it can change the acquiring order of locks/synchronization objects they may hold.

That means some threads could get an unfair advantage. With some basic real-world testing, the fairness issue could be seen, but a big difference in fairness was not found. This may be due to the luck of the draw in some cases evening out.

Not much can be done here, but it is just something to take into consideration.

Thread Race Conditions

Race conditions typically happen with access to memory that is not controlled properly by synchronization objects.

In cases like these, two threads simply doing i++; instead of the object being equal to 2 could be equal to 1 or some other value.

Sometimes, it can just be a timing issue of allowing a thread to do something before a resource is ready. That can happen if the thread isn't controlled by synchronization objects.

Race conditions are when two or more threads try to read/write a value and usually due to lack of synchronization between them results in an unexpected value/change.

To avoid this, use synchronization objects (e.g., lock/monitor.) to prevent it or appropriate atomic operations like the interlocked operations.

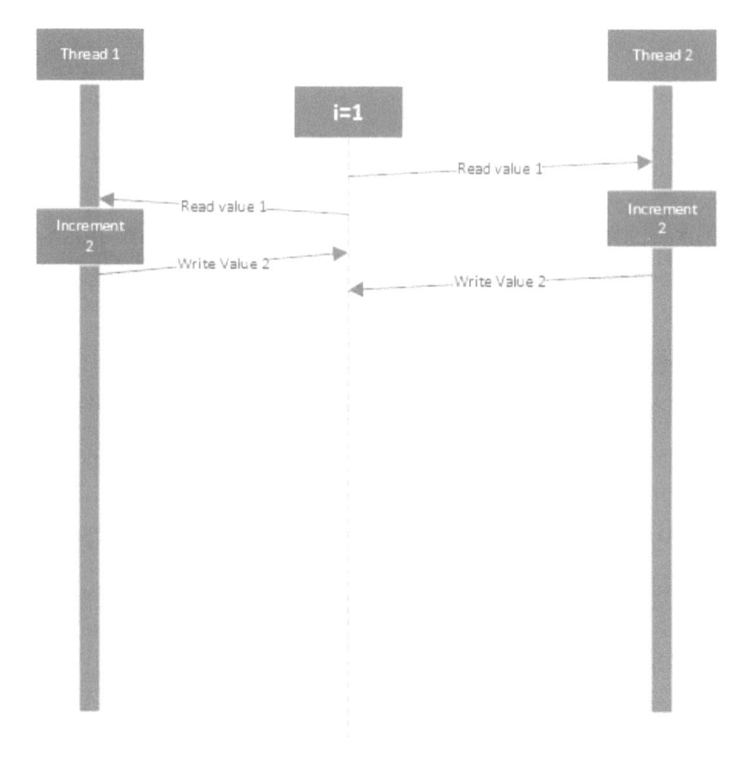

In the diagram above, thread 2 reads the value from memory (1). While it's trying to increment it, thread 1 is faster and reads, increments the value, and sets it to 2. Unfortunately, thread 2 doesn't know that happened and is also writing back a 2 to the memory location. What was expected was that it should equal 3, but due to a race condition (caused by no use of locking/synchronization), the value is 2.

Thread Priority Inversion

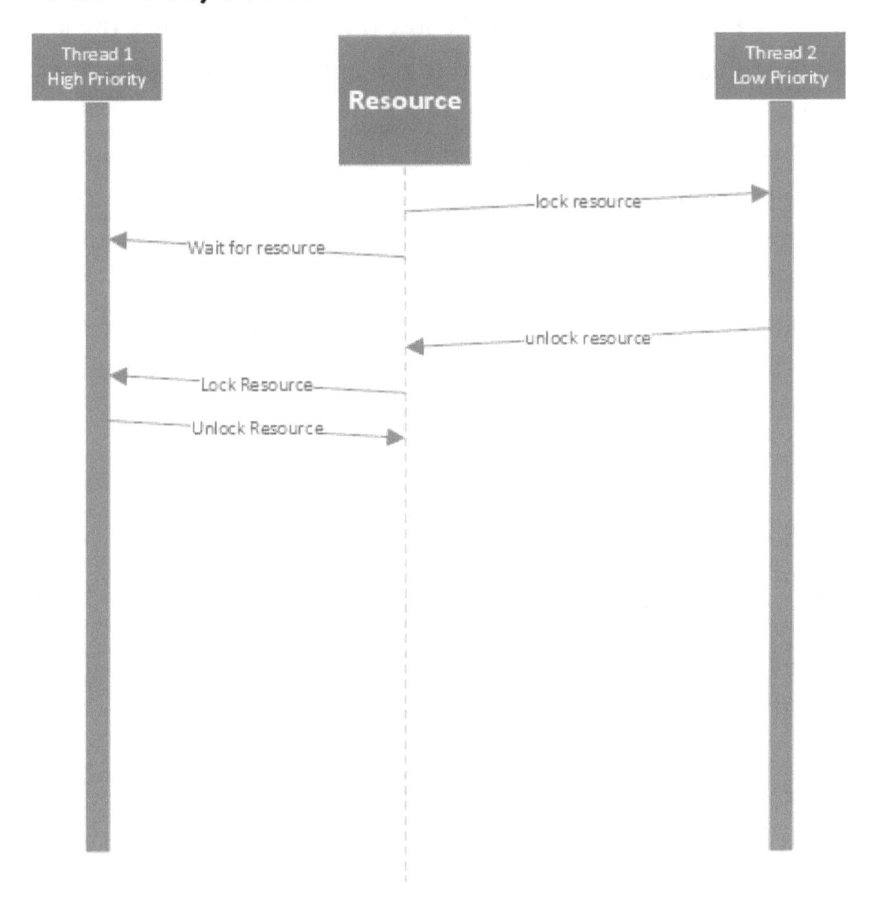

If a low-priority thread locks a resource a high-priority thread needs, the high-priority thread won't be able to run till the low-priority thread completes using the resource. This issue can be reduced through priority inheritance.

Thread priority inversion is when a low-priority thread owns a resource a high-priority thread needs.

Since the low-priority thread can't run due to the higher priority thread, this causes livelock (we're not deadlocked, but nothing can proceed), meaning the high-priority thread is given the processor to run since it's a higher priority than the low-priority thread. Since the low-priority thread can't be scheduled to run until the high-priority thread is done, we are stuck.

One methodology used on other operating systems (not on Windows) is priority inheritance, which would allow the lower priority thread to inherit the higher priority thread's priority so it would get time to run.

Unfortunately, Windows does not have this, so you would either need to find a way to implement something like it yourself if needed or avoid this scenario.

Deadlock

Thread 1: Acquires resource 1
Thread 2: Acquires resource 2
Thread 2: Tries to acquire resource 1
Thread 1: Tries to acquire resource 2

This leads to a deadlock, a.k.a. deadly embrace.

To avoid this, acquire locks and release in the same order on all threads, or detect the condition and release all resources.

Deadlock is the standard scenario where one thread acquires a lock that the other thread needs to continue. This involves two or more locks/synchronization objects, and they try to acquire them/release in different orders.

Thread 1 is holding object 1 lock and wants object 2 lock.

But thread 2 is holding object 2 lock and needs object 1's lock.

To avoid this, always acquire objects in the same order.

OR provide a way to detect deadlock and force one thread to give up its locks to allow other threads to proceed (SQL uses this method).

Livelock

Like deadlock, but threads continue to run but make no progress (keep trying to acquire resources, but never can).

We touched on this in the previous topic. Basically, livelock is where you are not deadlocked, but no progress can be made either due to priority, like we saw before, or we just can't acquire a needed lock, and the thread keeps trying.

Again, to handle this situation, detect the scenario and release locks from one thread or ensure the order they are acquired in.

Lock Convoy

Lock convoys are when multiple threads are waiting to acquire a lock.

When the arrival rate of requests for a lock is higher than the acquisition rate, many threads end up waiting to run results in that staggered (serialized) access through the lock.

This is natural for synchronization objects like lock/monitor/mutex, but it means the lock is highly contended in this time frame.

If this is causing performance issues, then consider finding a design where the threads are not waiting on just one lock, make locking more granular, or find a way to avoid locking if possible.

Thundering Herd

Thundering herd is when many threads get woken up, but only one or a few can proceed. This can cause higher CPU overhead as the herd tries to acquire resources it needs.

Ideally, the herd wouldn't be woken up unless they could proceed.

An example might be if you had a manual reset event that would let all threads through when you signaled, followed by an autoresetevent where only one could proceed.

In that case, a better design might be to have them all wait on the autoresetevent in the first place to avoid the thundering herd.

Thread Being Interrupted—Causes

Things that can impact your threads that can prevent them from running/interrupt them from running for some period of time.

- Interrupts
- DPCs
- Higher priority threads
- End of Quantum (end of a thread's allowed runtime)
- Cores put to sleep (power-saving modes)
- Too many threads ready to run for the available cores

Reference: http://msdn.microsoft.com/en-us/library/windows/hardware/ff545764(v=vs.85).aspx

There are many reasons why your threads might not run or be interrupted.

Interrupts: Software or hardware interruptions to processor activity to handle time sensitive events, such as network, disk activity. You can try to avoid scheduling on impacted cores. Interrupts may be caused by system, network, disk, video, etc., often having very high priority relative to normal or even real-time threads (<~25 microseconds per call, but there can be a lot) writing to disk or outputting to the network. (since this causes interrupts). ("Example 15 Measuring DPC/ISR Time—Windows Drivers" | *Microsoft Learn*, n.d.)

DPCs (deferred procedure calls): Similar to interrupts and are used for network, disk, and other activity. To reduce/avoid the impact, you can try to avoid scheduling on the same cores they run on if you are concerned. DPC Interrupts defer some work till later that runs at a slightly lower priority than interrupts but still above high-priority/real-time threads (<~100 microseconds per call, but there can be a lot of them).

Higher priority threads: Avoid this. Don't cause your own problems with higher priority threads, or test and make sure you have enough cores to handle your threads vs. OS higher priority threads. Higher-priority threads will get run before lower-priority threads. Threads can run if uninterrupted (~120 ms with default quantums) (OS Threads, etc.).

Thread scheduling (end of quantum): Make sure there are enough cores available to run threads.

Cores put to sleep because of power-saving mode: Don't use power-saving modes to avoid this.

Too many threads ready to run compared to available cores will delay execution of threads that are ready.

Thread Issue: Context Switching

A context switch is when one thread is swapped out for another thread by the operating system scheduler. This involves saving the current context for the current thread and then loading the context of the new thread to run.

A large amount of context switching can add overhead to the performance of an application/threads, since during this time, the previously running thread and the new thread are not really doing anything useful as far as the application is concerned.

A slightly worse variation of this is when threads switch cores as well. Windows prefers to run threads on the previous core it ran to help keep cache available. If that isn't possible, there can be additional overhead due to cache reloading and NUMA (depending on thread usage).

Thread Contention

Sometimes, two or more threads try to obtain the same resource (e.g., a lock/synchronization object, or a resource like memory, object etc.) (Goldin, n.d.).

When it's a lock/synchronization object, it might be referred to as a hot lock.

A highly contended lock/resource can be the cause for latency/delays, if using spin locks/lock-free implementations using CPU (aka burning CPU: using CPU with little positive benefit).

Switching from one thread to another requires context switching, which adds additional overhead.

Threading Patterns

- Swapping References: Swap references to an object atomically.
- Events: Event pattern to use for safe event usage with multiple threads.
- Double-Check Locking: Often used for lazy loading/singletons.

- Unprotected Flag: Good for signaling a thread to shut down with low overhead.
- Worker Threads/Thread Pools: A pool of threads to service tasks.
- Asynchronous Result: Use the asynchronous result pattern to collect the result information from threads.
- Background Worker: .NET pattern to make providing status updates from a background thread easier.
- Scheduler: Similar to how OS schedules threads.
- Watchdog/Monitor: A thread or threads to monitor other threads (e.g., deadlock monitor thread).
- Lock/Free: Example of non-blocking synchronization.
- Producer/Consumer: Simple threading pattern where one or more threads supply data and another thread or threads process the data.
- Serialized Workqueue: Similar to worker thread pools but serializes work on a resource.
- Task Parallel Library: .NET support for executing tasks with a thread pool.
- Parallel LINQ: Execute LINQ statements in parallel.
- Rx (Reactive extensions): Good for multithreaded streaming subscriptions.
- Disruptor: One of the lowest latency and lock-free multithreading patterns to date.

Swapping References

```
volatile List<int> _instance = new List<int>();
    public int Count { get { return _instance.Count; } }
    public void AddMyItem(int item) {
        lock (_lockObject)
```

```
        {
            List<int> items = new List<int>(_instance);    //copy
            items.Add(item);
            _instance = items;
        }
    } // ... delete methods, etc.
```

Swapping references can be thought of somewhat like snapshot or optimistic SQL access.

It usually boils down to copying the entire structure and just updating the reference to the structure everyone uses.

In this case, you can see the add method copies the current list, adds the item, and sets the current instance to the new array, so threads will either have the old array or the new array.

When adding , updating, removing items, a lock is taken to create a new list and assign it to the current instance.

Pro: Since effectively, the List is read-only because once it is created, it will never be modified after that, the entire array can be accessed lock free.

Con: The overhead for copying the array each change/update. Care has to be taken when using it to save the current reference so it doesn't change while you are using it (if that was important).

Events Pattern

```
public static event EventHandler MyEvent;
    var handlers = MyEvent;
    if (handlers != null)
        handlers(this, args);
```

Note: This means subscribers must always be robust and know they could be called even after they unsubscribe.

This is a thread safe pattern for handling events.

The key is to use a local variable to store the current event subscriber list, then compare to null. This avoids needing to lock and makes sure the event list is not null before calling it.

An important events reminder is that even after unsubscribing, your event could still be called since this is similar to the swapping references, where it is like optimistically saving a copy to use later.

Double-check Locking/Singletons: Lazy Initialization

This pattern was an optimization that won't work in all languages or platforms and therefore needs to be done with care. This was an idiom used in Java and C# and likely other places to improve performance for the access of singleton objects that need to be created on first use.

The pattern is to check if a variable is null outside a lock (since this is fast); if it's not null, return the value/reference. If it is null, then lock using a thread synchronization object and double check the value again (double check) to see if it's null this time inside the lock. If it is null, initialize the variable and return.

```
private static object volatile instance = null;
private static readonly object lockobj = new object();


public static Object MySingleton
    {
        get
        {
                if (instance == null) //First check outside lock
                {
```

```
                        lock (lockobj)
                        {
                                if (instance == null) //second check inside lock
                                {
                                        instance = new Singleton();
                                }
                        }
                }
                return instance;
        }
    }
```

.NET's Answer to Double-Check Locking:

```
Using System;
    private Lazy<EventWaitHandle> m_event;
```

This is basically double-check locking, or even minimal to no locking, depending on the initialization settings.

Unprotected One Shot Flag

```
volatile bool _done=false;
    Thread 1:
    Start thread 2
    //... Some work
    _done=true;
    Thread2:
    While (!_done)
    { //...
    }
```

This pattern is a way to use a flag to signal something to happen, sometimes used for things like signaling a thread to shut down if the flag is true.

Notice the flag is completely unprotected by synchronization objects like lock, which is why the volatile keyword is needed.

The key to the safety is the flag is only set to true and never changed back to false (thus, you only get one shot to change it). Otherwise, it would have required additional protection of a synchronization object.

Worker Threads/Thread Pools

System.Threading.ThreadPool

Thread pools are useful for short to medium running tasks that can run independently in parallel, where it doesn't matter which task is run first. The thread pool is beneficial, because it doesn't incur the cost of spinning up new threads for every task.

Worker threads/thread pools are a common pattern that allow you to queue an object with the task information, and one of the threads in the pool picks up that object and does the work.

Care should be taken, as long-running tasks could exhaust your thread pool or if your thread pool can expand oversubscribe your cores/memory.

Asynchronous Result

Run on another thread and retrieve the result

// Initiate the asynchronous call.

IAsyncResult result = caller.BeginInvoke(4000, out threadId, null, null);

// Wait for the WaitHandle to become signaled.

result.AsyncWaitHandle.WaitOne();

// Perform additional processing here. // Call EndInvoke to retrieve the results. string returnValue = caller.EndInvoke(out threadId, result); // Close the wait handle. result.AsyncWaitHandle.Close();

The IAsyncResult is a standard way for determining the result or waiting for the task to complete in .NET.

Background Worker C#

System.ComponentModel.BackgroundWorker

This provides the ability to run on a background thread while still providing status updates on the progress of the work and provides the ability to cancel the work.

Background worker was somewhat recently introduced to simplify the task of doing work on a background thread while still updating the UI with progress information.

It is particularly useful for WinForms/WPF. Given UIs are single threaded by default, it can proxy status updates to the UI thread.

This is also a general pattern, though, that a UI can kick off a background worker so that the UI does not get stuck waiting for something to complete.

Scheduler

Thread schedulers allow the control of the threads themselves that will be running jobs.

This allows the control of what thread will be running or not running. This allows fine grain control of when threads/jobs are run and how many and long they can run.

Scheduler is meaning like the thread scheduler in the operating system that coordinates what thread/task to run next. This doesn't need to be as elaborate as the operating system scheduler and could be as simple as using a thread pool or a little more elaborate by creating your own threads and having a controller thread that coordinates the other threads run times.

This can be useful when you need to more carefully control the way threading happens for task, or thread performance, or other control reasons.

Watchdog/Monitor

Sometimes, creating a thread to monitor other threads can be useful. One use, for example, is deadlock monitoring that can detect if threads are blocked for a specific time period and either free them or just log/warn that there is an issue. This pattern can also be useful for monitoring other thread activity and progress.

A watchdog/monitor could be something like a separate thread monitoring your other threads for deadlock, just as an example.

Lock-Free Interlocked Methods

- Interlocked Increment
- Interlocked Decrement
- Interlocked Exchange
- Interlocked Compare Exchange

Properly used, these methods can result in very fast atomic operations: 1 million iterations of lock(object) { increment++} compared to InterlockedIncrement produced 60 ms for lock (object), and 20 ms for Interlocked, three times as much. This is a single thread, thus no contention.

It is best to avoid using large numbers of Interlocked calls on different variables, as these lock 64 bytes in the processor cache line to handle SMP threading.

Lock free uses CPU resources to try to improve performance by not context switching away.

Some "lock-free" methods are sometimes used to implement synchronization-like capabilities. Notice that the performance is quite a lot better when uncontended for Interlocked calls compared to one of the fastest synchronization classes like lock.

Large numbers of interlocked calls can have a negative side effect though, since they can cause a higher amount of bus traffic (sending memory updates to main memory so they can be seen by other cores).

Lock-Free Threading

These methods provide atomic Read/Modify/Write operations:

- InterlockedCompareExchange
- InterlockedIncrement

Interlocked methods are often used to provide non-blocking synchronization for certain cases. It's actually possible to implement something like spin lock in terms of using methods like these.

Producer/Consumer

One thread adds items to a queue, another removes them.

Variations: Multi-producer, multi-consumer.

Producer-consumer pattern can have one or more threads producing data and one or more threads consuming (i.e., using) the data.

This can be as simple as a thread adding items to a list, and another thread removing items from the list and doing something with that data.

Serialized Workqueue w/Threadpool

Tasks are serialized to separate queues based on a resource ID. A workqueue task event is posted when there are items in a work queue. The next available thread wakes up, grabs the event, and locks the associated resource. This ensures only one thread will operate on an individual serialized queue at a time, ensuring event ordering for a particular resource.

Variations: separate thread pool for producers; separate thread pool for consumers

- A serialized workqueue with thread pool is similar to the task thread pool we talked about earlier.
- The difference though is tasks are serialized in the sequence they are added by resource.
- So one resource will only have one thread accessing it at a time and executing the tasks in sequence.
- In the financial world, for an implementation of stock trading, a resource might be a stock symbol, and they needed to ensure that market data or trades were updated in the sequence they came in.

C# Task Parallel Library

A set of public types and APIs to simplify concurrent task execution.

Example:

Parallel.Invoke(() => DoSomeWork1(), () => DoSomeOtherWork2());

The task parallel library was added to make creating threads a little easier. The syntax here launches some threads at the same time and runs the functions with a pretty simple syntax.

C# Parallel LINQ (PLINQ)

Parallel LINQ allows using multiple processors to process LINQ queries.

var source = Enumerable.Range(1, 20000);

//Opt in to PLINQ with AsParallel.

var evenNumbers = from num in source.AsParallel() where num % 2 == 0 select num;

Parallel LINQ can be used to try parallelize your LINQ queries.

The positives are you can easily try to use more cores if you are single threaded.

The negatives are you don't have a lot of control over thread execution, so if you have other threads running as well, it could oversubscribe your cores, making it execute slower rather than faster.

C# Rx: Reactive Extensions

Rx is a library for creating asynchronous event-driven code with observable collections.

Reactive extensions allow you to process streaming data in a multithreaded way and still allow it to propagate results back to a single thread as well as a UI thread if needed.

Again, similar here, the pros are easier parallelization, the cons are limited control the way your threads are used.

Disruptor Pattern Lock Free

Created by LMAX

The disruptor pattern is a relatively recent invention made of functionality that existed before.

It was invented in the last couple of years. It is probably the most performant single producer multi-consumer pattern that is available on the Pentium processor platform.

One comparison showed normal producer consumer was 6–7 million operations per second, compared to disruptor some claim 2 billion or more operations per second.

The design was created to perfectly match up with the underlying processor implementation.

The pros are that this is extremely fast for single producer multi-consumer, allowing for complex consumer dependencies.

The cons are that it doesn't work as well when there are multiple producer threads, and it's not an easy drop in replacement for a normal thread safe list/queue. The best performance is when used properly.

The disrupter is completely lock free with one producer and N consumers.

Benefits of using a Ring buff internally for Disruptor

- Cache coherency.
- Direct access for readers/writers.

- Smart design sizing the buffer up to the size of power of two so that variables don't need to use modulo to stay within the ring buffer.
- Best performance is with a single writing thread (producer) with batching of adding items to the buffer.

Cache coherency: By using a ring buffer memory, access can often be optimized in the L1 cache, making access very fast.

Readers/writers directly access the ring buffer to reduce overhead and keep cache coherency.

The buffers are sized to power of two to avoid needing to modulo the count for the ring buffer. By the nature of integers, it will auto-wrap.

Disruptor Avoiding False Sharing

False sharing is when two or more threads access memory close to the memory another thread is using (within a cache line), even though they are not using the same variable/memory.

When memory is written to another processor that is using the same cache line, then that cache needs to be flushed from that cache line and reloaded, which is fairly expensive.

Disruptor patterns spaces its variables out enough so variables that will be used by different threads will be in different cache lines to avoid false sharing.

Also, the disruptor pattern avoids false sharing by padding memory for variables.

If two threads access a similar area of memory (different variables but close in memory), the data needs to be passed back through the L1, L2, L3, and bus to notify the other cores caches that something changed.

If you pad variables to be at least the size of a L1 cache line, it can avoid thrashing memory updates.

Disruptor: Barriers/Fences

Disruptor code only uses memory barriers/fences when it needs them and tries to limit them to half fences (read or write but not both).

Disruptor also relies on the acquire/release semantics—half fences to provide thread safety and performance. Avoiding full barriers.

WinForms Update Control from Thread

This pattern is for updating the UI. This WinForms pattern of updating a control from a background thread has to send a message to the UI thread, and the UI thread picks it up and runs on its thread, because the UI code doesn't support multiple threads.

That's actually true all the way from .NET code to the underlying Win32/64 API.

Real-time Multithreading

Operating Systems:

Hard real time: If a time is not met, a system fails (e.g., airplane control systems).

Soft real time: Allows great variability in responses from the system (e.g., video game).

Windows consumer/server versions are not really considered a real-time OS, but it can function at a soft real-time level.

Windows CE, the foundation for Windows phone and other devices, is considered real time.

Other real-time OS are QNX, VxWorks, RTLinux, Interval Zero RTX.

Real-time operating systems break down into hard and soft real time. There aren't great definitions of what is real time or not, but generally speaking:

- Hard real time is where if a time is not met a system will fail.
- Soft real time allows more flexibility in response times/latency.

Windows consumer/server versions are NOT real-time operating systems, but they can be used for some soft real-time purposes.

Windows CE, the original basis for Windows phone, is considered a real-time operating system.

True real-time operating systems are available like QNX, VXWorks, RTLinux, and Interval Zero, which run with Windows as the UI.

Cycle time is the ability of a thread to respond to an event in a timely fashion and jitter is the variation in min/max times.

Real-Time Considerations

- CPU
- Interrupts
- Device/hardware
- Scheduler
- Static/dynamic loading
- Min, Max, Average: waiting time, processing times, context switch times, response times, slack time, deadlines
- Resources/sharing
- Processor/device utilization

When coding for real time, it is important to consider all aspects that can impact your threads:

- CPU in terms of speed, DPCs, cache sizing, context switch overhead.

- Interrupts (typically how long does it take min/max to service them).
- OS scheduling time, priorities, etc.

Real-Time Scheduling Anomalies

Just to give an example of various considerations:

Sometimes, even adding processors can increase your total processing time rather than decrease it, purely due to scheduling anomalies.

On three processors, everything fits nicely with only a small chunk of time where nothing is running.

However, on four processors, you can accidentally change the order of tasks if P4 doesn't have anything scheduled, and P3 runs out to hit a hard real-time limit.

Real-Time Thread Response Times

- Execution time
- Interrupt time
- Scheduler interference
- Blocked time (e.g., lower priority tasks, shared resources)

Things to consider for thread response times:

- How much impact from interrupts like network, disk, and so on.
- Scheduling context switch overhead
- Blocked time due to locks/resources, priorities, and so on.

Can .NET Do Real Time?

.NET can't do hard real time. It can sort of do soft real time.

Avoid GC. There are some low latency options built into .NET now to suppress GC (previous tests showed they didn't seem to work very well).

Use Object pools to reduce the need for garbage collections.

Create your own non-collected string class to avoid string collections or avoid strings.

Avoid Exceptions, as they are very slow.

Soft real-time .NET is used in financial trading systems and to drive real-time systems ran in Windows phone.

Some things you can do to avoid latency:

- Avoid GCs by creating object pools and allocating memory up front.
- Avoid exceptions when appropriate, as they can be slow.
- Test thoroughly and profile.
- Call out to more real-time languages like C/C++.

Can Windows Do Real Time?

Not exactly. More soft real time. There are third-party add-on products that can help do real time on Windows, sometimes with additional hardware.

There are some variants of Linux that are designed for real-time processing.

Measuring Latency for Machines across Threads/Cores

- Difference between the time the machine receives a request and sends a response.

- Normal time stamps can get to millisecond resolution.
- QueryPerformanceCounter (native API) can get to microseconds or better; works across processors and cores accurately on recent hardware on Windows 2008r2 and above.
- If your system receives a message and passes that between threads timestamping the message at each point, it is passed to another thread can help determine thread bottlenecks. Having checks at those points for a time difference exceeding a specified amount can be used to trigger an alert/log. That can be used to help narrow the area with the problem.
- An aggregate system can also be put in place to keep track of max times for each area for a certain time interval for individual threads that can be aggregated later at app shutdown, for example, or at timed intervals.

Computers receiving and sending packets to an external system won't be able to measure the overhead the operating system adds without an external tool (e.g., Tipoff, Corvil). Tracing with Windows event tracing might help trace within the OS to some level.

To measure latency within a machine, you can use the method QueryPerformanceCounter to get to microsecond or lower resolution and compare the results from two points in the code.

You can also use Visual Studio Profiler to measure performance of methods.

Or you can consider other third-party tools like dotTrace, or AQTime.

Measuring time between machines is more difficult. Normal time sync typically can only do about 10 ms between machines (sometimes, it can get it down to 1 ms).

Alternatively, different appliance can be used like Tipoff or Corvil to measure to microsecond or better accuracy between machines.

Testing Multithreaded Code

- Test on the types of systems where your code will run.
- Same number of cores as expected to run in production.
- Recommend testing with four cores at least and under significant load.
- Testing with a single core can be useful to help find threading issues, if that is reasonable for your app.
- Test with similar loads to what is expected and ramp up for expected loads x months/year out (financial markets typically test for thrice the current max volume, as an example).
- Tune the number of active threads you need for your workload when using thread pools.
- Use Visual Studio's Concurrency Analyzer to help analyze threads.

Careful with Static Variables/Types

Statics are often accessible to multiple thread.

Statics class field members, if using an initializer, will be initialized only once and static type constructors.

public static int _myField=5; // this is guaranteed to be initialized only once here

If a static method is called the first time, its field initializers will be run once first, then static constructor if it exists, then the method (the second or later thread will wait until initialization is done).

Initialization of different types of classes may occur in any order (e.g., Class A type could be initialized before or after Class B type for static type initialization). It's only guaranteed that they will be initialized before a method/member of the type is accessed.

Statics are often accessible to multiple threads, so if necessary, protect them with synchronization objects if needed or other appropriate methods if they can ever be modified.

In C#/.NET, public static initializers are guaranteed to be executed only once.

Note that there is overhead with static public methods, as they need to check if fields were already initialized.

Sleep(0) Problems

Sometimes, Sleep(0) is used to try to give up the current threads quantum to other threads. The problem is that it doesn't always work as expected. If the current thread is higher priority than other threads, it will not give up its time. While technically Sleep(1) might at least yield, it may yield a lot longer than you like since many systems clock granularity is set at 13–15 milliseconds.

Better to use proper synchronization objects or Thread.Yield().

Some people would say that using any sleep in code is inadvisable, as ideally, using appropriate synchronization, timers/events would probably better serve the implementation.

Sleep(0) typically doesn't just smell, it stinks, as usually, the intention is to temporarily give up the rest of a time slice so something else can happen. Unfortunately, this won't always work, as if this thread is a higher priority than other threads that need to run, then it may have no effect.

It is better to use Thread.Yield in that case.

Windows Disk Writes: Not Truly Asynchronous

Writing to disk either synchronously or asynchronously can block your threads when underlying Windows APIs are used. Windows asynchronous write functions are not truly asynchronous and can block (though often for much shorter periods of time than their synchronous counterparts).

Just a note that disk writes are the enemy of threads in terms of latency, as they can take long periods of time to write to disk for physical hard drives (SSDs are faster).

For example, if your logger writes directly to disk, it could delay your thread execution.

If latency is a concern, a better option might be to write a logger that just queues the message, returns immediately, and writes the log lines later.

Better Multithreading

Reduce the need for shared resources/objects. Shared objects require locking/and loss of cache coherency, for example if it's possible for a single thread to never touch a shared object by processing work as a task that is handled entirely within a thread.

If your threads use shared objects from an object pool, consider having separate pools per thread.

How Many Threads?

Consider the following:

- How much CPU time does each thread take?
- How much time does each thread wait (I/O, blocked on a synchronization object, etc.)?
- How many cores does your production machines have?
- How are threads used? Sometimes, creation of a certain number of threads can make sense, other times a thread pool.

- What is the memory impact/cost of threads? Too many threads ready to run or blocking on synchronization due to contention can decrease performance.

Deciding how many threads to use can be tricky.

If your threads use 100 percent CPU each, then it's pretty easy. One thread per core is probably best.

If your threads like most are a mix between CPU and I/O bound tasks, you can try to calculate to get a rough idea of the mix, then test to see the actual best number for throughput and responsiveness.

Some Final Tips

- Remember: Finalizers run on different threads (C#/.NET).
- Design to avoid synchronization when possible.
- If you need it, use the simplest, most appropriate locking that is effective for your requirements (i.e., lock() is a lot harder to mess up compared to dealing with volatile/atomics, lock-free implementations).
- CLEARLY indicate/separate out shared state classes/fields. Knowing what needs protection is half the battle.
- Keep your API surface area for requiring locks small/narrow to reduce the potential for missing synchronization.
- If possible, design your framework so that the code that deals with multithreading/shared state is designed once in the framework. If reasonable, design to pass data as part of a task instead of sharing it. If the app is properly designed, it can make it seem like you are coding for only one thread in most cases, reducing complexity.
- Limit shared state wherever it is reasonably possible.

- If data will not need to be modified, consider making it immutable.
- Reminder that finalizers run on different threads, so if you use them, you are multithreading.

Useful Tools for Windows

- Visual Studio: Profiler/Concurrency Visualizer
- VTune: Can profile the entire machine at once/CPU level profiling
- AQtime: Profiler
- Xperf/Windows Performance Analyzer (WPA): Windows event tracing

Some References:

"Common Patterns for Poorly-Behaved Multithreaded Applications—Visual Studio 2015" | *Microsoft Learn*. (n.d.). Retrieved September 17, 2022, from https://learn.microsoft.com/en-us/previous-versions/visualstudio/visual-studio-2015/profiling/common-patterns-for-poorly-behaved-multithreaded-applications?view=vs-2015&redirectedfrom=MSDN, earlier reference http://msdn.microsoft.com/en-us/library/ee329530.aspx

"C#—The C# Memory Model in Theory and Practice" | *Microsoft Learn*. (n.d.). Retrieved September 17, 2022, from https://learn.microsoft.com/en-us/archive/msdn-magazine/2012/december/csharp-the-csharp-memory-model-in-theory-and-practice, earlier reference http://msdn.microsoft.com/en-us/magazine/jj863136.aspx

Multithreaded Events

First, let's start off with saying that there is no perfectly safe multi-threaded event handling, as there are caveats/conditions that must be handled. So it's really if the particular method you plan to use is safe for the uses you require.

There is a great article here about this:

http://www.codeproject.com/Articles/37474/Threadsafe-Events ("Threadsafe Events," *CodeProject*, n.d.).

The one suggested solution the author mentions is to not use events in a multithreaded way. This can be a good solution when possible.

I'm going to show that there is another problem to contend with, and I will offer some classes to help handle some scenarios, plus propose some alternative options you could use, but it depends on if your events can be used that way. Ultimately, it depends on what you need to do, and the implementation/use and complexity you wish to manage.

What does this information present that is new?

1. There is an additional problem without a sequence of events (see problem #7), and we will show how to solve it.
2. Show a potential improvement that can help resolve problem #6 (might not have the most recent subscriber list).
3. Demonstrate a class to wrap events to make them safer.
4. Demonstrate true multithreaded events and a class to use them.

The Problems

To start, let's define the types of multithreading problems that come up with trying to solve this problem:

1. Possible Deadlocks adding and removing event due to lock(this) or lock(type) for static events.

2. Race condition calling a null event.
3. An added (subscribed) event handler is not immediately called.
4. A removed (unsubscribed) event handler is still called.
5. Deadlocks trying to subscribe/unsubscribe.
6. Might not get the most recent list of delegates to fire.
7. Problem/Feature: Events could be fired to delegates out of sequence.

The consensus is that there is no way to solve all of these issues. Perhaps, but let's see the ways we can work with these issues.

Problem Details

Problem #1: Possible Deadlocks adding and removing events

This should not be a problem in recent versions of .NET 4.5 as they reportedly use using lock-free constructs that should avoid this type of issue. If you need to handle this in earlier versions, you could implement your own add/remove handlers with your own lock object to avoid some potential for deadlock scenarios.

Problem #2: Race condition calling a null event

The problem is an event by default is null until you add a handler to it. If one thread is trying to add as another is trying to raise the event, or the last handler is trying to unsubscribe, when you try to call the event, you could get a null reference exception.

Problem #3: An added event handler is not immediately called

In this scenario, one thread adds a handler, but an event gets raised in the middle, and this handler doesn't appear to be immediately called.

Therefore, either controlling your event source is needed, not needing to worry much about a missed event, or you would need something more like a message bus that replayed events that already happened before subscribing.

Problem #4: An event handler is removed, but it is still called
In this scenario, one thread removes a handler, but an event is raised on another thread while this is happening, and it still gets called even after it was thought to have unsubscribed.

Problem #5: Deadlock due to an event calling a handler that interacts with another thread that subscribes/unsubscribes
This scenario causes a deadlock because if the event mechanism holds a lock while subscribing or unsubscribing and while calling events, it might be possible to deadlock (see this article for more details: http://www.codeproject.com/Articles/37474/Threadsafe-Events).

Problem #6: Might not get the most recent list of delegates to fire
We will see in the recommended solution that first the code tries to take a copy of the delegate event list to fire. When it does this, it's possible it might not get the most recent list because another thread already updated the list. This might not be that big an issue. It is similar to problem #3 in that the net result is an added event subscription that might not receive a notification immediately after subscribing.

Problem/Feature #7: Delegates might receive events out of sequence due
NOTE: This is more of an issue with the publisher of events controlling event ordering properly.

This can happen if multiple threads fire events at the same time. It's possible that they appear to the subscriber out of the expected sequence if there was an expected sequence. Once you have decided that multiple threads can fire events, this could happen at any time, even with proper locking. One thread beats another to firing an event, so it appears first.

A slight variation #7(B) of this is where the list of delegates starts to get one event sent to the list and then gets another event sent to it even before the first event has completed firing to the full list. If you really wanted multithreaded events, you might consider this a feature to truly support multithreading. Many events do have a typical order, such as Got focus, Lost focus, Session start, Session end (either indicated with EventArgs in your event or via separate events for each of those). The safest way to avoid this is to always fire your events from one thread if this matters and/or control the controller that decides on firing events with multithreaded synchronization to avoid it sourcing multiple events at the same time. Thus, this problem will exist in any multithreaded scenario where that is not done, since those are actions that need to be controlled by the publisher, likely with some type of state management that is not covered here.

At the end of the article, an example is shown of how to address event ordering between two events where the sequence matters.

We can exclude problem #1 since, as mentioned, it is not really an issue anymore. Problem #3, as mentioned, will be present in almost all implementations, unless you control your source of events/timing or implement your events like a message bus to send new subscribes all the previous events. .NET events typically aren't used that way.

Example of Basic Problem Multithreading Issue for Events

```
public ThisEventHandler ThisEvent;
```

```
protected virtual OnThisEvent (ThisEventArgs args)
    {
        If (ThisEvent!=null)
          ThisEvent (this,args); // ThisEvent could be null so you could get a null reference exception
    }
```

Problems	
#2 Null exception race condition	X
#3 A new subscriber might not get called immediately	X
#4 A handler is still called after unsubscribe	X
#5 Possible deadlock	
#6 Might not get the most recent list of delegates to fire	
#7 Problem/Feature: Events could be fired to delegates out of sequence	X

Normally Recommended Solution

Let's start with the recommended solution to understand what it handles and what it doesn't.

```
    public ThisEventHandler ThisEvent;


protected virtual void OnThisEvent (ThisEventArgs args)
    {
        ThisEventHandler thisEvent=ThisEvent; //assign the event to a local variable
        If (thisEvent!=null)
        {
          thisEvent (this,args);
        }
    }
```

Solution Summary

This solves problem #2 and does not have problem #5

This has problems #3 and #4. Thus, if you add a new handler, it might not get called immediately; if you remove a handler, it may still get called for a short time. This is better, as at least we got rid of one problem. We also see this solution introduces a possible #6 issue. It takes a copy of the list of handlers in the local thisEvent variable, but because this variable is not volatile, it may not get the most recent copy of the handler list.

Problems	
#2 Null exception race condition	
#3 A new subscriber might not get called immediately	X
#4 A handler is still called after unsubscribe	X
#5 Possible deadlock	
#6 Might not get most recent copy of handlers to call	X
#7 Problem/Feature: Events could be fired to delegates out of sequence	X

One way you can work around problem #3 (adding a new handler, it doesn't get called immediately) is to add your handlers early if possible, before it is likely that multiple threads will be calling your event. This avoids issues with #3.

For #4, when you are unsubscribing, set a bool flag that your event handler can check to see if it is being unsubscribed, if it is to do nothing, or just have smart handling in your event handler to know when this has happened. The problem is that there is no safe way to do this without locking.

Let's see if we can do better:

Example Fix for Normally Recommended Solution (Publisher)

In the event publisher, if we use this code:

```
[ThreadStatic] volatile ThisEventHandler _localEvent = null; // need volatile to ensure we get the latest

public virtual void OnThisEvent (EventArgs args)
{
   _localEvent=ThisEvent; //assign the event to a local variable – notice is volatile class field
   if (_localEvent!=null)
   {
     _localEvent(this,args);
   }
}
```

When not using locks in the event publisher, notice the variable _ localEvent. Many examples you might see on the Internet save a copy of the event into a variable and then call it if not null. They typically don't use a class volatile field. They should, otherwise they might not be getting the latest copy. The net effect may not be that much of an issue using a class field versus a local variable, as it would generally be expected when a method is called that the local variable will be initialized at least once. In C#, local variables can't be volatile, though, so to ensure reads/writes are directed to memory, a volatile class field can be used.

Example Improvement for Subscriber #1

In the event subscriber class, if we use this:

```
private object _lock = new object();
private volatile bool _unsubscribed=false;

private void MethodToUnsubscribe()
{
    lock(_lock)
    {
    _unsubscribed = true;

    ThisEvent -= new ThisEventHandler(ThisEventChanged);
      }
}

public void Subscribe()
{
    lock(_lock)
     {
       _unsubscribed = false;

       ThisEvent += new ThisEventHandler(ThisEventChanged);
    }
}

//Event handler
private void ThisEventChanged(object sender, ThisEventArgs e)
{

    lock(_lock)
    {
    if (!_unsubscribed)
    {
```

```
                    //Do work here
        }
        }

    }
```

Example Improvement for Subscriber #2 (Nonsequential True Multithreaded)

In the event subscriber class, if we use this:

```
    Private ReaderWriterLockSlim _rwLock = new ReaderWriter
LockSlim();

    private volatile bool _unsubscribed=false;

    private void MethodToUnsubscribe()
    {
        _rwLock.EnterWriteLock();
        _unsubscribed = true;

        ThisEvent -= new ThisEventHandler(ThisEventChanged);
        _rwLock.ExitWriteLock();
    }

    public void Subscribe()
    {

            _rwLock.EnterWriteLock();
            _unsubscribed = false;
```

```
            ThisEvent += new ThisEventHandler(ThisEventChanged);
            _rwLock.ExitWriteLock();

    }

    //Event handler – due to read lock could get called out of sequence
by multiple threads
    private void ThisEventChanged(object sender, ThisEventArgs e)
    {

    _rwLock.EnterReadLock();
        try
        {
        if (!_unsubscribed)
        {
                        //Do work here
        }
        }
        finally
        {
        _rwLock.ExitReadLock();
        }
    }
```

Solution Summary

This unfortunately puts some burden on the subscriber of the event.

IMPORTANT: This example code also allows for multiple threads to fire calls at the same time, which might not be desired. If not desired, just use a regular lock instead of the reader/writer lock otherwise your events could come out of sequence.

If you implement the publisher and subscriber code:

Problems	
#2 Null exception race condition	
#3 A new subscriber might not get called immediately	
#4 A handler is still called after unsubscribe	
#5 Possible deadlock	X
#6 Might not get most recent copy of handlers to call	
#7 Problem/Feature: Events could be fired to delegates out of sequence	X

If your events can be handled this way then some of the above issues are either solved or worked around. If your code cannot handle the limitations of this method, there are other implementations, but they will suffer from one or more of the problems listed. So it will come down to your code requirements and implementation complexity about how you wish to handle multithreaded events. (Or potentially as the first article mentions, don't do that and only use events from a single thread).

If you implement just the event publisher code and not the subscriber code:

Problems	
#2 Null exception race condition	
#3 A new subscriber might not get called immediately	X
#4 A handler is still called after unsubscribe	X
#5 Possible deadlock	X
#6 Might not get most recent copy of handlers to call	
#7 Problem/Feature: Events could be fired to delegates out of sequence	X

Both solutions solved the problem #6 shown in the standard recommended solution by using a volatile field in the publisher code to ensure the most recent copy of the event handlers is copied.

The above method shows how to handle this problem in the code that uses an event rather than in the code that publishes the event.

Let's look at an example that wraps up the logic to handle events a bit more safely:

SafeEvent Class

Let's look at wrapper class implementation that puts this all together so that the implementer of an event can handle most of the issues to not burden the listeners/subscribers. The below code is an implementation that can be used for event publishers. This implementation supports multithreaded nonsequential events being fired.

```
/// <summary>
/// SafeHandlerInfo - used for storing handler info, plus contains a

flag /// indicating if subscribed or not and the reader writer lock
/// for when the subscription is read or updated.
/// </summary>
/// <typeparam name="TArgs">Event args</typeparam> internal
class SafeHandlerInfo< TArgs> where TArgs : EventArgs {


    public EventHandler<TArgs> Handler;
    public bool Subscribed = true;
    //public object LockObj = new object();
```

```
    public ReaderWriterLockSlim Lock = new ReaderWriterLockslim();

     public SafeHandlerInfo(EventHandler<TArgs> handler)
     {
        Handler = handler;
     }

  }

  /// <summary>
  /// <summary>
  /// SafeEvent class provides safety for unsubscribing from events, so
even with
  /// multiple threads after unsubscribing it will not get called.
  /// Also makes sure that a null exception won't happen due to the
removing of
  /// events. Only one event is fired at a time, so single threaded through
this event.
  /// </summary>
  /// <typeparam name="TArgs">The type of the event args</
typeparam>
  public class SafeEvent<TArgs>
     where TArgs : EventArgs
  {

     private object _lock = new object();

     private event EventHandler<TArgs> _event;
```

```
public event EventHandler<TArgs> Event
{
  add
  {
    Subscribe(value);
  }

  remove
  {
    Unsubscribe(value);
  }

}

/// <summary>
/// Used to fire this event from within the class using the SafeEvent
///
/// </summary>
/// <param name="args">The event args</param>
public virtual void FireEvent(object sender,TArgs args)
{

                lock (_lock)
  {
                EventHandler<TArgs> localEvents = _event;
                if (localEvents != null)
                localEvents(sender, args);

          }

   }
```

```
        /// <summary>
         /// Unsubscribe - internally used to unsubscribe a handler from
the event
        /// </summary>
          /// <param name="unsubscribeHandler">The handler being
unsubscribed</param>
                  protected void Unsubscribe(EventHandler<TArgs>
unsubscribeHandler)
        {

                              lock (_lock)
                  {
                              _event -= unsubscribeHandler;
                  }

          }

        /// <summary>
        /// Subscribe - Called to subscribe the handler
        /// </summary>
         /// <param name="eventHandler">The handler to subscribe</
param>
        protected void Subscribe(EventHandler<TArgs> eventHandler)
        {
          lock (_lock)
          {
            _event += eventHandler;
          }
        }
    }
```

Solution Summary

The above code solves similar problems from the publishing side.

Since we added our own lock here, problem #1 of potential deadlock adding and removing subscribers is back.

Problems	
#2 Null exception race condition	
#3 A new subscriber might not get called immediately	
#4 A handler is still called after unsubscribe	
#5 Possible deadlock	X
#6 Might not get most recent copy of handlers to call	
#7 Problem/Feature: Events could be fired to delegates out of sequence	X

This code is susceptible to deadlocks under certain scenarios.

Potential Deadlock: If they unsubscribe an existing handler of the event currently being fired, there could be the potential for deadlock, so the best rule to follow is don't try to unsubscribe while in the middle of the event being called and avoid that in any downstream functions that are called by that event.

This hopefully should be very controllable, because as the subscriber of the event, you should know when you want to unsubscribe. This would only happen if a separate thread than the one being fired caused the unsubscribe of the current event being fired, so fairly limited chance.

Next, let's have an example of how to use the SafeEvent class:

```
/// <summary>
/// TestEventUser
/// Test the SafeEvent class for implementing an event using
SafeEvent
```

```
/// </summary>
public class TestEventUse
{
  //declare our private event
        private SafeEvent<EventArgs> _myEvent = new
SafeEvent<EventArgs>();

  /// <summary>
  /// MyEvent - proxy the add/remove calls to the private event
  /// </summary>
  public event EventHandler<EventArgs> MyEvent
  {
    add
    {
      _myEvent.Event += value;
    }

    remove
    {
      _myEvent.Event -= value;

     }

   }

  /// <summary>
  /// OnMyEvent - standard example idiom of how to fire an event
  /// </summary>
  /// <param name="args"></param>
  protected void OnMyEvent(EventArgs args)
  {
```

```
                    _myEvent.FireEvent(this,args); //call our private
event to fire it
        }

        /// <summary>
        /// FireEvent - This we provided on our test class as a quick way to
fire the event from another class.
        /// </summary>
        public void FireEvent()
        {
            OnMyEvent(new EventArgs());
        }

    }
```

Truly Multithreaded Event Handling (SafeEventNS Class)

Most implementations of event handling you'll see around either have many of the multithreading issues mentioned or will allow only a single thread in to fire a single event from a single thread at a time.

SafeEventsNS will allow multiple threads to fire the event at the same time, and the subscriber can get multithreaded calls at the same time. This means that notifications might not come in sequence. This is not the normal way most events are handled; most event handlers probably care about the sequence of events that come in. However, if you don't, and you need a relatively safe way to fire an event from multiple threads to multiple subscribers at the same time, this class might be useful.

SafeEventNS class

```
/// <summary>
/// SafeHandlerInfo - used for storing handler info, plus contains a
flag /// indicating if subscribed or not and the reader writer lock
/// for when the subscription is read or updated.
/// </summary>
/// <typeparam name="TArgs">Event args</typeparam> internal
class SafeHandlerInfo< TArgs> where TArgs : EventArgs {

    public EventHandler<TArgs> Handler;
    public bool Subscribed = true;
    //public object LockObj = new object();

   public ReaderWriterLockSlim Lock = new ReaderWriterLockslim();

    public SafeHandlerInfo(EventHandler<TArgs> handler)
    {
        Handler = handler;
    }

}

/// <summary>
/// SafeEvent class provides safety for unsubscribing from events
/// so even with multiple threads after unsubscribing, it will not get
called.
```

```
    /// Also makes sure that a null exception won't happen due to the
removing of events
    /// </summary>
    /// <typeparam name="TArgs">The type of the event args</
typeparam>
    public class SafeEventNS<TArgs>
      where Targs : EventArgs

    {

      Dictionary<EventHandler<TArgs>,
                    SafeHandlerInfo<TArgs>> _handlers = new
Dictionary<EventHandler<TArgs>,
        SafeHandlerInfo<TArgs>>();
              private ReaderWriterLockSlim _rwLock = new
ReaderwriterLockSlim();

      public event EventHandler<TArgs> Event {
        add
        {
          Subscribe(value);
        }

                remove
        {
          Unsubscribe(value);
        }

      }
```

```
/// <summary>
/// Used to fire this event from within the class using the SafeEvent
/// This reads a copy of the list and calls all the subscribers in it that
are still subscribed.
/// Anything that was unsubscribed gets removed at the end of the
event call. It was handler here since
/// The copy of the list might be held by multiple threads unsub-
scribe flags a handler unsubscribed and removes it.
/// that way if it is still in the list it will not be called
///
/// </summary>
/// <param name="args">The event args</param>
public virtual void FireEvent(object sender,TArgs args)
{
  _rwLock.EnterReadLock();
  List<SafeHandlerInfo<TArgs>> localHandlerInfos = _handlers.
Values.ToList();
  _rwLock.ExitReadLock();

  foreach (SafeHandlerInfo<TArgs> info in localHandlerInfos)
  {
    info.Lock.EnterReadLock();
    try
    {
      if (info.Subscribed)
      {
        EventHandler<TArgs> handler = info.Handler;
        try
        {
          handler(sender, args);
        }
```

```
            catch { };
          }

                    }
        finally
        {
          info.Lock.ExitReadLock();
        }
      }

    }


    /// <summary>
     /// Unsubscribe - internally used to unsubscribe a handler from
the event
    /// </summary>
      /// <param name="unsubscribeHandler">The handler being
unsubscribed</param>
            protected void Unsubscribe(EventHandler<TArgs>
unsubscribeHandler)
    {

            _rwLock.EnterWriteLock();
      try
      {

        SafeHandlerInfo<TArgs> handler = null;

        if (_handlers.TryGetValue(unsubscribeHandler, out handler))
        {
```

```
            handler.Lock.EnterWriteLock();
            try
            {

               handler.Subscribed = false;

               _handlers.Remove(handler.Handler);

                }
            finally
            {
               handler.Lock.ExitWriteLock();
            }
         }
      }
      catch (Exception e)
      {
         throw e;
      }
      finally
      {
         _rwLock.ExitWriteLock();
      }

   }

   /// <summary>
   /// Subscribe - Called to subscribe the handler
   /// </summary>
    /// <param name="eventHandler">The handler to subscribe</
param>
```

```
protected void Subscribe(EventHandler<TArgs> eventHandler)
{

  _rwLock.EnterWriteLock();
  try
  {

    SafeHandlerInfo<TArgs> handlerInfo = null;

    if (!_handlers.TryGetValue(eventHandler, out handlerInfo))
    {
     handlerInfo = new SafeHandlerInfo<TArgs>(eventHandler);


      handlerInfo.Lock.EnterWriteLock();
      try
      {

        _handlers.Add(eventHandler, handlerInfo);
      }
      finally
      {
        handlerInfo.Lock.ExitWriteLock();
      }
    }
    else
    {
      handlerInfo.Lock.EnterWriteLock();
      try
      {
```

```
                handlerInfo.Subscribed = true;
            }
            finally
            {
                handlerInfo.Lock.ExitWriteLock();
            }

        }
    }
    catch (Exception e)
    {
        throw e;
    }
    finally
    {
        _rwLock.ExitWriteLock();
    }

}

}
```

Let's show an example of how to use this, which is the same way as the previous SafeEvent class.

```
/// <summary>



    /// TestEventUser
        /// Test the SafeEvent class for implementing an event using SafeEvent
    /// </summary>
    public class TestSafeEventNS
```

```
{
  //declare our private event
        private SafeEventNS<EventArgs> _myEvent = new
SafeEventNS<EventArgs>();

    /// <summary>
    /// MyEvent - proxy the add/remove calls to the private event
    /// </summary>
    public event EventHandler<EventArgs> MyEvent
    {
      add
      {
        _myEvent.Event += value;
      }

      remove
      {
        _myEvent.Event -= value;

      }

    }

    /// <summary>
    /// OnMyEvent - standard example idiom of how to fire an event
    /// </summary>
    /// <param name="args"></param>
    protected void OnMyEvent(EventArgs args)
    {
```

```
            _myEvent.FireEvent(this,args); //call our private event to fire it
        }

        /// <summary>
        /// FireEvent - This we provided on our test class as a quick way
to fire the event from another class.
        /// </summary>
        public void FireEvent()
        {
            OnMyEvent(new EventArgs());
        }

    }
```

SafeEventNS Solution Summary

The SafeEventNS class still suffers from the potential for deadlocks, but offers the benefit of true multithreaded event support, if needed.

Since we added our own lock here problem #1 regarding potential deadlock adding and removing subscribersis back.

Problems	
#2 Null exception race condition	
#3 A new subscriber might not get called immediately	
#4 A handler is still called after unsubscribe	
#5 Possible deadlock	X
#6 Might not get most recent copy of handlers to call	
#7 Problem/Feature: Events could be fired to delegates out of sequence	X

Reminder: Problem #7 has to be handled by the publisher of the event only publishing in the correct sequence using multithreaded synchronization.

Single-threaded Access

So, as mentioned in the code project article and the original author John Skeet, there is a way to solve many of these problems: don't subscribe/unsubscribe or fire the events from multiple threads; only use one thread. That will avoid the locking overhead and some of the complexity and solve all the problems (sort of). It does add some complexity to the threading model. Also, it is arguable if it solves #3 and #4 problems, because if subscription is put into a queue to be handled on another thread, then you don't know when you will finally be subscribed or unsubscribed.

If you built an asynchronous notification to when you were subscribed or unsubscribed, that might be the one way to try to solve that.

For other potential implementations, take a look at the previously mentioned article. It explains the implementations and the problems each of them has:

http://www.codeproject.com/Articles/37474/Threadsafe-Events

Solving Problem #7

As mentioned, this problem is when events can be fired out of sequence. To solve that, the source of events must be controlled. Therefore, if there is a required sequencing of events, you protect your state machine and the firing of those events with synchronization if multiple threads could be firing it.

```
/// <summary>
/// TestEventUseSolveProblemSeven
/// Test the SafeEvent class for implementing an event using
/// SafeEvent – we want StartEvent to be fired before EndEvent
/// This shows how to solve problem #7.  If FireEvent() is that
/// only thing that could be used to fire events then
/// that will guarantee a StartEvent is called before an EndEvent()
/// </summary>
public class TestEventUseSolveProblemSeven
{
  //declare our private event
        private   SafeEvent<EventArgs>   _startEvent   =   new
SafeEvent<EventArgs>();
        private   SafeEvent<EventArgs>   _endEvent   =   new
SafeEvent<EventArgs>();
  private object _lock = new object();
  bool _started = false;

  /// <summary>
  /// StartEvent - proxy the add/remove calls to the private event
  /// </summary>
  public event EventHandler<EventArgs> StartEvent
  {
    add
    {
      _startEvent.Event += value;
    }

    remove
    {
```

```
        _startEvent.Event -= value;

      }

    }

    public event EventHandler<EventArgs> EndEvent
    {
      add
      {
        _endEvent.Event += value;
      }

      remove
      {
        _endEvent.Event -= value;

      }

    }

    /// <summary>
    /// OnStartEvent - standard example idiom of how to fire an event
    /// </summary>
    /// <param name="args"></param>
    protected void OnStartEvent(EventArgs args)
    {

      _startEvent.FireEvent(this, args); //call our private event to fire it
    }
```

```
        /// <summary>
        /// OnEndEvent - standard example idiom of how to fire an event
        /// </summary>
        /// <param name="args"></param>
        protected void OnEndEvent(EventArgs args)
        {

            _endEvent.FireEvent(this, args); //call our private event to fire it
        }

        /// <summary>
        /// FireEvent - This we provided on our test class as a quick way to
fire
        /// the event from another class.
        /// </summary>
        public void FireEvent()
        {
            // by using a lock to prevent other events from being fired and
managing our
            // state we can guarantee event ordering.
            lock (_lock)
            {
                if (_started)
                    OnEndEvent(new EventArgs());
                else
                    OnStartEvent(new EventArgs());
                _started = !_started;

            }
        }

    }
```

Summary

As we have seen, there is no straightforward, easy answer to all multithreading issues. You will need to pick the best answer for your purpose/requirements and handle the scenarios that can occur properly to avoid event/multithreading issues.

Does Your Sleep(0) Smell?

Why yes, it probably does. Code smell that is. (Thread.Sleep(0))

Code smell is a term that was coined to refer to something that just doesn't seem right. Examples of smelly code were given when this was coined. This one wasn't in that list, but it probably deserves its place in there.

The reason this is likely a code smell is because the usual intent of Thread.Sleep(0) is to give up the rest of your thread's time slice (quantum) to give other threads a chance to run.

This is often attempted in some producer/consumer scenarios or used to try to prevent "burning CPU," which refers to 100 percent CPU usage.

In reality, Sleep(0) will only give up your time slice (quantum) if there is an equal priority or higher thread ready to run. So if your thread is higher priority, nothing happens and your thread continues to burn CPU.

If you really needed to do something like this, win32 SwitchToThread or the Thread.Yield will yield to any threads on the same processor ready to run. But if nothing is ready to run, your thread will continue to run and burn CPU. If you are a consumer, and there is no data, it's using CPU needlessly in this case.

To prevent burning CPU, instead, code could use a multithreaded synchronization object that can notify a consumer when data is ready, like an AutoResetEvent or ManualResetEvent (or new slim versions).

If your app doesn't need super-high performance that can be the best way to go rather than trying to use Sleeps.

Alternatively, if the situation calls for Sleeps and SwitchToThread or Yield, it doesn't sound like the right answer for you. Sleep(1) will yield to any and all threads ready to run, but depending on your timer precision setting, that could wait 1–13 milliseconds, so it is rather slow.

In general, some would argue that even using Sleep regardless of the value is a smell all on its own, and alternatives include synchronization objects or a timer.

Another alternative is using async and await with Task.Delay, which won't technically hold the thread and will continue when it gets a notification:

```
async Task MyTask()
    {
      await Task.Delay(5000);
    }
```

Possible items to try to find out if it really smells when you see a Sleep:

- Is it holding up a thread that could do work needlessly? Could the thread be used to do other work rather than waiting?
- Is it waiting on something that could instead be triggered off a notification or event?
- Is it some place that you could have used a synchronization object because you are waiting on another thread to do something?
- Is it some place that might have made sense to use async await with Task.Delay?

There are Some Somewhat Legitimate Places for Using Sleep

Some examples that might be ok (non-smelly or at least less smelly) include:

- A delay on a dedicated thread due to deadlock that the thread couldn't progress anyway, and since dedicated won't be doing work otherwise.
- A delay when launching numerous threads (especially ones that will simultaneously access the database and update similar tables), when on a dedicated thread that couldn't do anything else, anyway.

Ok, time to get some sleep. Goodnight . . .

CHAPTER 31

Time Management

Time Management

Developers need as much uninterrupted thinking or coding time as possible as only with enough time they can get into "the zone," where they are efficiently thinking about or coding/working on the problem at hand. Every time they get interrupted by managers/people asking questions, the next endless meeting, or the countless other items that crop up during the day, it can take many minutes for them to get back into "the zone." Those minutes can add up to significantly reducing the effectiveness of your development staff.

Some ways to combat the problem:

- Block off time where there are no meetings.
- Set aside one time of the day for meetings and the rest; perhaps leave an hour open for a possible meeting to be inserted if absolutely necessary.
- Aggregate meetings.
- Don't interrupt your development needlessly and don't let others do it either.

Meetings

Tips to have better meetings:

- Only call a meeting if it's really needed.
- Only include the people for the meeting who really need to be there; perhaps some people just need to see the meeting summary.
- Have an agenda and stick to it.
- If people go off topic, ask that it be taken offline after the meeting.
- Produce a specific action plan if appropriate.
- Consolidate meetings if possible to avoid calling meetings for small items.
- Consolidate meetings toward the beginning or end of the day. Try to give people as much consecutive uninterrupted time in meetings as possible to increase their productivity.
- Make sure someone is taking notes so they can send out a summary.

E-mail

How to Manage Your E-mail Inbox

I presume many of you are, like me, are flooded with e-mails and tasks to do. Some of you have probably heard about various methods like GTD (Getting Things Done) that have quite a following as well as numerous other plans.

Through the necessity of being swallowed by my tasks and e-mail, I started using variations of different techniques from many of the well-known methodologies. I'm used to getting hundreds of e-mails a day. This methodology has helped me manage my e-mail and my work.

Change your Gmail settings: Go to labs and enable preview pane in the labs tab. Also in labs you might want to enable the mark read button. Go to the inbox tab and change the inbox type to Unread first. You'll then notice some settings below you can change

I changed my default view to only show unread e-mails. This way, when I read them or mark them read, they fall out of my view. Ctrl+Q will mark them as read using a shortcut from the main outlook view for the selected items (or click the little mail icon in the headline section as you hover over it).

I keep them unread in my view until I have done something with them. You should change your view to not automatically mark them read when just viewed in the reading pane. I added a mark unread button to my toolbar to allow me easily to mark items unread to keep in my view. You can also use the mark unread option from the edit menu.

Categories/Labels:

1. Create four main categories for tasks: daily, weekly, monthly, yearly.
2. Create four labels for each of the categories: daily, weekly, monthly, yearly.

Calendar Items:

1. Add to your calendar an appointment for weekly, monthly, and yearly reminder to review the category items.

Guidelines:

1. Don't read your e-mails all the time: Set up times if your job allows. I typically choose around three main times a day to go through e-mail: morning, midday, and about an hour before I need to leave. Yes, I sometimes read them more often than I should, and occasionally just glance to see if something looks urgent or not; if not, I let it go until my regular review times.
2. Couple minute rule: Like another popular method, if the e-mail that came in requires only a couple minutes, do it then to get it off your list.
3. Delegate: If you can totally delegate something and it's quick (a couple of minutes), do it to get it off your list.
4. Read: If you just needed to read it, read it if it's quick, and let it fall out of your view as read.

What to do if you could not do any of the above?

- Is it something you need to schedule, like a meeting? Add it to your calendar and invite the appropriate folks.
- Is it something you need to do that has specific target dates and times you need to do something? Schedule them in your calendar the time you need.
- If you need to keep track of the above items for any reason, then add a task.

After the below items have been done, you can mark your e-mail read:

1. Assign the categories/label to the task based on the period you wish to review: daily, weekly, monthly or yearly.

2. Also, add any additional categories for the task that are appropriate.
3. If you like organizing tasks by time, you could also create categories (like 5 minutes, 15 minutes, 30 minutes, 1 hour, 4 hours, 8 hours) to be able to quantify how much time a task may take.
4. If this task is critical and has important specific date deliverable, add calendar items for those.
5. If the task is fairly important and you want tickler reminders, you could add the reminder for the task; just make sure the number of these you do is limited, or you will be flooded with reminders.
6. Create Project labels to add e-mails to you want to keep track of/organize (or instead use Google Desktop or another product to easily find your e-mails; I don't use Google Desktop).

For people who always work on the same project, create a rule that always labels mail. Use other rules and keywords to sort e-mails into appropriate project folders, if possible. Manually label other e-mails you care about organizing to the right folder.

Daily review: Pick a daily time to review your daily items. I usually pick the morning, since it's easy to remember and helps you think about what you want to do for the day.

Free time: As per a popular method, use your daily, weekly, monthly, yearly lists as well as if you tagged items with a category of approximate time to complete, you can easily pick tasks that match your available current free time.

General: Just work your e-mail box, and add your calendar items and tasks. Review your weekly, monthly, and yearly items based on your recurring calendar items for those review times you added.

Keeping track of your tasks anywhere: I use my mobile phone to keep track of any home items I need to do. At the office, I'm usually sitting in front of a PC. I needed something that was always with me to keep track. The Android calendar works well, and it syncs with your Gmail calendar, so can keep everything up to date.

If you need a to-do list app, Todoist is one to look at for Windows, Android, or iOS.

I hope these ideas can help you dig out of your pile of e-mails, appointments and tasks and make you more productive.

Which Communication Method to Use?

E-mail, text/instant, voice/video call message etiquette—don't annoy your friends and coworkers!

Today, we have so many communications tools at our disposal, it can be hard to pick just one to use, since they can often have different purposes.

For example, text messages are limited in text and have an implied indication that you are looking for an immediate response. Other message platforms are not quite as limited but have this sort of instant implied response (e.g., Hangouts, Slack, Skype).

E-mails, on the other hand, can be written very detailed and don't usually have an instant notification, so folks sending e-mails probably don't expect an immediate response.

Voice calls also expect people to answer and talk to them NOW!

Method	Implied Immediacy	Conversation Complexity	Recommended need response time
Email	Today-Tomorrow	Low-Medium	4-8 hours or a day or so (depends on recipient/etc)
Text Message/IM	Soon	Low	< 2 hours
Voice/Video call	NOW!	Medium-High	NOW!

E-mail time can range based on whether the person you are e-mailing is in the office or not, and if it's near the end of the day or not. If your question/query can wait till tomorrow, and the person you are e-mailing will be in for work, perhaps e-mail will be just fine.

If instead it's near the end of the day in less than two hours and you need the answer before they leave, you might decide to text/instant message to get their attention now.

If the conversation is complex, you might want to choose a meeting with voice/video call to be able to relay the complexity more easily.

The key is to not choose methods that require a response NOW for something that can wait. You are interrupting your coworkers or friends for something that doesn't need immediate attention.

I know many people who are just used to texting, Hangouts, and so on, but at least give a thought for the communication method you are using to not interrupt people more than needed. Plus, use the right communication method for your conversation complexity. You probably shouldn't discuss brain surgery via text message or e-mail, for example. :)

Your friends/coworkers will thank you. You're welcome!

CHAPTER 32

Management

Intro

At some point in your career, you may either be looking to move to a management path or be given some level of responsibilities in management. This section will provide some guidance for you to achieve this goal and describe methodologies for management. This section won't describe everything about being a manager, though it will outline high-level areas. It will provide some specific aspects related to being an engineering manager that might be different from a non-engineering one. It will also cover things that you might not learn from traditional management training sources.

How to Become a Software Engineering Manager

Learning about the things a manager does can help your understanding of the role first. One factor is to think like an owner of the business (narrowed of course to within the confines of your role). Ask yourself what the CEO/owner would want you to do and what your manager would want you to do. Be able to solve issues yourself or with your team whenever possible, and engage with others when necessary. Showing you can handle issues without having to engage with your manager helps show you have the capability to manage issues. Part of a manager's job is keeping their manager informed of issues that they might want to know or need to know, so understanding what they would want or need to know about is important. Engineering managers, while they don't need to be technical to be effective, can be more effective when they have some degree of technical knowledge.

Being a manager requires having or learning things, such as:

- People/soft skills.
- Leading by example.
- Leading with empathy.
- Good organizational skills.
- Understanding how to work within the software development life cycle (SDLC).
- Some project management skills.
- Understanding how to coach/mentor.
- For technical managers, perhaps architecture/design skills/ technical skills.
- Understanding the technical roles of the team and their capabilities.
- For technical managers, asking the right questions to help their team make technical decisions or even for non-technical managers, helping teams come to the right conclusions.
- Initiative, passion/energy.
- Ability to influence/negotiate with people.

It will be easier to become a manager if you already demonstrate some of the above skills. You could potentially help set yourself up for a management position where you would be the obvious senior lead developer for a project, and a possible natural progression might be a management position (either by finding a new job in that role or by finding an internal role you can take to help play that position). Also, if you are demonstrating the above items and have relayed your desired career path to your manager, if opportunities present themselves, you might be given the opportunity at some point.

Don't just think a management role is the natural progression for development roles. There are plenty of jobs that have progressive development roles with decent pay scales. Not everyone is ready to be a manager. If you are short-tempered, complaining/criticizing others, constantly have heated arguments, or are quiet and not leading by example, management might be a challenging career path for you.

It can be easier to become a development manager if you have good technical skills that folks are calling on to help guide others and you are already forming good vision, technical architecture to guide people, strong but flexible opinions in the face of new facts/information that counter your opinions.

Pay attention to how not just your manager but other managers talk in meetings with their staff. It's also easier to have an authoritative voice if the team respects your technical skills, ideas and direction. So if you are planning to become a manager, really take stock of your skills and how others perceive your skills/experience to see if you feel you are really ready. If not, work on those skills so that you become a natural technical leader, which is one step in heading toward a technical lead and possibly eventually a management role if you have or can acquire the other skills as well.

Read more books/online information on being a manager to make sure you understand the principles and best practices for a manager.

Make an effort to learn about your business and your product area very well. Understand the company and product vision and plan. Understand the focus on meeting customer needs and positively impacting the financials where appropriate for your role. This is part of the background to help you become a natural leader by having expertise that others can call on.

Do you need to be an extrovert to be a manager? No. However, it might be easier for extroverts. Many managers are probably somewhere between introvert and extrovert, and they may be anywhere across the entire spectrum.

Pros of Being a Manager:

- Having some flexibility in tasks if your days aren't too crazy busy with meetings.
- Being able to help lead a team to successes can be gratifying.
- Being able to share your skills and expertise in ways that help to guide a team can also be fulfilling.
- Sometimes, management pay can be better than technical, though not always.

Cons of Being a Manager:

- You are responsible for your team's execution. When things go wrong, management will look to you to solve it and be responsible.
- Dealing with personnel issues can be quite taxing.
- Hiring/firing can be some of the most trying/draining tasks.
- People are looking to you for often hard/gray area decisions that need to be made that can have significant consequences on the success/failure of the team.
- Lots of meetings can be common for managers.
- If you wanted to stay technical, it can be difficult with many meetings.

- There are fewer management jobs than there are individual contributor jobs.

Leading Teams

Ideally, you should be an example for your team to follow (leading by example) in all matters including work ethic. Lead with vision and empathy.

Remember, what you say and do can set the tone for your team. If you treat something as noncritical or trivial, so will they. Use good moral values in your decisions. If you are leading an Agile team, ask questions if needed to lead them toward a solution. For an Agile team, have the team help make important decisions whenever possible. Whenever possible, make decisions that your team will respect.

One on Ones

One on Ones

One-on-one meetings are with just you and one of the team. The most important concern of one on ones is allowing time for a team member to discuss with you anything they feel they need to.

These should happen every one to three weeks with each team member. It is recommended that most of these meetings are kept informal.

Some example topics that might be covered in some of these meetings:

- How are they doing at home and work?
- Concerns they have.
- Career path.
- At the end of the year or organizational times of review, discuss reviews, goals/objectives, etc.

- Discussing topics they are interested in (it's a time for connecting with team members).
- Criticisms, if any (follow the rule: Praise in public, criticize in private).

How Is the Person Doing?

Ask about home and work life and balance.

Career Plans

What career path is the person looking for?

Do you think they have realistic expectations?

If your org has a list of skills and expectations for a job role, use that for the employee to fill in over time of how they have demonstrated meeting that expectation.

Problem Areas

Make sure you address any problematic concerns that have come up so that these are not a surprise when the time comes for compensation review.

Personnel Issues

At times, there might be issues caused by your team or others. One thing to remember is a standard management principle: praise in public, criticize in private. If you need to have conversations with someone, if it is a critique, make sure you do that in private, not public. When a concerning thing happens, it is important to bring it up as soon as possible, BUT take a step back first.

Does the situation need immediate action? Immediate physical violence threats/harassment? Of course, yes. But if the concern is regarding a process or just generally interpersonal, take a step back and think through the issue/concern.

Think about if it's possible from a process issue standpoint and see if it is a process issue. If it is, determine if staff needs more training or experience. Or have staff been given very sufficient training and time, and you still feel things are not handled right? It's best when things can be approached from a process standpoint if possible rather than blame, as folks are then more inclined to approach it with constructive thought. Ask questions from the team member about how they think "we" could improve a situation and prevent it from happening.

Also consider if there is something going on in your team member's life that might be impacting their work or working relationships. If so, talk to them. If there is something that can be done from a work/benefits standpoint to help them, you can discuss it.

For example, someone might not be doing their best work and seem tired all the time. You could say, "Hey, I've noticed you've seemed kind of tired. Anything going on? Is there anything I can help with?"

A response could be something like, "I've been really tired, because my wife has been ill, and I've been taking care of the baby all night."

After discussing, perhaps if your organization allows it, you could allow them to start work a little later so they could get some rest, perhaps temporarily cut back hours that could be made up on weekends.

There might be other cases where your organization's benefits might offer help with child care that you could suggest (if offered by the organization).

You get the idea, though. Think through from the point of view of how you can help your team member if possible, if that makes sense.

For another example, imagine you have an on-call policy for dealing with customer critical issues, and you call the team member on call, and they don't respond. Later, you ask them, "Why didn't you respond to the call?" You find out they were on the way to the hospital for their spouse. It's best to understand situations completely before deciding on what went wrong and determining what to do about it.

Performance Discussions

These conversations go easy when everything is good, but can be some of the toughest conversations when there are employee issues that need to be addressed. First thing to start out with is that if you don't know the cause of performance issues, ask questions. You might discover there are good reasons behind the issues, and perhaps you can help the team member with them in some way. For example, imagine an employee that is not getting their work done on time. You could say, "I've noticed that your work output is a little less than usual. That's not like you. Is everything ok?" The team member might say, "I've been going through chemo treatment, so I haven't been feeling well."

If you had been accusatory, it would have made the team member resent you, and most certainly you would feel pretty bad once you learned the reason things weren't as usual. As a manager, you might need to decide how to handle this, hoping it's a short-term impact until they can feel better and perhaps temporarily offer distributing work to help them through what is a trying time in their life.

Of course, there could be other times a staff member has no good explanation, and you might want to be more compelling about them improving their performance. It's all going to depend on the situation. If you have an ongoing problem with a team member that isn't improving, you should engage your HR team if you think you may eventually need to let someone go. Give them the opportunity to improve, though. Sometimes, they will surprise you once they understand the expectations better.

Compensation Discussions

These conversations can be easy when your company is making money and meeting/exceeding expectations of the team member. Of course, these get much harder if the company isn't doing well, or the performance of the team member has not been good. Before you go into these conversations, it's best to have good background information on why things are how they are that the team member can identify with. If pay increases were smaller than usual this year, why? You might say if true, "The company had a bad year. Sales were down by 50 percent, revenue down by 80 percent, so our budgets were decreased for the coming year, which reduced our compensation pool."

When it's a company impact, folks can understand if they have been hearing about the issues. If it's performance related, hopefully, you have been having the conversations about performance all year. That way, it's no surprise at compensation time that they are not going to receive a full bonus or increase due to performance.

Sometimes, to award an excellent contributor, you may have to take money from others to do so, so you might have to explain to those others why the comp is lower without saying specifically you took money and gave it to other people. Yes, this is the reality of management, so if you haven't done this before, be prepared. Usually, you would try to make it so the amount wouldn't be too noticeable, so you don't have to offer an explanation of any kind, if possible. If not, you could just say that was the best we could do based on the bonus pool this year. A kind of general statement.

When you have compensation conversations, you want the team member to feel valued for their efforts, so be sure to call out the great work they did for the year and thank them for it. Hopefully, the compensation your company can offer is fair market value or better so that it helps the staff member feel this way too.

Don't Micromanage

No one wants to be watched constantly about what they are doing. No one wants comments on every little thing they do. So try to find a balance of maintaining an appropriate direction without needing to do this. It is better to give your folks the information they need so they can be successful, and check with them at reasonable intervals (like the daily scrum). As you get closer to significant release time frames, you might need more frequent updates depending on your circumstances, but these should be short-term, rare usage, very limited, and only when necessary and kept to the absolute minimum needed.

Planning a Project

Help create sensible, ambitious plans that you can actually achieve with your team. This doesn't mean overworking them till they leave or allowing so much slack that they can take it easy. This is about finding the happy medium of having the right people, resources, time, features to be able to meet the goals in a timely fashion. This can involve helping set reasonable expectations with many stakeholders, such as business analysts, your manager, the management team, customer reps and your team.

Time Off

You need to manage the team's time off to make sure there is coverage for all the tasks and projects the team is required to handle. Make sure your team members take a reasonable amount of time off a year so they can recharge, not feel burned out, and can be renewed to work with passion on your projects. Don't make people work on their PTO. Let them have their time off so they can relax and recharge. Don't require them to monitor e-mails or be on call in any way on PTO if you can at all avoid it.

The Power of Questions

Use questions to lead and guide your team. Carefully choose your questions to be open and empowering. If you need a team member's work done by Wednesday, don't ask, "Will you be done by Wednesday?" Ask instead, "Is there anything the team can do to support your work to complete by Wednesday?" (Obviously, if the team has some spare time to support and it's critical work to be done by Wednesday). One question gives the person yes or no answers and a trapped feeling, and the other is empowering and helpful.

If you have concerns about the team's direction, rather than saying, "That's no good, do it this way," ask questions that gently expose your concerns to the team, so that they can come to the conclusion on their own.

Wherever possible, the above is a preferable method of leading teams. There might be times where timelines are tight and the risks are too high to spend the time guiding the team, and there might need to be times where you have to give explicit direction due to indecision and timelines, but those should be very infrequent, and the great majority of leading should not be that way and instead be guiding and leading by example.

Role in Scrum

Surprisingly, in Scrum, there is no official role for a manager. Though it is recommended that a manager not be the Scrum master, that can be ok sometimes, depending on the manager and the team's comfort level with them. A better role is just more of the management tasks that managers do for the team (hiring, firing, reviews, etc.) but also like a Scrum master helping unblock a team that is blocked. Also, help guide a team not by mandating a direction if it can be avoided, often just by asking the right questions so that the team can make the best choices.

Role as Architect

Technical engineering managers sometimes find themselves in the role of helping design or decide on architecture. This can depend on how technical the engineering manager is and the design skills of the teams involved. If the skills of the team are up to the task, it might be best to let them design, or the manager contribute some tidbits of information to help design, ask questions to help clarify good and bad design and help figure out which is which.

People Reviews (Yearly or Ideally More Often)

A formal review is held at least every year at most companies. This is often used to document goals achieved or missed, overall summary of how the employee did for the year, and follow-up criticisms/concerns to summarize. This meeting's data is sometimes directly or indirectly used to help inform end-of-year raises and bonuses. Criticisms should not be a surprise at this stage, since throughout the year, there should have been one-on-one meetings, so the employee should be well aware of any criticisms prior to the final review (unless they came up between the last one on one and the final review, perhaps).

Project Management

Managers are often called on to be project managers as well, even when there are dedicated or part-time project managers assigned to teams or projects. This usually means being part or primary planning person, as well as executing the plan and meeting the project time lines. Managers are often held responsible for these time lines.

Using Agile, you or your project manager might calculate the story points and the team's velocity and estimate when the project might be completed, taking into consideration team time off/holidays and potential story expansion. You could estimate a buffer of 0–30 percent extra points, based on risk/estimated possible expansion. That estimate presumes, though, the team can keep executing at full speed, and all dependencies are managed so that it doesn't slow the team, or those discrepancies can be absorbed by the buffer points. However, sometimes, that can be tricky.

The other item to consider is points estimate effort but not necessarily time. For example, imagine a mostly automated test that needs to be run but requires monitoring by a team member is estimated at five points (let's say roughly a typical week of effort), but it will take actually several months to execute the tests due to the amount of data that needs to be processed.

So sometimes, raw point calculations aren't enough, and you might need, in addition, a sprint plan: a plan of the tasks that will need to happen in each sprint through the release time. On top of that, analyzing the dependencies of work items on a team and between teams can help try to work through dependency concerns.

A tool you could use is a Gantt chart to help work through different stories, sprints, and dependencies.

Mentoring/Career Path

This can take the form of constructive suggestions on how to perform their current job. Sometimes, it is best to lead in the form of questions.

There might even be some people in the team that are looking to get into a management role, perhaps as part of a team reporting to you or a different management chain. Offering some suggestions on learning material online training can help. Help find opportunities to help your staff move forward, improving their skills/career.

Employee Concerns

One of the most challenging aspects of management is when someone on the team is having some trouble or isn't performing well. Perhaps it's someone always getting on everyone's nerves, or slow work, poor work, late to work, or even HR issues like harassment. With the exception of perhaps HR issues, sometimes it's best to start out by just asking general questions about how the employee is doing at home or work to see if they might offer some insight to you about what might be going on without the criticism yet. If you don't get any clues, ask about the situation in a very non-biased way.

Instead, you chat with the employee and say, "Hi, is everything going ok, today?"

The response, "Hi, sorry this morning I missed an alert. I was on the way to the hospital."

So we can see with a delicate approach without blaming the employee. We discovered there was a perfectly valid reason for not being on time. If we had started with blame, we would have found ourselves on the wrong side of things, caused bad feelings needlessly for the employee, perhaps souring a working relationship, instead of approaching with questions and empathy with the assumption initially, there might be good reasons for employee action or inaction.

Project Details

Confirm with your team on a regular basis that all requirements are being met. Actually, walk through the requirements and ask about how each is being met. Make sure each one is covered to your satisfaction. Dig into the details until you are sure.

Assess the status of the project regularly to make sure the team will meet the targets at least each sprint, or two, depending on project length. When possible, use an MVP philosophy, and don't allow expansion of functionality/changes if your product can survive without it. It's very easy to allow expansion and then spend time fixing things that didn't need to be there in the first place. Make sure functionality is tested when it's created and doesn't wait till the end. That will be difficult when it's hard to test without all of a project being together, but build and test in logical chunks. This will avoid massive test time near the end, when you hope you should be done. It also means finding issues early rather than later.

Example: Day in the Life of an Engineering Manager

Day X:

- Review team planned work for the week.
- Review time off to see how it can impact future sprint planning/releases.
- Go through e-mail and new support tickets, and assign to teams as appropriate.
- Meet with the team for scrum/post-scrum talks.
- Meeting with business analysts on current/future plans.
- One-on-one meeting with a team member.
- Respond to various Slack messages from business analysts, engineers, and managers throughout the day.

- All-manager meeting for all managers to cover any management related items like year-end reviews, purchasing, high-level release concerns.
- Daily Feature meeting for an in-flight feature for the current release (or following release).
- Go through and respond to any e-mails of the day.
- Review any resumes that came in for open positions on the team.
- Schedule screening calls if needed.
- Plan for tomorrow.

Team Size

There is a term "span of control," meaning the number of people a manager can effectively manage. A similar concept is used in the military to command armies. The size that you can effectively manage can range based on a lot of factors, such as the type of work, the caliber of people, and more. The range is usually 1–12.

Managing Management Expectations vs. Team Capability

If your team is like most, management always wants more delivered faster. Your job will be to manage their expectations while keeping your team on a reasonable schedule/work-life balance. This can be tricky. Explain what you are constantly doing/looking at to reduce tasks and decrease time while still providing the best realistic estimations that you have.

For example, if management kept pushing to deliver by June. The team kept communicating how they could consolidate tasks, improve testing time effort, and decrease the estimates over time, but the estimates were still indicating it was too close to call if it would make the release, so we might miss it. That was reported to management as well as the attempts to improve, adding more staff where they could to reduce time even more. Ultimately, it was very close. The team nearly missed the release but made it with part of the functionality into the release.

Delegating

When you are starting out as a new manager, it can be a little difficult to decide what and when you should delegate. It can feel unnatural asking people to do something. As a manager, it would be hard to carry out all of your management tasks all the time if you were stuck doing individual contributor tasks, so figure out what makes sense to delegate to people on the team or what still makes sense to do yourself.

Staffing/Hiring

I have very mixed feelings about the effort to hire people for a job. I feel thankful for the opportunity. It's great when you can bring on talented people. The problem is that you often have to go through tens of people or more to find the ones that are the right fit. That requires spending hours of your and your team's time. It's very draining when phone screens and interviews don't work out. I imagine it is even worse for the interviewee, but it was very draining for our teams as well. Some of the only things more draining are personnel issues and firing.

If you don't have the right interview questions, interviewing can feel like a crapshoot. We had a case where we asked mostly knowledge questions in an interview, and the candidate knew everything we asked. We felt we had a great candidate. We hired him, and he wasn't motivated to do any work, barely any at all. Some things can be very hard to interview for, like motivation. All the references were good, so those didn't help either.

Referrals

Employee referrals can often be one of your best sources of candidates. Not all will work out, but usually, the rate is significantly higher than random folks off the street. The percent of good candidates is even higher when the referral is from teams in your area of expertise who know capable candidates that would be a fit for your technology stack. This is good news, as your employees are willing to suggest to friends or former coworkers your office is a good place to work. It's a nice endorsement of your workplace and of the candidates.

Candidate Prescreening

Make sure the resume has all the keywords you expect. Check the tech stack. Check that their education/background seems reasonable. Check that their previous experience in the types of work they have done seems reasonable. Look for red flags: missing time, different fields of work, odd or unrelated tech stacks, etc.

Phone Screens/Online Tests

On a phone screen, you want to cover some basic areas:

- Clarify any potential red flags or exclusions.
- See if the description of what they say they actually worked on themselves matches what your job needs.
- See if they have the personality traits and team fit you are looking for.

- Check in a very simple way if they can code, review code, and have a reasonable thought process.

In-Person Interviews

Personality/Learning questions

Knowledge-Based Questions

- Computer Science/Algorithms/Data Structures:
  - Evaluating what folks learned about computer science can be good. Though a lot of folks are out of school for a while, only remember some of this. I would definitely say candidates with a multi-year computer science degree who have been given a solid background in data structures and algorithms will be more equipped to build solutions to a wide variety of problems that are faced in developing applications/services.
- Networking
- Operating Systems
- Design Patterns
- Technology stack understanding (e.g., C#, .NET, C++, Java, ASP.NET)

Problem-Solving Scenarios

- Architecture
- Find the cause of a problem

Coding

Come up with a coding scenario that the best people can finish in 15 minutes, and others might take 30–45. Longer doesn't necessarily mean worse if they are methodical, careful, perhaps even implement unit tests. Try to make this coding challenge something that would possibly actually be done on a typical day in your office. The more practical, the better the test.

Code Reviewing

Come up with a practical code review scenario, perhaps even an old bit of code that is ok to share that was really bad, so there are lots of things for people to comment about it. You can rate people by the number and type of things they find.

Make sure the code review example has trivial issues as well as significant actual bugs to find. This should be something related to what someone might actually review on your team.

Debugging/Fixing

Come up with a debugging scenario, something your developers might encounter doing their job on your software. Describe a bug the customer found. The candidate must debug the problem and come up with a solution, fix, and test the fix.

For example, we would set up a coding scenario, let's say, to debug an application. The candidate gets a list of bugs and the code base, with the Visual Studio IDE for C# apps, similar to what a developer would need to do in real-world scenarios. We told candidates they can look up whatever they need on Google to help them. We told them up front that they would be expected to code in Visual Studio IDE for C#. We would still get a few candidates who came in seeming to barely know their way around the IDE at all, so it was pretty obvious that those candidates probably were not going to do well, which was the case. If they had a different favorite editor, they could have used that as well.

Passion

Ask them what they find exciting in the world of computing. Ask them why. Have they worked on any projects outside of work they would share? If they can't offer too many things, you can kind of get an idea for their passion for the field. This isn't a deal breaker, but it can sort of separate the star performers from folks who just look at it as a job.

Usually, folks with a deep passion have dug into various technologies deeper and have a richer understanding of the tech and how to use it.

Onboarding

Mentoring

Assign a mentor to assist with onboarding so the person has someone to go to and ask for things. It's better if this is a regular team member rather than a manager so they don't feel it's too much to ask.

Training

Provide training on:

- How to use your products like your customers.
- How to set up the development environment.
- How to make changes to the software SDLC process.
- An overview of the internals of the software and data models.
- How to debug the software.

How do you get more headcount for your team?
Showing need is the number one way. If you have a new project, estimate when it will get done without headcount vs. with. If you support customer investigations, show that you can't keep up with the incoming investigations with the current staff. Basically, collect relevant data, and show how the headcount would benefit the company/team/timeline/time to market, business, etc. Sometimes, it can come down to as simple as that and asking for it. Other times, it can be an ongoing effort showing the data and making those requests.

Outsourcing of Development Work

This can also be relevant if there is a region in another time zone, and onboarding a new team there could have some similar concerns. For business leaders, looking at outsourcing (sometimes called offshoring when done in a different country) is a great idea on paper. Sometimes, the pay can be one-third the price for developers in another country. That seems like it would be three times the work for the price.

In reality, while it can be beneficial, it's never as easy as it sounds on paper and probably doesn't save as much money as it seems.

Don't disregard the time difference. Depending on the way your team works, a significant time difference can greatly slow down team work hand offs if they need to work closely with other teams in a different time zone.

Leadership

Make sure in the region, the outsourced teams have management you can trust to guide the day-to-day work. Having someone you can trust to direct work when you can't be there means your projects stay on task.

Allow for sufficient training and knowledge transfer time. Just bringing people onboard doesn't mean they can immediately do everything you need. Many products and processes are very complex and require some onboarding time, sometimes from many months to a year or more, before they can operate on their own sufficiently. Don't discount the time and effort it will take for knowledge transfer/ongoing training, as this will utilize some of your onshore team's time for a while. Make sure training materials are created (videos/PowerPoints) so the outsourced team can start to train new folks themselves.

If you have the option, employees in a region will be more dedicated than consultants. Churn rates for consultants in some regions can be very high, meaning you need to keep retraining people, and they never become sufficiently trained before they leave.

Types of projects

It's easier to hand off either work that doesn't require a lot of knowledge or context, or well-documented work with a lot of detail on requirements so that there doesn't need to be a lot of back-and-forth discussion across regions. Also, maintenance work could be easier to outsource/offshore, since it's in small, usually better-defined pieces. The training for support work can be high depending on the size of the software, areas that need to be covered, and team sizes.

Schedule regular meetings when the outsourced team can have discussions with the existing teams so they can ask questions as they continue to learn. Like grooming/planning sessions.

Offer ad hoc meetings as needed to fill in knowledge gaps.

Just remember that outsourcing could appear negative to local folks who think you will hire cheaper labor in another region and let the local folks go. Hopefully, that's not the case, and you can assure them that is not the plan. It's become a sort of the standard at some firms to have some full-time employees, some offshore, and some consultants to offer a mix of staffing to allow taking advantage of better labor costs.

Team Collaboration

Create a map of the teams your team works with or should. Come up with a plan to meet on some semi-regular basis that's an appropriate time relative to the amount of interaction and discussion that might be needed. A development team would hopefully include the operations team in reveals, but it still might be good to have a biweekly or monthly meeting to go over planned changes, concerns, or issues between the team leads.

Your company might have a group of DBAs for production that might be another team you want to engage, for example.

Even dev teams on the same product should probably have a meeting to go over different issues/concerns that come up.

Managing Large Multi-Team Projects

Make sure the project is set up for success

Make sure each of the teams involved is committed to delivery, and this project has appropriate senior management backing, so that each of the team's priorities is appropriately prioritizing this project to not interfere with other team's deliverables. Without a reasonably shared priority and commitment, if one team needs to deliver a dependency for other teams but isn't giving the project an appropriate priority, it can derail the whole project. This requires getting an understanding of the priorities of each team and a discussion with them to be sure their understanding of priorities and yours match.

If you don't think that priority is going to work, have a discussion with the stakeholders of the project and/or more senior management if appropriate to try to get the priorities or timeline to the point where you feel the project can be successful. Monitor this throughout the project in terms of priorities, timelines, and so on.

Project Manager(s)

It's always good to have a project manager if your company/team has the support of one for these types of projects. They can collect the time lines, estimates, and dependencies and help coordinate them. If you don't have a project manager and you are in charge of coordination, congratulations, you are the project manager. :)

Hold teams/leads accountable for providing estimates and dependencies, and try to keep commitments for dependencies to help keep teams on track.

Dependency Management

Make sure you have a list of all dependencies and how they interact between the teams. A Gantt chart may be useful for laying out the time lines and dependencies to make sure that estimates and time lines match up well with the dependencies. Microsoft Project can be a good tool to work through Gantt charts to figure out how all the priorities/tasks need to line up to get them to completion.

Scrum of Scrums Meetings

This is similar to a Scrum meeting but not held every day, possibly just once a week or every two weeks, if further out timeline, where there is a read out of status for entire teams/areas on what was done that week, what is planned, and what are the blockers, if any. Usually, one person represents a team or set of teams.

Dependencies can be brought up in this meeting as well when they are inter-team.

Have someone keep track of meeting minutes, updates, to-dos, dependencies, timeline changes, and so on.

Be an Advocate for Your Team/Members

All sorts of business decisions get made around everything from seating to pay. Advocate for your team members effectively so they have a productive environment that minimizes process, allows them to work effectively, and pays them fairly.

If any situations come up that might go against any of those principles, do the best you can to advocate for your team/members.

Sometimes, the default business action isn't the best action, and you might be able to influence that outcome.

Compensation

Hiring

When hiring someone, don't try to get the person at the lowest possible salary. Try to pay fairly relative to the market and your team. If you don't, it will be easy for them to find a competing job for more money. Once they realize that, all the time they spent learning your environment would be wasted if they decide to leave and go to another firm. Use your company's market survey information to guide you on fair pay. Also, it can be hard to fix this problem if you hire someone at too low a salary. Organizations are often resistant to large increases once hired, so your best bet is to get someone in at the most appropriate salary from the beginning.

If a person gives you a range for their salary, if it's within reason and makes sense for the role, consider it. It's much harder to change later, and if that person is happy with their pay, they are more likely to stick around. Think a little bit into the future a few years on about how you will manage this person's pay year to year. Will it be easy or hard to get them increases? Will that impact the person's desire to stay?

Base Pay

Each year, if you are lucky, your company offers some sort of increase, possibly 0–3 percent. Hopefully, that is funded fully so you can give base increases to all staff. Sometimes, though, that's not the case, and you need to decide who gets what money. How do you decide?

- Give more to your best performers first.
- Give more to someone below the average salary midpoint to get them more inline.
- Give less to people who didn't perform well during the year.
- Be as fair as you can with the obvious parameters of pay for performance, and so on.

None of these are easy decisions, usually. And it gets worse when you have less money to allocate.

Bonus

This sort of depends on your org and history. Some orgs offer 0–15 percent or more bonus. If the bonus is so regular that it's treated like salary, a lot more care needs to be taken with the allocation to keep it as consistent as possible. If bonus is treated as never a guarantee and often not a guarantee, you obviously have a lot more flexibility in the allocation of bonus.

Some strategies:

- Give more to your best performers first.
- Give more to someone below the average salary midpoint to compensate a little for the salary if you were not able to make it up in base pay and they are performing well.
- Give less to people who didn't perform well during the year.
- Be as fair as you can with the obvious parameters pay for performance

Almost always, you are given a limited amount of money for a bonus pool and need to decide how to distribute it among your staff. You could possibly do it all the same, but many orgs want to see it based on performance.

Stock

Some companies offer a stock purchase program, where you can pay or use a portion of your salary to buy company stock, often at a discounted price. They might do something like take the lowest price of a quarter and even subtract 15 percent. So if you sold as soon as you got the stock, it's not guaranteed because the stock can move quickly, but there is a chance you can make 15 percent or more of your money. That's a pretty good deal for a short time, so it is something worth considering if you can afford it. Just remember that all stock has risks. It can drop before the shares are available to you to sell, so only risk what you can afford to lose.

Also, some companies will offer stock to employees as part of compensation. For some companies, this is a regular activity; in some others, it is offered only to certain employees to incentivize them to stay. Remember, you will owe taxes when you sell. Some companies take the tax out for you, so check if they do or don't. Sometimes, when this is offered as part of compensation, it is similar to a 401k in that it has a vesting schedule over a few years. The idea is to have an added incentive for employees to stay with the company.

You can hold the stock if you like if you think your company's stock will increase in value. Of course, it could go down too, so you could lose the 15 percent or more that you made. One way to play it could be set a stop-loss at your 15 percent and keep that in place so you try to avoid losing what you made. You should know stop-losses aren't perfect, though, since stocks can drop before they open or not have enough liquidity to fill your order at a good price, so as with almost anything related to the stock market, there is risk.

Options

Some companies will offer options to new hires and employees. An option is the right to purchase stock at a particular strike price (or just sell the option for the difference in money). So when you are granted these, there will be a strike price. Hopefully, they will offer it in the money by a certain percentage.

For example, if your company stock was 100, if they gave you options with a strike price of 100, then your options are worth nothing until your stock goes higher than 100. If it goes lower, it's worth nothing.

If you were given 100 options and the stock went up $2, it would be worth $200. Often, there is a vesting schedule for these over a few years to keep an incentive for employees to stay with the company.

If you exercise your options, you owe the FULL price of the stock. So if the strike price was 100 and stock was at $101, if you exercised 50 of your options at 100, you would have to pay $5000 to purchase the 50 shares of stock at $100. If you just sell the options, you would get the difference in price between the strike price and the current price of the stock. So sell 50 options with strike price 100 and stock being at $101 will get you $50.

Remember, you will owe taxes when you exercise or sell based on the value at the time of exercise/sale. There were many stories during the dot-com boom of employees being granted options, and they exercised them to stock (options, I think, were done a little differently then), making them millionaires. They held the stock, and it went to zero . . . They said, "Damn, I lost all that money, but I guess I'm ok . . . "

Then later, they realized they owed taxes on the millions, and they had no money to pay. That's why most firms today will take out taxes for you when you sell/exercise to avoid this issue, but you should double check to be sure.

The Gray Area

Many business decisions will need to be made in what you might call the gray area, meaning not everything is just black or white, right or wrong. Some of these decisions can be easy, but some of these can be incredibly difficult to determine the right direction to go.

How do you decide in these situations? There is no one right answer, but I can provide some guiding principles to help you come to a conclusion.

Start by Asking Yourself These Questions:

- What are the costs, benefits, and risks of each of the possible decisions? Is there one that has the best cost/benefits/risk ratio?
- Think if you were the CEO of the business, how would you make your decision? Which one would you choose and why?
- If your manager were to decide, what do you think they would choose and why?

- If you chose X decision, what would your manager/CEO/team think and why?
- Are there long-term consequences to the decision one way or the other?
- What is the cost/impact of not making this decision now?
- When considering costs and benefits, did we cover the total cost of business/revenue gained/lost and people's time/salary used?
- Does this decision have an ongoing cost, and if so, is it worth paying it?
- Is there an alternate acceptable process solution?

What can you offer your team as a manager?

Perhaps you have as much or more experience than most or at least different experiences. Perhaps you have had a lot of failures and successes to draw from. Exposure to a lot of technology areas, problems, and solutions can provide a good basis for the decisions that need to be made. Use your experience to make sound technical or management decisions to remove roadblocks, decide on a path forward, and take responsibility for those decisions made. Making reasonable decisions that help your team deliver on time can be key. It could, for example, be helping them come to an agreement on a test strategy that the team and you believe in that can deliver quality software without being overly burdensome. This often takes into account the technical risks associated with the change to align well with the test strategy.

There are many cases where it's impossible to test all possible scenarios. The key is testing the main scenarios and the most likely edge cases, along with a statistically significant set of data/scenarios that provides a reasonable cover for reducing your risk.

What is acceptable risk? That can vary greatly, depending on the software, the change being made, the users, the regulatory environment, and more.

What are the consequences of not finding some issues? If the app was a game, the consequence might be the game plays a little funny or, in some odd scenarios, crashes. Definitely, no fun at all in those cases, but the risks may be pretty low. If, instead, you are building a brain surgery robot, you might have a lot more on your mind in terms of risks.

Management decisions in other areas can be similar. They have some risks that need to be managed. Helping your team keep their scope reasonable for a release so delivery is possible is one of those management tasks you can help with. Don't overbook your team if at all possible. No one likes to miss dates, especially when they feel they have no control over making a date due to there being more work than is possible in the time frame. Realize that you will never have all of the right ideas or answers. Listen to your team. They will often have ideas that you never thought of. If you don't know what to do, ask your team what to do, take their input, and if there is no consensus, help forge a path forward. That could be asking to collect more data to help make a decision, investigating a potential solution, or perhaps picking the best available option. A lot will depend on the urgency of a path forward, what is involved, and the benefits and risks.

Sometimes, not being involved in the actual implementation task lets you see more options available or can help you think outside of the box. For instance, imagine there is one day before code freeze, and your team discovers a performance issue on some customers' databases where an upgrade script could run for one year. The natural question comes: How many customers would this impact? After analysis, it is determined it only impacts 5 percent of customers, and for those cases, the customer used the software incorrectly and caused their own issues. Given the findings, you decide it's ok to upgrade, but on a customer by customer basis, a diagnostic can be run to determine if their database has an issue that they would have to correct or if they could be upgraded. This might not be ideal for the long term, but it can help 95 percent of customers today.

- Help keep scope reasonable.
- Make reasonable management decisions that your team believes in and trusts that help them make release dates.
- Remove blockers so the team can make progress. When a person or the team is stuck, help them past what is blocking them.
- Help manage risk for implementation, testing, deployments, process and resources.
- Think about if a process can solve an issue or concern rather than software as a short-term solution. Plan for better solutions for future releases if needed.

Clean Up Your Backlog

There are two variations of this.

1. If we are talking about your normal Agile backlog, you should be cleaning that up once a sprint to keep it tidy and ready to groom items for the next and a couple of future upcoming sprints.
2. If we are talking about items in your enhancement/issue tracking tool even beyond your Agile backlog, you should probably schedule a regular meeting that happens on an interval you are comfortable with for reviewing and closing or marking reviewed (or asking questions, etc.). This way, you are making sure there aren't any high-priority items sitting around or other items you want to get done. Plus, this will help you reduce the clutter in your system, so when you do have time to find more

items to pull into the first backlog, it's easier to find what you want to work on.

Aligning Code with Your Teams

You may have lots of code. Who should work on which code? Should everyone work on everything, or should there be some form of ownership? What makes the most sense?

The reality is there are many factors that come into play when aligning code/responsibilities with teams. For example, if you have a lot of code but only four people and changes to be made all over the code, there probably is no choice but everyone works on everything.

Why should you worry about how code is aligned with responsibilities?

- Code expertise can speed up implementation.
- Code expertise can reduce defects.
- Code expertise can reduce support times.

How Can You Achieve Code Expertise?

How does someone become a subject matter expert (SME)?

Someone who works in the same code areas more often tends to become an expert in that area.

(See background reference article: "An Analysis of the Effect of Code Ownership on Software Quality across Windows, Eclipse, Firefox" by Christian Bird, Nachiappan Nagappan, Brendan Murphy, Harald Gall, and Premkumar Devanbu. https://www.microsoft.com/en-us/research/wp-content/uploads/2016/02/ownership.pdf) (Bird et al., n.d.).

What Do We Mean by Alignment?

Aligning code functional areas to a team or one or more people who would increase the likelihood they work in the area more often to develop expertise in that area. So if you had a small client-server app with a small app UI and a small server, if you had two people, you might have one handle most of the UI work and the other handle most of the server work.

There are many other factors that can come into play. These are the main ones, but there are others. One team or team member may have skills in the UI area, while the other team or team member on the server side. Teams/people have different skills and levels of skills, and it can make sense to align code with skills.

Some choices are easy: One code base has Ruby code, one code base has .NET code. If you have a team that knows Ruby, your first choice probably shouldn't be to align them with the .NET code if they don't know that and you have other teams with that expertise. But, of course, there are lots of circumstances and caveats in business situations to consider.

Subject Matter Experts/Backups

For any code area, it can often be useful to have more than one person who can work in a particular area. This is just in case someone is out sick or leaves the company. This means that we need a way to build expertise in more than one person for coverage.

Code Ownership or Other Variations

You might hear the term "code ownership." This is a style of where one person or team(s) own code areas, and only they can make changes. Rarely does it make sense to have one person's own code, since in business, you should always have a backup. But in a startup or a small company with a small code base, perhaps this could survive for a while. The general concept, though, is that one owner becomes an expert, so they know how to make the changes in that area. It's better when this can be multiple people or a team.

Other styles might just align most work to be done this way, but other teams could make changes in the area if needed. Or it might require or recommend if other people or teams make changes that they have them reviewed by the owner or subject matter experts. This is somewhat a balancing act of allowing parallel work by multiple teams but trying to reduce the potential for quality issues by having subject matter experts work with them or at least review code.

Cross-training/Knowledge Transfer

You can have a subject matter expert train other people. Training can be done with staff in lieu of a person being able to work in an area enough to build expertise themselves. But the likelihood is that they won't be an expert initially unless they work on that code area, and the longer they don't work on that area, the more things they will forget. So it is often good to get people started on a code area as a backup person, but not a great substitute, for building expertise.

Team Size/Code Size/Areas

The size of the team and the size of the code base can influence how code is aligned. If the code size is small and you have one or two people or a small team, perhaps everyone can work on everything and build expertise in all areas, since there isn't too much to learn. But imagine a large product with six million lines of code and only six developers. Everyone would probably have to work on everything, because if you have lots of bugs or feature requests, you might need to let people just work across different areas to cover everything. Perhaps there are subareas you could break down to align two people per area to try to develop some expertise, but the code size is so vast and the team so small that the likelihood is that the team will have to jump back and forth in the code and become a jack-of-all-trades and master of none.

Product Life Cycle

This can play a role in alignment of code. For example, if a product is mature but large and perhaps only gets very few bug reports or enhancements in some specific areas, maybe a small team could concentrate on a small area. But if the product still has lots of bugs and enhancement request all over the code base, we are back to possibly jack-of-all-trades, master of none with a small team. In large, mature products, there can be large areas of code that rarely get touched, and so by the time a change is actually needed there, people who were experts at one time may have forgotten a lot about the area and need to relearn/remember if they get back into that code.

Large Products/Code Base and Teams

A more realistic approach for large products is aligning teams of people with areas of code so they can handle the support and features in a particular area of code. Not too much code, so there are not areas developers never work in (otherwise they won't develop expertise in it).

This probably can never be achieved perfectly, but at least getting close will help developers develop expertise in areas, and if it's teams handling areas, there will be multiple people who can learn areas and become experts in them hopefully. In reality, even within these subareas, there are often individuals who develop greater expertise by doing more work in even smaller subareas.

Looking at areas and adding up the support incidents and feature requests for last year and/or expectations for the next year could help the teams decide how much code/areas they can handle and keep up the support and increase expertise.

References:

Bird, C., Nagappan, N., Murphy, B., Gall, H., & Devanbu, P. (n.d.). *An Analysis of the Effect of Code Ownership on Software Quality across Windows, Eclipse, and Firefox.* 14.

When/What To Escalate?

On the whole, managers are expected to handle their area and not need to escalate things very often. There are some obvious items like the need to adjust compensation outside of your budget that would need discussion.

It gets more difficult with other people outside your team or management chain. Again, it would ideally be better to handle this without the need to escalate through meetings. and only escalate if absolutely needed. It gets even more tricky when a disagreement occurs with someone on another team and they are at one management level above or higher. Then it might be worth a discussion with your manager regarding whether you should have a discussion with them directly or with your manager so they are at least in the loop on the decision (because if there is some reaction from the meeting, your manager wouldn't be surprised that it happened without them). Scenarios like these require lots of thought and some discussion to try to steer clear of political pitfalls. Check all your facts and make sure they are solid before having these discussions. Think through the opposite side of the argument to make sure you aren't missing something to see it from the opposite point of view. This can help you avoid missteps and possible arguments/discussions. Make sure you have clear, logical reasons why your position is what it is.

Agile Team Management

Agile teams are supposed to be self-forming, and the team should be deciding on the things they are working on. If you work with business analysts and the team to prioritize the work correctly in grooming and planning meetings, the team should hopefully be able to guide and manage itself. This is a different way than traditional managers have worked on telling people what tasks to do. The Agile way is far better for most tasks. People like to have some say in the work they do, even if that's limited to who works on which items in the backlog next. This can make life much easier for a manager, since you don't have to worry most of the time about who gets what work.

Occasionally, you may need to help with guidance. Ask questions to help the team focus on what they need. That is the much better approach when time allows. There might be some occasions that don't have time for consensus or to gather the team. In those cases, you might need to pick someone for a task and to drop something else. Hopefully, that is the exception rather than the rule though, as it robs people and the team from self-direction.

Even though teams are supposed to be self-managing, there are a lot of items as a manager you can assist with. Meetings tend to be the lifeblood of management. However, sometimes, meetings can feel like a vampire sucking the life out of you. If you are relatively new to management, the transition into a massive number of meetings can be harsh. Coming from a development background, you might think, "Am I even doing work if I'm in meetings all the time?" The answer is yes. Meetings might not feel like productive work all of the time, but depending on the meetings, they can be surprisingly important. You might not even think a meeting is important until you get asked a question days or even weeks and months later that you know the answer to because you were in the meeting. Sometimes, those answers can make a huge difference in the trajectory of the team.

CHAPTER 33

General Topics

When Good Architecture Isn't Good Right Now

In a galaxy not too far away, imagine our fine products. Imagine we have two similar products. Let's call them Old Product and New Product—both maintained by the same set of teams. New Product relies on libraries from the Old Product. The New Product has been mostly a new interface and SIMT that relies on all the libraries for the Old Product to act as core libraries.

The dependency is a little painful, but all the core libraries were shared so they were at least maintained in one place.

Let's say the company wants to push the New Product and get customers off the Old Product. The company decides it wants to differentiate the New Product more and build significant new functionality and make sure the architecture can be clean, free of old code, no feature flags, and unencumbered by the old code.

To facilitate the new architecture, a decision is made to split the two products. They were already each in their own source control, where the New Product had a reference to the Old Product's libraries to use as the core.

A new source control is created for the New Product, and the source code from the Old Product is copied into the New Product's source control (where it used to have library references for core, it now has the full build of source code so that it can diverge from the old code).

The initial plan is to issue changes to both source control repos when modifications are needed to the core libraries (but the plan is most changes would only go to the new product source control) for at least six months and review then. The concern is obviously that if there is large divergence for the core libraries, increased merge pain and more significant testing is needed. But if most changes only go to the New Product, it is not a big deal.

All seems good in the world, except for one thing. More than 90 percent of the customers still use the Old Product. A tool was built to upgrade from Old Product to New Product, and few customers are interested due to concerns about the difference in features in the New Product.

Oh wait, we do need legacy changes for a little while? Next, let's imagine the news comes that nearly all changes for the next six months will impact both products/source control, meaning nearly all work will be duplicated/merged with different source controls. Basically, bugs need to be fixed in the core libraries, impacting both products and need to be fixed in both and both will be supported.

Ok, much more ugly, but still only six months . . .

Ummm . . . ok, legacy changes for a "little while" = years?! Of course, only about a month later, the news comes that the entire year will need most changes to both products. Many folks figure it may be years before customers upgrade, and support for both products will remain for some time.

But how can good architecture be bad for now? In this scenario, it seems like the products would have been better off staying the way they were for a while with New Product relying on the Old Product's core functionality as a reference (not copied) until there was at least a well-defined (and realistic) time frame to limit the amount of manual, or source control driven code copying, merging/dual testing needed.

Of course, then the architecture wouldn't be clean and free of flags for the core libraries if they were shared. However, significant duplicated effort would be prevented, affecting the work of perhaps dozens or more of staff. Feature flags, dependency injection, and hooks/events could have allowed the core libraries to remain mostly unchanged but allowed all the functionality that was needed for the New Product, while minimizing the work effort.

This shows that there are a lot of things that can affect architecture decisions and source control plans, and sometimes the ideal architecture may not be the best at the moment.

Considering the business objectives can be key, but they must be viewed within the full context of what your company is trying to do and the reality of the situation, not what the business hopes to accomplish. The question is more about what can be realistically accomplished, and what are the costs of the change we are making.

What were the possible cons of the decision: In this example, the cost would have been that multiple development teams would have their progress slowed initially by maybe only 10–25 percent. As time goes on, the effort required could double the time needed to fix a bug or deliver a feature. Think about if your company could only produce half the features it used to a year. That would lose opportunity cost and cost up to twice as much to implement the same functionality.

What's even worse is that as code diverges, it would be harder and harder to revert and change your mind if the plan did not go as expected.

What were the possible pros of the decision: The possibility of getting a clean architecture unencumbered by the old code. Possibly produce new features faster since the old code could be removed. Maybe customers might want to upgrade if the features built were good enough and big enough. The possibility of reducing code complexity and support effort.

What was the likely reality? Both pros and cons, but remember that we said 90 percent of the customers were still on the Old Product. Thus, 90 percent of the revenue was coming from the Old Product customers. Those customers wanted at least equivalent features to upgrade, but they were not there and likely would diverge further. Developers would have to spend extra time developing the same fixes twice, and that was most of the development work.

Alternative examples: Now, of course, there could be reasons to do dual code changes (not seemingly in that scenario), but imagine both products were going to have their own life with no upgrade path, and we wanted to accelerate both of them. Split the source controls, copy the code, and hire new teams so they would separate into Old and New Product teams to allow clean acceleration and direction for both products. That could be a valid reason to go that path.

If, as the original scenario mentioned, minimal changes would be made to the Old Product, things could be fine utilizing dual code changes only as needed for emergency hot fixes, perhaps.

Even if every change needed dual code changes, and if they had been limited to six months or so, dual code changes could be managed probably without too much difficulty, knowing there would be light at the end of the six-month tunnel.

Thus, there clearly are scenarios in which the original plan could have worked under the right conditions, if they existed.

How to Reduce Overhead Costs for Your Business—Keep Processes under Control!

More process than needed, or just right? Agile and more

How to reduce overhead costs for big businesses like *Fortune* 1000 companies? They already make a lot of money, and they have a lot to lose if things go wrong. These businesses reduce risk by adding processes that are designed to compensate for potential risks. The upside is that it will hopefully really reduce risk, and the downside is that it may also reduce productivity and increase costs (processes often have costs, in terms of staff time it uses to follow and maintain).

In big firms, the processes often grow organically over time or are instituted when big failures occur and management wants a process in place to reduce the chances of it happening again. Over time, the rules and regulations build up. For each noted failure, a new process is added. Over time, the original people who made the changes are no longer with the firm, but their processes continue on, often continually increasing. Also often, the firm forgets some of the original intent of individual processes and the balance of the cost of instituting new processes vs. risk.

Smaller and medium-size firms have an advantage that there is often one person in charge who can make a decision: Is this process really needed for this?

A larger business often has so many groups that there is no one person or even group to talk to about how processes may have overcompensated for the risk (or even to discuss rationally if they have) or have gone into areas that don't have significant risks. It is also hard for large businesses to manage so many differences of scale in their organizations.

Even if an organization is big or huge, often the departments/divisions responsible for maintaining specific products are smaller subsets that could be stressed or crumble under the weight of heavy process unless augmented to support it.

Here is how to reduce overhead costs for your business:

1. If in a large organization in management, what can you do to ensure reasonable processes: Ask the questions for each process:
   - Is this process really needed?
   - How much will this process cost to implement (money, people's time, materials, opportunity time lost)?
   - What is the real chance of the risk occurring?
   - What would the real cost of not implementing the process be?
   - Is this process worth the implementation cost?
   - Is this a process that really needs to be followed globally or can it been done in just isolated divisions/groups?
2. Scale the processes based on cost to do the job (thus the risk), complexity, and scope/size in enough granular detail to handle all size groups and tasks it is likely to encounter.
   - Consider that often, there may be very small tasks. How much overhead will the process add? Is the overhead worth it?
   - Think about tasks at different scales: hours, days, two weeks, a month, two months, three months, etc. Cover all the scales you are likely to encounter. Breakdown the granularity to limit unneeded overhead at each scale.
3. If you are a senior manager, appoint or suggest there be one person or group who understands the reasons for the process, so

it's clear who people should talk to about the process. It should be clear what the processes were intended to address and not address. If flexibility can be allowed, as long as the spirit of the process is allowed, then allow it. If it is ok, the process can be altered to allow either informal or formal exceptions (depending on what is needed).

- Have the team request feedback specifically on the processes—informally and formally—perhaps twice a year to ensure feedback is collected. Have the feedback aggregated and circulated to all, and have the person/team responsible for the process work through the process with people that live it daily (or often).

4. If new processes are suggested, have people do the following:
   - Estimate the cost of following the process (money, productivity, time to market).
   - Estimate the cost of not following the process (money, risk, other).
   - Decide if the benefit of the process outweighs its cost.
5. Think about how to make a process fit naturally in with people's workflow.
   - Automate it if possible.
   - Put it in a natural workflow so people don't have to go outside of an interface/app they normally work with.
   - If the process requires or would benefit from implementation of a tool, consider if an off-the-shelf best of breed tool might be the best option. Often, large firms try to build their own, and if it's not their core business, they often don't have the experience, motivation, or resources to build a world-class tool. Instead, they get a version 1 product that they have to live through the usability trials and tribulations that will likely never equal the best of breed tool. Consider

if best of breed tools can be used and feed the processes needed, or build into the workflow to seamlessly integrate with the way people work.

Why Did I Mention Agile?

This whole thing doesn't sound too Agile. To compensate for the overwhelming process, many businesses seemed to have seized upon a relatively recent ALM management methodology: Agile for software development processes. They seized upon this, as Agile methodologies like Scrum and XP nearly mandate limited process. People have pointed to Agile partly to get out of a process mess, partly as it has gotten some acclaim as being beneficial, and because it can work. Businesses with a lot of processes often put a lot of processes around Agile projects. In highly regulated businesses, there could be some need for that.

Agile can be useful in improving productivity in these environments to get back to the minimum that is needed to do the job. Ideally, it shouldn't require Agile to achieve this, and the process would instead be improved overall. Agile did seem to help push back some of the unneeded processes a little, though often, it's not enough on its own in large process laden organizations, and real change as described above is needed.

Companies that have a large product that all or many other internal products integrate into

This can be very challenging to scale, since every additional integrating product adds additional load to the main product in terms of potential product, dev, QA, and support. Ideally, you could architect out some of the concerns, but some of those would still remain.

One approach that seems to work well is the integrating team be responsible for the end-to-end support of their product, including supporting the main product for their integration area. That way, the resources billed for the integrating product to your main one are billed to the right cost center, and it keeps those costs in line with the integration for development and support.

If you did not do it that way, you would basically have a huge amount of resource needs on your main product to support all of your integrating products for each one you add. On top of that, in that scenario, it's likely that the main product engineers wouldn't know the full end-to-end processing to the integrating product, so there would be gaps in knowledge of supporting a full end-to-end workflow, and that can result in a lot of bugs and slow support. Having the integrating team own the whole integration from the main product all the way through to the integrating product means they know the whole end to end and can support it all the way through.

Reinvention

Don't reinvent the wheel unless you really need a new wheel

With some developers, there seems to be a problem with accepting other people's work, and they often need to rewrite something themselves for some reason. Maybe they think they are improving it; maybe they don't understand it till they rewrite it.

Don't rewrite something for reasons like the code isn't clear to me. If it's unclear to most developers, then a rewrite may be in order. If another team member had written the code, they would wonder why you felt the need to rewrite it unless there was a good reason. Refactoring could be a good reason. Just make sure you are able to explain it to the code author and it's something you believe they would accept.

Rewriting code can introduce new bugs, and unless there was a reason to do so, you may have introduced new bugs for basically no benefit to the software or customer.

If there is good third-party open-source software available, and the licensing is suitable, perhaps use that rather than reinventing something yourself. It would save time/money. Even if you have to purchase a library, consider if it's worth your time to write and maintain that versus buying or using to see what the cost/benefit ratio is.

Generating Ideas/Solutions

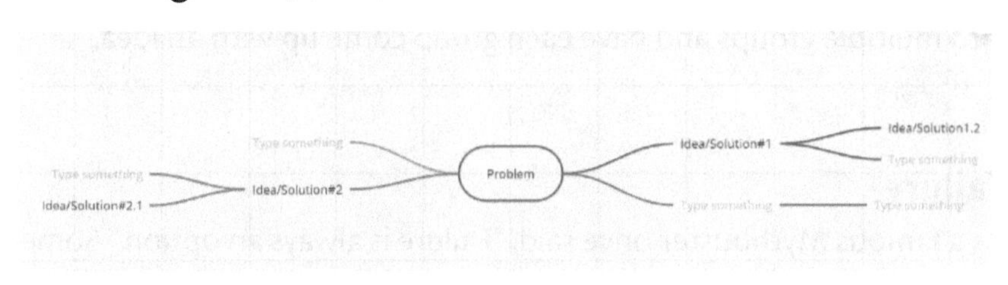

(Mind map created on https://miro.com/)

Mind Maps

You can try using a mind map like the image above to help generate ideas or solutions. There are lots of tools you can use to help you online. Or just use a whiteboard or paper.

Concentration

Just let your mind flow and write down any ideas, no matter how crazy or dumb they seem. Don't filter yourself. Sometimes, a dumb/crazy idea can work out or be modified to work out.

Do Something Else

Sometimes, you can come up with ideas in the craziest places: in the bathroom, shower, while driving, taking the train, for example. Giving your mind the chance to wander sometimes produces results.

Brainstorming

Get a few folks in a room, and let them come up with ideas unfiltered without anyone criticizing them, and just write all of them down, no matter how silly or crazy. Again, sometimes, those ideas may work or can be transformed into something workable. Sometimes, even split into multiple groups and have each group come up with an idea.

Failure

As a famous Mythbuster once said, "Failure is always an option." Sometimes, things fail spectacularly badly. Software developers should think of the responsibility and the consequences of failure and mitigate these risks as much as possible through a good software development process to go out with quality software. Still, sometimes, things fail. The following are some examples of software bugs and stories of when things fail due to bugs or other reasons.

One day that started normally didn't end quite so normally when it was announced that a major stock had stopped trading that day due to order anomalies. Then you find out it was your company's order system entering duplicate orders that caused it. It wasn't a normal workflow. There were particular conditions that could cause it, but the net effect was that a lot of orders were duplicated. The good news is that spectacular failure wasn't mentioned in the news that announced the trade halts.

One of the folks on our teams was researching a failure of order processing for a trading system. The bug had existed for over 10 years but wasn't hit. Apparently, it only got hit on February 29 under certain conditions. Always test your leap years and other exception cases!

Not a software bug, but another scenario for a trading system servers went down, and some trading through the system stopped and didn't failover to backups. It was found that someone entered the data center and accidentally kicked the plug out of a rack of servers, and it was noted that some of the primary and backup servers were in the same rack, which should not have been the case.

In 2003, working at a financial firm in NYC, I was on a call interviewing someone who was in New Jersey when the app support team yelled out, "Data center in Connecticut is down." Then the person on the call said they just lost power in New Jersey. Then a few seconds later, we lost power in the NYC office and data center. The backup batteries and generators came up, but some trading was not working. We learned later by the Extranet network carriers that the firm used lost power on both their primary and backup lines because they were both on the same generator that failed. Confirm with your vendors and test whenever possible. We also saw later ("Northeast Blackout of 2003," *Wikipedia*, n.d.) that the power failure was actually attributed to a software bug that an alarm failed to go off when a feeder line was overloaded, so operators did not know to redistribute power. (See Wikipedia https://en.wikipedia.org/wiki/Northeast_blackout_of_2003) (Genscape Inc, 2003) (NERC Steering Group, 2004).

Turning Failure into Success

Some projects you work on may be executed like clockwork and delivered on time. Other projects can be bit of a struggle. If you try to do everything you possibly can to deliver value to your customer/user as early as possible without compromising quality, you might find a way to turn your struggle into at least a partial win instead of a delay or a failure. While failure is always an option, it doesn't necessarily have to be your final one.

There was one project that was working on an API performance enhancement. To do this, performance enhancement required re-implementing the rendering of the output and building a better table in the database to join on. The first attempt copied a lot of data and improved performance an incredible amount. The data architects reviewed and said this doubled the size of the database, so they rejected it. So the schema needed to be reworked, and they tested the performance with a slim join table. The performance dropped by a factor of 10 or more but was still in a reasonable range. The team parity tested, and all looked good.

The last part was filling the backfill table. The team tested it and found it ran for up to 48 hours on large amount of customer data. This would mean it probably wouldn't be reasonable to deploy for all customers by default with the regular release. This was a roadblock. The team could have given up and spent time trying to improve the performance, but they analyzed there would be few customers to pick this up soon, and the ones that did would be fine installing over a weekend. What could have been a project failure through some decisions, they could still release.

Customer data was tested on the script, and a worse problem cropped up. Some customer data had unexpectedly high amounts of certain data, which caused the query to slow down so much that it was estimated it could take 1 year for the script to complete. Some optimizations were done, but it was still estimated that it could take close to a year for 100 or so customers.

This could have been the end of the road for the project until it could be fixed. Instead, the team looked at the data and found that the customers with issues had customizations that caused their own issues. It was decided the data they created was likely bad, erroneous data, and they would have to clean it up, which they should do regardless if they wanted to upgrade, since the data was duplicated and bad. It was only 100 customers who weren't a large percentage, plus few planned to upgrade any time soon. So the plan was to have a diagnostic script that would check for any customer and check before upgrading. Once again, what could have caused a failure to deliver through some reasonable decisions was still able to deliver value to a large set of customers sooner rather than delaying for a perfect solution.

Try to plan your project to avoid these situations, but if you end up in them, work through every idea and option to deliver value and quality to your customer sooner rather than later. Some might argue that wasn't quality, but hundreds of customers are now using the new, much faster API with no errors. As long as you deliver it without increasing risk or reducing the quality of what was delivered.

The next time you are in a bind, think through the data, the customers, and your options carefully. Tenacity can pull you through to perhaps a compromise solution. Don't ignore the real risks, and plan how to deal with them. If everyone agrees the plans are sound, then you might have an option to turn what could have been a failure into a success.

Integrity and Playing Fair

As a developer, you can design some software the way users expect, or you could design software in a way that is perhaps easier, but it would make it unfair. What would you do?

For example, imagine you create a simple Blackjack game. You could just use a random number generator to generate a new card on the fly, making sure you don't repeat the same number more than there could be cards in the deck. Or you could design internally that it simulates 52 cards and shuffles them once and then deals out of the shuffled deck.

Why is this so different, you ask? Well, there are aspects people care about that computers do not. People have a mental model of how games are played, and they want to have some expectation that it works that way. For example, if it was a two-player card game, and one player just got a 10 of hearts, the other player could be saying, "Wow, good thing I didn't hit on my hand." But if you were using just a random number generator rather than selecting the next card on a shuffled deck, that probably wouldn't have been the card they would have got.

Try to match people's mental model to be fair and meet people's expectations. Otherwise, at least explain to them that your software doesn't work as they expect.

Don't write viruses, malware or Trojans. These can cause great harm to people and society.

Have integrity with your software. Don't fool or mislead people. Software is integrated with the fabric of society today. Use your talent with integrity and for bettering society.

Do No Harm

When developing software or changing software, your intent should be morally and ethically guided. As mentioned above, don't harm people or things. How would you feel if a virus destroyed all of your photos and videos or took over your bank account, and you lost all your money? Empathy is important. Make sure you consider the impact of your software and changes on people and society that will use it. This can relate to keeping private information private or pretty much any topic of this area. Do no harm is from a doctor's Hippocratic oath. If you think about it, it doesn't mean it quite so literally. For instance, a medicine given to a patient might have side effects that could be considered harm, but the benefits to the patient should significantly outweigh the side effects. The same thought process should apply to software developers. Just make sure you are thinking about it from the best interest of your users and society, not for you.

Cryptocurrency

Cryptocurrency might seem like a strange topic to include, but crypto only exists because of software and software engineers/developers. If you didn't believe developers have an outsized impact on the world, crypto should give you a better picture. Developers literally made money out of nothing. There are still plenty of people who don't believe in crypto and think it is worth nothing. Perhaps they will be proven right. At the moment, though, it is worth something, depending on the coin you are thinking about.

Cryptocurrencies are built on public/private key cryptographic codes. That allows encryption to another person/wallet/crypto exchange in a secure way. Then the transaction is usually recorded from multiple servers that make up the crypto, and they each generate a cryptographic ledger (blockchain) that provides proof of exchanging an amount of crypto with another crypto wallet.

Because the ledger is open, all the machines on the network can confirm, and it's possible to verify who is the owner of the coin.

If you want to understand this at the deepest levels, first learn about public key cryptosystems, then read up on cryptocurrency.

You can start trading/speculating in crypto if you are ok with the very significant risks. If you want to learn the basics of what Bitcoin is and how to trade, it starts here.

Crypto has a lot of risk associated with it and potentially a lot of reward. It's been both praised and maligned in the media. No matter how you consider it, though, crypto is volatile and high risk, so don't speculate with any money that you can't afford to lose.

Take it slow with very small amounts of money so you learn the process and procedures required.

Cryptocurrencies like Bitcoin, Etherium, Lightcoin, and others are sort of like a different currency maintained by networks of different organizations/computers to securely record transactions.

Understanding Crypto Basics

If you want to buy some crypto coin like Bitcoin, you need to exchange some other currency for Bitcoin, like US dollars, or even a different crypto currency. They all have exchange rates that change all the time. It's somewhat similar to exchanging for foreign currencies, because when you trade, there is usually an exchange rate, and the company doing the exchanging for you extracts a percentage fee. For crypto, there is usually a network fee that is somewhat similar.

When you buy crypto, you usually have to buy it through a service or some type of exchange (like Bittrex). You can think of Bittrex sort of like a broker/exchange for the stock market like TD Ameritrade letting you trade Nasdaq stocks on the exchange.

Once you buy crypto, it needs to be stored somewhere, often called a wallet.

Crypto Wallets

To put crypto coins into your wallet, you usually want to receive the coin in your wallet by providing your wallet's address (a large number generated by your wallet that can be used for you to receive your crypto coin).

Sending someone or a business your crypto coin is similar. You need to use a receiver address (large number generated) to send to the receiver.

When you purchase crypto on an exchange like Bittrex, they try to make that easy for you by automatically handling the large numbers from your account so you do not need to worry about that. Great care must be taken when providing those numbers, as a missed digit/typo could result in your money disappearing forever.

Also know that different cryptos typically have their own account/wallet/address, so Bitcoin would be stored in a different wallet address than say Etherium. Wallets can support single or multiple types of crypto.

The downside of not having your own wallet (like using only the exchange), though, is similar to a bank or broker holding your money. You won't have access to it unless you withdraw it to receive in your personal wallet. Also, crypto is probably easier to steal online than money from your local bank.

Crypto wallets can be software like an app on your computer or phone, or a hardware device (with related software) to keep the digital keys off any Internet connected device for safety.

Because crypto is digital if a wallet is stored on your computer, phone, or even the exchange, it's possible for someone to hack it and steal your cryptocurrency. Crypto exchanges or your computer/phone aren't like your local bank. If they get hacked, they may not be insured to recover your money (kind of like someone stealing your credit card number, if you want to think of it that way, but there is no fraud limit for crypto). Hardware wallets (Like the Ledger Nano S or X) were invented to keep those important private numbers off devices directly connected to the Internet to reduce the chance of your crypto being stolen.

It's kind of equivalent to hiding your money in a safe you control. But you better not forget your passwords to your crypto wallet, or you may never see your money again.

So folks with lots of crypto might decide to buy some on an exchange and then send it to their offline hardware wallet. Each time you move money, unlike a bank, there is a transaction cost/network fee. Think of it like extracting your money from an ATM that charges you a mandatory fee/percent of the transaction. Just moving money from one wallet to another is similar in cost.

You can sign up at Bittrex to be able to buy and trade your own crypto.

Note that due to the risks, banks and credit cards have made it more difficult to buy crypto. Example here uses a debit card. Many credit cards prevent crypto transactions from certain sites to avoid the risks.

If you think you are ready to take the plunge/risks, you can sign up at Bittrex.

Some important notes: Crypto exchanges act like banks now and require KYC (Know Your Customer). They often require identification like driver's license, picture (Bittrex even does face recognition against your license).

Storing your money on the exchanges faces other risks. For example, your account could get disabled because they add new KYC requirements, and you won't have access to your money until you prove you are you. Having your own wallet can be nice to avoid some of that. I've had my account disabled at least twice at Bittrex already for no other reason than they wanted more verification information, even though they didn't require any when the account was originally opened. And it can take some time to get that worked out.

There are other exchanges, but Bittrex is one of the most popular with many crypto coins to trade. Coinbase is US based and has much fewer coins. There are other services as well.

Proof of Work

Some cryptocurrencies use proof of work algorithms for a miner to prove they expended energy to calculate an appropriate hash that is considered to be good by the network. It's sufficiently hard to create but easy to determine if it's correct. This method has been under scrutiny due to the large amount of energy required for it. The nice part about it is that people can buy some hardware for some cryptocurrencies, and they can mine and get some cryptocurrency in exchange for their work. This makes the network much more open and distributed. Another algorithm that doesn't take as much time or energy to calculate is called proof of stake ("How Bitcoin Mining Really Works," n.d; Lachtar et al., n.d.).

Ideal vs. Practical

Software Developers: Idealism Software vs. Practical Software vs. Business Software (i.e., Real World)

Background

Software developers taught classically in either mathematics or computer curriculums learn languages, algorithms, error handling, and all about the little things that can make your program go wrong. Things like not checking all of your return values, inconsistent data or unexpected data, and not handling/throwing exceptions properly can all potentially result in disaster for your software.

Developers' Ideas on Ideal Software

Developers are often taught or otherwise learn some ideals, perhaps not to these extremes all the time:

- All bugs are bad, and they must all be fixed.
- All code must be 100 percent tested (well, perhaps this isn't always taught in school).
- Data must match expectations exactly or the program may fail.
- We must have complete requirements to write software.
- Developers must be told by business analysts exactly what the requirements are (maybe this is learned at certain companies).
- The software should not be released until everything is tested and all bugs are fixed.
- Code must be well designed (i.e., fill in your favorites here: SOLID, Tier solutions).

Business Software

This is not quite the same as the ideal software. Business-driven software has a different set of values than ideal software. This is not saying this is a good set of things to consider; it's just often the reality of the situation at many companies.

- Software must deliver value to its users (otherwise no one will pay for it).
- Software must deliver enough value for the company (this could be profit or something else for a non-profit). Thus, software should have more value than support/maintenance costs
- Software should not cause enough harm to the user that the company would be sued (and the counterparty win significantly), should not cause significant loss of reputation

We can tell from some companies that this isn't a hard and fast rule.

- Software should not cost more to develop than the company is willing to or able to spend.
- Software must be delivered at the best speed possible to avoid losing opportunity cost.

Practical Software

What is good software?

An idealistic developer might say:

Developer Idealism + Business Software = Good Software

A developer might say well designed/architected software. A business might consider any software that satisfies what we mentioned for business software to be good. Another business might consider some reasonable cross between business software and developer ideal software to be good software. A company may view the software as good, while some users or others may consider it bad. It's possible even for the company to view it as good software and developers to view it as bad software.

From looking at it, the developer ideal software would seem to fit all the criteria. Unfortunately, the business software concerns tend to not fit all the time with the ideal software concerns. Practical software does not preclude ideal software/good software, though achieving that level is probably rare for most commercial software.

There is undoubtedly a lot of software that developers with the ideal software view would not consider good software but make a ton of money.

Here is one example of how quite often Business Software conflicts with Ideal Software:

Developer ideal software: All bugs must be fixed.

Fixing bugs takes time, and as a result money, either through development cost or lost time opportunity cost (i.e., need features now to sell a contract). Some bugs are just more important than others, and the business is often willing to balance it so the software can be released as long as the bugs remaining are minor or at least don't conflict with the business software guidelines.

Bugs that users are rarely ever likely to hit, or cosmetic bugs, might all take a back seat to releasing the software.

So if a lot of software doesn't match the ideal developer expectation of good software, doesn't that make for a lot of unhappy developers?

Maybe?

What can we do about it? (Developing Good Software and Developer Happiness)

- Realize getting to the ideal developer good software plus business software is a rare goal to reach.
    - There is nothing wrong with reaching and striving toward that goal. Just realize that the practical software aspects must be weighed as well. This is more often a path rather than a goal that can ever be achieved. Just realize that the business pays your bills, so compromising for the best ideal software versus practical software takes some continuous attention.
- Make progress toward your goal of better software each release
    - Ideas

§ This could mean you add a little refactoring/maintenance time to each story to make slow/steady progress, being careful to remain practical. Perhaps this means taking advantage of resolving technical debt when there is some extra time. Sometimes, this might be between release cycles, at the beginning of releases and light releases. It's often easier to add an extra day to a story than to ask for a month for the entire team to spend refactoring your architecture. If you really need that month and can explain it in practical terms to the business, perhaps that can be a better route. If not, perhaps a bit more slow and steady approach may help.

§ Work on a culture of refactoring and improving your software wherever changes are made. If your app is monolithic and doesn't have good test coverage, this can be risky. To reduce risk, do bigger refactors in smaller chunks and closer to the beginning of a release rather than the end to allow for some more burn in/testing time. Just build a little into your estimates to allow for at least a little refactoring for any story. Still try to build any new code to be unit testable (this can be tricky in a monolithic app). You might need to use some heavy tools like Typemock to help you mock your monolithic hard to test objects if you can't do anything about them at the moment.

- **Are you tying your emotions in the state of your software? Why?**
  - You should not tie your emotions to the perceived state of the software. It's great to be passionate about software, but realize that not everyone has your passion. As we've discussed already, it is probably rare to get to the nirvana of

truly ideal software. If you tie your emotions this way to it, you may be setting yourself up for a lot of less than happy times. Perhaps we should just be happy on the path to "try" to get closer to the ideal.

- Stay positive. Don't let the prospect of not having ideal software get you down. Just work on it methodically, knowing you are on an improving path. You are in the same boat as a lot of other developers, so you have plenty of company.
- Don't gripe about how bad the software is all the time to the business folks. First, they quite literally probably don't want to hear it if they are selling millions of dollars' worth of software to customers. That can get you the label of the negative person from the business folks. If the architecture is bad, that's a developer discussion. Use some of the other constructive suggestions in this post to improve it. Unless you translate it to business terms, you not might find much sympathy or help.

- **Think about both the ideal view and the practical view of the software**
    - § Weigh the cost, risk, time, opportunity, and benefit ratios of things. If you can describe tech debt changes that you need to do within a way that shows a benefit for practical software, your ideas will more likely be accepted. If you can't make a good case for it, maybe you know someone who could.

        - o Example: the website is slow:
    - § If the cost of website SLA violation fines is exceeding the cost/time it would take to fix it, it's a much easier sell to the product folks or business folks. It's not always this cut and dry, though, so making a case can be a lot harder.

  - § Especially when discussing with product and business folks, they may not care much about the "monolithic" architecture you keep complaining about. You'll need to phrase things carefully in terms they do care about For example, there is a lot of code that is hard to change that takes longer for us to get you what you want. Of course, they will want to know how long to improve the situation or what it will cost to improve it compared to continuing as is. If the cost versus benefits ratio isn't right for the business, your improvement ideas may not be given much importance, though.
- **How to solve an issue of tech debt like monolithic software?**
  - § Let's say you have a web app that is suffering using old ASP.NET web forms. Explaining your monolithic software architecture issue to the business may not produce much results. Instead, the pitch might be that customers have been complaining about web pages that don't load fast and look old, and the UI is unresponsive. Instead, propose to replace one of the modules with a more state-of-the-art MVC Razor implementation. That will help give them the fast/responsive UI they need with the ability to test faster so there are fewer bugs in the future. This is pretty close to what happened at a company I know of.
  - § Some firms are moving toward breaking up their applications into microservices. They can allow you to break out one area of your application at a time into different services to help break up your application to more logical chunks that are easier to build, support, extend, and test. Maybe you can't do all the work to do this at

once. Instead, build it in steps. Start out with just creating the framework of some initial classes and moving the functionality into these classes, perhaps providing a proxy class that can later be used for the messaging layer between your application and service or in the future just taking advantage of something like WCF in .NET, for example. At least this starts to refactor and organize your code, providing better testability as well. You might be able to build smaller refactors like this into your existing software schedule. If not, and some justification is needed, you could mention the benefits of future scalability/redundancy that microservices can bring.

- **Have the right conversations with the right people**
  - § Arguing low-level technical details with business folks is often not as fruitful as you would like, unless you can explain it in terms that matter to them. Perhaps the improvement ideas can be handled within just the development team scheduling instead of engaging the business folks. In general, you probably shouldn't argue low-level technical deals with business folks unless you are really sure it's going to matter to them. That means it makes sense in the practical software way of thinking. Ok, sure, if the software is going to collapse or a bug is going to be super bad, then you should be able to convince them something needs to be done from a practical software perspective. They may not care if some data is inconsistent unless it impacts one of the practical software concerns. If you fail to heed this advice, you might be tagged as not a team player, bringing up inconsequential issues, not being collabor-

ative. My standard recommendation is that if you think you should bring up the concern based on this information, bring it up. If they don't agree, see if it's because they don't understand. If so, you can give an explanation another gentle try. Once it's clear they understand but don't agree, it's important to drop it (if they are the main decision maker for your project). If it's really that important (i.e., could kill someone on a self-driving car, etc.), you owe it to make sure you've escalated to other appropriate parties such as your manager to make sure there are other responsible parties that understand the concern to see if others agree with the importance/ corrective measures needed. Make sure it's logged in your bug tracking system. While there is no official Hippocratic oath for developers, we should consider the "do no harm" philosophy (no physical, financial, psychological, legal, or moral harm). If you really feel something will violate one of those in a significant way, by all means, keep escalating. Also, if it's something you can fix without engaging the business folks, and it won't impact schedules, perhaps you can slipp it in any way while discussing with your dev manager.

- **Build your reputation as someone who can make the magic happen.**
  - Why?
    - § Once you have built some good will, getting people to agree to your improvements will be easier.
  - How?
    - § When the business folks come and ask if you do "this," for whatever "this" is, the answer shouldn't be no.

- § Stay positive. Focus on what you can do. Be collaborative with a solution.
- § Offer options, even if some of them can only in varying degrees provide the solution they are looking for.
- § When you say you can do something, make sure you can deliver.
- § Even when you don't know how to solve it, say we're going to look into this to get you some options.
- § If their schedule allows it for your solution, build in some time for improvements.

Rant on Why Software Architecture Is Not Exactly Like Building Architecture

Building software is not exactly like building a home or a building. On the surface, there would seem to be many similarities between building software and a building, and there are. But there are critical differences that change everything. (I don't architect buildings, only software for a living... so if I get building architecture wrong, cut me a break, please. :))

It's fine to use this description that software architecture is like building architecture where it makes sense, but it shouldn't be used to malign software development due to the noted differences.

For example, it's fine to say that we need a solid foundation of our software architecture like a building.

It's NOT fine to say something like, "Why do you keep changing your architecture?! Did the Empire State Building change their architecture? No!" Or like, "The Empire State Building architects got it right the first time. Why didn't you?!"

Let's examine the differences.

Static vs. Dynamic

Building software compared to building homes or buildings is like comparing old, fixed type printers to movable type and these days compared to a word processor. Certain things are much easier to do once you can change things extremely easily, changing economies of doing tasks. They had to plan printing to the last detail early on, because there was no choice. Again, I'm not an expert on printing, so if I said something out of place, let it slide.

A building once built is a relatively static object from an architecture perspective. It can have walls and things moved on the inside, or additions made within available space. When architecting a building, there is an end goal, a point when you are pretty much done. With software, there is often no "done," only done for this release.

"Infinite" Space

Building software is like building a home/building that has seemingly infinite dimensions of space inside—a building you can specify down to the last nail because you eventually run out of space (most building architects probably stay above the subatomic level!). With software, the economics are entirely different. From memory being relatively cheap compared to physical space in a building, it's almost like having infinite dimensions of possibilities. When you finish a room in a building, you could paint it and have tables. but physical space starts putting limitations on what is workable to add. In software with memory being plentiful, it always "seems" ok to add another chair table, or even another room inside a room! In some cases, this is amazing, and in other cases, this is just a mess in software development (but it is a reality we must deal with). When you have the ability to construct seemingly alternate dimensions to fit things in your code, things start to be very different from buildings. (Ok, memory is not infinite, but you get the point . . . When you have 4 or 8 billion of something (4 GB/8 GB), that's a lot of something!) Go ahead and ask your building architect to build you an entirely new building inside your already existing building after it is already complete and make both buildings still usable!

Virtually unlimited dimensions means it is very difficult to plan for future things or even architect for some changes. How do you plan to build another entire building inside your existing building?!

Cost/Economics

With buildings, there are obvious costs to changing things:

- Labor costs
- Time costs
- Materials costs
- Land costs
- Space use/limitations
- Permits

With software, these costs are much less or often at least less obvious. Time and labor costs still exist, but most companies don't employ building contractors year round. They employ them to finish a building, and then they are done. Often, developers are employed year round, so the costs are already built in and less visible for labor; only time cost is often visible. The rest of the costs such as materials, land, and space are often virtually unlimited, or costs economies are so different from buildings that you can't really compare (yes, computers cost money).

Base of Knowledge

Building architects work from well-known bases of knowledge that have been honed for tens of years (and some information even thousands of years—think the pyramids, irrigation/aqueducts, etc.).

They can rely on many things being standard: water pipes, toilets, electrical systems, gas piping. Rooms typically are . . . well, rooms. Sure, you can give them some architectural spiffiness, but many of the aspects stay the same. Go ahead and ask your architect if they need a different sewerage protocol for every building?!

With software, almost everything about the next "building" is different, and that matters. Sure, on a computer on Windows, your network might stay the same (but what is going to go over that network?! Protocols are often different for each application), on a computer writing to disk is pretty much the same (but what is the file structure/format?!).

Building architects have basically swappable materials with known variations for brick/wood. (some more appropriate for one task than another). But in software, we don't often have those building blocks (yes, an argument for component software, but it's not that easy, as we'll see). In software, there are many reusable components, but often, they are not the meat of what makes your application. Sure, there are list boxes, combo boxes, check boxes, text boxes, all types of readily available components and controls to use. But the part that makes your application do something useful is often times new and different, specifically designed for your business needs. It's like a super customized building just for your needs, where there are some familiar elements, but everything down to even the building materials could be different almost to the point of it being like a building architect doing architecture with materials from a different planet. One app gets built with C#, the next with C++, perhaps the next with HTML5. While they can all produce a "building" (i.e., software product), they often work differently with different strengths and weaknesses. It's so different, it's like a specialization of doctors from brain surgeon to general practitioner. Building architects, I don't believe, have this level of newness going on in each of their buildings. Software is like one project building a ship, and the next project building a house, and the next one a submarine. Ask your local building architect to try that!

Ok, so maybe you now buy that building architecture/construction is not like software architecture construction, but what should we do to make things better?

I certainly don't have all the answers, because as we've shown, software is often different each time.

Some Ideas

Agile vs. Waterfall: As noted earlier, it is often hard to do true waterfall, because unless it's a contract job, developers are often on staff and need work while the "architect" is still doing their work. The Rational Unified Process years ago helped start some of the ideas that architecture tasks don't need to be done before development can start. Agile went even further. What is the right answer? All of it really depends on the project.

If you are building a fighter jet for contract, you'll probably architect/design/specify as much as you can up front; same for a heart-lung machine. For your little tool app, maybe a one-line description. TDD or Agile are just fine. Match your project with your SDLC, risk adverseness, costs and structure. At our location, we architect the major components and define "just enough" for the team to understand what they are building. Sometimes, that can be a sentence; other times, it can be a 100-page document. If there are components that can be worked on, as soon as we're all comfortable, we'll give the developers a go ahead to implement portions or the whole. We'll run iterations of functional versions to demo or release to produce ROI as soon as possible.

Improved Languages/Tools: In the Windows world, tools have come a long way since the old vi editors (no flames from vi masters, please!). Built-in refactoring tools, code/object visualization and visual debugging is helpful.

More Common Components: Build into the languages similar functionality, whether it is observable collections, common/standard threading pattern support, and so on.

Design Patterns: Design patterns clearly help start providing a foundation/base of knowledge to work from. Having languages support standard patterns where appropriate may help.

Common Platforms/Tools: To allow building a base of knowledge, if the ground gets pulled out from under you or changes to mud, it's hard to keep your footing and build a base of practical knowledge rather than more abstract patterns. .NET is a nice concept providing a base framework that many languages can run on, providing some commonality between them.

Code Libraries: Sure, we have specific DLLs, SO files, or what have you already. Sometimes, these are generic enough to be used on multiple projects. Much more of what's out there needs to be assembled into usable libraries to be available to all languages. One example was STL for C++ that became the C++ standard library. Also, smaller snippets/templates/patterns of code and design patterns that can be pasted, filled in, and shared with all would help provide some of the standard reusable building blocks.

Building architecture and construction is not that close to software architecture construction

- A building is static while code is more dynamic/changeable (think non-movable type vs. the word processor).
- There is seemingly infinite space for software with infinitesimal costs; not so for buildings. Real space costs lots of money. Ask your building architect to build in infinite dimensions. I bet they will look at you funny!
- Buildings for the most part reach a "done" state; non-contract software rarely ever is really done.
- Costs/Economics
  - There are only time/labor costs for software mostly, and labor costs tend to be hidden, because unless it's a contract dev staff, developer pay is already built into the companies costs.
  - Minimal materials cost (yes, computers cost money, but not as much as a truck full of wood, pipes, and so on, and computers can be reused by multiple programs; buildings don't really work like that).
  - Often, costs drive action before completing a full architecture plan, because companies are often already paying developers and are not going to have them sit around doing nothing.
  - Architecture is mostly an upfront cost for buildings, while it is an ongoing cost for software projects.
- Base of Knowledge
  - Defined inputs and outputs: Your building architect probably doesn't have vastly different sewerage protocols to worry about. Every new software product probably does have different formats of data it needs to send or receive.

  - Known materials, tools, strengths, loads for buildings: A hammer used on one job probably looks a lot like a hammer on another job, but does C++ really look F# and work the same? And could you use each with little to no training? Not quite!

So go ahead, keep using the concept that software architecture is like a building when it makes sense, but remember the significant differences, and don't let someone use this to malign your development process.

Operations and DBA Teams

How developers typically work with DBAs and operations teams

DBAs

These folks maintain the production and other databases.

They might work on things like:

- Optimizing databases.
- Analyzing and solving database issues: Performance, replication and space.
- Assisting with designing replication options for scaling and more.
- Applying fixes to programs SQL stored procedures.
- Working with developers on designing performant software solutions that will work well in production.
- DBAs assist developers with pulling data from production databases to analyze support issues.
- DBAs work on capacity planning to make sure the databases for the applications keep running well.

Database folks probably work with and analyze databases more than most developers. They have great experience in helping you solve performance or other issues with the application. The development team would work with the DBA team anywhere in the product life cycle. DBAs are invited to the team reveals and other development meetings where it makes sense to work with or have DBA input.

Operations Team (Ops)

The operations team is responsible for all the machines in production. They help create the images for the operating systems and software that forms the base of each machine or virtual machine deployed. They are responsible for configuring and securing all the machines in production. They would handle capacity planning for the production machines. They are responsible for the deployment of company and third-party software. The networking team would be involved in designing, upgrading, diagnosing, and maintaining connectivity.

The development team works with the ops team throughout the development life cycle. They are invited to the team reveals and are invited to other meetings where it makes sense to work with or get ops input. For example, if the ops team is responsible for the deployment tools, and new functionality or configuration is required with the deployment tools, then they would work with the development team to implement and test the new functionality.

Why Patch Rather Than Fix?

Why do companies (sometimes) patch rather than fix code? Is there anything we can do about it?

First, let me define a "patch." A patch is when you make a very isolated, narrow change to handle a particular circumstance rather than addressing the issue holistically.

The primary answer is likely time. It will seemingly take too long to either properly fix or test a change, so we build the minimal change needed to satisfy.

If we do this all the time, then our code will obviously be littered with patches.

There are two primary reasons why the time will take too long, usually too long to fix or too long to test. There can be other reasons, of course, but those are likely the common ones.

It will be hard to discuss either of these in lieu of specific examples. Through testing, we might be able to cover some scenarios.

What are some of the reasons it can take a long time to test something:

- Complex test setup.
- Not reproducible (unknown data/sequence of events or unknown load).
- Complexity in the data/large number of variables.
- Long test run times.
- Creating the tests will take a long time.

There are probably more, but let's focus on the first three.

Not Reproducible (Unknown Data/Sequence of Events)/ Complexity in Data

I'm not sure if everyone's testing is like this, but with all of the organizations I've worked with, most of the tests were scripted to basically replay the exact same tests as before. So the tests were useful only for regression, testing for previously found bugs, and existing functionality worked the same as it did before under very specific scenarios of coded tests.

What if, in addition to that, we had a test suite that could generate random data of every variety and sequence and order possible? It would use every possible Unicode character or ASCII character randomly for data inputs. It would be coded to vary the order, sequence, and even speed of its tests.

The longer you run the test, the more variability you've tested. It's not repeating the exact same tests; it still is a form of regression, as if it had worked before, it should work now. But it's a different trying order and different data. You might have had to rely on tons of customer data before to get the same combinations. This could be at least an option to consider to reduce the customer-specific data you need to test with. This is probably similar to fuzz testing. Honestly, the teams I worked with have not built many of these, but there definitely seems to be a need for them, and they would be worth considering.

Creating Tests Will Take a Long Time

Sometimes, for some scenarios, a solution to this can be a generic parity test. Imagine you need to make a change to your code and realize you have no specific tests at all in your multiple thousands of regression test suites. You realize, though, that lots of tests probably use related functionality but aren't specifically testing anything.

One idea in this scenario is to ask if you built a generic parity test that could compare the data from a version of the app without your change to the new version with your change. If the application stores data in a database, for example, you could just compare the version of the database where the old code ran to the version where the new code ran.

Basically, that way, you are using your thousands of tests to confirm your old and new code results in the same data output. If your change could affect that, then this type of test could be useful to build for future scenarios where you might need this. This proved very useful in some scenarios that would have otherwise been too expensive to build tests for relative to the change benefit.

Sometimes, a Patch Is Ok for Now

Customers need to do their work, and the businesses need to continue to make money, or you and perhaps many other people won't have jobs. Sometimes, we do need quick solutions when we need something now, and we can't wait for a better solution. If a ship is sinking, it's probably not going to make it back to port for the fix and retrofit of the ship. You could bet if the crew onboard had a way to save it, they would use whatever they had, even if it caused some additional damage they had to fix later. So don't feel too bad about these patches that you need to do occasionally. You can't afford to let your ship sink. That doesn't mean you shouldn't look into improving your testing, implementation, and architecture to handle things better in the future.

Computer Science and Life

Sometimes, you find that your regular life can benefit from your computer science info.

One of the principles of memory management is having the size of a new memory block fit the smallest space available.

I noticed my refrigerator was not very organized this way, but it could be. So I proceeded to put the smallest items in the smallest spaces to make room. Obvious, it works, but it is still a random crossover.

Another scenario is just trying to find something and dividing things in half until you do, like a binary search. This is another aspect I've found useful in circumstances outside of computer science.

I'm sure there are many more. What have you noticed?

Third Party Products/Libraries

When you are using third-party products and libraries, you should maintain active support on them if at all possible. If that means upgrading the plan for it at reasonable intervals to stay within supportable versions, do it. If you don't, you might end up finding your system falling apart in production, and you can't figure out why, and you can't get any help from your third-party vendor since your program/library is no longer supported.

Yes, this happened. Don't let it happen to you. Keep track of supported versions and keep upgraded at regular intervals. What made it worse was that it was even hard to upgrade the almost 10 years of versions, as the old version was not compatibility running on the same machine as the new version. Even worse, almost all the servers in production depended on the library. An upgrade would require duplicating almost every server and having the additional hardware on hand for upgrading thousands of websites. That just seemed too much, so a plan was hatched to reduce the need for dependencies to just one type of server to make upgrades more manageable. That would reduce the hardware costs for upgrading. Still, this plan crossed multiple teams and would likely take many months to pull off.

Don't end up in the same boat. Stay up to date.

Why Is X More Reliable Than Software?

Why can X be pretty reliable while software seems less so?

There was a joke that suggested automobiles were more reliable than software, because if they were like software, they would crash every day.

Back when that was said, software was much less reliable than today and did crash more often; perhaps once a day or week. While it was kind of funny, it also made me ask the question: Why?

This is a question I occasionally think about.

Let's think through this a little in terms of the differences between software and a car.

A car has to be built in a sort of waterfall process. Every part and specification must be designed and created upfront. Sure, there can be prototypes, quick manufacturing, or use of existing components to prototype a vehicle, but at some point, they need a complete design down to the last screw on the car to be able to manufacture it. Even each part may be specified down to 0.0005 inches more or less, depending on its purpose, the material, and recreating a process to make all of these parts in the hundreds of thousands or more. Factories and machines are designed and built to manufacture all of these parts with very detailed specifications. They will often create and use automation to test the moving parts for wear. All of this is needed, because they need to make hundreds of thousands of these same parts/cars in a quality way.

Car parts usually have a very specific purpose and can only perform a limited set of operations or functions. Take, for example, the steering wheel. It can just go left or right. You can unlock or lock a door. You can turn the wipers on or off. Other than the car's infotainment system, individual functionality for car parts have limited function. That can help with testing. Cars once designed typically aren't redesigned where they have to upgrade everybody's car after it has been sold! They just update cars for the next model year and make people buy new ones.

You also won't have 1 million people trying to drive the car at the same time. With software and cloud services, that or more can happen.

Car parts and systems aren't generally changed after they are made. They might support slightly varied components for the low-end trim versus the premium trim, but you probably won't be changing out the chassis or anything like that.

So How Might Automotive Production Compare to Software?

Software Architecture Designs are rarely like automotive designs. Usually, the high-level design is created, and the details are left to an individual or small teams of developers.

- An individual developed part of software likely isn't scrutinized to the detail of individual car parts, because for software, we only need to create something once. We don't need to make hundreds of thousands of the same thing, so each part does not warrant that level of design scrutiny. It could be a very costly mistake if they have to redesign a car part later (recalling cars, recreating a new manufacturing process, etc.). With software, change is much easier, so the economics of investing as much effort up front isn't "seemingly" there.
- A lot of software construction parts do more than simple functions like a door that just locks or unlocks.
- Manufacturing specification has a very specific blueprint design and process for creating many of the same components. Software doesn't have the same commonality. There are many programming languages to code in. Even within the same language, the functionality is even slightly complex. Each solution created could be a little different for certain aspects of development.

There are some car part-like components in software (e.g., textbox, password field, label).

- Cars don't need to support being upgraded in place.
- Cars don't need to scale to thousands of millions of drivers for the same car.
- Software architecture is about designing for scale, functionality, resiliency, and change. If your engine dies, there is no backup engine that takes over as there could be in a software implementation.

We can learn some things about our craft and understand that complexity differences, economics, individual building of functionality, and more all add up to determine why reliability can differ from physical products.

Can We Make Software More Reliable?

- Yes, we can. If we spent as much time and resources as car manufacturers do, I'm sure we could. It's been suggested that a new model of a car might cost a billion dollars to create. That's a lot of money! If you spent that much on most software to create, I'm sure we could do better. One hundred software engineers, even if you paid $200K each a year, would only be $20 million. One billion could support 5,000 software engineers at that rate. How many software projects do you know with that many engineers? Of course, the economic benefits/reward would have to justify this before businesses would do it.
- One obvious item is to componentize things that make sense. Don't require people to re-implement the same functionality in more than one place. For example, use an API client library

rather than requiring users of the API to roll their own each time.

- Perhaps machine learning could be used to identify repeated functionality that could be reused.
- NASA enhances reliability by having multiple software or hardware components that do the same thing. For example, they might have three flight control modules to report on a critical system. Each one implements a slightly different algorithm that should produce the same result. They would vote, and it would use the value of the two that were the same if one produced a different value. On smaller bits of code, they would work on proofs that the code is correct, along with tests. That's not your ordinary code review. It's either testing EVERY possible permutation and/or logically proving the correctness of code or algorithms via math/proofs.
- Code generation is also a possibility, presuming a generator could be designed to output useful code that didn't need changing once output.
- By automatically generating code, once you have tested and proved the generation is correct, it should generate very reliable code. The downside is that these systems are often not very flexible. There were many attempts at low-code or no-code generation of user interface with the backing database, and they often needed modification to handle the functionality users desired.
- Teach AI/machine learning to generate code for us.

Diagnosing Windows Issues

Inevitably, something will go wrong with your computer while you are working or while you are developing. You may have been working with Windows for a while and learned a lot about fixing and diagnosing some issues. As a developer, there can sometimes be a bit more that you can understand and do to solve problems in certain situations. Having a better understanding of the way software works can help with troubleshooting issues.

A Windows Service Won't Start

Check the Windows event log at the time of the attempted start and see if there are any issues noted. If the service you are trying to start creates its own logs (like IIS), you could check to see if those exist as well.

If a Hardware Device Isn't Working Properly

Check the Windows Device Manager to see if any devices have a little yellow triangle next to them. If they do it right, click it and uninstall the device (don't uninstall the software). Then, after it's uninstalled, reboot and see if it's better. Check your computer hardware makers website for software and driver updates that may help.

Blue Screen of Death (BSOD)

If you get a blue screen, see if there is any information on the screen about why it failed. Google for that information to see if it helps identify the issue. When it blue screened, it probably created a crash dump file. You can Google to see for your version of Windows where that would be. Then you can use Microsoft Visual Studio to open it. Look at the call stack and try to find any names of drivers you can recognize to determine a possible cause. If you see names *.dll, look them up on the Internet to see what driver might use them. If you discover it looks like a graphics driver., go find the one on your computer manufacturer's site and try to update to the latest version. You can research if others had a similar issue as well with the stack details and see what they did. Also, try removing any plugged-in USB devices you don't need plugged in to see if this prevents an issue.

Slow Computer

If your computer is slow, try bringing up the Task Manager. Look at how much the CPU is being used and memory is used. If the CPU is high, go to the processes tab and sort on CPU to see what is using up your CPU time. If you don't know what the process is, research it on Google to see if it's something you need or could consider removing. Also, scan your computer for malware with your antivirus program. Malwarebytes is a good program to try if you are worried your computer being infected. Check on the processor tab if your processor is running at full speed or not. Some laptops, if they don't recognize the power adapter properly, will throttle the CPU to as low as one-quarter speed. If you see that happening, try unplugging and plugging back in the power adapter and see if it helps. If it doesn't, double check your Windows power settings are correct. Suppose the computer runs at a reasonable speed without the adapter but is slow if plugged in, consider getting a new power adapter to try to see if that is the cause.

Staying Safe in the Digital Age

You are very likely leaking data and leaving a digital trail about yourself online whenever you use your computer or smartphone. Computers don't show you all of the information you are leaving behind. On top of that, if you are letting viruses and malware in, you are leaking even more information but, even worse, to people who are likely to do you some type of digital harm, like stealing your financial information or identity, credit card numbers, and so on.

So what can you do to make yourself and your data safer? Let's look at the protection of your privacy and data. Following these recommendations below can help.

On Your Computer

Use an admin account separate from your regular account: This can significantly reduce viruses and other threats to your computer. The account you use normally should not be an admin account; only use the admin account for installing software/devices that need it, then log out and log into your non-admin account to do everything else.

Only install the applications you need: uninstall the ones you don't. Don't install any software unless from a well-known, trusted company.

Limit the access allowed by the programs on your PC: If they don't need access to the camera, microphone, information, identity or credit card numbers., disable them for the app. On Windows 10, in the search bar, type privacy settings and select it. Then you can go and set permissions on apps for location, camera, microphone, voice activation, notifications, account info, contacts, calendar, phone calls, call history, e-mail, tasks, messaging, radios (Wi-Fi/Bluetooth), other devices, background apps, diagnostic and data.

Don't install browser plug-ins: They have access to anything you can see or type in your browser. If you must use them, configure them for only certain sites or disable them when you don't need them, or at least only use plug-ins from well-known companies you trust. Given how much our trust is breached these days, that can be a big question. Norton/McAfee antivirus plug-ins are probably ok, for example, or a plug-in from directly Microsoft or Google, figuring they have so much access to what you do anyway, they wouldn't need a plug-in to siphon info, so probably safe for those big companies.

Browser Incognito Mode: Use incognito mode to access sensitive sites like banking. Reminder, Incognito only prevents leaving traces of information on your PC, but your Internet provider still knows what you accessed, plus any sites you accessed have data (and really any computers between you and the site you visited, in theory).

TOR Browser to keep your browsing information safe: If you want to reduce your data kept on your computer from as many others as possible, use the TOR browser (https://www.torproject.org/) for anything you want to search on the Internet. It's slow but pretty secure about preventing tracking of your data. Obviously, if you use an account on a website, the website will know that account. But if you create anonymous accounts while using the TOR browser, then it's unlikely sites would have any data you did not provide them, nor anyone else in between. TOR is a complex network designed to aggregate requests so that no one can tell who initiated a specific request from which source and also keeps the data sent and received securely. Default settings keep most information from being stored on your system. You don't need to use this all of the time; just when you feel your search results are sensitive, like searching about medical conditions you wonder if you might have or any other sensitive topic).

Browsers/Apps/VPNs: Another way to reduce data on the Internet of your browsing habits is to use a VPN. Think of a VPN as a secure connection between you and your VPN provider. In theory, no one else in between can see your data, only that you are connecting to a VPN provider. Only your VPN provider would know where you connect from if they log or keep records, so you need to find a provider that does not and you trust and that is based in a country you trust. You don't need to use this all of the time, just when you feel your search results are sensitive, like searching about medical conditions you wonder you might have or any other sensitive topic.

USB Drives/Devices: Don't plug in USB drives or anything USB to your computer that you did not buy or receive from a source you trust, as they can infect your computer.

Install a good, trusted antivirus/antimalware scanner (Recommend Norton Antivirus or McAfee) AND on-demand use of Malwarebytes once a week to scan for anything concerning.

- https://www.malwarebytes.com/
- Bitdefender

Browsing on the Internet giving sites info: Have more than one e-mail account. For sites you don't trust and are not critical, give them one e-mail address you use for noncritical sites. For other, more critical sites like your bank account, use your other e-mail address. Be sure to use different passwords for each.

Don't give personal info to sites that don't really need it: If they force you to log in to use their service and don't prevent you from receiving the service, you need to provide some standard false information. Things like your birthdate, address, and phone number are all bits of information used to identify you, and many sites that don't even need that information ask for it. If they have no legitimate need or right to it, then don't provide it.

Don't visit non-legit sites on the Internet: I know it's tempting to visit that video site that has literally every TV and movie online for free. You should have learned by now that very few things in life are truly free, and free means there is likely a hidden cost of risking being infected by viruses from that site or giving up other information. Try to stick to well-known sites that are legitimately run businesses to reduce your risk.

Use multifactor authentication: On important sites like your critical e-mail account, be sure to use two-factor authentication (authenticator app, like Google Authenticator or less ideally, SMS Text messages). That way, logging in requires more than your password but also a code provided from the app or text message. SMS messages are less ideal, as phone companies have been known to be tricked into transferring a phone number to someone else who can then get the text message with the code. Many sites, while they shouldn't, use that as the primary method of authenticating you are you (one factor, instead of more than one). That sort of blows the idea of using multiple factors to authenticate you.

Use a Password Manager

A password manager can store and keep all of your passwords securely so you only have to recall one password to unlock the password manager, and it can auto-fill your username and password on sites for you. It can even generate more secure passwords for you and remember them. 1Password is a good password manager. They support online and offline password management, depending on which product you buy. Offline is probably safer than online, as offline stores your passwords only on your machine, which is less convenient but hopefully more secure. LastPass is a well-respected online password manager that you can use, and it can sync with all your devices.

https://1password.com/
https://www.lastpass.com/

On Your Phone

Many of the same things mentioned above apply.

Install only the apps you need. Almost any app you install can get your phone number and account info. If you don't trust the app with that, don't download it.

Limit permissions of the apps you install to only what they need when they need.

Use incognito mode to keep info off your device.

If you need truly private browsing, try the TOR browser

Use a VPN to keep your information safe (from a VPN provider you trust), when needed.

Install a good antivirus software like Norton or McAfee.

Only install apps from the approved app stores.

Lock your phone with a code and keep it secret

Turn off the location on your device and only enable it when you need it.

On Android, disable ad personalization in the settings, and reset your Android advertiser ID once in a while. This is a unique ID used to track you across sites, also found in settings.

Don't use Siri, OK, Google, and so on. They store your voice sometimes, even without the wake-up word, and in some cases, you can't control how long.

Websites You Use

Visit their privacy settings, and disable or opt out of any ad personalization.

For example, Google and other sites may track your location and websites you visit. Disable all of the history tracking.

E-mail

Most of us probably use Gmail. Gmail is free to use for a reason. They possibly use your e-mail information to target ads for you. They possibly keep track of things you buy probably anywhere, since you get an e-mail about it. All of that information is stored online, and if Gmail ever got hacked, they would have all of that information.

An alternative e-mail called Proton Mail encrypts e-mails to you and from you if the person you are sending to supports it (if not, it sends a regular e-mail and receives regular e-mails). The difference is that it stores your e-mails encrypted, and only you can decrypt them with your password.

Proton Mail is considered one of the most secure e-mail services. Their base level is free, but you can upgrade for additional features.

Devices

Recommend against using Google, Alexa, and other home speakers and devices. They do have mechanisms not to keep history for long now, but why take the potential risk that they could record audio in your home of you and your family?

Backups

We know no one likes to think about backups. Do something to make this as easy as possible. Just buy an external USB hard drive big enough to hold at least one or two copies (perhaps more) of your data. Consider buying a backup program like Acronis. Perhaps set it up to copy once a month so it's not too onerous, and when it's done copying, it unplugs the USB drive. Leaving it connected could allow ransomware to encrypt your entire drive and prevent you from accessing it. If you keep this offline until you do the backup once a month and then disconnect, it should hopefully give you a way to recover if your computer is ever hit by ransomware malware.

I know a lot of services are selling cloud backups, but they are slow and cost a lot for the storage you may want or need each year, and if you forget to pay, your data is gone. Also, if they aren't encrypting your data well, more data could leak online.

Of course, if your only copy is at home and there is fire or water damage, you could be in trouble. If you buy a hard drive that protects from fire and water damage, this could help. Check out: https://iosafe.com/.

NOTE: Even adhering to all of these things, your computer and devices can leak information.

For example, your phone has a radio in it to be able to take calls. The towers can still, even without location on, probably pinpoint your location to within a few hundred feet, maybe less. This data is collected by your cell provider and is sometimes sold to third parties.

If you browse without a VPN or TOR, your IP address is sent out, and it is like a phone number to find out who you are.

Your browser gives away some information all the time, including OS (e.g., Windows, Apple OS X, Linux), browser (Chrome, Safari, Explorer, etc.), and size of the browser, which could be used as partial information to start to identify a user.

It can be really difficult to nearly impossible to limit all data from leaking out, but the instructions here should serve as a guide to help you keep your information safer and less leaky.

Your Own Website

Maybe you want to set up your own blog or just play around on the web. One of the most flexible platforms out there is WordPress. Don't get confused, though. There is a site called wordpress.com that lets you get a basic blog for free with limited features or pay a lot more money to get some features. But that is not the full power of WordPress. WordPress is also software you can use, download, and install yourself. More likely, though, you can find a less expensive web hosting company that has WordPress support that they can install for you.

WordPress can go from a basic blog to a full-fledged e-commerce site. There are plug-ins for nearly anything you could want to do. As a developer, you could even figure out how to extend it further since it's written in PHP and can be modified.

WordPress software is free, but a hosting server that supports it will cost you some money if you want to do more than the limited free blog on wordpress.com.

Smaller Releases

There is a trend toward releasing small changes more often, perhaps doing a software release every week or every other week. To do this, ideally, use comprehensive automated regression tests. But the smaller releases do mitigate some risk by changing only a smaller part. If you can be sure to identify the risks and impact, smaller releases can potentially reduce risk and deliver value earlier for customers.

At one company, I was at some products that released changes almost every week with deployments several times a week. We had hundreds of deployments a year across SIMT infrastructure and probably dozens or more releases. Narrowing the scope can reduce the tests that need to be run for a release. Validated software would still need to have some comprehensive regression, but if the automation is good, perhaps that is enough. The downside of this can be that there is obviously some overhead to releasing very often. But the change risks can be significantly reduced. If a performance issue is noticed, it may be the only one thing that can be easily identified and rolled back. If it were a much larger release, the underlying cause would need to be identified first, which could be much harder for performance-related or intermittent issues, depending on the area.

Impact on Society

The Internet

Wow... even thinking about this topic, I suspect entire books could be written about it.

For those who grew up in the age of the Internet, you didn't get to experience the transformative nature that it has had. The mix of computers and the Internet has changed everything. From a software developer's perspective, when I had an issue prior to the Internet, I had to read the manual, ask colleagues, or call the company if it was a third-party product. Being able to search the Internet and find a knowledge base of articles possibly related to your topic is amazing. Going from basically having to go it on your own to now being able to research the world's knowledge or ask people around the world is an incredible change from what it once was. Need to order something? Just go online and order it. Before the Internet, there were some big stores you could call to get items delivered by viewing the offline catalogs and ordering over the phone.

Cell Phones

Having a computer in your pocket, possibly hundreds or thousands of times more powerful than the original personal computers that could only fit on a desk, is stunning. On top of that, being able to connect to the Internet and get information from around the world from nearly anywhere is incredible. Got lost and need directions? No problem. Need to order pizza? No problem. Need a calculator? No problem. Pay at the register? No problem. None of this was available years ago and has created incredible opportunities.

Social Media

Staying in touch with friends, followers, or whomever, this is definitely new. Before this, there was no way to easily reach hundreds, thousands, or millions of people easily. Only newspapers or TV media perhaps had that kind of power. There are obviously some good points and bad points about this. As developers, you have a surprising amount of influence on the creation of technology. When you are involved in the creation of technology, consider how it may help or hurt the users of society.

Business

For years and years, businesses would talk about the paperless office when computers came out, but that was a pipe dream rather than a reality. Fast forward to today, and it seems we have arrived. There is very little paper being circulated around. Instead, it's e-mails or links to sites and documents. Businesses have been transformed from slow to get updates on data surrounding the business to near instantaneous sales numbers. Now, businesses can concentrate on using the massive amounts of data they have access to for a competitive edge over the competition.

How to Be the Worst Software Engineer
(Please Don't Do These)

- Write your entire program on a single line of source code to see if you can.
- Name your base classes nonsensically different from the derived class (no airplanes derived from animal!).
- Estimate the story 1 sprint effort but actually finish it in one day, the last day!
- Drink and code.
- Say you can't help with the coffee maker because you do software, not hardware.
- Write a 1,000 line regex in Perl.
- Wait till the last day of the release to tell your manager it's going to take one more month to complete.
- Use both tabs and spaces.
- Play *Game of Thrones* with bugs to see who can get the most in a release.
- Tell QA: "It worked fine on my machine."
- Write an endless loop stored procedure.
- Code like it's 1984, and try to fit everything in 16K.
- Write your own Array, LinkedList, or Dictionary, cause you like yours better.
- Make reading a property of a class causing it to delete everything from the database.
- Name every method starting with your name or initials.
- Rewrite the entire class because you just didn't like its style.
- Write your source code using all 159 possible Unicode character sets, because that seems fun.
- Create pop-up web advertisements.
- Change spaces to an empty Unicode control character.

- Assume all code you get from the Internet is good code.
- Catch every exception and do nothing. {} catch {}
- Wait till the end of your 6-month release before you test any code.
- Wait three months before you check-in/commit ANY code.
- Write your entire program in binary.
- Invent your own cryptographic algorithm, then, you know, protect passwords with it and a nuclear reactor.
- Create 50-level derived classes with a polymorphic method called process that do completely different things.
- Code like no one is watching.
- Create one-third screen ad banners or full-screen pop-up ads.
- Create fake "download here" buttons that bring up ads.
- Make the user read the manual.
- Write two methods in C# or any language with the same name and same parameters that differ only by case and do different things.
- Use more newlines to decrease your bugs to lines of code count.
- Use acronyms for all method and property names, and name all variables x1, x2, x3 . . .

Useful Tools and Websites

Useful Tools

Visual Studio

    Visual Studio Code

Jetbrains Resharper add-on for Visual Studio. Great refactoring tools https://www.jetbrains.com/

Jetbrains DotPeek is a .NET decompiler. great for learning how code works.
https://www.jetbrains.com/

WinDbg from Microsoft. A great for debugging windows dump files, even kernel level.

Windows Performance Recorder and Windows Performance Analyzer: Analyze down to context switches over the entire OS and all running processes on windows.

Intel VTune Profiler: Very detailed statistics down to the process level (cache misses, etc.).
https://www.intel.com/content/www/us/en/developer/tools/oneapi/vtune-profiler.html#gs.46pgp9
Notepad++: Good text editor
https://notepad-plus-plus.org/
7zip: Free zip file app.
https://www.7-zip.org/

Jira: Widely used issue tracking system
https://www.atlassian.com/software/jira

Postman: Great for testing REST APIs
https://www.postman.com/

Websites
Github.com

Amazon.com and Microsoft Azure: Cloud computing
https://aws.amazon.com/
https://azure.microsoft.com

Docker
www.docker.com

Stackoverflow.com
Codeproject.com
Codeguru.com

Useful Environment/Platforms
Eclipse: Good for Java/Android and more
https://www.eclipse.org/ide/

Unity Game IDE: Great environment for creating 2D and 3D games; even the pros use it.
https://unity.com/

GameMaker: Great for 2D games, simple enough older kids/teens probably can create their own games
https://gamemaker.io/en

Best Developer Blogs

Scott Guthrie's blog EVP of Microsoft Cloud and Enterprise group
https://weblogs.asp.net/scottgu

Scott Hanselman Microsoft Web platform team
http://www.hanselman.com/blog/
Brain Harry Visual Studio ALM
http://i1.blogs.msdn.com/b/bharry/
Jeff AtWood Windows/web developer
http://blog.codinghorror.com

Scott Allen Consultant/Pluralsight author – windows, web technologies

http://odetocode.com/blogs/all

John Skeet

https://codeblog.jonskeet.uk/

Joseph Albahari

https://www.albahari.com/

Mike Brind

https://www.mikesdotnetting.com/

Derek Comartin

https://codeopinion.com/

Reading List

There are many great books to read for software developers. Here are some. Many are older but still supply some great details even if not up to date on the latest version or framework (perhaps a newer edition will be out for the framework you need).

Windows Internals (Part 1 + Part 2) by Pavel Yosifovich, Mark Russinovich, David Solomon, Alex Ionescu.

For .NET/C# folks

CLR via C# by Jeffrey Richter

For Microsoft SQL Server

Pro SQL Server Internals by Dimitri Korotkevitvh

General

Code Complete by Steve McConnell

Cracking the Coding Interview by Gayle Laakmann McDowell

Psychology of Everyday Things by Donald Norman
About Face by Alan Cooper
Usability Engineer by Jakob Nielsen
The Phoenix Project: A Fictional Novel about IT/DevOps

CHAPTER 34

Notable Software/Technologies

While the software field is still very young, there is a lot of software out there. Some of it is lost to the time of changing hardware/software platforms, but a large portion is available and still able to run.

Windows

Windows is the most popular desktop OS on the market, holding about 74 percent of the market share. OS X holds about 15 percent, and Linux is about 2 percent ("Desktop Operating System Market Share Worldwide" | *Statcounter Global Stats*, n.d.).

For general servers, the claims are about 72 percent Windows and about 18 percent Linux/Unix. ("Global Server Share by OS 2018–2019" | *Statista*, n.d.).

For public facing Internet servers, data suggests Linux (37%) ("Linux vs. Windows Usage Statistics," *September* 2022, n.d.) servers have more market share than Windows (20%). Those numbers sound off, though. If we look at it by language as a rough proxy of OS platform (PHP vs. ASP.NET), it ranges around 57–77 percent for PHP, and we can guess most are Linux, compared to ASP.NET (7–18%), most we can guess are Windows. For the top 1,000 websites, it's the higher end for Windows and lower end for Linux.

Of course, these numbers don't take into account the mobile device OS market.

The point is there are plenty of Windows desktop/server OS and platform usage.

The Windows development tools are the best in the business. Visual Studio and Visual Studio Code make development a lot more manageable along with dozens of developers' tools/diagnostics.

Windows has a lot more GUI applications for point and click access to tools, compared to Linux, which has way less and is more command-line driven.

Having worked at the division of the company that made Unix, even they used Windows as their desktop OS back in the 90s, prior to selling their Unix group. Even today, I would guess, many but not all Linux developers probably also have a Windows box for their desktop OS. That definitely was the case at a major financial company in the 2005–2014 time frame.

(See references so you can judge how accurate this data is or not.)

Benefits

- Largest availability of desktop software.
- Most desktop users.
- Best development tools on the market.
- Used in almost every business.
- Usually included when you buy a computer.
- Supports millions of devices, USB, video cards.

- Allows you to run your desktop apps and some Linux apps as well if you desire with the POSIX subsystem.
- Best game support/driver availability.
- Great support available if you need it.

Cons

Compared to Linux, you don't have source access to the OS for Windows, but most folks don't need that.

Windows requires a bit more memory by default than stock Linux

Linux/Unix

For the desktop market, OS X (based on Unix) holds about 15 percent, and Linux about 2 percent. ("Desktop Operating System Market Share Worldwide" | *Statcounter Global Stats*, n.d.).

For general servers, the claims are about 72 percent Windows and about 17 percent Linux/Unix. ("Global Server Share by OS 2018–2019" | *Statista*, n.d.).

Pros

- Uses less memory than Windows on average.
- If developing websites, PHP one of the most used web languages often runs on Linux servers.
- Open source, so you can view all the source code.
- OS X has one of the best Unix/Linux desktops.
- Control over the OS if you need it. You could update the kernel yourself if needed.

Cons

Linux only has community support unless you buy one of the vendor products like Red Hat.

Games support is not as good as windows

Android

Android is a mobile OS created by Google (now Alphabet). Android is the most popular OS of any on the market, holding more than 50 percent of the OS market and more than 50 percent of the mobile market. As of this time, the Google Play Android app store has more apps than the iOS store by at least 50 percent. ("Mobile Operating System Market Share Worldwide" | *Statcounter Global Stats,* n.d.).

If you are looking for a popular market to get into mobile device software, Android definitely has the market share.

Apps are often written in Java. It is relatively simple to write basic applications.

Pros

- Open source, so you can access all the code and create your own.
- Less expensive to create apps than iOS.
- More flexible app store than iOS.
- More devices/hardware are available to run it than iOS.

Cons

- Some would say not quite as secure as iOS, but that's questionable.
- More apps in the app store may mean more competition.

iOS

iPhone was really the first breakthrough smartphone device. Windows mobile lost out to iOS, as did Blackberry and more. Then Android came along and matched and in some ways succeeded iOS.

To write for IOS, you will need a Mac. Apple doesn't like you to write for their devices without a mac so they don't even want you emulating without a Mac device.

Pros

- Uses Apple hardware.
- Uses has a large ecosystem following.

Cons

- More expensive to create apps for the app store than Android.
- Apps store is more restrictive than the Google Play Store.
- Apple doesn't like you side loading and bypassing their store.
- Fewer hardware options than on Android.
- Closed ecosystem, so you can't customize the OS or device to your liking like Android.

- Costs for iOS devices are typically higher for their premier hardware than many Android devices.

Machine Learning

Machine learning is a set of technologies that allow training your machine on a set of data to solve different types of problems.

Some examples of the problem areas machine learning is used for:

- Grouping things together (e.g., similar products/images).
- Ranking information to find the most relevant.
- Finding unusual events in a set of data.
- Predicting the value of something based on input data.
- Finding things that interest you.
- Classifying objects/images (e.g., dog, car, etc.).

Machine learning has all sorts of uses. Those are just some examples of the ways it can be used with data.

Machine learning is done with something called neural networks. Neural nets are made up of nodes that have inputs and outputs. There are typically input nodes and output nodes and can have one or more layers in the middle. This can create a layered graph-like structure.

Each node can be thought of as having a certain weight and bias values, and based on the input data, if they exceed a threshold, it outputs 1, or if it's below the threshold, it outputs 0.

There are networks that learn through forward propagation only and some that use back propagation to improve on the results.

Usually, some existing data is used to train the network and record the weighted values to use for later. Then the network can be tested with new data to see how it performs.

Figuring out the number of layers needed for neural nets is a bit of both science and intuition at the moment. It's thought to represent complex functions. If more complex than linear, then more than one internal layer is needed, at least two. Sometimes, this needs to be tried. Just see the results if they help or not. When you don't know, trying more depth and testing could be tried. Creating a system that tests different depths to find the optimal depth can help. Different depths can impact the training time needed.

Machine learning is used in everything from the recommendations you see on websites to self-driving cars and more. Machine learning is a technology that will probably find its way into more and more business processes.

Docker Containers/Kubernetes

Containers like Docker allow running software in an isolated environment like a virtual machine but much more slimmed down and efficient.

Containers are easy to configure with a base and then deploy new software into on the fly.

You can use an orchestrator like Kubernetes to deploy a set of containers together, changing the state from one set to another set.

Kubernetes also has the ability to help with redundancy if it can configure a load balancer to balance the load between containers.

Kubernetes also has the ability to scale containers up and down based on criteria like CPU, memory, etc.

Containers are often used in the Linux or Windows variety.

Visual Studio now has built-in support for deploying to Docker containers and debugging in them.

NoSQL

This is a newer type of document store technology similar to a database. The difference between this and SQL technology is that in SQL, you have denormalization where you break information into different tables and then create SQL statements that join all of that information back together.

With NoSQL, you can just think of information as being stored in documents in terms of a json document. Queries are to find documents that have the information you need.

Document storage is in some ways easier. You don't need to create a complex table design with references. Everything you need is just stored in a document together.

Sometimes, if there is a lot of information, you still might need to break out information to multiple documents to avoid performance issues.

Querying is done in software like MongoDB, a NoSQL type database in more of a programmatic way than using SQL. It's very function like json and beyond is to find the documents you need.

The performance of pulling data out this way can be faster than a SQL database, since the granularity is the document for pulling data. Unlike SQL, it won't need to lock multiple rows or entire tables of data when handling transactions in most cases.

NoSQL can make a lot of sense for configuration or storage of other things that are very document-like. As long as you don't require joining lots of information from multiple documents, NoSQL could provide nice performance gains.

The other benefit is software like MongoDB even supports automatic sharding and even replication, so it is able to scale much easier than many SQL databases like Microsoft SQL.

CHAPTER 35

Appendix

About Ruby. (n.d.). Retrieved September 26, 2022, from

Acquire and Release Semantics—Windows Drivers | Microsoft Learn. (n.d.). Retrieved September 23, 2022, from https://learn.microsoft.com/en-us/windows-hardware/drivers/kernel/acquire-and-release-semantics?redirectedfrom=MSDN

Agile—Why Do We Use Story Points Instead of Man Days When Estimating User Stories? - Software Engineering Stack Exchange. (n.d.). Retrieved September 17, 2022, from https://softwareengineering.stackexchange.com/questions/182057/why-do-we-use-story-points-instead-of-man-days-when-estimating-user-stories

Algorithm—Token Bucket vs Fixed Window (Traffic Burst)—Stack Overflow. (n.d.). Retrieved September 17, 2022, from https://stackoverflow.com/questions/65868274/token-bucket-vs-fixed-window-traffic-burst

Announcing Rate Limiting for .NET—.NET Blog. (n.d.). Retrieved September 17, 2022, from https://devblogs.microsoft.com/dotnet/announcing-rate-limiting-for-dotnet

Apple Reveals Windows 10 is Four Times More Popular than the Mac—The Verge. (n.d.). Retrieved September 19, 2022, from https://www.theverge.com/2017/4/4/15176766/apple-microsoft-windows-10-vs-mac-users-figures-stats

Beck, K., Beedle, M., van Bennekum, A., Cockburn, A., Cunningham, W., Fowler, M., Grenning, J., Highsmith, J., Hunt, A., Jeffries, R., Kern, J., Marick, B., Martin, R. C., Mellor, S., Schwaber, K., Sutherland, J., & Thomas, D. (2001). Manifesto for Agile Software Development. http://agilemanifesto.org/

Bird, C., Nagappan, N., Murphy, B., Gall, H., & Devanbu, P. (n.d.). *An Analysis of the Effect of Code Ownership on Software Quality across Windows, Eclipse, and Firefox.* 14.

C# Coding Conventions | Microsoft Learn. (n.d.). Retrieved September 17, 2022, from https://learn.microsoft.com/en-us/dotnet/csharp/fundamentals/coding-style/coding-conventions

C#—Double.Epsilon for Equality, Greater than, Less than, Less than or Equal to, Greater than or Equal to—Stack Overflow. (n.d.). Retrieved September 17, 2022, from https://stackoverflow.com/questions/2411392/double-epsilon-for-equality-greater-than-less-than-less-than-or-equal-to-gre.

Chistory. (n.d.). Retrieved September 26, 2022, from http://www.bell-labs.com/usr/dmr/www/chist.html

Codd, E. F. (1970). *A Relational Model of Data for Large Shared Data Banks.* https://web.archive.org/web/20070612235326/http://www.acm.org/classics/nov95/toc.html

Collation and Unicode Support—SQL Server | Microsoft Learn. (n.d.). Retrieved September 17, 2022, from https://learn.microsoft.com/en-us/sql/relational-databases/collations/collation-and-unicode-support?view=sql-server-ver16

Common Patterns for Poorly-Behaved Multithreaded Applications—Visual Studio 2015 | Microsoft Learn. (n.d.). Retrieved September 17, 2022, from https://learn.microsoft.com/en-us/previous-versions/visualstudio/visual-studio-2015/profiling/common-patterns-for-poorly-behaved-multithreaded-applications?view=vs-2015&redirectedfrom=MSDN

Compiler Basics, Part 2: Building the Scanner—Visual Studio Magazine. (n.d.). Retrieved September 17, 2022, from https://visualstudiomagazine.com/articles/2014/06/01/compiler-basics-part-2.aspx

Concurrent Affairs: Build a Richer Thread Synchronization Lock | Microsoft Learn. (n.d.). Retrieved September 23, 2022, from https://learn.microsoft.com/en-us/archive/msdn-magazine/2006/march/concurrent-affairs-build-a-richer-thread-synchronization-lock

COS-418, Fall 2016: Distributed Systems. (n.d.). Retrieved September 17, 2022, from https://www.cs.princeton.edu/courses/archive/fall16/cos418/

C#—The C# Memory Model in Theory and Practice | Microsoft Learn. (n.d.-a). Retrieved September 17, 2022, from https://learn.microsoft.com/en-us/archive/msdn-magazine/2012/december/csharp-the-csharp-memory-model-in-theory-and-practice

C#—The C# Memory Model in Theory and Practice | Microsoft Learn. (n.d.-b). Retrieved September 17, 2022, from https://learn.microsoft.com/en-us/archive/msdn-magazine/2012/december/csharp-the-csharp-memory-model-in-theory-and-practice

C#—The C# Memory Model in Theory and Practice, Part 2 | Microsoft Learn. (n.d.). Retrieved September 17, 2022, from https://learn.microsoft.com/en-us/archive/msdn-magazine/2013/january/csharp-the-csharp-memory-model-in-theory-and-practice-part-2

Desktop Operating System Market Share Worldwide | Statcounter Global Stats. (n.d.). Retrieved September 17, 2022, from https://gs.statcounter.com/os-market-share/desktop/worldwide

Dhar, V. (2013, December). *Data Science and Prediction | December 2013 | Communications of the ACM*. https://cacm.acm.org/magazines/2013/12/169933-data-science-and-prediction/fulltext

ECMA-335—Ecma International. (n.d.). Retrieved February 6, 2023, from https://www.ecma-international.org/publications-and-standards/standards/ecma-335

Example 15 Measuring DPC/ISR Time—Windows Drivers | Microsoft Learn. (n.d.). Retrieved September 22, 2022, from https://

learn.microsoft.com/en-us/windows-hardware/drivers/devtest/example-15--measuring-dpc-isr-time

Explained: Neural Networks | MIT News | Massachusetts Institute of Technology. (n.d.). Retrieved September 17, 2022, from https://news.mit.edu/2017/explained-neural-networks-deep-learning-0414

Extensible Markup Language (XML) 1.0 (Fifth Edition). (n.d.). Retrieved September 26, 2022, from https://www.w3.org/TR/REC-xml

Fearless Concurrency—The Rust Programming Language. (n.d.). Retrieved September 26, 2022, from https://doc.rust-lang.org/book/ch16-00-concurrency.html

File:NIST Enterprise Architecture Model.jpg—Wikimedia Commons. (n.d.). Retrieved September 17, 2022, from https://commons.wikimedia.org/wiki/File:NIST_Enterprise_Architecture_Model.jpg

Filesystems. (n.d.). Retrieved September 26, 2022, from https://tldp.org/LDP/sag/html/filesystems.html

Gamma, E. (Ed.). (1995). *Design patterns: Elements of reusable object-oriented software*. Addison-Wesley.

Garbage Collection: Automatic Memory Management in the Microsoft .NET Framework. (n.d.). Retrieved September 17, 2022, from https://web.archive.org/web/20130310021543/http://msdn.microsoft.com/en-us/magazine/bb985010.aspx

Garg, V. K., & Mittal, N. (n.d.). Time and State in Distributed Systems. 9.

http://users.ece.utexas.edu/~garg/dist/wiley-encyc.pdf Access time originally was 9/17/2022 9pm

Genscape Inc. (2003, August 15). *What Caused the Power Blackout to Spread So Widely and So Fast? Genscape's Unique Data Will Help*. https://web.archive.org/web/20160518020430/http://www.prnewswire.com/news-releases/what-caused-the-power-blackout-to-spread-so-widely-and-so-fast-genscapes-unique-data-will-help-answer-that-question-70952022.html

Global Server Share by OS 2018–2019 | Statista. (n.d.). Retrieved September 17, 2022, from

Goldin, Maxim. (n.d.). MSDN Magazine: Thread Performance—Resource Contention Concurrency Profiling in Visual Studio 2010 | Microsoft Learn. Retrieved September 23, 2022, from https://learn.microsoft.com/en-us/archive/msdn-magazine/2010/june/msdn-magazine-thread-performance-resource-contention-concurrency-profiling-in-visual-studio-2010

Google Testing Blog: Code Coverage Best Practices. (2020, August 7). https://testing.googleblog.com/2020/08/code-coverage-best-practices.html

Historical Yearly Trends in the Usage Statistics of Server-Side Programming Languages for Websites w3techs.ashx (1504×555). (n.d.). Retrieved September 17, 2022, from https://visualstudiomagazine.com/articles/2021/09/14/~/media/ECG/visualstudiomagazine/Images/2021/09/w3techs.ashx

How Bitcoin Mining Really Works. (n.d.). Retrieved September 17, 2022, from https://www.freecodecamp.org/news/how-bitcoin-mining-really-works-38563ec38c87

How to Configure the Number of Layers and Nodes in a Neural Network. (n.d.). Retrieved September 17, 2022, from *https://machinelearningmastery.com/how-to-configure-the-number-of-layers-and-nodes-in-a-neural-network*

How to Write Your Own Compiler, Part 1: Mapping Source Files—Visual Studio Magazine. (n.d.). Retrieved September 17, 2022, from https://visualstudiomagazine.com/articles/2014/05/01/how-to-write-your-own-compiler-part-1.aspx?m=1

HTML Basic. (n.d.). Retrieved September 17, 2022, from https://www.w3schools.com/html/html_basic.asp

HTML Standard. (n.d.). Retrieved September 26, 2022, from https://html.spec.whatwg.org/multipage/#toc-dom

Hull, R., & Peter, Dr. L. J. (n.d.). *The Peter Principle: Why Things Always Go Wrong: As Featured on Radio 4.*

Hunt, C. (n.d.). *1. Overview of TCP/IP—TCP/IP Network Administration, 3rd Edition [Book]*. Retrieved September 26, 2022, from https://www.oreilly.com/library/view/tcpip-network-administration/0596002971/ch01.html

Intel® 64 and IA-32 Architectures Software Developer Manuals. (n.d.). Retrieved September 17, 2022, from https://www.intel.com/content/www/us/en/developer/articles/technical/intel-sdm.html

Job Search | Indeed. (n.d.). Retrieved September 17, 2022, from indeed.com

Kikama Jr, K. (2010). Securing the Rapid Application Development (RAD) Methodology. 55.

http://cs.lewisu.edu/mathcs/msis/projects/msis595_KividiKikama.pdf

Krasner, G. E., & Pope, S. T. (1988). *A Description of the Model-View-Controller User Interface Paradigm in the Smalltalk-80 System*. https://web.archive.org/web/20100921030808/http://www.itu.dk/courses/VOP/E2005/VOP2005E/8_mvc_krasner_and_pope.pdf

Lachtar, N., Elkhail, A. A., Bacha, A., & Malik, H. (n.d.). *A Cross-Stack Approach Towards Defending Against Cryptojacking | IEEE Journals & Magazine | IEEE Xplore*. Retrieved September 26, 2022, from https://ieeexplore.ieee.org/document/9170774

Linux vs. Windows Usage Statistics, September 2022. (n.d.). Retrieved September 17, 2022, from https://w3techs.com/technologies/comparison/os-linux,os-windows

Manifesto for Agile Software Development. (n.d.). Retrieved September 17, 2022, from

Beck, K., Beedle, M., van Bennekum, A., Cockburn, A., Cunningham, W., Fowler, M., Grenning, J., Highsmith, J., Hunt, A., Jeffries, R., Kern, J., Marick, B., Martin, R. C., Mellor, S., Schwaber, K., Sutherland, J., & Thomas, D. (2001). Manifesto for Agile Software Development. http://agilemanifesto.org/

Martin, R. C. (2000). *Design Principles and Design Patterns*.

http://staff.cs.utu.fi/~jounsmed/doos_06/material/DesignPrinciplesAndPatterns.pdf

Mobile Operating System Market Share Worldwide | Statcounter Global Stats. (n.d.). Retrieved September 17, 2022, from https://gs.statcounter.com/os-market-share/mobile/worldwide

NERC Steering Group. (2004, July 13). *Technical Analysis of the August 14, 2003, Blackout.* https://web.archive.org/web/20120318081212/http://www.nerc.com/docs/docs/blackout/NERC_Final_Blackout_Report_07_13_04.pdf

Norman, D. A. (1988). *The psychology of everyday things.* Basic Books.

Northeast Blackout of 2003—Wikipedia. (n.d.). Retrieved September 22, 2022, from https://en.wikipedia.org/wiki/Northeast_blackout_of_2003

One Big Fluke › Simplest Explanation of the Math behind Public Key Cryptography. (n.d.). Retrieved September 17, 2022, from https://www.onebigfluke.com/2013/11/public-key-crypto-math-explained.html

Ōno, T. (1988). *Toyota production system: Beyond large-scale production.* Productivity Press.

OSI Model. (n.d.). Retrieved September 17, 2022, from https://www.imperva.com/learn/application-security/osi-model

Overview of Synchronization Primitives | Microsoft Learn. (n.d.). Retrieved September 23, 2022, from https://learn.microsoft.com/en-us/dotnet/standard/threading/overview-of-synchronization-primitives

Performance Considerations for Run-Time Technologies in the .NET Framework. (n.d.). Retrieved September 17, 2022, from https://web.archive.org/web/20111105031300/http://msdn.microsoft.com/en-us/library/ms973838

PHP vs. ASP.NET vs. Ruby Usage Statistics, September 2022. (n.d.). Retrieved September 17, 2022, from https://w3techs.com/technologies/comparison/pl-aspnet,pl-php,pl-ruby

Primality Test—Wikipedia. (n.d.). Retrieved September 17, 2022, from https://en.wikipedia.org/wiki/Primality_test

Processes, Threads, and Jobs in the Windows Operating System | Microsoft Press Store. (n.d.). Retrieved September 22, 2022, from https://www.microsoftpressstore.com/articles/article.aspx?p=2233328&seqNum=7

Programs—Khoury College of Computer Sciences. (n.d.). Retrieved September 17, 2022, from https://www.khoury.northeastern.edu/programs/#jump-0)

Rate-Limiting Strategies and Techniques | Cloud Architecture Center | Google Cloud. (n.d.-a). Retrieved September 17, 2022, from https://cloud.google.com/architecture/rate-limiting-strategies-techniques

Rate-Limiting Strategies and Techniques | Cloud Architecture Center | Google Cloud. (n.d.-b). Retrieved September 17, 2022, from https://cloud.google.com/architecture/rate-limiting-strategies-techniques#techniques-enforcing-rate-limits

Ries, E. (2010, April 30). *The Five Whys for Start-Ups*. https://hbr.org/2010/04/the-five-whys-for-startups

Sarkar, R. (n.d.). *Distributed Systems Clocks, Ordering of Events.*

https://www.inf.ed.ac.uk/teaching/courses/ds/slides1718/time2.pptx.pdf

Schwaber, K. (1990). *Ken Schwaber | Scrum.org*. https://www.scrum.org/team/ken-schwaber

System.Threading Namespace | Microsoft Learn. (n.d.). Retrieved September 23, 2022, from https://learn.microsoft.com/en-us/dotnet/api/system.threading?view=net-6.0

The Absolute Minimum Every Software Developer Absolutely, Positively Must Know About Unicode and Character Sets (No Excuses!)—Joel on Software. (n.d.). Retrieved September 17, 2022, from https://www.joelonsoftware.com/2003/10/08/the-absolute-minimum-every-soft-

ware-developer-absolutely-positively-must-know-about-unicode-and-character-sets-no-excuses

The Fallacy of Premature Optimization. (n.d.). Retrieved September 17, 2022, from https://ubiquity.acm.org/article.cfm?id=1513451

The World's Second-Most Popular Desktop Operating System isn't macOS Anymore | Ars Technica. (n.d.). Retrieved September 19, 2022, from

Thomas, D., & Hunt, A. (2019). *The pragmatic programmer, 20th anniversary edition: Journey to mastery* (Second edition). Addison-Wesley.

Threading in C#—Part 4—Advanced Threading. (n.d.). Retrieved September 17, 2022, from https://www.albahari.com/threading/part4.aspx

Threadsafe Events—CodeProject. (n.d.). Retrieved September 17, 2022, from https://www.codeproject.com/Articles/37474/Threadsafe-Events

TOGAF | The Open Group Website. (n.d.). Retrieved September 26, 2022, from https://www.opengroup.org/togaf

Tools And Techniques to Identify Concurrency Issues | Microsoft Learn. (n.d.). Retrieved September 23, 2022, from https://learn.microsoft.com/en-us/archive/msdn-magazine/2008/june/tools-and-techniques-to-identify-concurrency-issues

Traveling Salesman Problem | Solve the Traveling Salesman Problem. (n.d.). Retrieved September 17, 2022, from https://www.popularmechanics.com/science/a30655520/scientists-solve-traveling-salesman-problem

Understanding Low-Lock Techniques in Multithreaded Apps | Microsoft Learn. (n.d.). Retrieved September 17, 2022, from https://learn.microsoft.com/en-us/archive/msdn-magazine/2005/october/understanding-low-lock-techniques-in-multithreaded-apps#S10

Uses for the Lex and Yacc Utilities—IBM Documentation. (2021, April 8). https://www.ibm.com/docs/en/zos/2.4.0?topic=yacc-uses-lex-utilities

var—C# reference | Microsoft Docs. (n.d.). Retrieved September 15, 2022, from https://docs.microsoft.com/en-us/dotnet/csharp/language-reference/keywords/var

Volatile—C# Reference | Microsoft Learn. (n.d.). Retrieved September 23, 2022, from https://learn.microsoft.com/en-us/dotnet/csharp/language-reference/keywords/volatile

What Are Neural Networks? | IBM. (n.d.). Retrieved September 17, 2022, from https://www.ibm.com/cloud/learn/neural-networks

What Is a GPU? Graphics Processing Units Defined. (n.d.). Retrieved September 27, 2022, from https://www.intel.com/content/www/us/en/products/docs/processors/what-is-a-gpu.html

What Is Scrum? | Scrum.org. (n.d.). Retrieved September 25, 2022, from https://www.scrum.org/resources/what-is-scrum

What Is the Difference between MVC and MVVM?—Stack Overflow. (n.d.). Retrieved September 17, 2022, from https://stackoverflow.com/questions/667781/what-is-the-difference-between-mvc-and-mvvm

(N.d.). https://docs.microsoft.com/en-us/dotnet/csharp/language-reference/keywords/var

Sites/Links/Information

This book provides links to many sites. Given the ever-changing nature of the Internet, we cannot be responsible for what may appear or not appear on those sites. We did our best to provide quality links at the time this information was written, but this document will probably be more static than the Internet that it links to. So will not be updated to reflect changes in what may or may not appear at those links in the future.

Information can be inaccurate, incomplete, or simply wrong.

Thanks for reading this book. If you liked it, please review it on the site you bought it from. Thanks!

More Information/Errata

You can visit our website to find the information we didn't have time to get into the book. There may be new information that came out after we published. You can also report errors or missing information on our website.

Any Errata we will add to the GitHub repo.

Please visit www.essentialsoftwaredevelopment.com to join our e-mail list.

https://github.com/AppJungle/EssentialSoftware Development Career-TechnicalGuide

Please leave a review on Amazon if you enjoyed this book.

Made in United States
Troutdale, OR
11/06/2024

24493304R00385